VENTURE CAPITAL DEVELOPMENT IN CHINA 2018

中国创业投资发展报告 2018

主　编　胡志坚　张晓原　张志宏　副主编　房汉廷　沈文京　郭　戎　张明喜

经济管理出版社
ECONOMY & MANAGEMENT PUBLISHING HOUSE

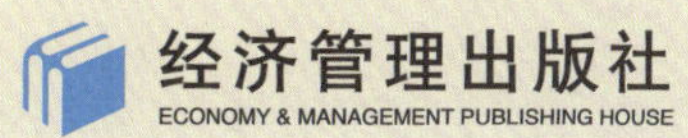

图书在版编目（CIP）数据

中国创业投资发展报告 2018/ 胡志坚，张晓原，张志宏主编 .—北京：经济管理出版社，2018. 7

ISBN 978-7-5096-5906-9

Ⅰ . ①中… Ⅱ . ①胡… ②张… ③张… Ⅲ . ①风险投资—研究报告—中国—2018 Ⅳ . ① F832. 48

中国版本图书馆 CIP 数据核字（2018）第 166490 号

组稿编辑：陈 力
责任编辑：陈 力 钱雨荷
责任印制：高 娅
责任校对：王淑卿

出版发行：经济管理出版社
（北京市海淀区北蜂窝 8 号中雅大厦 A 座 11 层 100038）
网 址：www.E-mp.com.cn
电 话：（010）51915602
印 刷：北京印刷集团有限责任公司印刷二厂
经 销：新华书店
开 本：880mm × 1230mm/16
印 张：15.75
字 数：509 千字
版 次：2018 年 9 月第 1 版 2018 年 9 月第 1 次印刷
书 号：ISBN 978-7-5096-5906-9
定 价：150. 00 元

委员会

主编

胡志坚　张晓原　张志宏

副主编

房汉廷　沈文京　郭　戎　张明喜

常务编委（按姓氏笔画排序）

丁飞燕　马　敏　马德庆　王　元　王　磊　王　飙
王　衡　王一军　王守仁　王松奇　王树勋　王品高
王秋颖　王俊艳　王振伟　王晋斌　王润田　王朝平
王雄武　方国银　邓天佐　卢秀峰　卢道真　付剑峰
白瑞明　冯治库　成　功　朱星华　华裕达　向　兵
刘　阳　刘维华　次仁平措　关春祥　许　强　孙晓芸
寿学平　李　庆　李　鑫　李文雷　李希义　李爱民
李雪婧　李银安　杨国荣　吴利军　何国杰　何勇军
沈文京　宋高堂　张　伟　张　华　张　健　张　萌
张世杰　张自强　张明喜　张建红　张俊芳　陈　千
陈　伟　陈　玮　陈工孟　陈云波　陈振权　陈晓明
陈海涛　范　毅　尚朝秋　金弈名　赵　雯　荆树山
俞志华　胥和平　秦　勇　倪泽望　倪振东　高　兵
郭　戎　郭滕达　唐永明　黄慰萍　彭　元　董　梁
韩　亮　韩　珺　傅丽枫　谢　岩　谢照杰　靳晓云
蒲毅蘋　路　辉　解　鑫　蔡久田　熊仁章　黎苑楚
魏世杰

调研分析组

组　　长：郭　戎　**副组长：**张俊芳

执笔分工：

第 1 章　张俊芳　　第 2 章　姜艳凤
第 3 章　赵淑芳　　第 4 章　魏世杰
第 5 章　朱欣乐　　第 6 章　李希义
第 7 章　李明珠　　第 8 章　郭滕达
第 9 章　孙奥林

附录整理　张俊芳（附录 1、附录 2，附录 5~ 附录 8）
朱欣乐（附录 3）
马国超（附录 4）
王秋颖（附录 9）

创业风险投资调查员（按姓氏笔画排序）

马　宁　马　肖　马晨征　王　娜　王　铀　王　皓
王子铭　邓　凯　邓韵然　卢　慧　叶　竞　田　园
兰定成　邢慧婧　巩耀亮　毕朝阳　华巢苹　刘　丽
刘　明　刘　淼　刘其榕　祁　阳　孙　婷　纪博乐
苏淼淼　李　哲　李　根　李昊坤　李国源　李莲靖
李晓鹏　杨　燕　杨继涛　汪瑞民　宋蜀玉　张　艳
张　捷　张　婷　张小莉　张雪梅　陈　诚　陈　娟
陈坤鹏　武　赟　苗　红　林维柒　金　戈　金　湛
周利平　孟雄伟　赵　婧　赵　璐　赵文君　郝殿伦
胡　焱　胡诗悦　胡雷华　钟慧敏　郗丽娜　姜宁鹏
祝　涛　晋美诺布　徐　佳　徐　茜　徐东升　徐锦娟
徐溪红　郭璐璐　曹建胜　博晓秋　董　婷　董　键
韩巧娟　谭艺平　潘荣翠　潘懿文　薛　润　霍利华

参与和支持单位（排名不分先后）

科学技术部资源配置与管理司
中国科学技术发展战略研究院
科技部火炬高技术产业开发中心
科技部科技经费监督管理服务中心
国家科技风险事业开发中心
商务部外国投资管理司
国家开发银行投资业务局
中国进出口银行业务开发与创新部
中国社会科学院金融研究中心
中国科技金融促进会
中国台湾创业风险投资商业同业公会
亚洲创业基金期刊集团（中国香港）
中国风险投资研究院
《中国科技投资》杂志社
北京清科创业风险投资顾问有限公司
辽宁大学工商管理学院
北京市科学技术委员会
北京创业投资协会
北京市科技金融促进会
北京首都科技发展集团公司
天津市科学技术委员会
天津市创业投资协会
上海市创业投资行业协会
重庆市科学技术委员会
重庆市科技创业投资协会
河北省科学技术厅
河北省科学技术情报研究院
河北石家庄高新技术产业开发区科技局
山西省科学技术厅
山西省风险投资协会
山西省科技基金发展总公司
内蒙古自治区生产力促进中心
内蒙古科技风险基金管理办公室
四川省科学技术厅
四川省高新技术产业金融服务中心
四川省成都生产力促进中心
四川省成都高新区金融办
四川省绵阳高新技术产业开发区创业服务中心
贵州省科学技术厅
贵阳国家高新区科技创新创业局
贵阳高新区金融办
贵州省科技评估中心
云南省科学技术厅
云南省科学技术院
辽宁省股权和创业投资协会
辽宁省沈阳市科学技术局
辽宁省沈阳科技风险投资有限公司
辽宁省大连市生产力促进中心
辽宁省大连高新技术产业园区金融办
吉林省长春市科学技术局
吉林省高技术创业服务中心
黑龙江省科学技术厅
黑龙江省科力高科技产业投资有限公司
黑龙江省哈尔滨市创业投资协会
湖北省科学技术厅创投引导基金管理中心
湖北省创业投资同业公会
湖北省武汉市科技局
湖北省武汉市科技金融创新促进中心
湖北省襄樊高新技术创业服务中心
河南省科学技术厅
湖南省科学技术厅
湖南省科技交流交易中心
山东省科学技术厅
山东省科技服务发展推进中心
山东省青岛市科技局
山东省青岛生产力促进中心
江苏省科学技术厅
江苏省创业投资协会
江苏省南京市科技局
江苏省无锡新区科技金融投资集团
浙江省科学技术厅
浙江省风险投资协会
浙江省杭州市科技局
浙江省宁波市科学技术局
安徽省科学技术厅
安徽省科技成果转化服务中心
江西省科学技术厅
福建省高新技术创业服务中心

福建省高新技术产权交易所有限公司
福建省厦门市科技局
福建省厦门火炬高技术产业开发区管委会
广东省科学技术厅
广东省风险投资促进会
广东省广州风险投资促进会
广东省佛山高新区经济发展和科技局
广东省珠海高新区科经局
深圳市创业投资同业公会
深圳市科技金融服务中心
海南省科学技术厅
甘肃省科学技术厅
甘肃省科技风险投资有限责任公司
甘肃省兰州高科创业投资担保有限公司
宁夏回族自治区科学技术厅
宁夏回族自治区科学技术厅生产力促进中心
陕西省科学技术厅
陕西科技控股集团
陕西省西安高新技术产业开发区管理委员会金融服务办公室
陕西省宝鸡高新区高技术创业服务中心
陕西省杨凌农业高新技术产业示范区管委会金融工作办公室
新疆维吾尔自治区科学技术厅
新疆新科源科技风险投资管理有限公司
广西科学技术厅
广西科技情报研究所
西藏自治区科学技术厅
西藏自治区科学信息研究所
青海省国有科技资产经营管理有限公司

目　录

摘 要

创业投资为我国经济高质量发展赋能
——2017 年中国创业投资发展的新态势、问题与建议

全国创业投资调查写作组[①]

创业投资在国家创新体系建设中扮演着重要角色，成为助推高科技企业发展的重要动力。本文结合科技部第 16 次全国创业投资专项调查数据，分析了 2017 年我国创业投资行业发展的新态势，调查了行业发展的景气指数；同时，结合相关调研情况，对行业面临的发展障碍提出了初步思路。

近年来，业内不少人士声称“炒房时代已经过去”“中国已经进入股权投资时代”“全民皆 PE”等，这些言论听起来不免有“夸张”“博眼球”的嫌疑，但实际情况是，近年来以创业投资（又称风险投资，以下简称创投）为代表的私募股权投资[②]的确取得了长足快速的增长，据中国证券投资基金协会备案数据显示，截至 2017 年底，全国已备案私募股权基金（含“创投”）66418 只，同比增长 42.82%，管理规模 11.1 万亿元。

2017 年，IPO 审核加速带动了创业投资基金的募集、投资和退出，政府引导基金的进一步扩容引导了社会资金更多地流进创投基金和实体经济，港股、美股的窗口期为具有国际视野的创业投资基金带来更大的机会，整个中国创投行业呈现出良好的发展态势。无疑，创投行业的快速发展，已经成为破解中小企业融资难问题、加快金融供给侧改革的重要手段。

1. 2017 年创投发展的新态势

结合统计数据分析，2017 年我国创投行业发展呈现出以下新态势：

1.1 总量持续增长，增速略有下滑

2017 年，中国创投总量持续增长，活跃的创投机构数达到 2296 家，较 2016 年增长 12.3%。其中，创业投资基金 1589 只，增幅 11.8%；创业投资管理机构 707 家，增幅 13.3%（见图 1）。

从资金规模来看，2017 年，全国创业投资管理资本总量达到 8872.5 亿元，较 2016 年增加 595.4 亿元，增幅为 7.2%，较前两年明显放缓（见图 2）。此外，基金两极分化的现象较为严重，管理资本规模超过 5 亿元的机构虽然仅占 10.2%，但掌握了 72.1% 的管理资本总量。

① 全国创业投资调查写作组人员：张明喜、李希义、张俊芳、魏世杰、朱欣乐、郭滕达、薛薇等。本报告执笔人：张俊芳。

② 私募股权基金主要指从事私人股权（非上市公司股权）投资的基金，包括投资非上市公司股权或上市公司非公开交易股权两种。广义的私募股权基金包括风险投资基金，但由于风险投资主要以投资高科技企业并扶持企业成长为主业，投资阶段偏早前期，在投资阶段、持股比例、投资目标，以及退出方式等方面与一般私募股权基金明显不同，因此各国政府在制定政策时有所倾向，并进行单独统计。

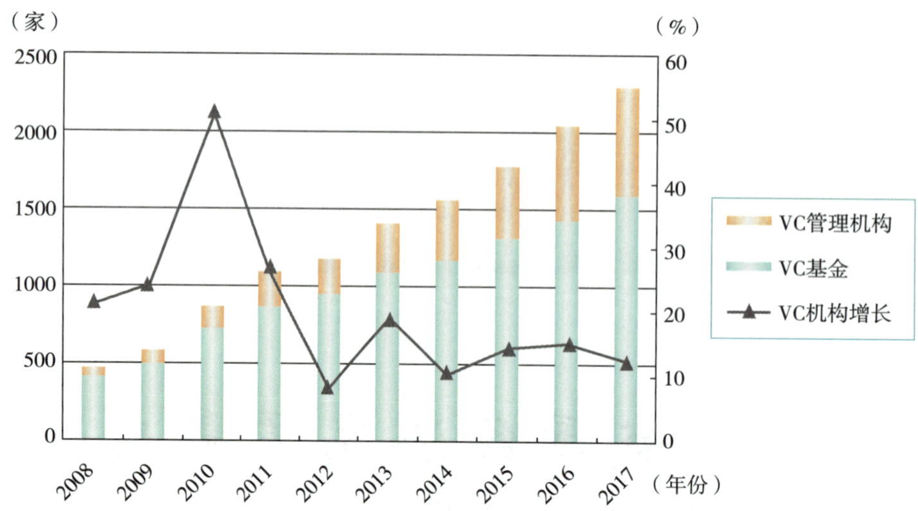

图 1　中国创业投资机构总量、增量（2008~2017）

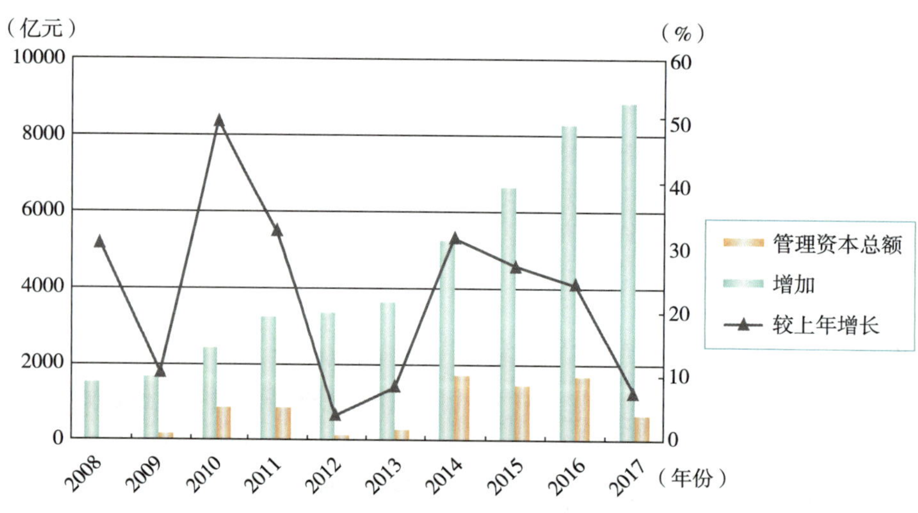

图 2　中国创业投资管理资本总额（2008~2017）

1.2　基金形态日益多元化，母基金成为重要的参与主体

近年来，创投机构的表现形式日益丰富，越来越多的创投基金通过委托创投管理机构进行专业化管理，或是通过母子基金进行层级管理。2017 年统计显示，母基金已经成为重要的创投参与主体，共有 79 家创投机构以母基金的组织形式存在，占比 3.44%，包括 51 只创投基金，28 家创投管理机构；管理资本规模达到 503.7 亿元，占比 5.7%。其中，最大母基金管理资本总量达到 241 亿元，投资的子基金数量达到 58 只。此外，公司化的创投基金与个人天使投资基金等组织形式也快速增长。

1.3　资金募集渠道不断丰富，政府引导基金与高净值人群快速增长

按照资金来源的机构性质进行划分，2017 年创业投资资本构成中，政府引导基金出资占比 7.28%，其他政府财政资金出资占比 6.29%，国有独资投资机构出资占比

12.47%，三者合计占比 26.04%，较 2016 年下降了 10.1 个百分点；高净值个人投资占比 9.73%，上升了 2.65 个百分点；外资企业占比 3.38%，下降了 1.04 个百分点；此外，社保基金占比 0.04%（见图 3（a））。

按照资金来源的金融属性进行划分，银行、保险、证券等金融机构资本合计占比 11.99%，较 2016 年大幅增长 5.81 个百分点。其中，银行资本较上年大幅上升；其他金融资本占比 27.85%，较上年上升 5.3 个百分点；主要资金仍来源于非金融资本，占比 60.15%（见图 3（b））。

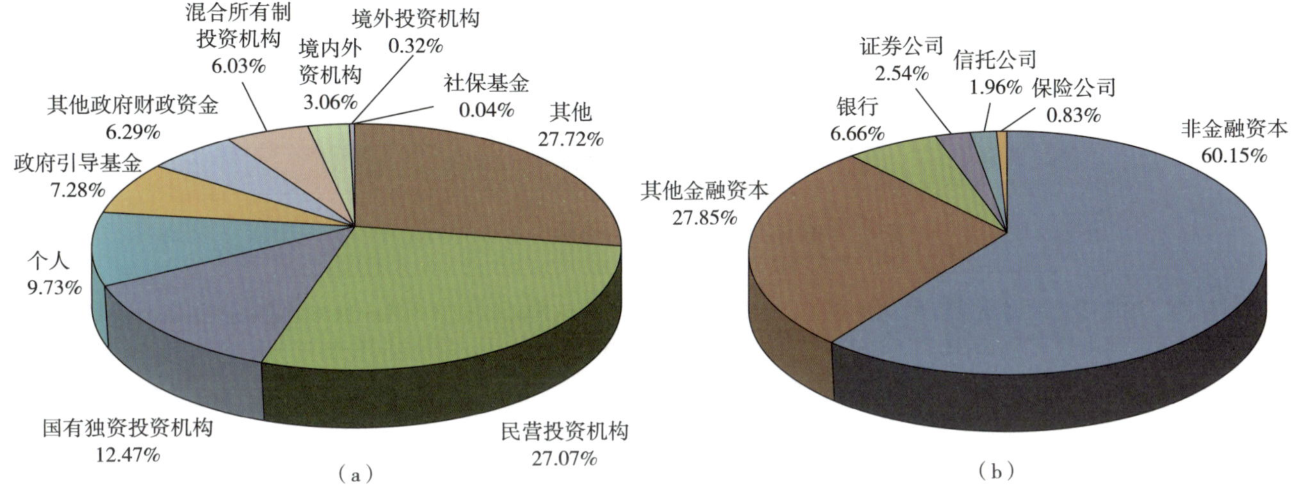

图 3　中国创业投资资本来源（2017）

1.4　累计投资突破两万家，扶持了一批“独角兽”企业快速成长

据统计，截至 2017 年底，全国创业投资机构累计投资项目数达到 20674 项，累计投资金额 4110.2 亿元。其中，2017 年当年披露投资项目 2687 项，投资金额 845.3 亿元，平均投资额为 3145 万元 / 项，较 2016 年大幅增加。

创业投资的发展成功助推了一大批高新技术企业成长。统计显示，截至 2017 年底，创投机构投资的高新技术企业（项目）达到 8851 项，投资金额 1627.3 亿元，分别占比 42.8% 和 39.6%。其中，2017 年投资的高新技术企业（项目）825 家，较 2016 年增加 30.1%；投资金额 153.8 亿元，增幅 67.0%。投资于科技型中小企业（项目）858 家，投资金额 97.5 亿元。据“独角兽”俱乐部盘点①，2017 年国内入围的 124 家“独角兽”公司背后共有 200 多家机构投资，其中不乏红杉资本、IDG 资本、启明创投等创投机构的身影。

1.5　为经济高质量发展赋能，引领物联网、绿色经济、人工智能等前沿领域

按传统行业划分，2017 年中国创业投资行业的投资项目主要集中在软件和信息服务业（18.27%）、新能源和环保（11.61%）、生物医药（11.38%），以及其他行业（10.44%）等领域。其中，软件和信息服务领域内的投资金额出现大幅下降，占比由 2016 年的 47.55% 缩减到 2017 年的 7.11%。

值得一提的是，由于近年来新技术的出现，传统的行业划分已变得模糊。比如，金融科技可能属于网络产业，也可能属于金融保险行业，而人工智能则可能分布于多个行业内。因此，2017 年增加了对热门行业板块的统计。从统计结果来看，除其他板块以外，2017 年中国创投的热点主要分布在物联网与大数据、绿色经济、人工智能、金融科技等领域，引领科技发展的前沿领域（见图 4）。

1.6　区域发展不平衡加速，创投向北、上、广等科技资源相对丰富地区聚集

区域发展不平衡一直是我国创投发展的基本特征。由于创投主要以高新技术企业为投资目标，在科技资源发达的地区，大多也具备丰富的创投资源。统计显示，2017 年，全国创投仍然主要集中在北京、江苏、广东、浙江等地，四个地区集中了全国 62.5% 的资金。此外，安徽、山东、

① IT 桔子发布的《2017 年独角兽俱乐部》报告。

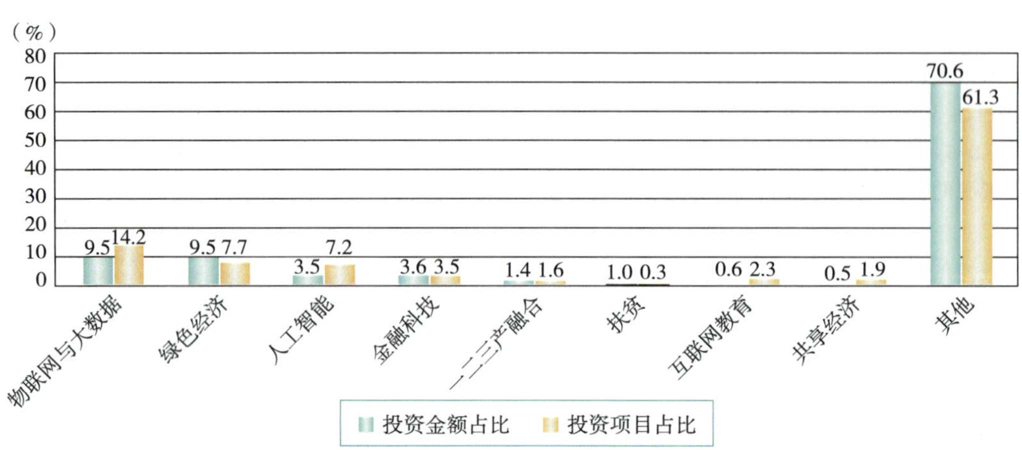

图 4 中国创投业投资的行业板块分布（2017）

天津、湖南、湖北等地的创业投资也发展迅速，规模增长较快（见图 5）。

相比而言，内地欠发达地区的资金来源主要以国有资本、政府财政资金为主，获得政府的直接资助较多，而沿海经济发达地区的民间投资更为活跃，大多为间接资助方式。

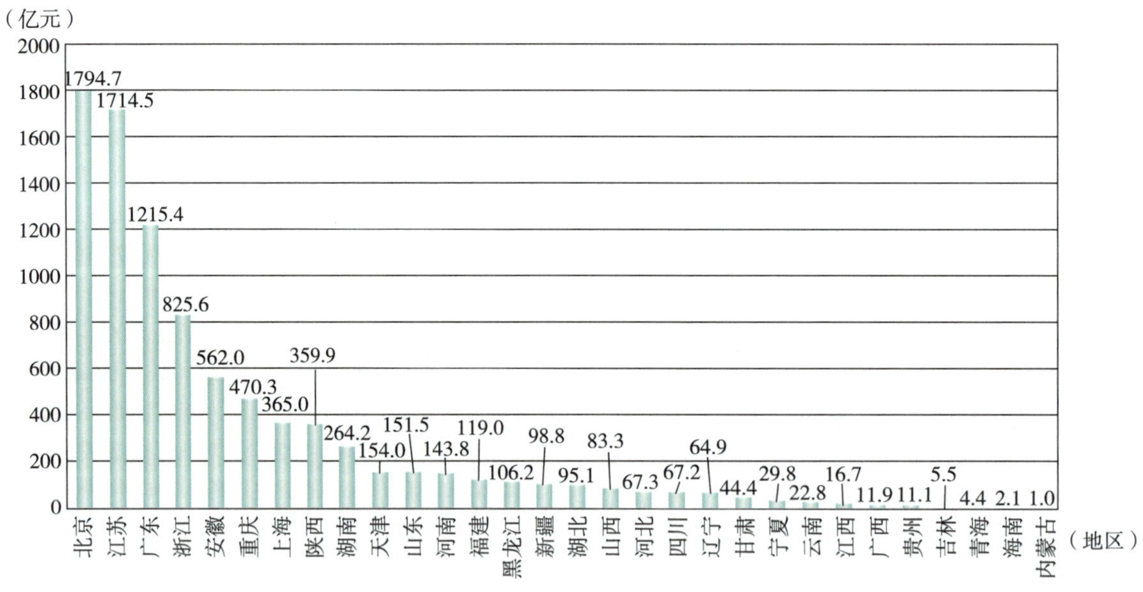

图 5 中国创投业投资的地区管理资本分布（2017）

1.7 资本市场运行平稳，行业退出总体表现良好

2016 年以来，为防范金融风险，证监会发审呈现从严监管的态势。市场数据显示，2017 年当年 IPO 项目 436 项，总融资额为 2301.53 亿元；其中，120 项项目受到创业投资企业投资，占比 27.5%。相对而言，并购与回购仍然是创投企业实现退出的主要渠道，整个创投行业实现退出项目共 878 项，其中，通过并购、回购退出项目分别为 286 项、306 项，合计占全年退出项目的 67.5%；此外，近 10% 的

项目通过“新三板”实现退出，增加了5.17个百分点。

从行业退出收益表现来看，总体退出收益率表现良好，全行业平均投资收益达到243.35%。整个行业投资退出步伐略微放缓，退出时间增加到4.4年，行业年均收益率达到38.33%（见图6）。

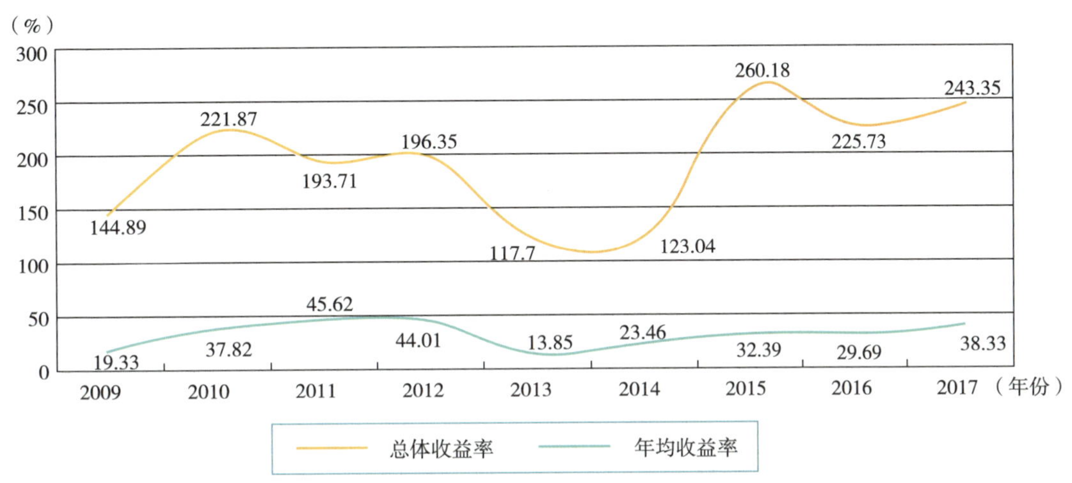

图6 中国创投业退出收益率（2009~2017）

1.8 早前期投资不足，行业急功近利倾向有所增加

按投资项目的发展阶段进行划分，2017年中国创投的投资金额主要集中在成长（扩张）期和成熟（过渡）期，占比分别为44.7%、29.9%，相比往年有所增加。相应地，对起步期项目的投资下降较大，资金占比由2016年的30.30%下滑到2017年的20.8%；种子期项目投资变化较小。投资阶段整体后移，行业“急功近利”倾向有所增加（见表1）。

此外，统计显示，2017年创投项目的R&D投入达到279.7亿元，项目平均研发投入资金为1261.7万元/项。相比而言，种子期、起步期的项目处于重要的研发投入阶段，但由于绝大多数企业尚未盈利，不能用销售收入弥补R&D投入成本，因此创投资金成为其重要的投入来源。

表1 中国创业投资项目所处阶段分布：投资金额与投资项目（2016~2017）

成长阶段	投资金额占比（%）		投资项目占比（%）	
	2016年	2017年	2016年	2017年
种子期	4.33	4.5	19.6	17.8
起步期	30.3	20.8	38.9	39.5
成长（扩张）期	38.5	44.7	35.0	36.2
成熟（过渡）期	26.3	29.9	5.7	5.9
重建期	0.6	0.2	0.8	0.6

1.9 科技金融服务平台作用日渐凸显，成为重要的项目来源渠道

近年来，创业投资的项目来源呈现出多元化的发展趋势，调查显示，2017年中国创投的项目来源仍然以“政府部门推荐”（21.9%）、“朋友介绍”（14.0%）和“项目中介机构”（16.0%）三个渠道为主。但三者占比之和从2013年的64.5%下滑到2017年的51.9%。

值得注意的是，随着“双创”的环境营造与科技金融服务业的发展，“科技金融服务平台”的重要作用日渐凸显，已经成为创业风险投资项目来源的重要渠道，2017 年来源于该渠道的项目占比达到 11.0%（见表 2）。

表 2 创业投资机构获取项目信息来源渠道（2013~2017）

单位：%

年份＼信息渠道	政府部门推荐	朋友介绍	项目中介机构	股东推荐	项目业主	银行介绍	媒体宣传	众创空间（孵化器）	科技金融服务平台	其他
2013	25.5	19.9	19.1	13.2	10.1	6.0	2.6	—	—	3.6
2014	24.9	17.7	17.1	14.3	11	7.4	3.9	—	—	3.6
2015	21.3	14.6	15.2	13.9	11.3	7.1	3.5	10.4	—	2.7
2016	20.2	15.4	15.1	14.1	11.5	6.1	3.5	11.3	—	2.7
2017	21.9	14.0	16.0	11.4	9.5	2.5	1.4	9.1	11.0	3.2

2. 行业景气分析

2.1 2018 年行业发展总体呈乐观态势

对于 2018 年投资前景，中国创业投资界整体上给出了相对乐观的预测。认为 2018 年投资前景“非常好”和“好”的机构分别占比 7.4% 和 53.7%，合计较上年提高 2.5 个百分点，持乐观预期的机构比重连续两年提高。此外，对 2018 年投资前景持“不确定”态度的机构比重有所增加，达到 4.8%。对于复杂的国际经济形势，特别是中美贸易摩擦的影响，80.2% 的机构认为宏观经济对行业影响较大（见图 7）。

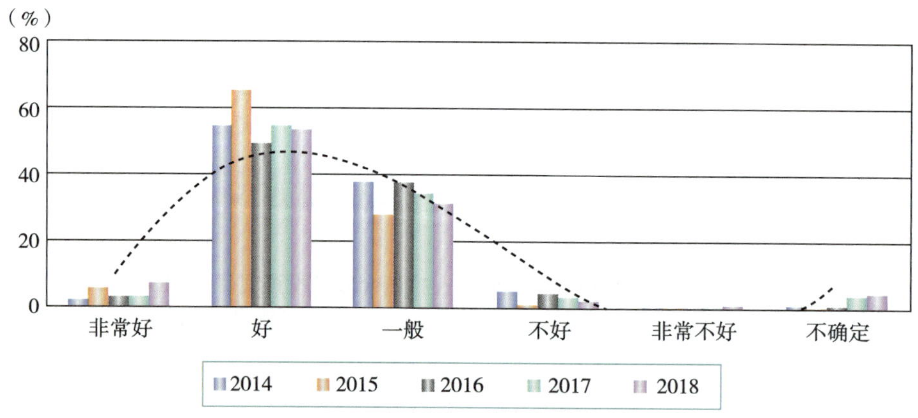

图 7 创投机构对投资前景预测（2014~2018）

2.2 行业环境向好，市场竞争进一步加剧

2017 年调查显示，认为中国创投机构投资效果不理想的主要原因集中在“退出渠道不畅”（18.5%）、“政策环境变化”（17.3%）、“市场竞争”（18.3%）、“内部管理水平有限”（17.1%）等方面。与前几年相比，“退出渠道不畅”与“政策环境变化”影响占比明显下降，而“市场竞争”与“内部管理水平有限”占比呈现出较大幅度上升。此外，“影响机构进行决策的因素”调查显示，“市场前景”“管理团队”和“技术因素”仍然是三个最主要因素，但“市场前景”影响因素大幅上升了 12.2 个百分点，达到 30.5%。这在一定程度反映出，我国创投行业整体环境日益改善，随着机构数目的增加，行业市场竞争态势不断加剧。

2.3 人工智能等高科技领域将成为未来投资新热点

2017 年调查显示，“人工智能”“新能源、高效节能技术”“生物科技”将成为 2018 年创投机构最看好的领域，占比分别为 23.4%、21.9%、19.8%，占比较往年大幅上升。此外，“金融科技”和“科技服务（教育）”占比也略有上升，分别为 5.5%、5.4%。从投资趋势可以看到，网络产业、共享经济等领域的投资热度大幅下降，而高科技前沿领域的投资将成为投资的主战场。

3. 困惑与问题

3.1 大资管时代来临，造成创投行业发展的短期阵痛

2018 年 4 月 27 日，中国人民银行、中国银行保险监督管理委员会、中国证券监督管理委员会、国家外汇管理局联合印发了《关于规范金融机构资产管理业务的指导意见》（银发〔2018〕106 号），开启了大资管行业的统一监管的新时代——金融机构的业务调整和数十万亿元的资产“腾挪”将成为金融市场最大的变量之一。从长远来看，更加标准化、净值化的资产管理行业对基础市场的稳定发展是积极的，但短期必将带来创投行业发展的阵痛。主要表现为，银行理财对接券商、基金子公司甚至私募投资基金等载体上的私募 FOF 产品模式将不再存在。这意味着创投的募资来源将受到限制，直接影响到创投行业募集的资金体量。据业内反映，业内小规模的创投基金受到的冲击最大，募资难将成为行业短期发展的主要瓶颈。

3.2 监管政策尚未明确，影响创投行业发展

2014 年以来，为防范金融风险，相关部门加强了对证券投资基金业的监管，但将“创投”行业视同一般证券基金业纳入监管范围，在很大程度上造成了行业发展的障碍。2016 年 9 月，国务院印发《关于促进创业投资持续健康发展的若干意见》，提出“对创业投资企业在行业管理、备案登记等方面采取与其他私募基金区别对待的差异化监管政策”。2017 年 8 月，国务院发布《私募投资基金管理暂行条例（征求意见稿）》，再次指出要对创投行业实行“差异化监管”，但目前尚未出台相关指导意见和办法，创投行业依然受制于一般证券基金的监管框架。

3.3 政策引导基金盲目扩张，隐患日渐凸显

为带动社会资本进入高科技领域，引导早期投资，近年来各地政府通过设立创投引导基金，优化资金配置方式、方向，支持了一大批创业投资机构和优质创业创新项目。调查显示，截至 2017 年底，全国设立政府创投引导基金共计 483 只；累计出资 620.9 亿元，引导带动创业风险投资机构管理资金规模合计 2913.2 亿元。然而，快速扩张使政府引导基金日渐暴露出一些问题。比如，部分政府引导基金募资受阻，没有按照约定条款募集到足够的社会资本；部分引导基金难以寻找到好的项目投资，造成财政资金结存现象严重；部分地区在设立政府引导基金时尚未考虑发生投资损失时的坏账准备，存在财政资金审计的风险；部分地区尚未采用市场化的运作模式，投资效率较低；等等。

3.4 行业发展尚未形成良好的创投生态链

从整个创投行业发展的生态链来看，国内好“种子”相对不足，导致创投行业发展缺乏“源头活水”。近年来，我国企业资金短缺问题从“绝对不足”转向“相对不足”，一些好的项目被众多创投机构“哄抢”，而另一些项目则仍然“嗷嗷待哺”。不少投资机构反映，目前已经不是缺钱的问题，而是缺乏好的项目投资。随着近期中美贸易战的持续，美国将加强海外并购的限制，而国内好“种子”的培育孵化机制的缺乏，在一定程度上影响了创投行业发展。此外，国内资本市场发育尚不完善，导致创投行业的退出渠道狭窄，影响投资收益。现阶段，我们依然存在 IPO 审核的制度障碍，“堰塞湖”现象严重。2017 年调查显示，“退出渠道不畅”一直是近年来创业投资不理想的首要原因。

3.5 相关税收优惠政策难以落地

为促进行业发展，2017 年 4 月，财政部、国家税务总局发布《关于创业投资企业和天使投资个人有关税收试点政策的通知》，在 8 个全面创新改革试验区 ① 和苏州工业园区进行试点，对符合条件的创业投资企业给予投资额 70% 的税前抵扣。2018 年 5 月，政策被推广至全国范围。然而，据 2017 年国家自主创新示范区 ② 内调查显示，由于存在备案管理和操作障碍、对天使投资人抵扣要求条件较为严格等问题，相关政策尚未落地。

---

① 包括京津冀、上海、广东（珠三角）、安徽（合芜蚌）、四川（成德绵）、湖北武汉、陕西西安、辽宁沈阳等地区。

② 其中，北京中关村、上海张江、广东珠三角、安徽合芜蚌、四川成都、武汉东湖、陕西西安、辽宁沈大、江苏苏南 9 个自主创新示范区属于政策试点范围。

4. 思考与建议

鉴于创投行业规模的迅速扩大，其发展对促进实体经济发展的影响日益增强，建议按照“放管服”的总体思想，进一步完善创投行业发展的内外环境。

4.1 不断培养行业内生能力，引导创业投资方向

近年来，伴随着投资环境的不断优化与高净值人群的增加，大量资本涌入创投行业。由于行业的急剧扩张，必然存在人才储备不足、行业发展不规范、投资追求“短平快”项目的现象，特别是政府引导基金的快速扩张，缺乏市场化的运作机制，隐忧日渐凸显等。鉴于风险投资行业发展的重要作用，建议进一步规范、提高基金运作管理水平，加快行业专业化人才队伍建设；同时，继续引导投资方向，更多地关注早期投资与价值投资，多渠道培育优秀的种子与项目源。

4.2 充分尊重行业属性，破除行业发展的制度障碍

现阶段，创投行业面临的各种制度障碍主要根源于尚未充分认识行业属性，没有从顶层设计的思路出发，建立与之相适应的管理制度。从国际情况来看，各国均认为，投资与证券投资基金是两种截然不同的投资业态，可以显著地提高市场配置资源的效率，主张由市场机制自发地加以调节。建议借鉴国际经验，按照“分类监管、适度监管”原则，尽快推动相关政策的制定与完善，明确界定免予证券监管的标准，从源头上建立信息共享机制，停止实质审批等不当做法；同时，结合我国国企分类改革要求，制定符合创业投资运作规律的相关管理办法，制定与创投管理规律相适应的财政资金管理制度。

4.3 继续完善创投发展的生态链，优化投资发展的生态环境

优秀的“源头活水”是创投发展的原动力，资本市场的改革与发展直接关系着投资的退出收益与自身供血的再循环。建议继续完善优秀项目的孵化培育机制，通过发展科技金融服务平台，建立国际合作孵化器、加速器、国际科技合作基地等方式，加快优秀项目的培养；学习借鉴美国等资本市场建设方面的先进经验，进一步加强多层次资本市场的制度建设，增强市场与政策的稳定性。同时，加快推进《关于促进创业投资持续健康发展的若干意见》等文件相关配套办法的制定，找准《关于创业投资企业和天使投资个人有关税收试点政策的通知》等税收政策的实施难点，推进政策落地实施。

Executive Summary

Venture Capital Energizes High-Quality Economic Development in China

—New Trends, Problems and Suggestions on the Development of China's Venture Capital Industry in 2017

National Venture Capital Survey Group①

Venture capital, which plays an important role in the construction of national innovation systems, has become an important driving force for the development of high-tech enterprises. Based on the data of the 16th National Venture Capital Survey of the Ministry of Science and Technology, this paper analyzes new development trends of China's venture capital industry in 2017 and investigates the prosperity index of the industry. In the meantime, it presents preliminary considerations for handling obstacles to the industry's development on the basis of related surveys.

In recent years, many people have claimed that "real estate speculation has ended" "China has entered the era of equity investment" and "private equity (PE) investment has penetrated into the whole nation". Although these statements sound exaggerated, PE investment ② represented by venture capital has indeed developed rapidly and considerably. According to the data of China Securities Industry Association, a total of 66418 PE funds (including VC funds) had been filed as of the end of 2017, climbing 42.82% from a year earlier and involving a management scale of RMB 11.1 trillion Yuan.

In 2017, the acceleration of IPO examination promoted the recruitment, investment and exit of VC funds, the further expansion of government fund-of-funds led social capital to invest in VC and real economy, and the window period of Hong Kong stocks and U.S. stocks provided great opportunities for VC funds with international vision. Overall, China's VC industry showed a favorable development trend in 2017. There is no doubt that rapid development of the VC industry has become an important means of solving financing difficulties of small and medium-sized enterprises (SMEs) and accelerating financial supply-side reforms.

---

① Members of the writing group: Zhang Mingxi, Li Xiyi, Zhang Junfang, Wei Shijie, Zhu Xinyue, Guo Tengda, Xue Wei, et al. The report was prepared by: Zhang Junfang.

② PE funds mainly refer to funds invested in private equities (equities of unlisted companies) and consist of funds invested in equities of unlisted companies and those invested in non-publicly traded equities of listed companies. PE funds include VC funds in broad sense. However, VC investment tends to take place in early prophase since VC is mainly invested in high-tech enterprises and used to support corporate growth. VC funds are distinctly different from general PE funds in investment stage, shareholding ratio, investment objective and exit mode. Therefore, governments should give preference to VC funds and carry out separate statistics when formulating policies.

1. New Development Trends in 2017

According to the statistical analysis, China's VC industry presented the following development trends in 2017:

1.1 The total amount continued to grow and the growth rate slightly decreased

The total amount of VC in China continued to grow in 2017. The number of active VC institutions reached 2296, increasing by 12.3% from the previous year. Among them, the number of VC funds and VC management institutions rose 11.8% and 13.3% from a year earlier to 1589 and 707 separately (See Graph 1).

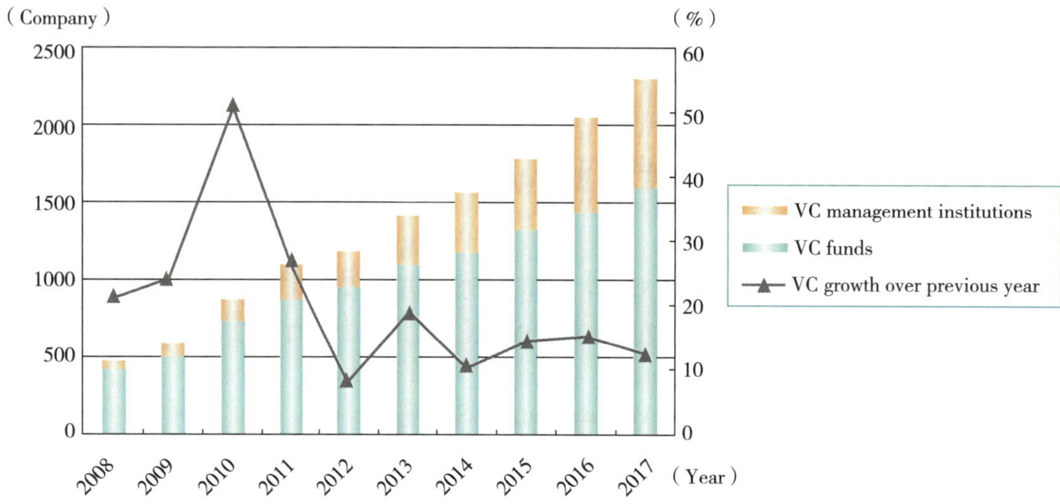

Graph 1 Total and Incremental Amount of VC Institutions in China (2008~2017)

Judging from the fund size, the managed VC funds totaled 887.25 billion Yuan in 2017, increasing by 7.2% (59.54 billion Yuan) from the previous year. It should be noted that the growth rate was significantly lower than that in the previous two years (See Graph 2). In addition, funds were seriously polarized. Although institutions with the management scale of more than RMB 500 million Yuan merely accounted for 10.2%, they mastered 72.1% of the total managed capital.

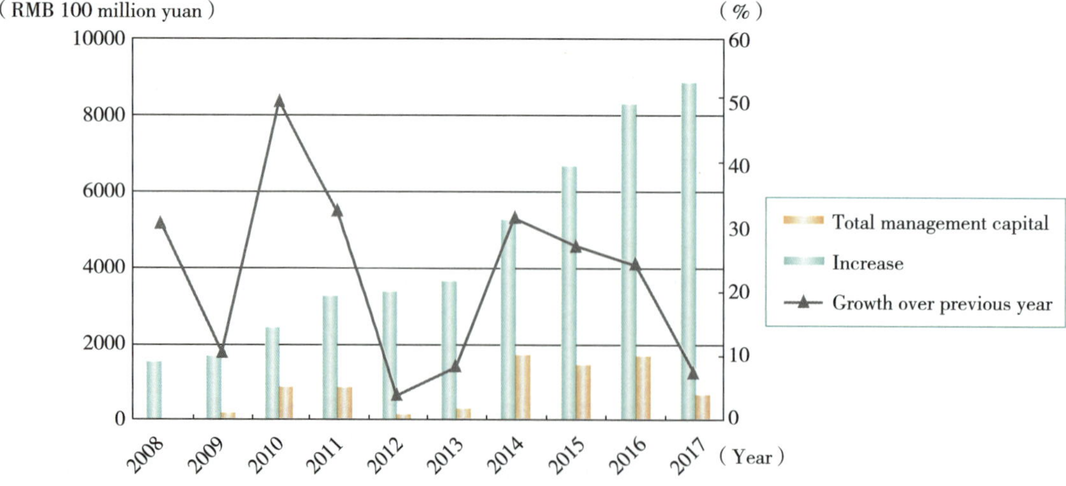

Graph 2 Total Amount of Managed VC Funds in China (2008~2017)

1.2 Fund forms became increasingly diversified and FOF became an important participant

Due to the increasingly diversified fund forms, a growing number of VC institutions have entrusted the professional management of VC funds to VC management institutions or carried out hierarchical management through FOFs in recent years. According to the statistics in 2017, FOF had become an important VC participant. A total of 79 VC institutions had existed in the form of FOF, including 51 VC funds and 28 VC management institutions and involving a management scale of RMB 50.37 billion Yuan (accounted 5.7%). Among them, management scale of the largest FOF reached RMB 24.1 billion Yuan and the number of sub-funds invested reached 58. In addition, corporatized VC funds and individual angel investment funds had developed rapidly.

1.3 Fundraising channels were constantly enriched and investment proportion of government-guided funds and high-net-worth individuals increased rapidly

Judging from the institution nature of fund sources, government-guided funds, other government financial funds and wholly state-owned investment institutions contributed to 7.28%, 6.29% and 12.47% of the total amount of VC respectively in 2017, totaling 26.04% and decreasing by 10.1% from the previous year. The investments by high-net-worth individuals and foreign-funded enterprises accounted for 9.73% and 3.38% of the total amount separately, up 2.65% and down 1.04% from a year earlier separately. In addition, social insurance funds occupied 0.04% of the total amount (See Graph 3 (a)).

Judging from the financial nature of fund sources, financial institutions such as banks, insurance companies and securities firms contributed to 11.99% of the total amount of VC, up by an impressive 5.81% from a year early. Among them, bank capital rose sharply from the previous year and the investment proportion of other financial capital increased by 5.3% to 27.85%. Major funds still came from nonfinancial capital, accounting for 60.15% of the total amount (See Graph 3 (b)).

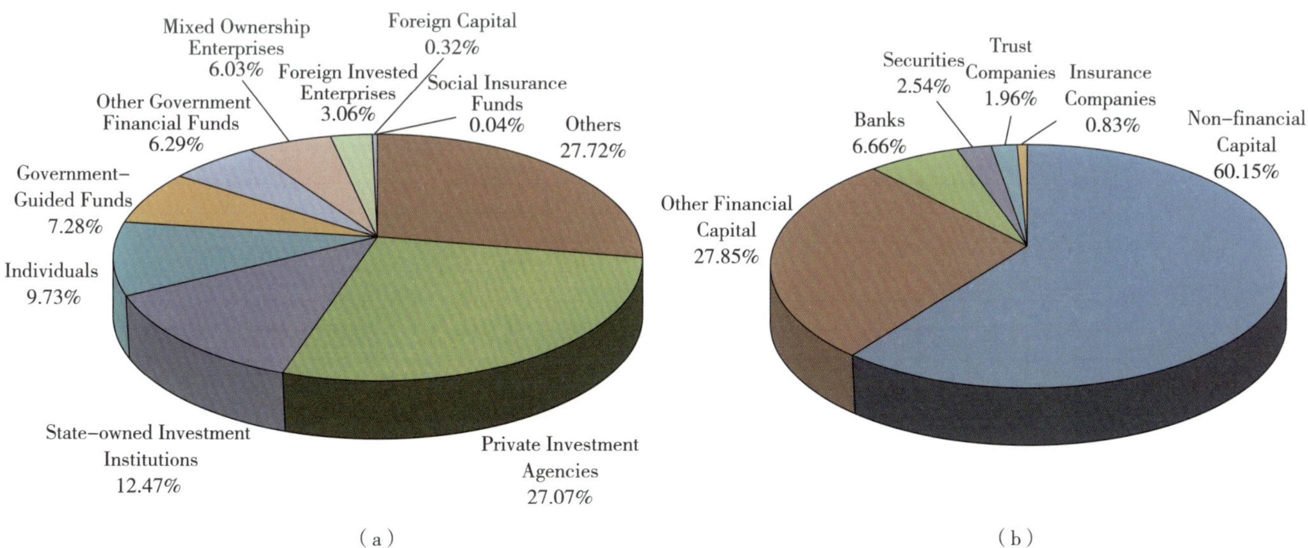

Graph 3 Fundraising Sources of VC in China (2017)

1.4 The cumulative number of investment projects exceeded 20000 and a batch of unicorn enterprises developed rapidly

According to statistics, the cumulative number of projects invested by VC institutions reached 20674 and the cumulative investment amount reached RMB 411.02 billion Yuan as of the end of 2017. Among them, 2687 investment projects were disclosed in 2017, with an investment amount of RMB 84.53 billion Yuan. In other words, the average investment per project was RMB 3.145 million Yuan, making a significant increase from 2016.

The successful development of VC had promoted the growth of a large number of high-tech enterprises. Statistics showed that the number of high-tech enterprises (projects) invested and the investment amount reached 8851 and RMB 162.37 billion Yuan as of the end of 2017, accounting for 42.8% and 39.6% separately. Among them, 825 high-tech enterprises (projects) were invested in 2017, with an investment amount of RMB 15.38 billion Yuan, up 30.1% and 67.0% from a year earlier separately; 858 high-tech SMEs were invested in 2017, with an investment amount of RMB 9.75 billion Yuan. According to the inventory of the Unicorn Club, the 124 unicorn companies shortlisted in 2017 been invested by VC institutions more over 200 units, including Sequoia Capital, IDG Capital, Qiming Venture Partners and Northern Light Venture Capital.

1.5 VC energized high-quality economic development and led frontier fields such as IOT, green economy and artificial intelligence

According to classified statistics by industries, China's VC institutions mainly invested in the software and information service industries (18.27%), new energy and environmental protection industries (11.61%), biomedical industry (11.38%) and other industries (10.44%). Among them, the investments in software and information service industries slumped considerably and the investment proportion decreased from 47.55% in 2016 to 7.11%.

It's worth noting that traditional industry classification has become blurred due to the emergence of new technologies in recent years. For example, financial science and technology belong to both network industry and financial insurance industry and artificial intelligence (AI) also involves multiple industries. Therefore, statistics was performed on popular industrial sectors in 2017. It can be seen from the statistical results that VC in China was mainly invested in frontier fields such as IOT and big data, green economy, artificial intelligence and Fin-tech (See Graph 4).

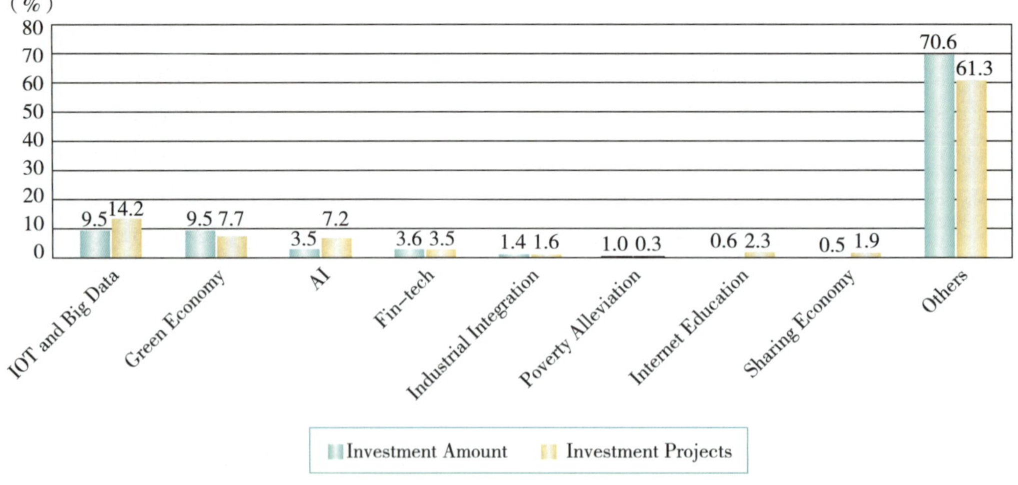

Graph 4 Distribution of Industrial Sectors Invested by China's VC Industry (2017)

1.6 Unbalanced regional development was accelerated and VC resources were abundant in technological resource gathering places such as Beijing, Shanghai, Guangzhou

Unbalanced regional development has been a basic feature of the development of China's VC industry. Since VC is mainly invested in high-tech enterprises, regions with rich technological resources tend to have abundant VC resources. Statistics showed that 62.5% of China's VC investments were concentrated in Beijing, Jiangsu, Guangdong and Zhejiang in 2017. In addition, VC investments in Anhui, Shandong, Tianjin, Hunan and Hubei also increased rapidly (See Graph 5).

Comparatively speaking, underdeveloped regions in mainland China were mainly directly subsidized by the governments (state-owned capital and government financial capital) while economically developed coastal regions were mostly indirectly funded by private capital.

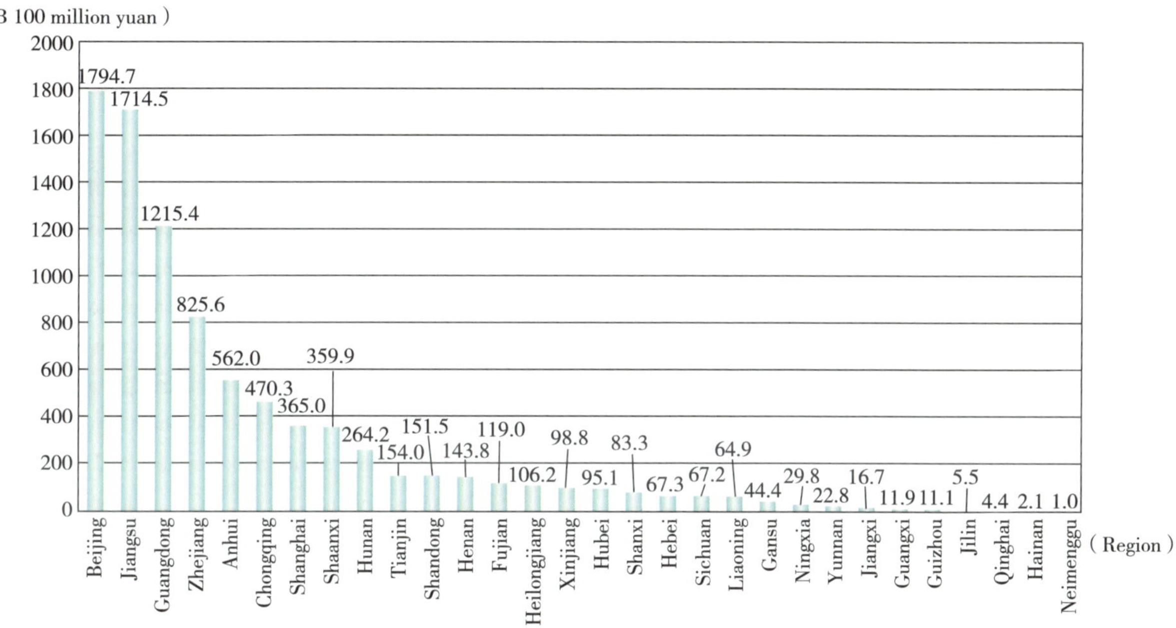

Graph 5 Regional Distribution of VC Investments in China (2017)

1.7 The capital market ran smoothly and the VC industry enjoyed outstanding exit performance

The Issuance Examination Committee of China Securities Regulatory Commission has implemented strict regulation to prevent financial risks since 2016. According to the market data, there were 436 IPO projects in 2017, involving a total financing amount of 230.153 billion Yuan. Among them, 120 projects (27.5%) were invested by VC enterprises. By contrast, M&A and repurchase still served as the main exit ways of VC enterprises. There are 878 projects achieve exit in the whole. Among them, 286 and 306 enterprises (totaling 67.5%) exited by means of M&A and repurchase separately. In addition, nearly 10% (a 5.17% increase) of the projects exited the industry through new OTCBB.

Judging from the exit returns, the VC industry enjoyed outstanding exit performance on the whole and the average rate of return on investment reached 243.4% in 2017. The industry slightly slowed down the pace of investment exit and the exit time increased to 4.4 years. The annual average rate of return reached 38.3% (See Graph 6).

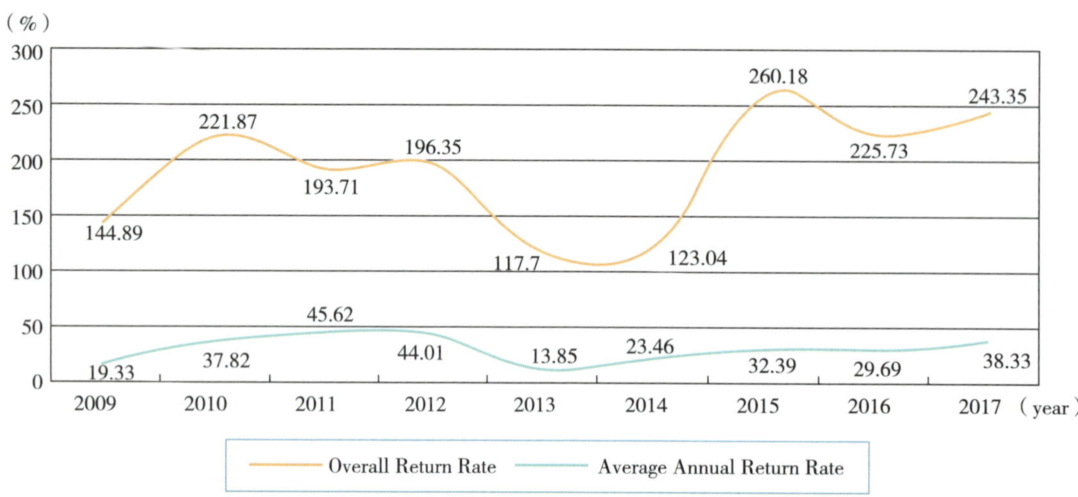

Graph 6 Exit Return Rate of China's VC Industry (2009~2017)

1.8 Lack of investment in the early stage, and the tendency to eargerness for quick results has increased

Judging from the development stages of investment projects, China's VC investment mostly took place in the growth (expansion) stage and the maturity (translation) stage in 2017, accounted 44.7% and 29.9% separately and the investment proportion slightly increased compared to previous years. Accordingly, the proportion of investment in start-up projects decreased from 30.3% in 2016 to 20.8%. The investment stages shifted backwards and the eagerness for quick success and instant benefit increased See-Table1.

On the other hand, the R&D input of projects reached RMB 27.97 billion Yuan, and the average R&D investment in project was RMB 12.617 million Yuan per project. In contrast, the projects in the seed stage and starting stage are an import stage of R&D input. However, as most enterprises are still not profitable, they cannot make up the R&D investment cost with the sales revenue, so the VC capital should become an important source of investment.

Table 1 VC Project stage (2016~2017)

Stage	Investment amount (%)		Investment project(%)	
	2016	2017	2016	2017
Seed stage	4.33	4.5	19.6	17.8
Start-up stage	30.3	20.8	38.9	39.5
Growth (expansion) stage	38.5	44.7	35.0	36.2
Maturity (transition) stage	26.3	29.9	5.7	5.9
Reconstruction stage	0.6	0.2	0.8	0.6

1.9 S&T financial service platforms gradually became an important project source

The sources of VC projects have presented a diversified development trend in recent years. According to the surveys, VC projects in China still came from the following sources in 2017: government recommendation (21.9%), friend recommendation (14.0%) and project agency (16.0%). Nevertheless, the total proportion of them decreased from

64.5% in 2013 to 51.9% in 2017.

It's worth mentioning that "S&T financial platforms" have become important sources of VC projects due to the creation of innovative and entrepreneurial environment. Projects came from this source accounted for 11.0% of the total number in 2017 (See Table 2).

Table 2 Information Sources of VC Projects (2013 ~ 2017)

Unit: %

Year \ Information Source	Government recommendation	Friend recommendation	Project agency	Share holder recommendation	Project owner	Bank recommendation	Media publicity	Maker space (incubator)	S&T financial service platform	Others
2013	25.5	19.9	19.1	13.2	10.1	6.0	2.6	—	—	3.6
2014	24.9	17.7	17.1	14.3	11	7.4	3.9	—	—	3.6
2015	21.3	14.6	15.2	13.9	11.3	7.1	3.5	10.4	—	2.7
2016	20.2	15.4	15.1	14.1	11.5	6.1	3.5	11.3	—	2.7
2017	21.9	14.0	16.0	11.4	9.5	2.5	1.4	9.1	11.0	3.2

2. Industry Prosperity Analysis

2.1 The industry has shown an optimistic development trend in 2018

China's VC industry offered upbeat forecasts about the investment prospects in 2018. Institutions with "very good" and "good" investment prospects accounted for 7.4% and 53.7% of the total number separately, 2.5% higher than the previous year. The proportion of institutions with optimistic expectations had increased for two consecutive years. On the other hand, the proportion of institutions that held an "uncertain" attitude toward the investment prospects in 2018 increased to 4.8%. 80.2% of the institutions argued that macro economy had a greater impact on the VC industry in comparison with the complex international economic situation, especially Sino-US trade conflicts (See Graph 7).

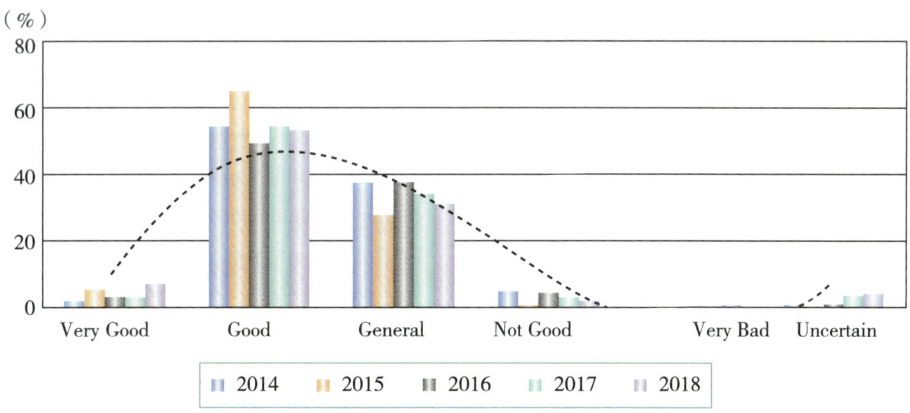

Graph 7 Forecasts about the Investment Prospects (2014 ~ 2018)

2.2 The industry environment has been improved and the market competitions have been further intensified

According to the surveys in 2017, the unsatisfactory investment results were mainly attributed to the following reasons: "poor exit channels" (18.5%), "policy environmental changes" (17.3%), "market competitions" (18.3%) and "limited internal management abilities" (17.1%). Among them, the proportion of "poor exit channels" and "policy environmental changes" had significantly decreased compared to previous years while that of "market competitions" and "limited internal management abilities" had drastically increased. In addition, surveys on "the influence factors of institutions' decision-making" showed that "market prospects", "management teams" and "technical factors" were still the three most important factors. Nevertheless, the proportion of "market prospects" had increased by 12.2% to 30.5%, which indicated the constant improvement of China's VC industry. Market competitions were constantly intensified with the increase in the number of institutions.

2.3 High-tech fields such as artificial intelligence has become new investment hotpots

According to the surveys in 2017, "artificial intelligence" "new energy and high-efficiency energy-saving technology" and "biotechnology" would become the most promising fields in 2018, accounting for 23.4%, 21.9% and 19.8% of the total number respectively. In addition, the proportion of "financial technology" and "technology service (education)" would slightly increase by 5.5% and 5.4% separately. It can be seen from the investment trends that the investment in network industry and sharing economy will decrease sharply while high-tech frontier fields will become the main investment battlefield.

3. Puzzles and Problems

3.1 The advent of the pan-asset management era has brought development throes to the VC industry

On April 27, 2018, People's Bank of China, China Banking and Insurance Regulatory Commission, China Securities Regulatory Commission and State Administration of Foreign Exchange jointly issued Guiding Opinions on Regulating the Asset Management Business of Financial Institutions (No.106 [2018] of the People's Bank of China), opening up a new era of unified pan-asset management supervision. The business adjustment of financial institutions and the transfer of trillions of assets shall become the biggest variables in the financial market. Standardized and netted asset management industry shall exert a positive impact on the steady development of basic market in the long run and bring development throes to the VC industry in the short term. Specifically, PE FOFs relied on carriers such as banking connection brokers, fund subsidiaries and PE funds shall no longer exist, which means that the fundraising sources of VC shall be restricted and directly influence the amount of funds raised. According to industry insiders, small-scale VC funds suffer the worst impact and fundraising difficulties serve as the main obstacles to the industry's development in the short term.

3.2 The regulatory policy has remained unclear, which influences the development of the VC industry

Related departments have strengthened the regulation on securities fund industry since 2014, so as to prevent financial risks. However, the inclusion of VC industry into general securities fund industry hampers the development of the industry to a great extent. In September 2016, the State Council issued Several Opinions on Promoting the Sustainable and Sound Development of Venture Capital, proposing to treat VC funds and other PE funds differently and adopt differentiated regulation policies in respect to industrial administration, filing and registration. It issued the Interim Regulation on the Administration of Private Equity Investment Funds (Consultation Paper) in August 2017 to once again put forward the implementation of differentiated regulation. However, relevant guidance and methods have not yet been issued. In other words, the VC industry is still subject to the regulatory framework of general securities funds.

3.3 The hidden dangers have become increasingly prominent due to the blind expansion of government-guided funds

To lead social capital to the high-tech field and guide early investment, local governments have supported a large number of VC institutions and high-quality innovative and entrepreneurial projects by establishing government-guided funds and optimizing fund allocation modes in recent years. According to the surveys, the number of government-guided funds had reached 483 as of the end of 2017. The total investment reached RMB 62.90 billion Yuan, guiding and stimulating RMB 291.32 billion Yuan of VC sub-funds. However, the rapid expansion of government-guided funds has gradually exposed some problems. For example, some government-guided funds are blocked from fundraising, eventually failing to raise enough social capital in accordance with the terms agreed. Some government-guided funds cause serious financial fund balances due to the difficulties in finding proper investment projects. There are risks of financial fund audit when government-guided funds are established without considering bad debts caused by investment losses. The investment efficiency is low in areas where market-oriented operation modes are not adopted.

3.4 There hasn't been a favorable development ecological chain for the VC industry

Judging from the development ecological chain of the entire VC industry, China lacks excellent "seeds", leading to the shortage of development "sources and impetuses" for the VC industry. Fund shortage in China has changed from "absolutely insufficient" to "relatively insufficient" in recent years. Some projects are "snapped" by lots of VC institutions while some projects are still "starving". Lots of investment institutions show that the current question is not the shortage of funds, but the shortage of wonderful investment projects. As the Sino-US trade war continues, the United States shall strengthen its restrictions on overseas M&A while the shortage of excellent "seed" incubation mechanisms in China shall influence the development of the VC industry to a certain extent. On the other hand, domestic capital market is still imperfect, which leads to narrow exit channels and influences investment returns of the VC industry. China is still faced with institutional barriers to IPO examination and dammed lake phenomenon at the present stage. According to a survey in 2017, "poor exit channels" has been the primary cause of unsatisfactory VC investment in recent years.

3.5 It is difficult to implement related preferential tax policies

To promote the development of the VC industry, the Ministry of Finance and the State Administration of Taxation jointly issued the Notice on the Relevant Pilot Tax Policies for Venture Capital Enterprises and Individual Angel Investors in April 2017, proposing to carry out pilot projects in 8 comprehensive innovation reform pilot zones ① and Suzhou Industrial Park and deduct 70% of the investment amount of eligible VC enterprises on a pre-tax basis. The policy was extended nationwide in May 2018. According to the surveys on national independent innovation demonstration zones ② in 2017, however, relevant policies haven't been implemented due to the obstacles to archival administration and operation, the strict requirements on deductions from angle investors and so on.

4.Considerations and Suggestions

Considering the rapid expansion of the VC industry and its increasing impact on the development of real economy, it is recommended to further improve the internal and external development environments of the industry in accordance with the overall idea of "streamlining administration, delegating power, strengthening regulation and improving services".

4.1 Constantly cultivating endogenous ability of the industry and guiding investment directions

Along with the continuous optimization of investment environments and the increase in high-net-worth individuals, a large amount of capital has flooded into the VC industry in recent years. Due to the drastic expansion of the industry, however, some problems will inevitably occur, such as insufficient talent reserves, non-standardized industry development and pursuit of projects with low investment, short investment cycles, and quick and high returns. In particular, hidden dangers of the rapid expansion of government-guided funds and the shortage of market-oriented operation mechanisms have become increasingly prominent. Considering the importance of VC development, it is recommended to further standardize and improve fund operation management and accelerate the construction of professional talent teams. In

① The 8 pilot zones include Beijing-Tianjin-Hebei, Shanghai, Guangdong (Pearl River Delta), Anhui (Hefei-Wuhu-Bengbu), Sichuan (Chengdu-Deyang-Mianyang), Hubei (Wuhan), Shaanxi (Xi' an) and Liaoning (Shenyang).

② Among them, 9 independent innovation demonstration zones fall within the pilot range, including Zhongguancun in Beijing, Zhangjiang in Shanghai, Pearl River Delta in Guangdong, Hefei-Wuhu-Bengbu in Anhui, Chengdu in Sichuan, East Lake in Wuhan, Xi'an in Shaanxi, Shenyang University in Liaoning and south Jiangsu.

the meantime, it is important to constantly guide investment directions, pay more attention to early investment and value investment and cultivate excellent seeds and project sources through multiple channels.

4.2 Fully respecting attributes of the industry and breaking institutional obstacles to the industry's development

At the present stage, the various institutional obstacles to the VC industry are mainly rooted in the insufficient understanding of industry attributes and the fact that corresponding management systems are not established from the perspective of top-level design. It's internationally believed that VC funds and securities investment funds are distinctly different from each other. VC funds can significantly improve the efficiency of market resource allocation and advocate the spontaneous adjustment of market mechanisms. It is recommended to learn from international experience, promote the formulation and improvement of relevant policies in accordance with the principles of "classified regulation and moderate supervision", clearly define the exemptions from securities regulation, establish information sharing mechanisms and stop inappropriate practices such as substantive audit. In the meantime, it is necessary to formulate relevant management systems according to the requirements of the classified reform of state-owned enterprises and the operation laws of VC, and establish financial fund management systems adapted with VC management laws.

4.3 Constantly improving the ecological chain of VC development and optimizing the ecological environment of investment and development

Excellent "sources and impetuses" are the original driving forces for the development of VC. Reform and development of the capital market are directly related to the exit returns and capital recycling. It is recommended to constantly improve the incubation mechanisms of excellent projects and accelerate the cultivation of excellent projects by developing science and technology financial service platforms and establishing international cooperation incubators, accelerators and international science & technology cooperation bases. In addition, it is advised to learn from the advanced experience of US Stock Exchange to further strengthen the system construction of multi-level capital markets and enhance the stability of markets and policies. In the meantime, it is important to accelerate the formulation of documents such as *Several Opinions on Promoting the Sustainable and Sound Development of Venture Capital*, study the difficulties in implementing tax policies such as *the Notice on the Relevant Pilot Tax Policies for Venture Capital Enterprises and Individual Angel Investors*, and promote the implementation of relevant policies.

1 中国创业投资机构与资本

1.1 2017 年度调查概述

2018 年 1~3 月，科技部、商务部、国家开发银行等部门联合启动第 16 次全国创业投资年度调查工作，按照国家统计局要求（国统制〔2017〕4 号），组织了全国 36 个省（市、自治区）、70 个调查实施机构和 141 名调查员进行网上填报。在此期间，各类创业投资机构认真贯彻落实国家《统计法》，积极配合调查工作。十余年来，本项统计调查工作为中央引导地方科技发展专项资金、科技成果转化引导基金申报，以及创业投资年度评奖等工作提供了有效的数据支持，也为我国创投业内重要政策的出台提供了有力支撑，成为我国科技金融工作的重要组成部分。

2017 年度报告所调查的创业投资机构主要包括以下两类：① 创业投资企业（基金），包括以政府资金直接投资项目，或采用引导基金的方式参股创业投资。② 创业投资管理企业，其受创业投资基金委托，筛选投资项目，提出投资决策建议，并受托进行投资后管理。组织形式主要包括公司制企业与合伙制企业。

根据创业投资的标准概念，我们剔除以下样本：①行业性和综合性投资公司，投资类公司等。②以基建、房地产等大项目投资为主业的产业投资基金。③以并购、夹层融资等为主业的私募股权投资基金（PE）。④主要从事担保业务、信托业务的金融机构，但持续地开展了创业投资业务的机构除外。⑤在境外注册设立、在境内仅以办公室形式开展商业活动的私募股权机构。

统计显示，截至 2017 年底，“中国创业投资信息系统”（www.ivcc.cn）中累计 6174 家机构参加过调查（包括关停并转等注销机构），其中 2017 年首次参与调查的新注册机构 949 家。

1.2 创业投资机构和管理资本

2017 年，IPO 审核加速带动了创业投资基金的募集、投资和退出，政府引导基金的进一步扩容引导了社会资金更多地流进实体经济，港股、美股的窗口期为具有国际视野的创业投资基金带来更大的机会，中国创投行业呈现出良好的发展态势。

2017 年，中国创业投资机构数达到 2296 家[①]，较 2016 年增加 251 家，增长 12.3%。其中，创业投资基金 1589 家，创业投资管理机构 707 家（见表 1-1、图 1-1）。

① 实际存量机构数，主要包括：创业投资企业（基金）、创业投资管理企业。该数据已剔除不再经营创投业务或注销的机构数。

表 1-1 中国创业投资机构总量、增量（2008~2017）[①]

项目 \ 年份	2008	2009	2010	2011	2012	2013	2014	2015	2016	2017
现存的 VC 机构（家）	464	576	867	1096	1183	1408	1551	1775	2045	2296
其中：VC 基金（家）	410	495	720	860	942	1095	1167	1311	1421	1589
其中：VC 管理机构（家）	54	81	147	236	241	313	384	464	624	707
当年新募集基金数（只）[②]	110	152	261	250	204	147	230	283	248	195
VC 机构增长（%）	21.1	24.1	50.5	26.4	7.9	19.0	10.2	14.4	15.2	12.3

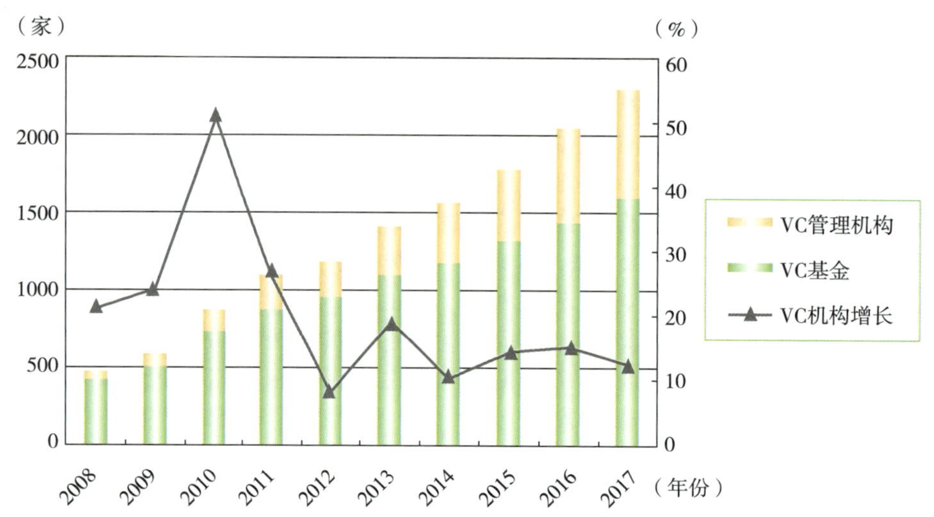

图 1-1 中国创业投资机构总量、增量（2008~2017）

近年来，创业投资机构运营模式日益多元化，创投基金采取委托管理的模式日益盛行，2008~2017 年，创投管理机构由 54 家增加到 707 家，增长超过 10 倍，最大基金管理公司管理资本量达到 450 亿元；此外，创业投资的分层现象日益增多，2017 年，以母基金形态存在的创业投资机构数达到 79 家，最大母基金规模达到 241 亿元，管理的子基金数达到 58 家。

2017 年，全国创业投资管理资本总量达到 8872.5 亿元[③]，较 2016 年增加 595.4 亿元，增幅为 7.2%；基金平均管理资本规模为 3.86 亿元，较前三年大幅下滑（见表 1-2、图 1-2）；披露当年新募集基金 526 亿元[④]。

① 由于我国创投行业的迅猛发展，基金形态的日趋多样，从 2010 年起，按照国际惯例区分基金和基金管理公司，并对前期数据进行了追溯调整。

② 在实际统计中当年新募基金数量存在一定偏差，存在当年进入统计而实际为前几年募集成立的基金，因此每年对前期新募基金数据进行调整。

③ 我国创业风险投资的业态不断复杂化，存在大量的资本嵌套。因此，在计算管理资本量时，我们对母子基金，以及基金与受托管理公司之间重复的资本量进行了剔除。

④ 共 44 家新募基金披露了募集资金总量。

表 1-2 中国创业投资管理资本总额（2008~2017）

项目 \ 年份	2008	2009	2010	2011	2012	2013	2014	2015	2016	2017
管理资本（亿元）	1455.7	1605.1	2406.6	3198.0	3312.9	3573.9	5232.4	6653.3	8277.1	8872.5
较上年增长（%）	30.8	10.3	49.9	32.9	3.6	7.9	31.7	27.2	24.4	7.2
基金平均管理资本规模（亿元）	3.55	3.24	3.34	3.72	3.52	3.26	4.48	4.66	4.05	3.86

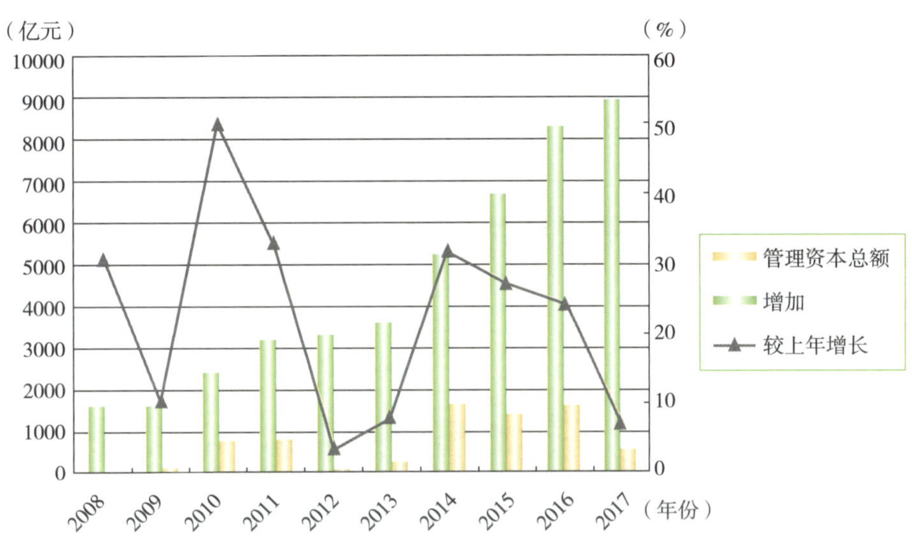

图 1-2 中国创业投资管理资本总额（2008~2017）

1.3 创业投资的资本来源

考虑到不同资本来源属性之间的交叉关系，以及近年来创业投资资金来源日趋多元化的特点，2017 年，我们按照两个维度对我国创业投资的资本来源进行划分。

第一个维度按照资金来源的机构性质进行分类如下：① 政府引导基金。② 其他财政资金，包括各级政府（包括事业单位）对创业风险资本的直接资金支持。③ 国有独资机构投资，指国有独资公司直接提供的资金，包括企业和银行等国有金融机构。④ 混合所有制机构投资。⑤ 民营投资机构投资。⑥ 社保基金。⑦ 高净值人群。⑧境内外资，指通过已在中国大陆境内注册并运作的外商独资（含港、澳、台）和合资合作企业取得的创业投资资本。⑨ 境外资金，是指境外机构获得的创业投资资本。⑩ 其他资金。

据统计，2017 年中国创业投资的构成中，政府引导基金出资占比 7.28%，其他政府财政资金出资占比 6.29%，国有独资投资机构出资占比 12.47%，三者合计占比 26.04%，较 2016 年下降了 10.1 个百分点；高净值个人投资占比 9.73%，上升了 2.65 个百分点；外资企业占比 3.38%，下降了 1.04 个百分点；此外，社保基金占比 0.04%（见图 1-3）。

第二个维度根据资金来源的金融属性划分，银行、保险、证券等金融机构资本合计占比 11.99%，较 2016 年大幅增长 5.81 个百分点。其中，银行资本较上年大幅上升；其他金融资本占比 27.85%，较上年上升 5.3 个百分点；主要资金仍来源于非金融资本，占比 60.15%（见图 1-4）。

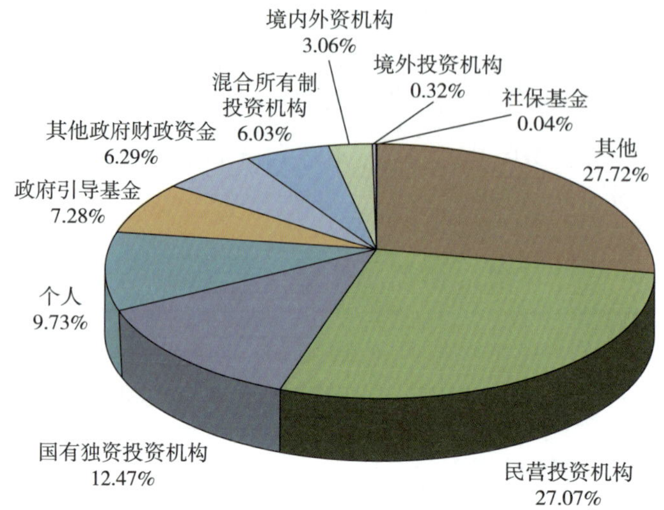

图 1-3 中国创业投资资本来源（2017）（维度一）①

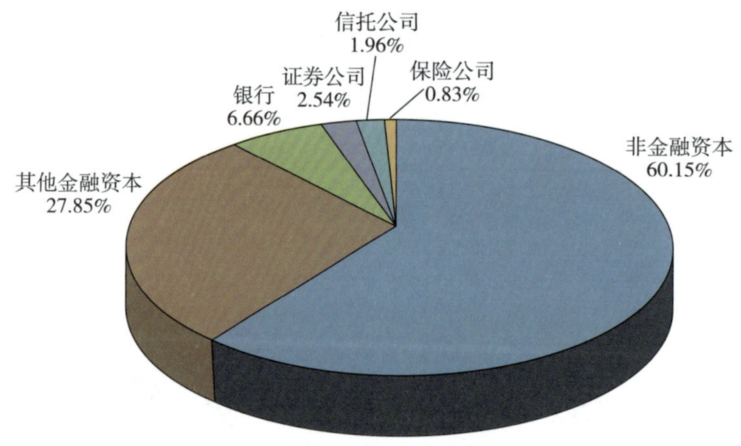

图 1-4 中国创业投资资本来源（2017）（维度二）②

1.4 创业投资机构的资本规模及分布

总体而言，2017 年创业投资机构的平均管理规模较前几年大幅下滑。从资金分布情况看，管理资金在 5000 万元以下的创业投资机构占机构总数的 32.3%，较 2016 年上升 1.8 个百分点；管理资金在 5000 万 ~1 亿元的机构数占比为 20.1%，较 2016 年略有下滑；管理资金在 1 亿 ~5 亿元的机构合计占比 37.1%，且规模在 1 亿 ~2 亿元，以及 2 亿 ~5 亿元的企业占比均较 2016 年略有上升；规模在 5 亿元以上的管理资金占到了 10.2%，较 2016 年下滑了 2.3 个百分点（见图 1-5）。

① 有效样本数为 1724 份。
② 有效样本数为 1711 份。

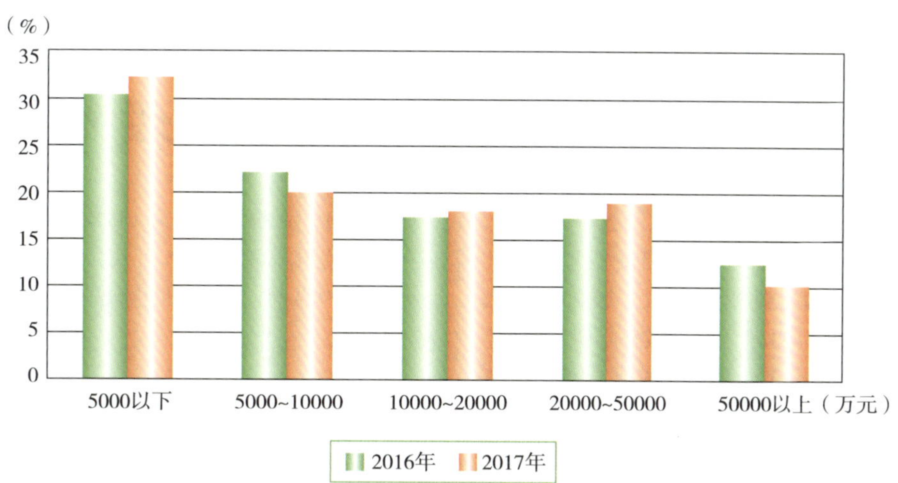

图 1-5　中国不同规模创业投资机构分布（2016~2017）①

按管理资金规模划分，2017 年创投机构管理资金规模继续下滑，管理资金规模在 5000 万元以下的机构掌握着 2.1% 的创业投资总资本，规模在 5000 万 ~1 亿元的机构掌握了 4.2% 的份额，规模在 1 亿 ~2 亿元的机构掌握了 6.9% 的总资金，规模在 2 亿 ~5 亿元的机构所占管理资本的份额为 14.7%，均比 2016 年的占比有所提升；大量的管理资本掌握在规模在 5 亿元以上的机构手中（见图 1-6）。

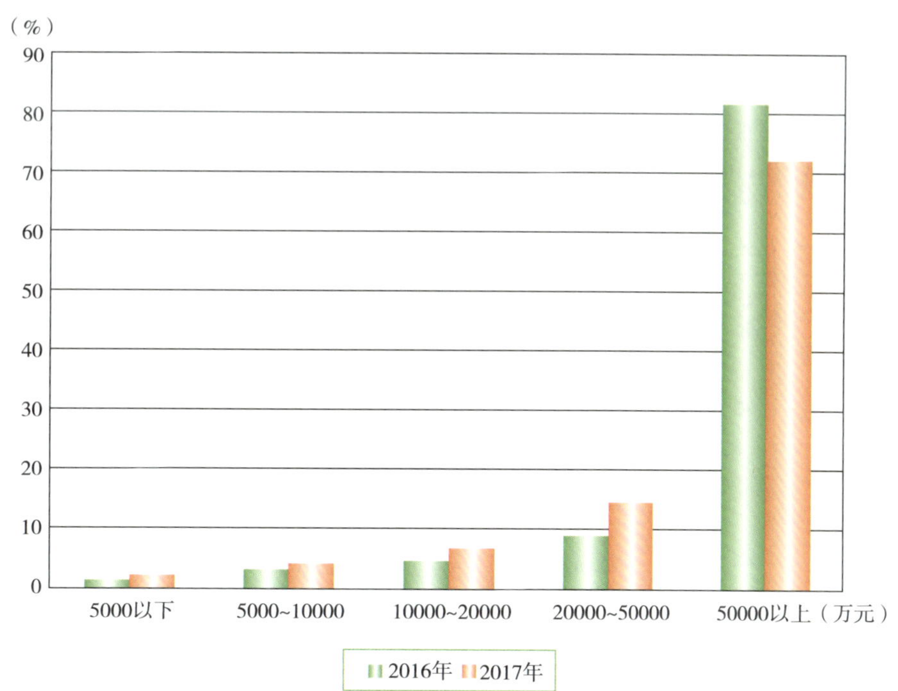

图 1-6　中国不同规模创业投资机构管理资本分布（2016）②

① 有效样本数为 3319 份。
② 有效样本数为 2968 份。

1.5 中国创业投资的总体投资情况

2017 年，披露的中国创投市场投资项目达到 2687 项，与上年相比基本持平；其中 1378 项为首轮投资，占比 51.3%。披露项目投资金额达到 845.3 亿元，较 2016 年大幅增加，项目平均投资额为 3145 万元，较往年明显增大。

其中，投资于高新技术企业项目 825 项，较 2016 年增加 30.1%；投资金额为 153.8 亿元，较上年增加 67.0%，项目平均投资额为 1865 万元，高新技术企业项目投资期可能较为靠前，单笔项目金额小于平均投资强度（见表 1–3）。

表 1–3　截至 2017 年底中国创业投资当年投资情况（2012~2017）

年份	当年投资项目总数（项）	投资高新技术企业 / 项目数（项）	当年投资金额（亿元）	投资高新技术企业 / 项目金额（亿元）
2012	1903	850	356.0	172.6
2013	1501	590	279.0	109.0
2014	2459	689	374.4	124.8
2015	3423	820	465.6	117.2
2016	2744	634	505.5	92.1
2017	2687	825	845.3	153.8

截至 2017 年底，全国创业投资机构累计投资项目数达到 20674 项，累计投资金额 4110.2 亿元，其中投资高新技术企业项目数 8851 项，投资金额 1627.3 亿元，占比分别为 42.81% 和 39.6%（见表 1–4）。

表 1–4　截至 2017 年底中国创业投资累计投资情况（2012~2017）

年份	累计投资项目总数（项）	投资高新技术企业 / 项目数（项）	累计投资金额（亿元）	投资高新技术企业 / 项目金额（亿元）
2012	11112	6404	2355.1	1193.1
2013	12149	6779	2634.1	1302.1
2014	14118	7330	2933.6	1401.9
2015	17376	8047	3361.2	1493.1
2016	19296	8490	3765.2	1566.8
2017	20674	8851	4110.2	1627.3

2 中国创业投资的投资分析

2.1 中国创业投资行业特征

2.1.1 中国创业投资行业分布①

2017年中国风险投资的行业分布发生了较大变化。从投资项目数看，主要集中在其他行业、其他制造业、软件产业、医药保健、科技服务，这五个行业集中了当年32.68%的项目，集中度较上年下降12.15%。

然而，从投资金额来看，主要集中在采掘业、建筑业、医药保健、生物科技与其他行业，这五个行业集中了59.08%的资金投资。特别是采掘业和建筑业，尽管投资的项目数很少，但主要为扩张期的大项目投资，因此金额占比很高（见表2-1、图2-1、图2-2）。

表2-1 中国创业投资项目行业分布：投资金额与投资项目（2016~2017） 单位：%

投资行业	2017年		2016年	
	投资金额	投资项目	投资金额	投资项目
采掘业	20.19	0.43	0.01	0.09
建筑业	14.37	1.39	1.98	0.56
医药保健	8.96	6.09	3.65	5.44
生物科技	8.04	5.26	1.89	4.37
其他行业	7.52	10.44	12.90	13.67
金融保险业	5.12	3.48	6.97	3.12
传统制造业	3.99	4.70	1.99	3.58
其他制造业	2.97	7.22	1.65	4.09
消费产品和服务	2.86	4.92	1.43	3.07
社会服务	2.70	1.87	0.90	1.95
IT服务业	2.68	5.13	3.30	6.70
农林牧副渔	2.37	1.78	0.96	1.91
软件产业	2.16	7.18	9.58	7.58
新能源、高效节能技术	2.02	3.74	1.97	3.77
网络产业	1.95	4.52	34.03	11.35
新材料工业	1.91	4.39	3.36	5.53

① 有效样本数为2299份。

续表

投资行业	2017 年		2016 年	
	投资金额	投资项目	投资金额	投资项目
传播与文化娱乐	1.85	5.13	3.02	5.26
环保工程	1.78	3.39	1.47	3.12
科技服务	1.33	5.35	1.61	4.51
交通运输、仓储和邮政业	0.89	1.39	1.60	0.88
半导体	0.84	3.09	1.27	1.30
计算机硬件产业	0.84	2.39	0.96	1.91
光电子与光机电一体化	0.80	1.74	0.85	2.14
通信设备	0.67	1.48	0.95	2.00
批发和零售业	0.47	1.44	0.43	0.70
其他 IT 产业	0.32	1.44	0.64	1.02
水、电、煤气	0.26	0.30	0.24	0.05
房地产业	0.14	0.22	0.37	0.23
核应用技术	0.01	0.09	0.04	0.09

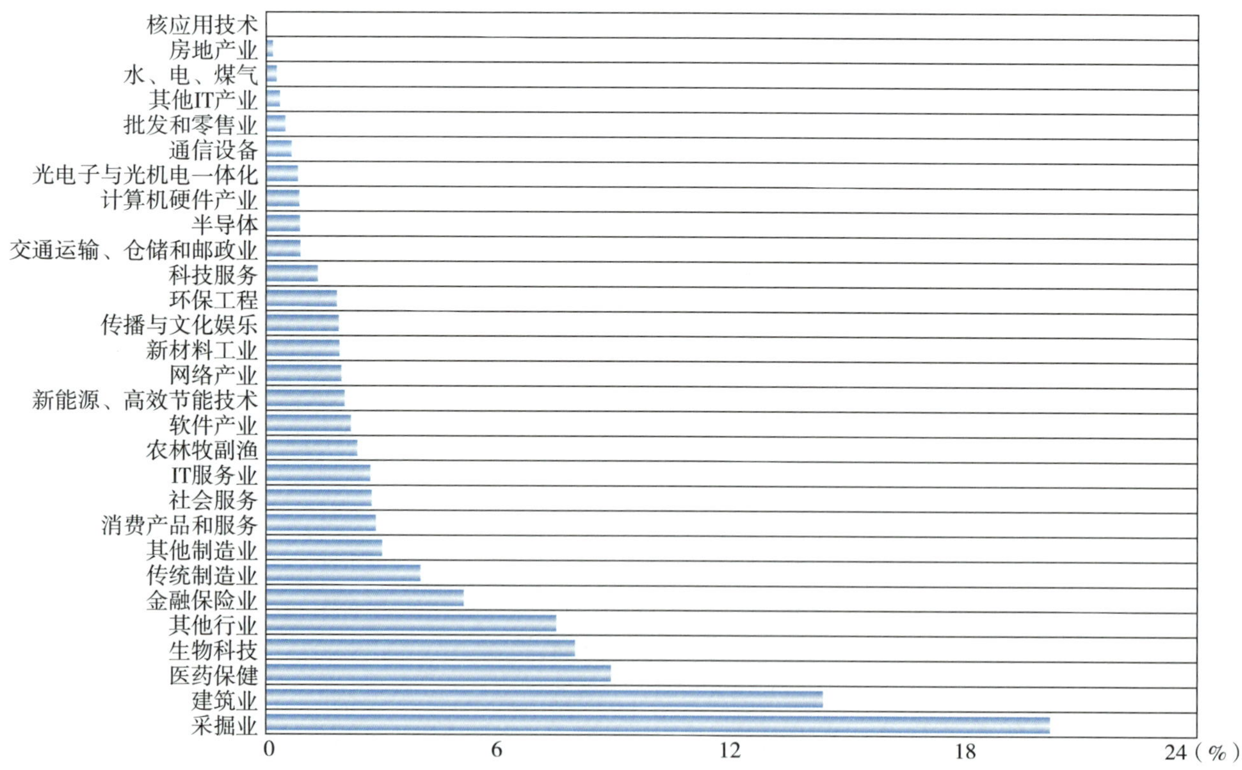

图 2-1 中国创业投资项目行业分布：投资金额（2017）

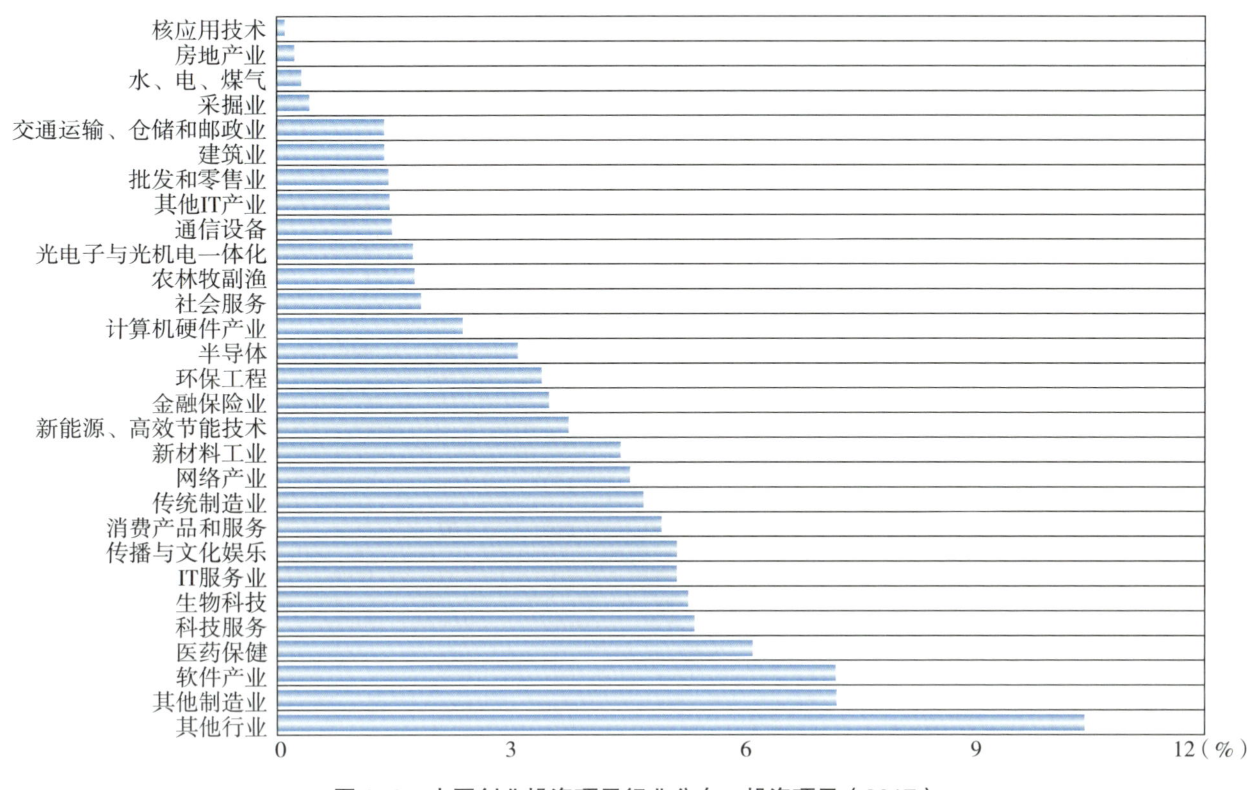

图 2-2　中国创业投资项目行业分布：投资项目（2017）

从我国创业投资行业变化趋势看，中国创业投资主要以行业热点为主。从投资项目分布来看，仍然以高新技术企业为主要投资对象，相比而言，2017 年投资于网络行业的热度大幅下降。而生物科技、其他行业和金融保险业等不断获得创业投资的青睐（见表 2-2、表 2-3）。

表 2-2　中国创业投资业投资项目投资金额行业分布（2008~2017）　　单位：%

投资行业 \ 年份	2008	2009	2010	2011	2012	2013	2014	2015	2016	2017
采掘业	3.60	1.50	2.50	0.60	1.30	0.51	0.00	0.06	0.01	20.19
建筑业	—	—	—	1.60	1.94	1.32	0.62	0.76	1.98	14.37
医药保健	2.50	4.90	5.30	3.80	4.85	10.04	7.35	5.37	3.65	8.96
生物科技	5.70	2.50	3.90	3.90	2.80	2.27	3.68	2.13	1.89	8.04
其他行业	12.70	10.00	15.70	11.20	7.62	2.65	8.45	10.41	12.90	7.52
金融保险业	8.20	15.20	7.80	2.40	5.42	10.12	2.86	5.71	6.97	5.12
传统制造业	15.60	11.90	10.10	7.70	10.10	7.19	7.64	3.77	1.99	3.99
其他制造业	—	—	—	8.20	4.83	5.30	3.31	3.67	1.65	2.97
消费产品和服务	3.90	4.30	7.10	9.40	6.27	5.00	1.57	2.14	1.43	2.86
社会服务	—	—	—	0.70	1.09	1.86	2.36	3.42	0.90	2.70

续表

投资行业＼年份	2008	2009	2010	2011	2012	2013	2014	2015	2016	2017
IT 服务业	4.60	1.50	3.20	2.80	3.14	3.58	3.00	3.03	3.30	2.68
农林牧副渔	2.60	3.50	4.10	4.10	6.07	6.33	2.00	1.94	0.96	2.37
软件产业	6.20	10.90	2.90	2.10	2.41	2.02	7.37	7.54	9.58	2.16
新能源、高效节能技术	7.70	8.50	8.30	6.20	7.19	8.69	2.94	2.95	1.97	2.02
网络产业	2.70	1.80	2.80	2.50	2.05	1.90	4.02	5.07	34.03	1.95
新材料工业	4.40	6.40	9.30	8.70	7.81	7.13	3.72	5.66	3.36	1.91
传播与文化娱乐	1.80	2.50	2.10	2.20	6.35	6.16	5.44	5.50	3.02	1.85
环保工程	1.30	1.80	3.30	2.60	2.81	2.89	2.83	2.31	1.47	1.78
科技服务	2.10	2.00	2.30	1.60	1.64	1.02	2.18	1.76	1.61	1.33
交通运输、仓储和邮政业	—	—	—	1.40	0.35	2.57	0.18	1.86	1.60	0.89
计算机硬件产业	3.40	0.10	1.10	0.70	1.10	0.68	4.15	1.65	1.27	0.84
半导体	2.90	2.30	1.20	1.30	1.44	1.40	1.35	0.65	0.96	0.84
光电子与光机电一体化	4.00	4.10	4.20	3.30	3.49	4.62	1.89	0.85	0.85	0.80
通信设备	1.80	1.90	1.00	2.80	3.63	3.11	13.76	18.59	0.95	0.67
批发和零售业	0.00	0.30	0.70	1.20	0.85	0.50	3.82	1.24	0.43	0.47
其他 IT 产业	2.30	2.20	1.20	1.50	1.68	0.36	1.02	0.48	0.64	0.32
水、电、煤气	—	—	—	0.10	0.29	0.25	0.44	0.46	0.24	0.26
房地产业	—	—	—	4.90	1.24	0.21	1.99	0.94	0.37	0.14
核应用技术	0.00	0.10	0.00	0.40	0.24	0.17	0.06	0.08	0.04	0.01

表 2-3 中国创业投资业投资项目行业分布（2008~2017）

单位：%

投资行业＼年份	2008	2009	2010	2011	2012	2013	2014	2015	2016	2017
其他行业	10.40	9.70	11.70	8.40	7.26	3.74	8.14	10.85	13.67	10.44
其他制造业	—	—	—	8.30	4.98	4.67	4.11	5.25	4.09	7.22
软件产业	9.70	13.90	7.00	3.50	3.12	5.32	9.40	7.41	7.58	7.18
医药保健	4.80	6.00	5.80	4.40	6.18	9.99	5.28	4.05	5.44	6.09
科技服务	4.50	2.70	2.50	1.80	2.58	1.94	2.60	3.05	4.51	5.35
生物科技	6.10	5.50	5.60	3.30	4.80	4.17	4.11	3.47	4.37	5.26
IT 服务业	3.80	3.30	4.20	4.10	3.42	4.17	5.67	5.75	6.70	5.13
传播与文化娱乐	1.70	2.10	1.90	2.40	5.28	5.24	3.81	4.32	5.26	5.13
消费产品和服务	2.80	3.10	4.10	7.20	3.54	3.45	2.56	2.66	3.07	4.92

续表

投资行业 \ 年份	2008	2009	2010	2011	2012	2013	2014	2015	2016	2017
传统制造业	14.20	9.40	7.30	8.00	8.82	6.03	4.98	4.44	3.58	4.70
网络产业	2.00	3.10	4.80	3.20	2.82	3.74	8.88	10.61	11.35	4.52
新材料工业	6.60	7.20	10.10	9.50	8.76	7.61	5.93	5.48	5.53	4.39
新能源、高效节能技术	5.10	6.30	7.80	6.00	7.20	6.75	4.16	4.17	3.77	3.74
金融保险业	4.90	5.40	4.10	2.00	4.20	6.54	3.59	5.17	3.12	3.48
环保工程	2.20	2.70	3.30	3.20	3.06	3.95	3.03	3.09	3.12	3.39
半导体	2.70	3.80	2.50	1.70	1.44	2.51	1.78	1.16	1.30	3.09
计算机硬件产业	1.30	0.40	1.40	1.30	1.50	1.22	1.69	1.81	1.91	2.39
社会服务	—	—	—	1.30	2.34	1.87	1.65	3.09	1.95	1.87
农林牧副渔	2.60	2.30	3.20	4.80	4.74	3.66	2.73	2.01	1.91	1.78
光电子与光机电一体化	5.90	5.10	6.00	4.60	3.78	4.89	2.86	2.05	2.14	1.74
通信设备	3.90	3.00	2.50	3.20	3.72	3.16	8.32	5.79	2.00	1.48
其他 IT 产业	3.20	3.70	2.30	2.40	1.92	1.01	1.60	1.04	1.02	1.44
批发和零售业	0.20	0.30	0.70	1.20	0.72	0.36	1.86	1.08	0.70	1.44
建筑业	—	—	—	1.80	1.62	1.22	0.56	0.58	0.56	1.39
交通运输、仓储和邮政业	—	—	—	0.80	0.24	1.15	0.17	0.89	0.88	1.39
采掘业	1.50	1.00	1.20	0.70	0.48	0.57	0.04	0.04	0.09	0.43
水、电、煤气	—	—	—	0.10	0.42	0.29	0.22	0.31	0.05	0.30
房地产业	—	—	—	0.30	0.54	0.29	0.22	0.35	0.23	0.22
核应用技术	0.00	0.10	0.00	0.50	0.48	0.29	0.04	0.04	0.09	0.09

按行业大类统计，信息软件行业、生物医药行业、其他行业、计算机通信行业依然是中国创业投资的热点领域。从趋势看，2017 年创业投资对信息传输、软件和信息服务业的投资金额大幅下滑（见表 2–4）。

表 2–4 中国创业风险业投资项目前十大行业分布（2016~2017） 单位：%

行业划分（代码）			2017 年		2016 年	
			投资金额	投资项目	投资金额	投资项目
C8	医药生物业	生物科技 医药保健	17.00	11.38	5.54	9.81
E	建筑业		14.37	1.39	1.98	0.56
O	其他行业		7.52	10.44	12.90	13.67

续表

<table>
<tr><th colspan="3" rowspan="2">行业划分（代码）</th><th colspan="2">2017 年</th><th colspan="2">2016 年</th></tr>
<tr><th>投资金额</th><th>投资项目</th><th>投资金额</th><th>投资项目</th></tr>
<tr><td rowspan="4">I</td><td rowspan="4">信息传输、软件和信息服务业</td><td>IT 服务业</td><td rowspan="4">7.11</td><td rowspan="4">18.27</td><td rowspan="4">47.55</td><td rowspan="4">26.65</td></tr>
<tr><td>其他 IT 产业</td></tr>
<tr><td>软件产业</td></tr>
<tr><td>网络产业</td></tr>
<tr><td rowspan="4">C9</td><td rowspan="4">新能源和环保业</td><td>核应用技术</td><td rowspan="4">5.72</td><td rowspan="4">11.61</td><td rowspan="4">6.84</td><td rowspan="4">12.51</td></tr>
<tr><td>环保工程</td></tr>
<tr><td>新材料工业</td></tr>
<tr><td>新能源、高效节能技术</td></tr>
<tr><td>J</td><td colspan="2">金融保险业</td><td>5.12</td><td>3.48</td><td>6.97</td><td>3.12</td></tr>
<tr><td>CA</td><td colspan="2">传统制造业</td><td>3.99</td><td>4.70</td><td>1.99</td><td>3.58</td></tr>
<tr><td rowspan="4">C7</td><td rowspan="4">计算机、通信和其他电子设备制造业</td><td>半导体</td><td rowspan="4">3.15</td><td rowspan="4">8.70</td><td rowspan="4">4.03</td><td rowspan="4">7.35</td></tr>
<tr><td>光电子与光机电一体化</td></tr>
<tr><td>计算机硬件产业</td></tr>
<tr><td>通信设备</td></tr>
<tr><td>C12</td><td colspan="2">其他制造业</td><td>2.97</td><td>7.22</td><td>1.65</td><td>4.09</td></tr>
<tr><td>N</td><td colspan="2">传播与文化娱乐</td><td>1.85</td><td>5.13</td><td>3.02</td><td>5.26</td></tr>
</table>

近年来，由于新技术的出现，许多行业已经难以再采用传统的行业分类方式进行划分。比如，金融科技产业可能部分属于网络产业，部分属于金融保险行业，而人工智能产业则可能分布于多个领域内。因此，从 2017 年调查起，我们除了按照传统的行业进行行业划分统计，另采用了概念板块进行投资分布统计。

从统计结果来看①，除其他板块以外，2017 年中国创业投资的项目主要分布在物联网与大数据、绿色经济、金融科技、人工智能等概念板块（见表 2–5）。

表 2–5 中国创业投资业投资项目的概念板块分布：投资金额与投资项目占比（2017） 单位：%

概念板块	投资金额占比	投资项目占比
物联网与大数据	9.49	14.21
绿色经济	9.48	7.68
金融科技	3.58	3.51
人工智能	3.46	7.24
一、二、三产融合	1.44	1.59
扶贫	0.98	0.27
互联网教育	0.55	2.30
共享经济	0.48	1.92
其他	70.55	61.27

① 有效样本数为 1823 份。

2.1.2 中国创业投资对高新技术产业与传统产业的投资比较①

按照高新技术产业和传统产业对被投资项目划分，可以看出，中国创业投资对高新技术产业的投资金额和投资项目占比在经历2016年短暂的回升后，2017年均在一定程度上有下降。其中，2017年中国创业投资对高新技术产业的投资金额占比大幅下降（见表2-6、图2-3、表2-7、图2-4）。

表2-6 中国创业投资项目年度行业分布：高新技术产业与传统产业（2008~2017） 单位：%

产业＼年份	2008	2009	2010	2011	2012	2013	2014	2015	2016	2017
高新技术产业	63.2	67.7	67.0	53.4	55.3	61.3	65.4	59.0	60.9	55.7
传统产业	36.8	32.3	33.0	46.6	44.7	38.7	34.6	41.0	39.1	44.3

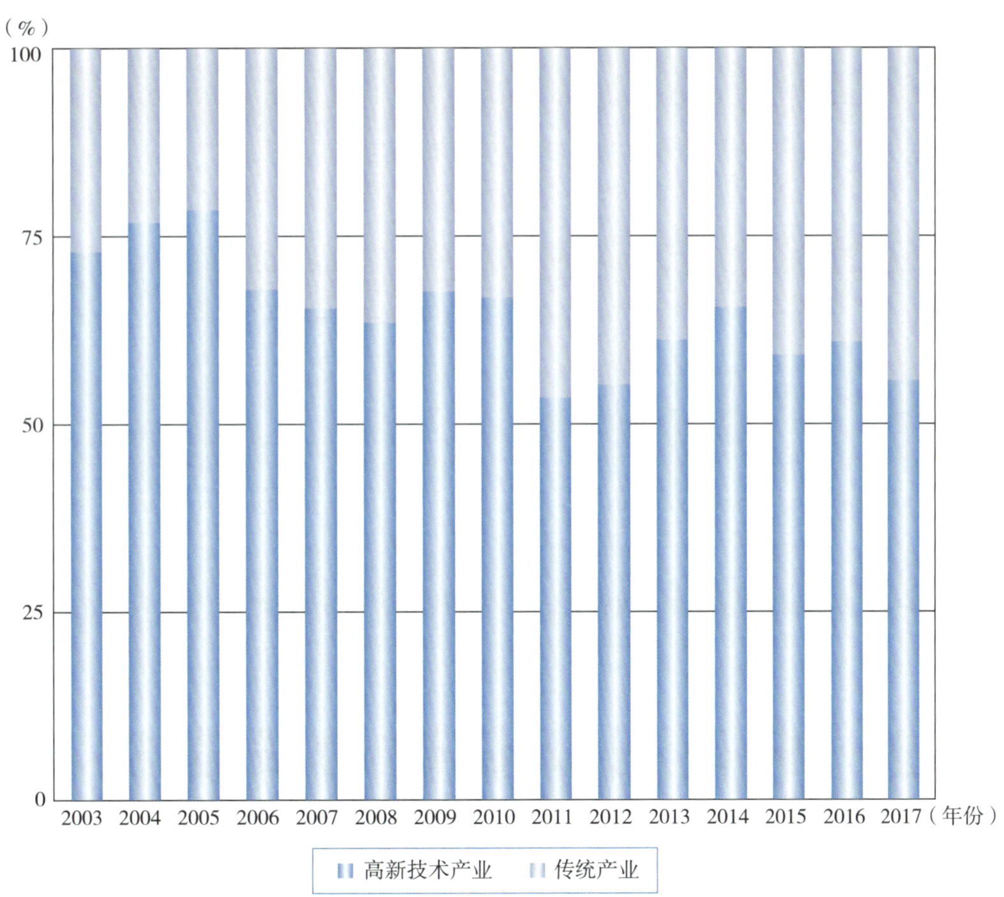

图2-3 中国创业投资项目年度行业分布：高新技术产业与传统产业（2003~2017）

① 有效样本数：高新项目样本数为1281份；传统项目样本数为1018份。

表 2-7 中国创业投资金额年度行业分布：高新技术产业与传统产业（2008~2017） 单位：%

年份 产业	2008	2009	2010	2011	2012	2013	2014	2015	2016	2017
高新技术产业	55.2	52.3	52.4	44.9	47.6	50.4	59.3	58.2	65.6	54.5
传统产业	44.8	47.7	47.6	55.1	52.4	49.6	40.7	41.8	34.4	45.5

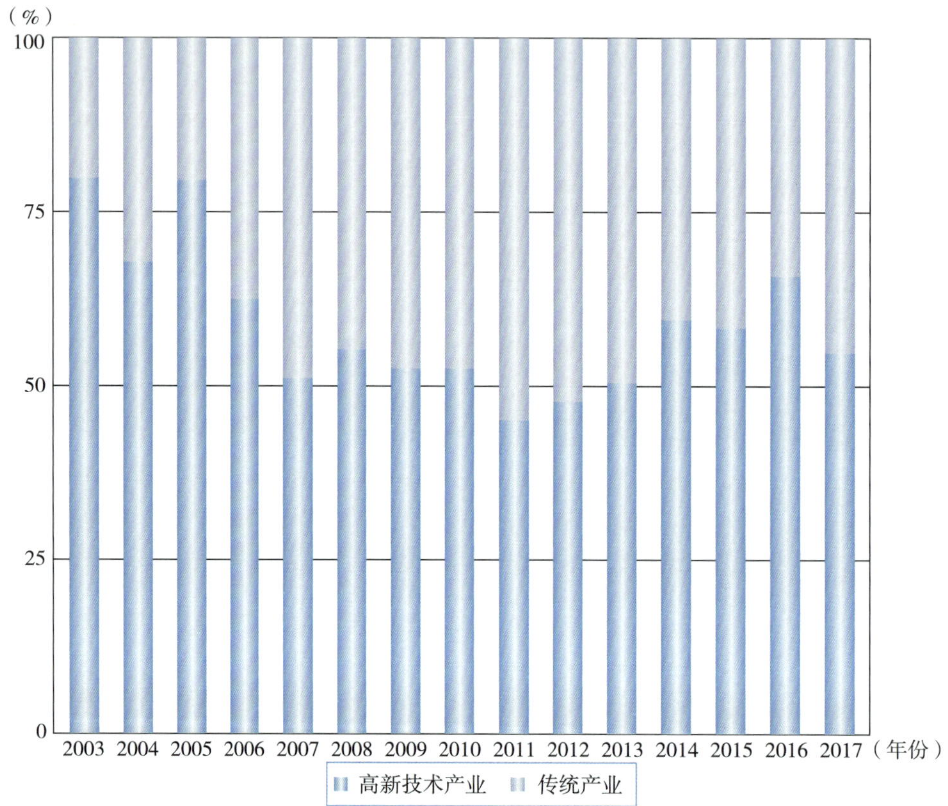

图 2-4 中国创业投资金额年度行业分布：高新技术产业与传统产业（2003~2017）

2.2 中国创业投资的投资阶段

2.2.1 中国创业投资所处阶段总体分布[①]

按照投资金额划分，2017 年中国创业投资机构的投资金额主要集中在成长（扩张）期和成熟（过渡）期。与 2016 年相比，成长（扩张）期和成熟（过渡）期的投资金额分别提高 6.16 个百分点和 3.55 个百分点，投资机构对成长（扩张）期的投资金额依然保持最多。相比而言，对起步期项目的投资下降最大，由 2016 年的 30.30% 下滑到 2017 年的 20.76%。

按照投资项目划分，2017 年中国创业投资机构的投资项目主要集中在起步期和成长（扩张）期，总体变化不大。相比 2016 年，创业投资对起步期和成长（扩张）期的投资项目数略有上升，对种子期的投资项目则下降 1.85 个百分点（见表 2-8、图 2-5、表 2-9、图 2-6、表 2-10、图 2-7）。

① 有效样本数为 2217 份。

表 2-8 中国创业投资项目所处阶段总体分布：投资金额与投资项目（2017） 单位：%

成长阶段	投资金额	投资项目
种子期	4.5	17.8
起步期	20.8	39.5
成长（扩张）期	44.7	36.2
成熟（过渡）期	29.9	5.9
重建期	0.2	0.6

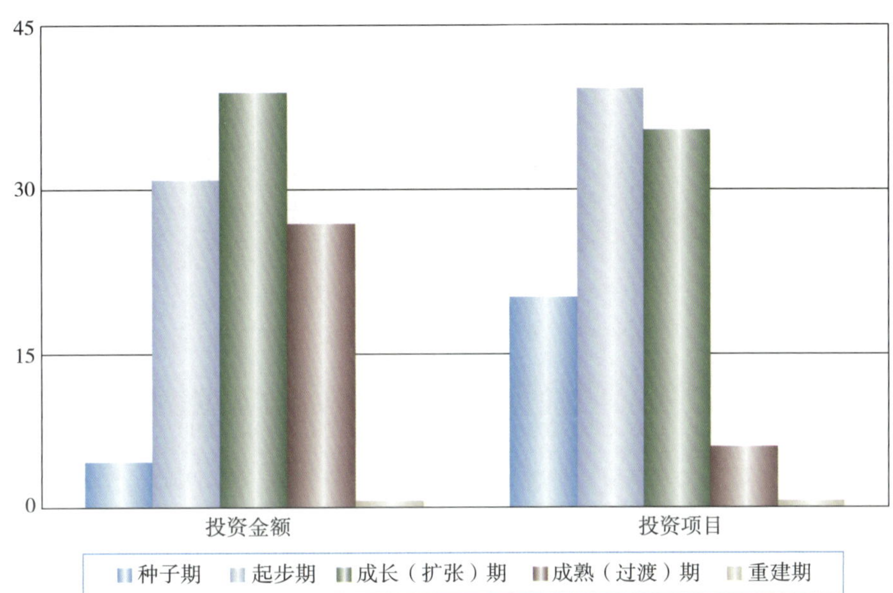

图 2-5 中国创业投资项目所处阶段总体分布：投资金额与投资项目（2017）

表 2-9 中国创业投资项目所处阶段分布：投资金额（2008~2017） 单位：%

阶段＼年份	2008	2009	2010	2011	2012	2013	2014	2015	2016	2017
种子期	9.40	19.90	10.20	4.30	6.55	12.22	5.63	8.11	4.33	4.54
起步期	19.00	12.80	17.40	14.80	19.32	22.38	25.23	21.53	30.30	20.76
成长（扩张）期	38.50	45.10	49.20	55.00	52.00	41.42	59.04	54.40	38.50	44.66
成熟（过渡）期	26.50	18.50	20.20	22.30	21.56	22.82	10.05	15.24	26.31	29.86
重建期	6.60	3.70	3.00	3.60	0.57	1.16	0.05	0.72	0.55	0.17

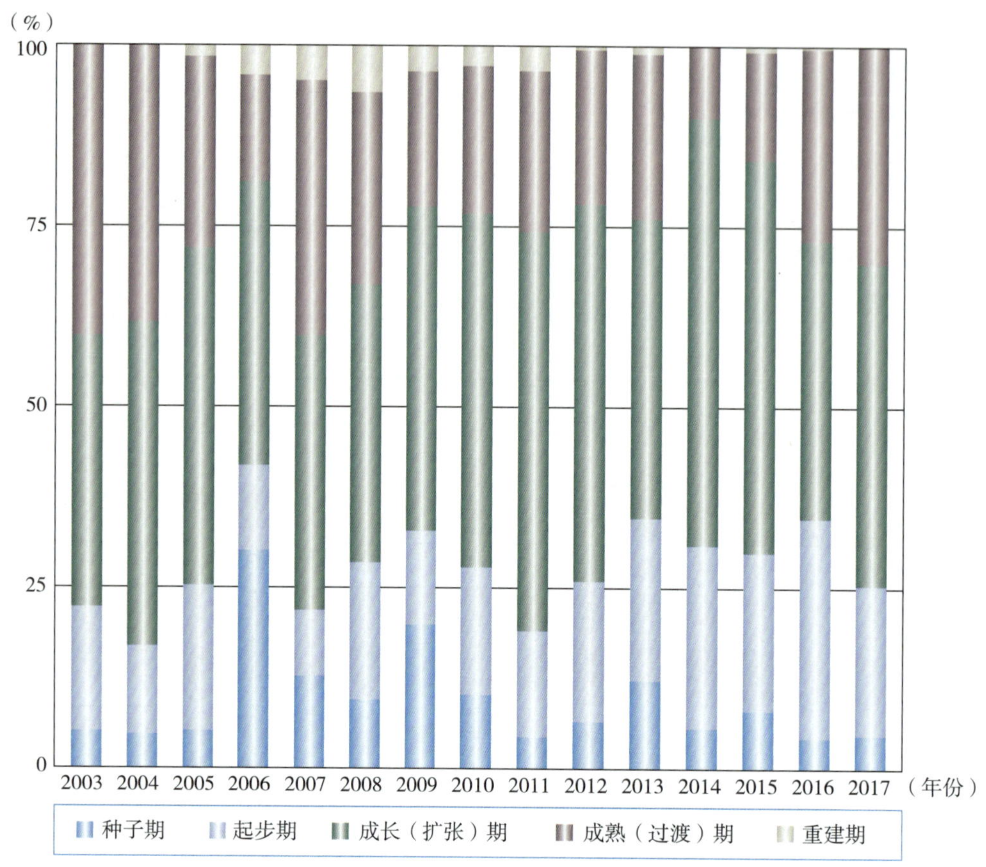

图 2-6 中国创业投资项目所处阶段分布：投资金额（2003~2017）

表 2-10 中国创业投资项目所处阶段分布：投资项目（2008~2017） 单位：%

阶段 \ 年份	2008	2009	2010	2011	2012	2013	2014	2015	2016	2017
种子期	19.30	32.20	19.90	9.70	12.33	18.36	20.76	18.22	19.62	17.77
起步期	30.20	20.30	27.00	22.70	28.66	32.46	36.55	35.55	38.92	39.51
成长（扩张）期	34.00	35.20	40.90	48.30	44.98	38.21	35.94	40.15	35.00	36.22
成熟（过渡）期	12.10	9.00	10.00	16.70	13.24	10.00	6.49	5.41	5.71	5.91
重建期	4.40	3.30	2.20	2.60	0.79	0.97	0.26	0.66	0.75	0.59

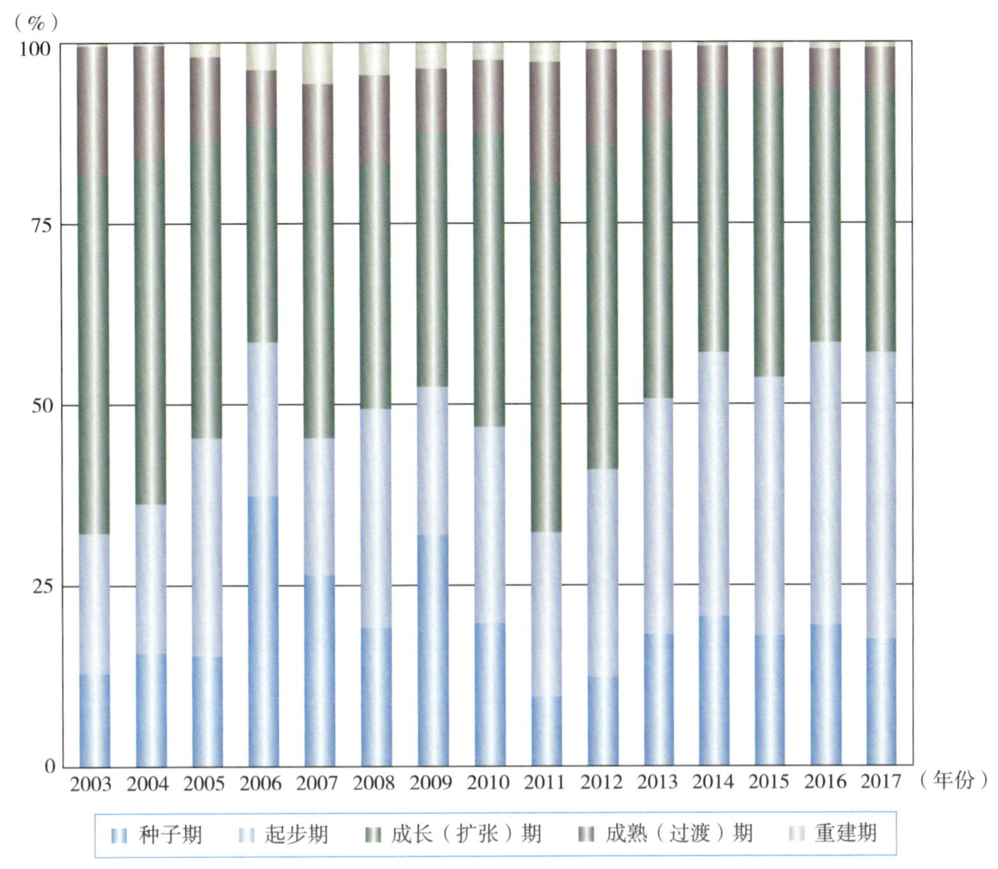

图 2-7 中国创业投资项目所处阶段分布：投资项目（2003~2017）

2.2.2 中国创业投资各投资阶段的 R&D 投入

2017 年，调查对投资项目的研发投入情况进行了统计，数据显示，① 2017 年创业投资项目的 R&D 投入达到 279.7 亿元，项目平均研究投入资金为 1261.7 万元 / 项。相比而言，种子期、起步期的项目处于重要的研发投入阶段（见表 2-11、图 2-8）。

表 2-11 中国创业投资不同成长阶段的 R&D 平均投入强度（2017）

单位：万元 / 项

成长阶段	平均投入
种子期	446.43
起步期	569.48
成长（扩张）期	2268.09
成熟（过渡）期	2257.20
重建期	983.00

① 有效样本数为 828 份。

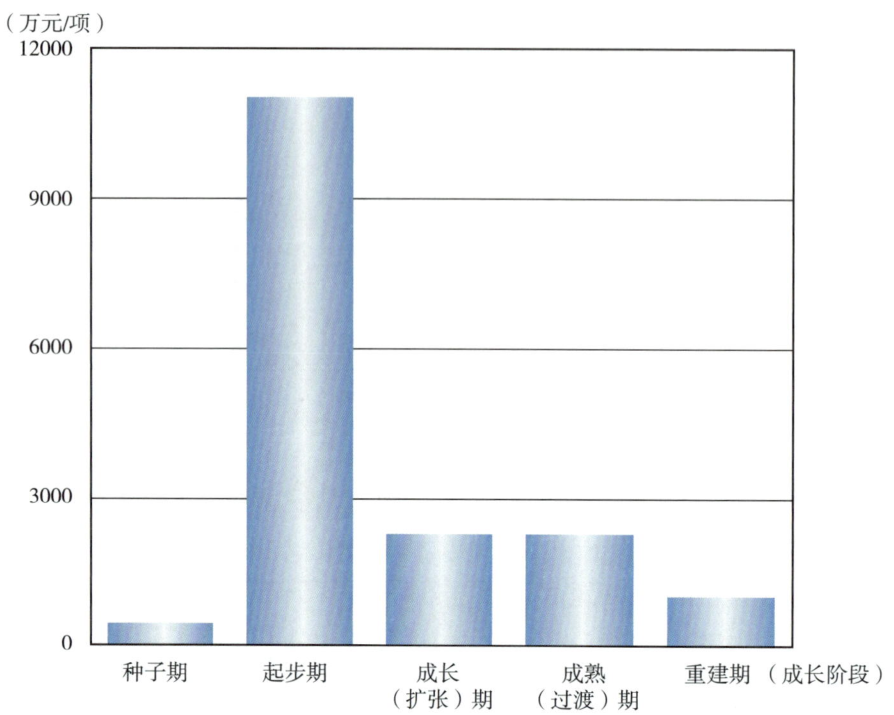

图 2-8 中国创业投资不同成长阶段的 R&D 平均投入强度（2017）

2.2.3 中国创业投资在主要行业投资项目的阶段分布

从分行业的投资项目阶段分布看，2017 年，核应用技术、消费产品和服务、传播与文化娱乐以及金融保险业等行业的种子期投资项目数较高；软件产业、通信设备、其他行业和金融保险业的种子期投资金额较高。而生物科技、环保工程、建筑业、消费产品和服务等产业的投资则主要集中在成长（扩张）阶段（见表 2-12、表 2-13）。

表 2-12 中国创业投资项目主要行业的投资阶段分布：投资项目（2017）[①] 单位：%

投资行业	种子期	起步期	成长(扩张)期	成熟(过渡)期	重建期
计算机硬件产业	16.67	38.89	40.74	3.70	0.00
消费产品和服务	29.52	36.19	30.48	3.81	0.00
网络产业	23.76	39.60	29.70	6.93	0.00
核应用技术	100.00	0.00	0.00	0.00	0.00
水、电、煤气	0.00	33.33	16.67	50.00	0.00
房地产业	20.00	40.00	0.00	40.00	0.00
社会服务	19.44	44.44	33.33	2.78	0.00
传播与文化娱乐	28.30	40.57	24.53	4.72	1.89
其他制造业	13.29	36.71	40.51	9.49	0.00
半导体	11.59	50.72	34.78	2.90	0.00

① 有效样本数为 2299 份。

续表

投资行业	种子期	起步期	成长（扩张）期	成熟（过渡）期	重建期
其他 IT 产业	22.58	32.26	35.48	9.68	0.00
农林牧副渔	7.32	26.83	60.98	2.44	2.44
金融保险业	24.32	55.41	16.22	4.05	0.00
医药保健	9.92	42.75	44.27	2.29	0.76
建筑业	0.00	18.75	71.88	9.38	0.00
新材料工业	13.83	40.43	38.30	6.38	1.06
环保工程	4.05	32.43	54.05	8.11	1.35
通信设备	2.94	44.12	47.06	5.88	0.00
光电子与光机电一体化	10.81	48.65	37.84	2.70	0.00
生物科技	18.58	46.90	30.09	3.54	0.88
传统制造业	4.00	26.00	54.00	15.00	1.00
软件产业	23.33	45.33	27.33	4.00	0.00
采掘业	10.00	20.00	20.00	50.00	0.00
其他行业	21.27	37.56	38.01	2.26	0.90
IT 服务业	16.35	37.50	34.62	8.65	2.88
批发和零售业	16.67	23.33	50.00	10.00	0.00
科技服务	25.00	53.57	20.54	0.89	0.00
交通运输、仓储和邮政业	15.63	37.50	25.00	21.88	0.00
新能源、高效节能技术	17.65	28.24	49.41	4.71	0.00

表 2-13　中国创业投资项目主要行业的投资阶段分布：投资金额（2017）[①]　　单位：%

投资行业	种子期	起步期	成长（扩张）期	成熟（过渡）期	重建期
建筑业	—	0.52	71.21	28.27	—
采掘业	0.03	0.07	0.25	99.66	—
其他制造业	5.53	24.80	56.09	13.58	—
医药保健	1.02	76.41	21.51	0.75	0.30
核应用技术	100.00	—	—	—	—
通信设备	19.73	17.64	58.18	4.44	—
批发和零售业	3.38	7.71	74.60	14.31	—
消费产品和服务	5.75	21.56	69.76	2.93	—
社会服务	0.61	7.20	76.60	15.59	—
金融保险业	15.42	31.07	44 75	8.75	—
传统制造业	0.42	43.29	47.75	7.86	0.68

① 有效样本数为 2146 份。

续表

投资行业	种子期	起步期	成长（扩张）期	成熟（过渡）期	重建期
计算机硬件产业	4.83	24.10	62.47	8.60	—
半导体	12.46	44.12	41.67	1.75	—
其他行业	16.07	26.71	56.60	0.56	0.06
新能源、高效节能技术	7.75	20.74	64.50	7.01	—
光电子与光机电一体化	2.81	34.19	60.56	2.44	—
水、电、煤气	—	19.87	17.77	62.36	—
农林牧副渔	6.66	5.60	84.95	1.67	1.11
软件产业	25.64	32.78	30.89	10.68	—
交通运输、仓储和邮政业	4.44	16.59	30.57	48.40	—
传播与文化娱乐	11.00	22.30	47.61	18.32	0.77
环保工程	0.86	20.49	73.84	4.15	0.66
网络产业	6.10	17.66	30.97	45.27	—
IT 服务业	3.39	26.71	56.43	11.86	1.60
其他 IT 产业	10.78	31.89	43.54	13.78	—
新材料工业	12.77	28.56	50.76	7.03	0.88
生物科技	2.12	18.45	76.85	2.53	0.05
科技服务	9.82	40.45	47.37	2.36	—
房地产业	2.78	4.63	—	92.59	—

按照行业概念板块进行划分，2017 年，在金融科技、互联网教育、人工智能等板块的种子期投资项目与投资金额均较多，而扶贫、一二三产融合、绿色经济概念板块的投资则主要分布在成长（扩张）期，其中扶贫成长（扩张）期的投资项目达 80%（见表 2-14、表 2-15）。

表 2-14 中国创业投资项目主要概念板块的投资阶段分布：投资项目①

单位：%

投资行业	种子期	起步期	成长（扩张）期	成熟（过渡）期	重建期
一二三产融合	17.24	31.03	48.28	3.45	0.00
人工智能	26.15	53.08	17.69	3.08	0.00
绿色经济	12.32	35.51	47.83	3.62	0.72
互联网教育	36.59	43.90	19.51	0.00	0.00
扶贫	0.00	20.00	80.00	0.00	0.00
物联网与大数据	18.99	45.74	30.62	4.65	0.00
其他	16.52	36.57	38.48	7.62	0.82
金融科技	32.76	46.55	18.97	1.72	0.00
共享经济	40.00	54.29	5.71	0.00	0.00

① 有效样本数为 1823 份。

表 2–15 中国创业投资项目主要概念板块的投资阶段分布：投资金额[①] 单位：%

投资行业	种子期	起步期	成长（扩张）期	成熟（过渡）期	重建期
物联网与大数据	11.64	23.24	49.97	15.15	—
绿色经济	5.37	14.47	69.08	10.85	0.23
共享经济	25.57	45.89	28.54	—	—
人工智能	11.40	34.22	51.99	2.39	—
金融科技	43.81	19.50	35.62	1.07	—
一、二、三产融合	3.98	28.13	65.12	2.77	—
扶贫	—	2.74	97.26	—	—
其他	4.95	19.79	64.27	10.66	0.33
互联网教育	30.69	43.14	26.17	—	—

2.3 中国创业投资的投资强度

2.3.1 中国创业投资强度的变化趋势与行业差异[②]

数据显示，我国创业投资强度自 1995 年以来总体呈上升趋势，到 2011 年达到顶峰，此后逐年下滑，到 2017 年略有回升，投资强度为 1085.55 万元 / 项（见表 2–16、图 2–9）。

表 2–16 中国创业投资的投资强度（2008~2017） 单位：万元 / 项

年份	2008	2009	2010	2011	2012	2013	2014	2015	2016	2017
投资强度	1041.25	1059.77	1356.53	1550.53	1322.66	1282.12	1129.53	1089.26	1014.76	1085.55

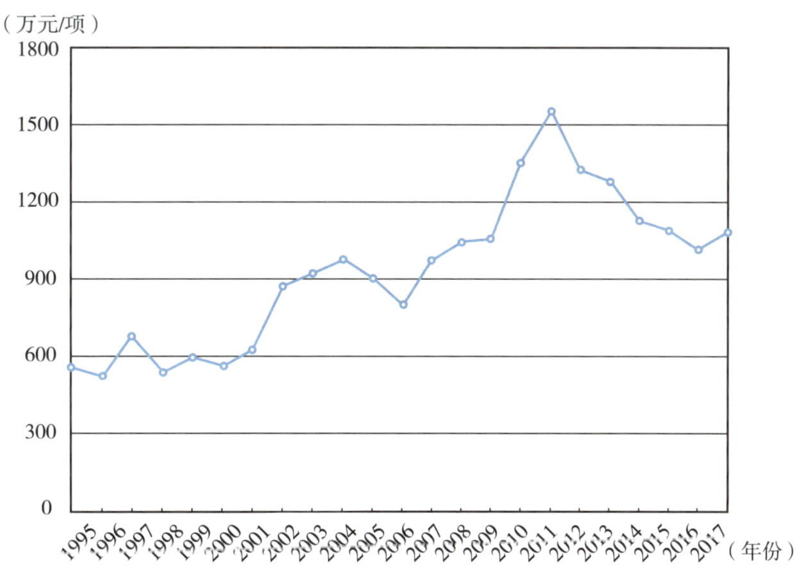

图 2–9 中国创业投资的投资强度（1995~2017）

① 有效样本数为 1796 份。
② 有效样本数为 2430 份。

按行业划分，2017 年创业投资对水、电、煤气，房地产业，采掘业，建筑业等行业的投资主要以扩张期项目投资为主，投资强度较大；而对网络产业、软件产业、生物医药等行业的投资则趋于早前期项目（见表 2-17、图 2-10）。

表 2-17 中国创业投资不同行业的投资强度（2008~2017） 单位：万元 / 项

年份 投资行业	2008	2009	2010	2011	2012	2013	2014	2015	2016	2017
医药保健	678.8	1052.5	1409.3	1444.5	1144.5	1351.0	1429.6	1190.4	1212.9	1321.3
新能源、高效节能技术	1447.4	1156.6	1302.8	1647.8	1373.0	1420.2	1059.2	1054.3	1089.9	1430.0
新材料工业	867.6	1212.9	1376.6	1639.7	1224.5	1444.0	1006.4	1416.6	1033.1	1194.9
消费产品和服务	1774.1	1435.8	2463.2	2102.0	2036.9	1712.8	1053.3	1260.2	781.0	877.3
网络产业	1186.7	805.5	925.8	1487.4	1028.8	721.0	742.8	794.4	1007.9	891.1
通信设备	580.8	671.0	726.0	1791.6	1439.3	1704.3	1540.4	1268.5	1200.5	948.5
生物科技	878.0	612.0	805.1	1369.0	904.5	960.5	1059.2	1130.9	1091.2	1110.0
软件产业	732.4	788.4	756.2	976.3	1029.8	677.8	945.0	907.7	751.3	939.7
其他行业	1155.6	1189.9	1542.2	1628.9	1110.4	1075.7	1400.5	1156.7	1179.8	1204.1
其他 IT 产业	942.3	827.4	980.7	1297.0	1171.2	616.4	971.1	849.4	695.7	729.3
批发和零售业	30.0	1673.3	1988.2	1642.8	1810.3	2410.0	1638.7	947.8	1075.6	1069.3
农林牧副渔	1327.8	1580.6	2054.7	1505.4	1836.0	1516.6	1036.7	1517.0	1073.9	1107.3
科技服务	600.8	785.9	1400.8	1391.7	842.4	944.0	903.1	854.1	708.9	709.2
金融保险业	1537.0	1964.0	1326.1	977.6	1653.0	1885.6	929.0	1216.9	1469.1	931.3
计算机硬件产业	782.1	495.0	997.3	1117.0	799.6	581.5	1225.9	1067.8	908.0	991.1
环保工程	760.8	893.7	1501.4	1368.9	1402.3	1268.6	1559.3	1311.4	1184.6	1291.8
核应用技术	—	1200.0	—	1517.3	757.4	1008.3	2500.0	4000.0	1176.0	352.5
光电子与光机电一体化	898.9	879.1	1075.8	1420.0	1288.3	1294.2	863.4	769.8	708.2	1290.4
传统制造业	1320.7	1481.1	2057.8	1754.9	1390.3	1409.1	1032.4	1115.1	1122.4	1356.7
传播与文化娱乐	671.5	1437.6	1413.1	1458.1	1398.6	1441.9	1543.3	961.0	907.5	872.3
采掘业	1850.5	1211.0	1633.2	1184.3	2130.4	1537.8	200.0	3002.0	290.0	1968.4
半导体	1407.6	688.7	895.4	1608.3	1312.6	963.9	1322.8	856.4	1064.9	892.6
IT 服务业	791.0	609.1	1002.1	1208.5	1216.5	963.0	843.4	895.5	854.1	1005.4
水、电、煤气	—	—	—	866.7	1050.0	1512.5	1232.5	1845.4	—	2790.0
社会服务	—	—	—	1150.3	728.5	1370.1	1147.2	752.7	771.4	977.3
其他制造业	—	—	—	1825.3	1483.5	959.4	1181.2	1107.6	921.1	1031.7
交通运输、仓储和邮政业	—	—	—	2163.9	2244.7	1432.4	1762.5	1633.9	1148.4	1198.3
建筑业	—	—	—	1466.7	1834.0	1989.3	1346.9	1181.1	700.3	1809.1
房地产业	—	—	—	1492.2	1523.9	1237.5	511.0	2193.6	365.0	2160.0

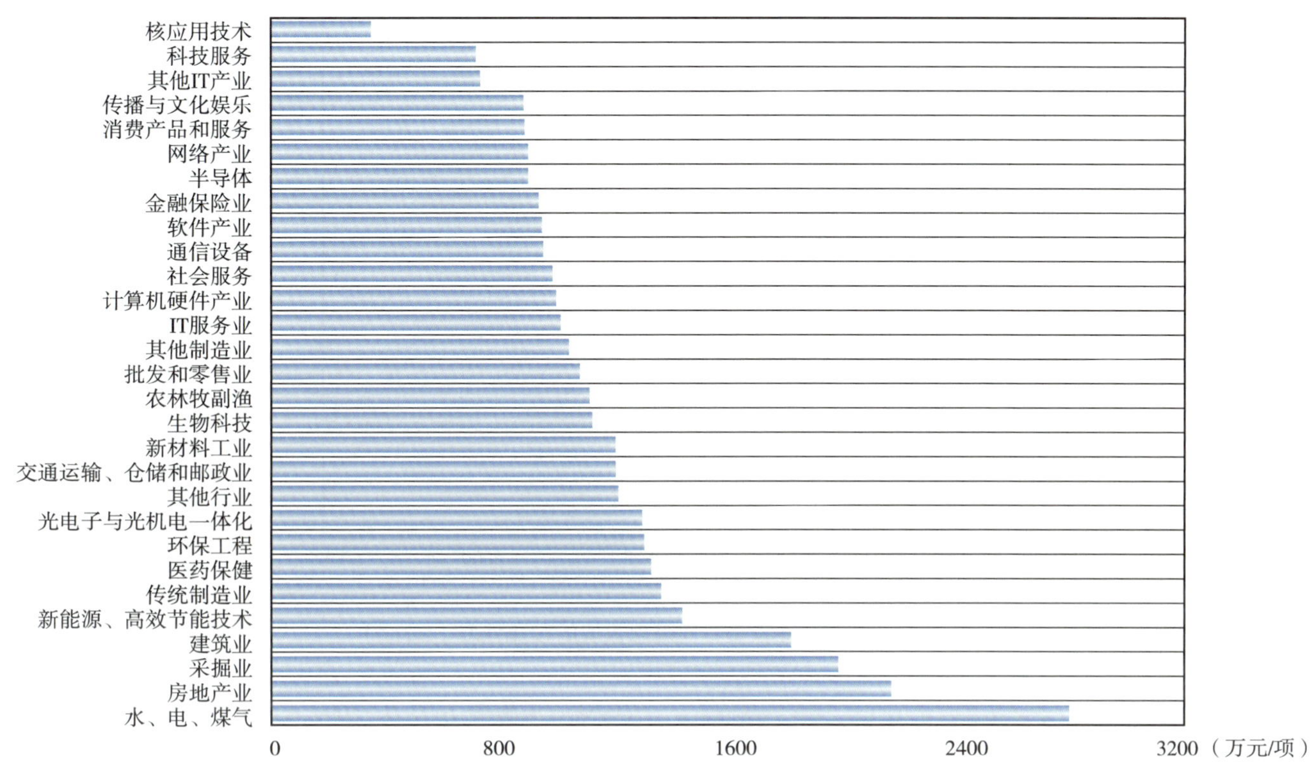

图 2-10　中国创业投资不同行业的投资强度（2017）

按照行业概念板块进行划分，扶贫板块的项目大多属成长期项目，单笔投资体量较大。相对而言，物联网、科技金融、人工智能等领域的投资阶段较为靠前，投资强度较低（见表 2-18、图 2-11）。

表 2-18　中国创业投资不同概念板块的投资强度（2017）　单位：万元 / 项

概念板块	投资强度
互联网教育	488.84
共享经济	512.94
人工智能	981.60
物联网与大数据	1370.61
一、二、三产融合	1864.43
金融科技	2093.61
其他	2363.56
绿色经济	2533.43
扶贫	7299.99

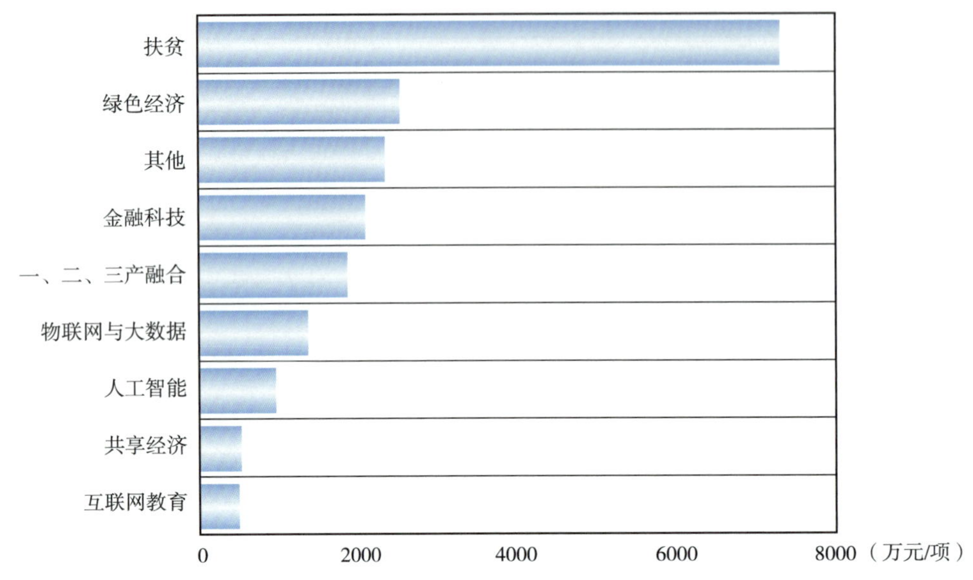

图 2-11 中国创业投资不同概念板块的投资强度（2017）

2.3.2 中国创业投资机构单项投资规模分布[①]

2017 年，中国创业投资机构投资项目金额分布如下：500 万 ~1000 万元的投资项目所占比例最大，达到 21.2%；其次是 1000 万 ~2000 万元的投资项目，占比为 18.1%。与 2016 年相比，投资强度有所上升，超过 300 万元的项目比重较 2016 年上升了 5.3 个百分点（见表 2-19、图 2-12）。

表 2-19 中国创业投资机构单项投资金额分布（2008~2017） 单位：%

年份 \ 金额（万元）	<100	100~300	300~500	500~1000	1000~2000	>2000
2008	17.1	22.0	11.7	15.0	18.9	15.2
2009	11.7	22.4	12.6	20.3	17.3	15.7
2010	13.4	15.5	8.9	17.5	21.5	23.2
2011	6.8	10.6	10.2	20.6	25.7	26.2
2012	10.2	13.1	11.3	21.2	24.7	19.5
2013	8.4	17.6	14.6	20.0	20.1	19.3
2014	12.3	19.1	13.9	18.3	20.4	15.9
2015	14.5	17.5	15.3	19.9	17.2	15.6
2016	15.9	18.1	15.5	20.9	15.8	13.8
2017	10.7	18.0	17.7	21.2	18.1	14.2

① 有效样本数为 2430 份。

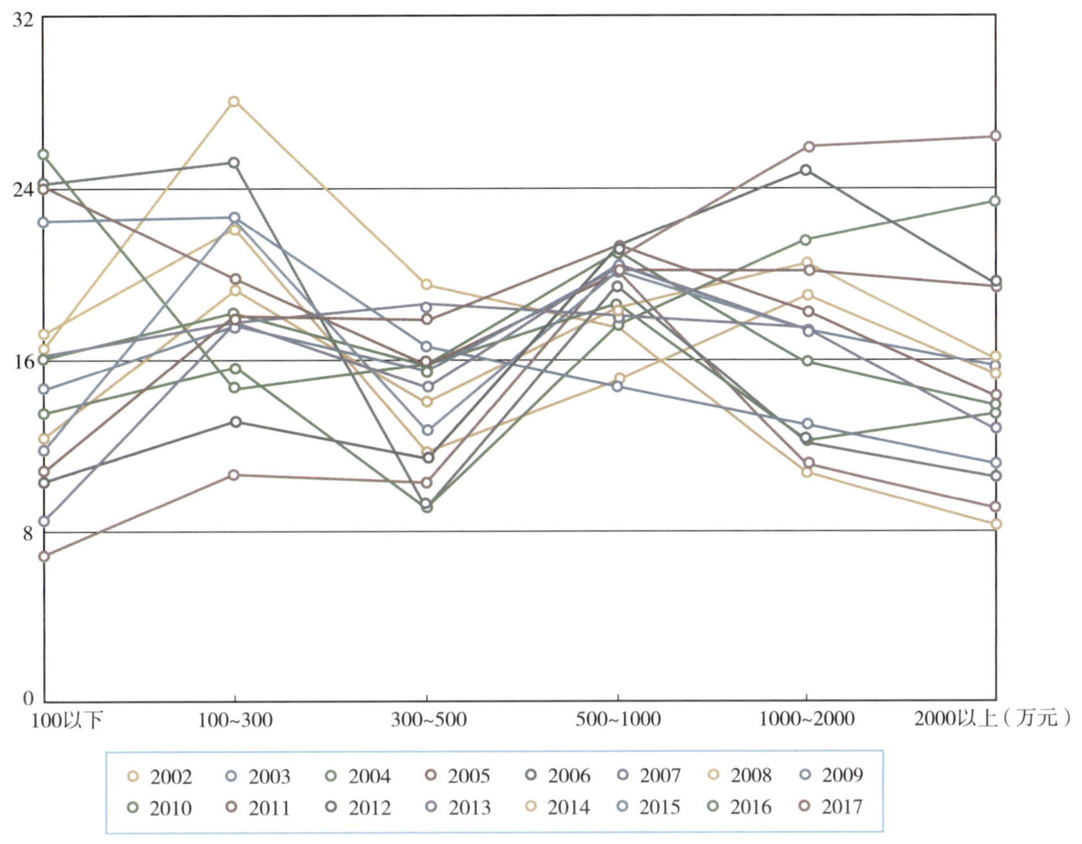

图 2-12 中国创业投资机构单项投资金额分布（2002~2017）

2.3.3 中国创业投资的投资策略（联合投资）

联合投资通过合作分享其他创业投资伙伴的专业知识和技能，有效分散创业投资机构的投资风险，实现资金使用效率最大化，最终优化项目选择，提升投资组合整体价值。数据显示：2017 年创业投资机构和其他创业投资主体联合投资的项目中，100 万~500 万元规模的项目所占比例最高，占比为 32.9%。其次为 500 万~1000 万元、1000 万~2000 万元的项目，分别占 19.6%。相比 2016 年，100 万~500 万元和 1000 万~2000 万元以上的项目占比有一定程度的提高，而 100 万元以下、500 万 ~1000 万元、2000 万元以上的项目占比出现下降现象（见表 2-20、图 2-13）。

表 2-20 中国创业投资联合投资的单项投资金额分布（2008~2017）① 单位：%

金额（万元）/ 年份	<100	100~500	500~1000	1000~2000	>2000
2008	19.00	31.60	13.90	20.30	15.20
2009	13.00	28.00	21.00	19.00	19.00
2010	10.30	15.40	24.10	23.10	27.20
2011	6.10	22.00	18.30	25.60	28.00
2012	13.00	28.70	20.90	20.00	17.40

① 有效样本数为 225 份。

续表

年份 \ 金额（万元）	<100	100~500	500~1000	1000~2000	>2000
2013	12.00	32.00	28.00	12.00	16.00
2014	16.00	27.60	10.40	23.30	22.70
2015	11.40	28.50	23.20	21.30	15.60
2016	14.60	32.50	20.40	10.70	21.80
2017	11.10	32.90	19.60	19.60	16.90

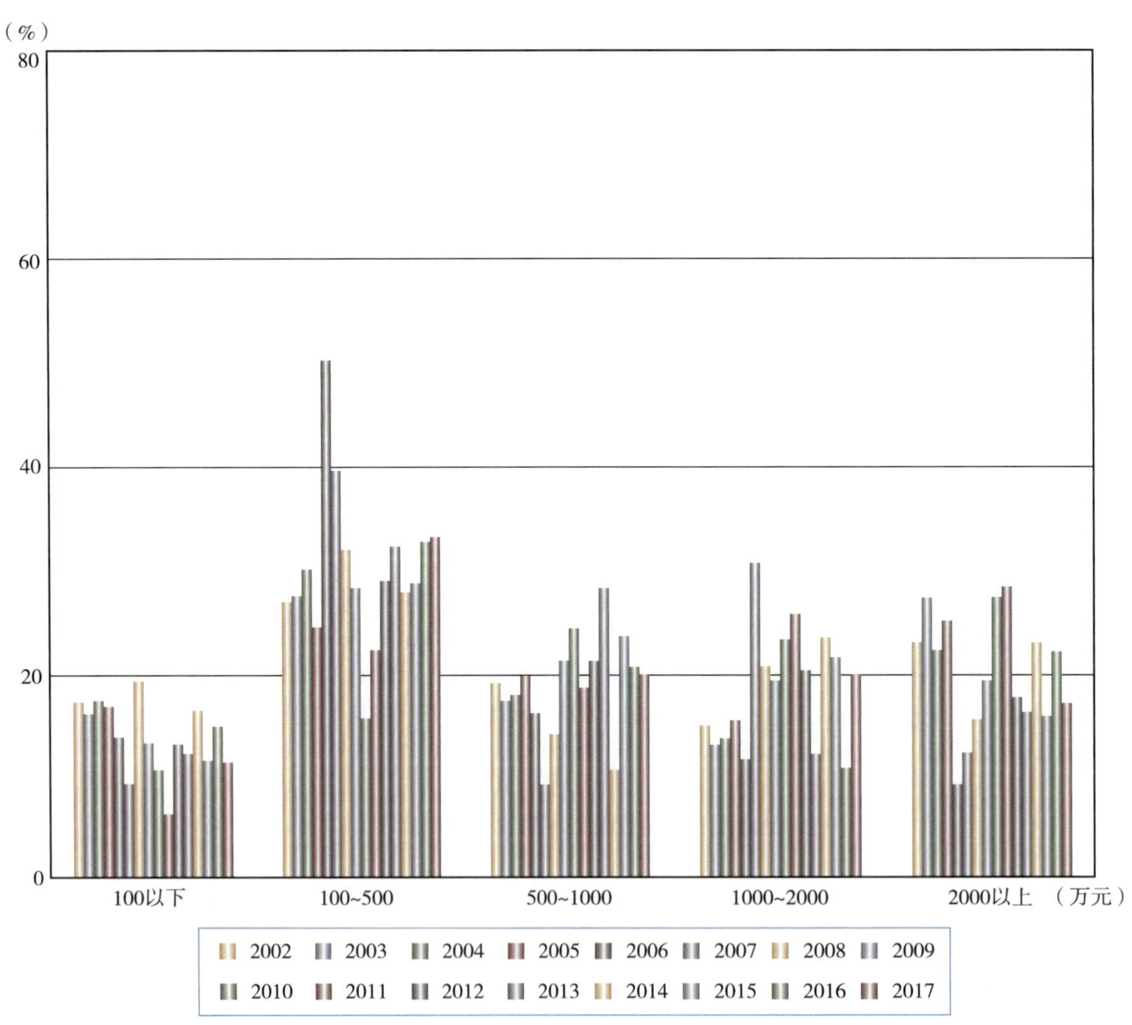

图 2-13 中国创业投资联合投资的单项投资金额分布（2002~2017）

2.4 中国创业投资的首轮投资与后续投资①

2017 年，中国创业投资项目的首轮投资和后续投资占比分别为 72.7% 和 27.3%。与 2016 年相比，首轮投资占比提高了 3.7 个百分点，提升幅度较大。可能的原因之一是 2017 年我国创业创新活动热情较高，投资机会增加。后续投资占比在经历 2010 年以来的持续上升后 2016 年、2017 年出现回落。总体而言，2017 年我国创业投资机构对被投资项目的首轮投资仍然居于主导地位（见表 2–21、图 2–14）。

表 2–21　中国创业投资的首轮投资和后续投资（2008~2017）　单位：%

项目 \ 年份	2008	2009	2010	2011	2012	2013	2014	2015	2016	2017
首轮投资	84.5	82.7	86.2	83.4	80.1	77.5	68.1	62.7	69.0	72.7
后续投资	15.5	17.3	13.8	16.6	19.9	22.5	31.9	37.3	31.0	27.3

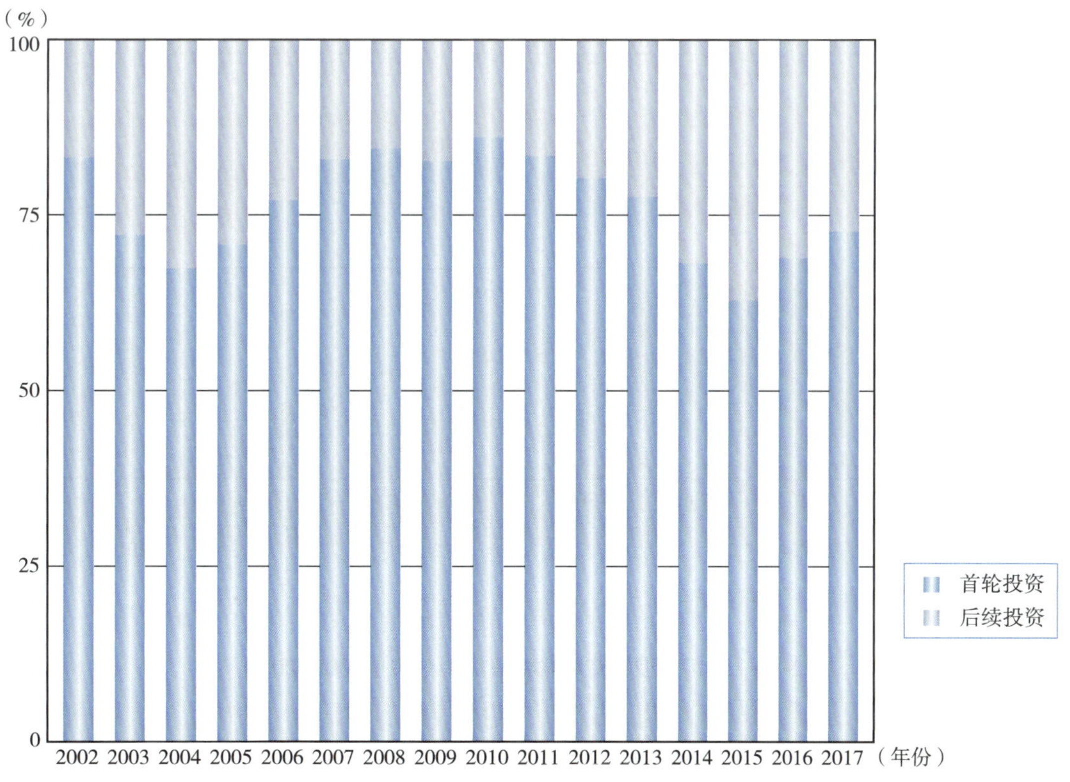

图 2–14　中国创业投资的首轮投资和后续投资（2002~2017）

① 有效样本数为 1592 份。

2.5 中国创业投资机构持股结构①

2017 年，中国创业投资机构的持股结构延续了原有的趋势，仍然以参股为主，不谋求控股始终是创业投资机构的主导经营策略。统计数据显示，2017 年创业投资机构的投资项目中，持股比例在 10% 以下的项目所占比例高达 68.57%，与往年相比，这一数据继续上升。而持股比例在 50% 以上的项目占比仅为 2.33%（见图 2-15、表 2-22）。

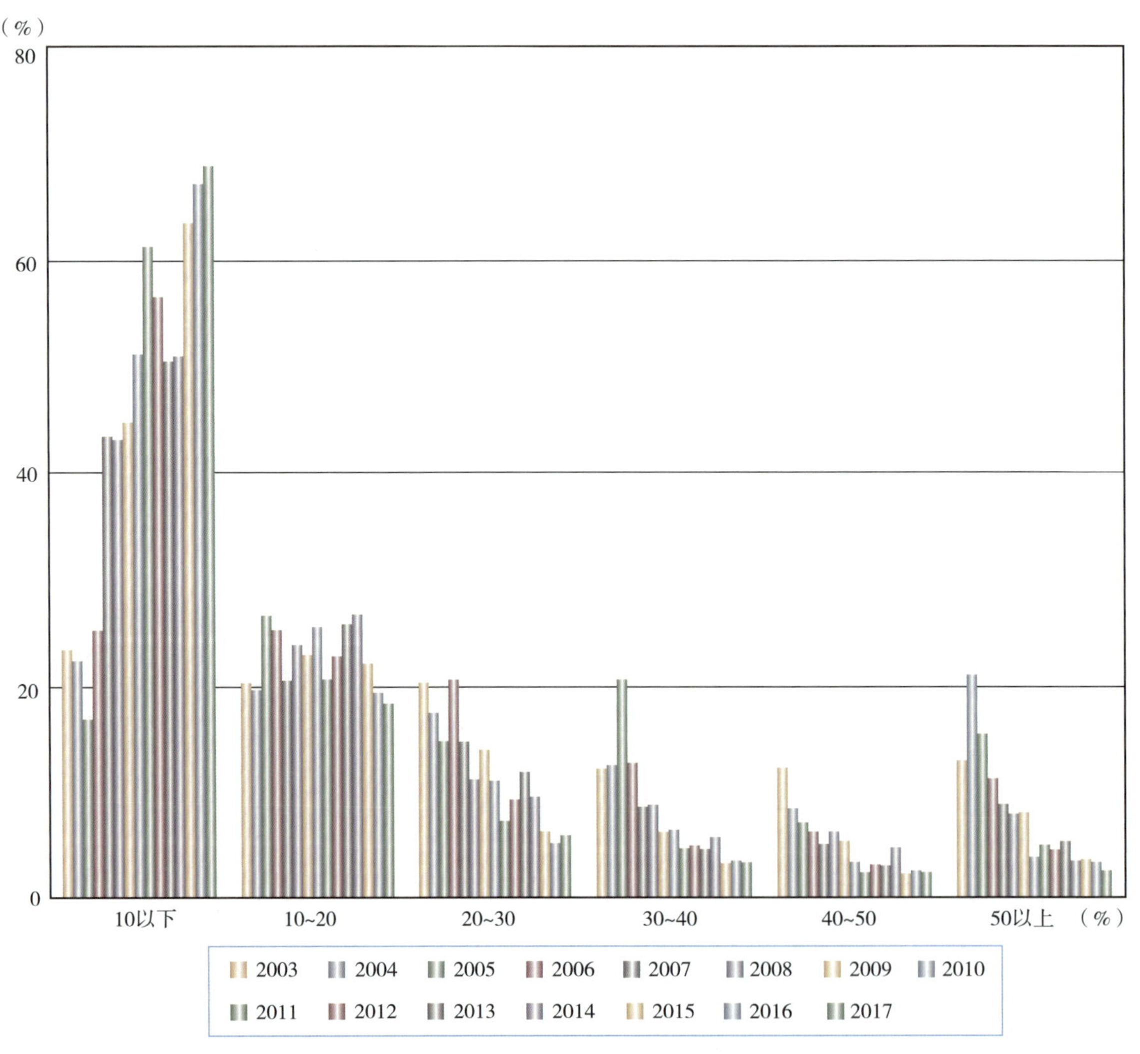

图 2-15 中国创业投资机构持股结构分布（2003~2017）

① 有效样本数为 2186 份。

表 2-22 中国创业投资机构持股结构分布（2008~2017） 单位：%

年份 \ 股权比例（%）	<10	10~20	20~30	30~40	40~50	>50
2008	42.92	23.65	10.95	8.61	6.13	7.74
2009	44.60	22.77	13.64	5.98	5.14	7.87
2010	50.99	25.15	10.85	6.17	3.14	3.70
2011	61.04	20.46	7.08	4.38	2.24	4.80
2012	56.29	22.57	9.07	4.70	3.00	4.37
2013	50.32	25.60	11.60	4.40	2.88	5.20
2014	50.79	26.43	9.30	5.55	4.60	3.33
2015	63.47	21.88	6.10	2.96	2.14	3.46
2016	66.97	19.16	5.03	3.29	2.41	3.13
2017	68.57	18.12	5.67	3.11	2.20	2.33

2.6 中国创业投资项目主要特征

2.6.1 中国创业投资项目的资本规模①

从被投资项目的实收资本来看，投资项目的规模总体呈上升趋势。与 2016 年相比，2017 年投资项目规模 500 万元以下的中小投资项目占比减少了 11.05 个百分点，而 5000 万元以上的投资项目占比大幅增加 24.29 个百分点（见表 2-23、图 2-16）。

表 2-23 中国创业投资项目的实收资本规模分布（2008~2017） 单位：%

年份 \ 资本规模（万元）	<500	500~1000	1000~3000	3000~5000	>5000
2008	18.90	15.70	26.50	12.20	26.70
2009	21.60	13.90	23.50	15.40	25.60
2010	26.40	12.43	23.42	13.06	24.68
2011	15.23	11.50	24.23	13.56	35.48
2012	16.93	14.49	26.09	13.18	29.32
2013	19.49	15.25	23.74	14.44	27.07
2014	35.38	12.07	20.82	9.77	21.97
2015	33.10	12.58	20.65	10.89	22.78
2016	31.74	12.53	20.69	11.05	23.99
2017	20.69	13.79	17.24	0.00	48.28

① 有效样本数为 29 份。

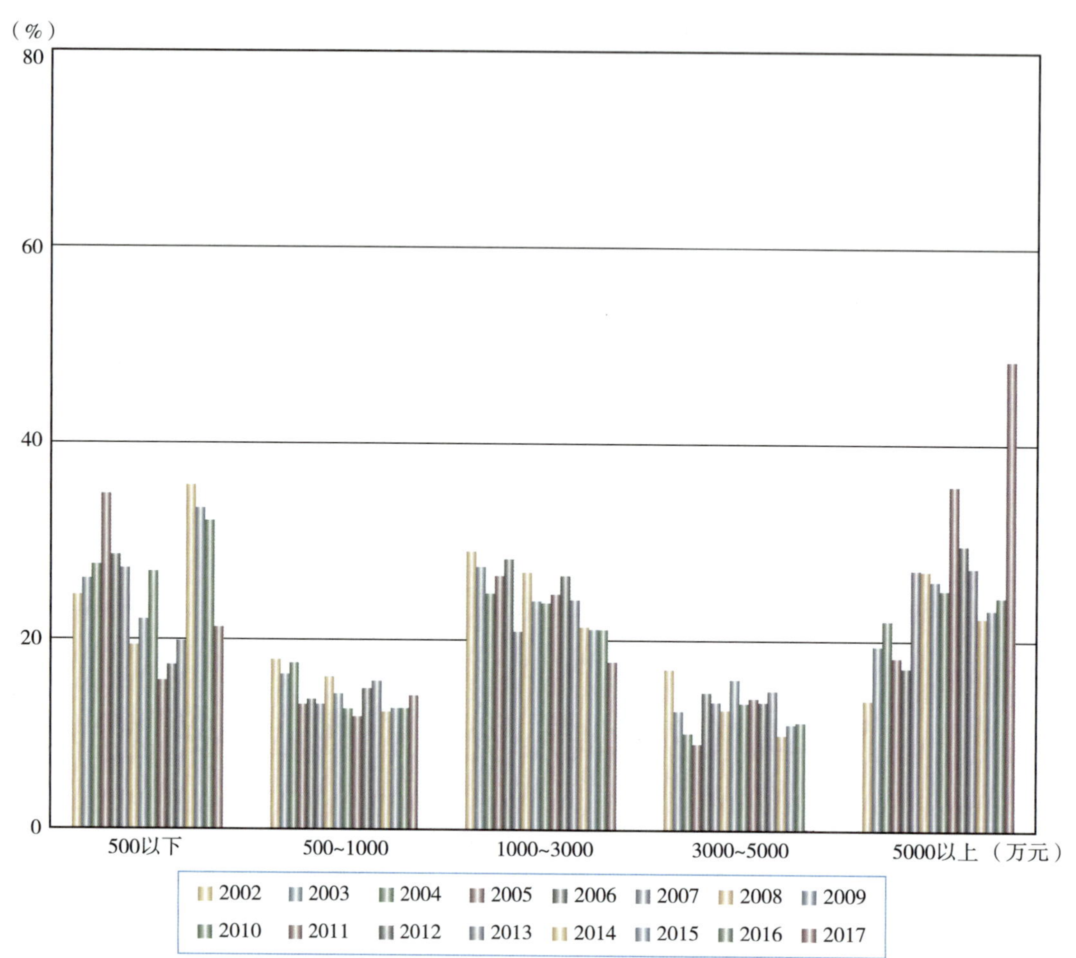

图 2-16 中国创业投资项目的实收资本规模分布（2002~2017）

2.6.2 中国创业投资项目的雇员规模[①]

从雇员规模分布来看，2017 年，中国创业投资机构投资项目中，雇员人数主要集中在 10~50 人，占比达到 32.88%；接下来依次为雇员规模在 200 人以上和 10 人以下的项目，占比分别为 20.02% 与 17.58%（见表 2-24、图 2-17）。

表 2-24 中国创业投资项目雇员规模分布（2008~2017）

单位：%

雇员规模（人） 年份	<10	10~50	50~100	100~150	150~200	>200
2008	14.60	29.90	14.40	7.50	3.40	29.90
2009	21.80	36.70	9.80	6.20	4.80	19.90
2010	14.60	28.90	13.90	8.20	5.90	27.50
2011	11.30	24.30	13.30	8.90	6.90	34.10
2012	12.88	25.96	13.39	11.76	8.62	27.38

① 有效样本数为 1053 份。

续表

雇员规模（人）/年份	<10	10~50	50~100	100~150	150~200	>200
2013	13.75	30.38	13.97	10.20	7.43	24.28
2014	18.52	32.46	14.78	8.75	5.10	20.39
2015	19.07	38.14	15.11	5.91	4.98	16.79
2016	21.84	37.89	14.06	7.79	4.18	14.25
2017	17.58	32.88	16.40	7.32	5.80	20.02

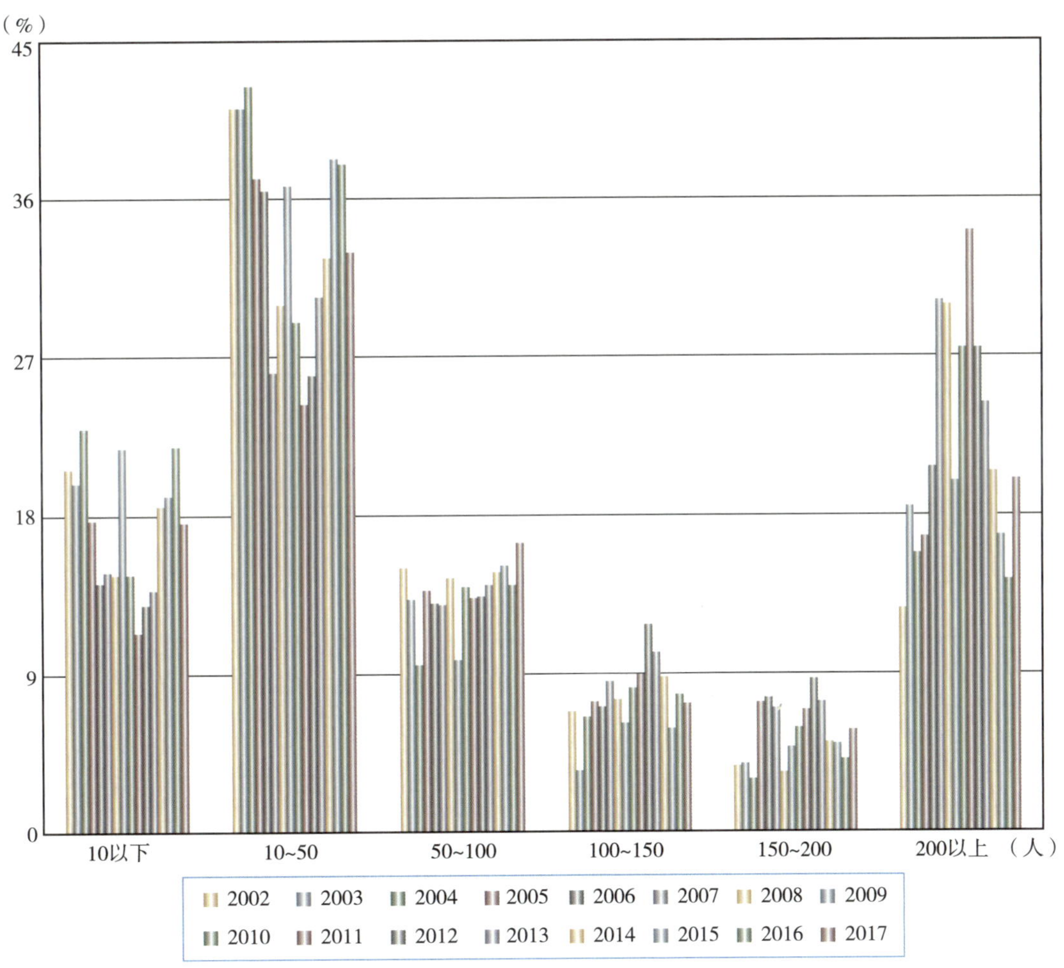

图 2-17 中国创业投资项目雇员规模分布（2002~2017）

2.6.3 中国创业投资项目的经营时间①

从企业经营时间看，2017 年创业投资机构仍然偏好比较稳健的成熟项目。其中，成立时间超过 5 年的企业投资占比最高，达到 53.13%，相比 2016 年该数据继续上升。然后是成立时间在 1~3 年的初创期企业和成立时间在 3~5 年的企业，占比均为 18.75%（见表 2-25、图 2-18）。

① 有效样本数为 2149 份。

表 2-25 中国创业投资项目经营时间分布（2008~2017） 单位：%

经营时间（年） 年份	<1	1~3	3~5	>5
2008	17.30	24.30	19.00	39.40
2009	40.20	16.70	12.30	30.80
2010	13.60	28.80	13.60	43.90
2011	11.80	20.10	16.30	51.80
2012	14.25	20.51	15.19	50.05
2013	19.54	21.54	17.21	41.71
2014	29.29	22.21	16.14	32.35
2015	21.01	27.95	14.95	36.09
2016	20.38	29.31	12.46	37.85
2017	9.38	18.75	18.75	53.13

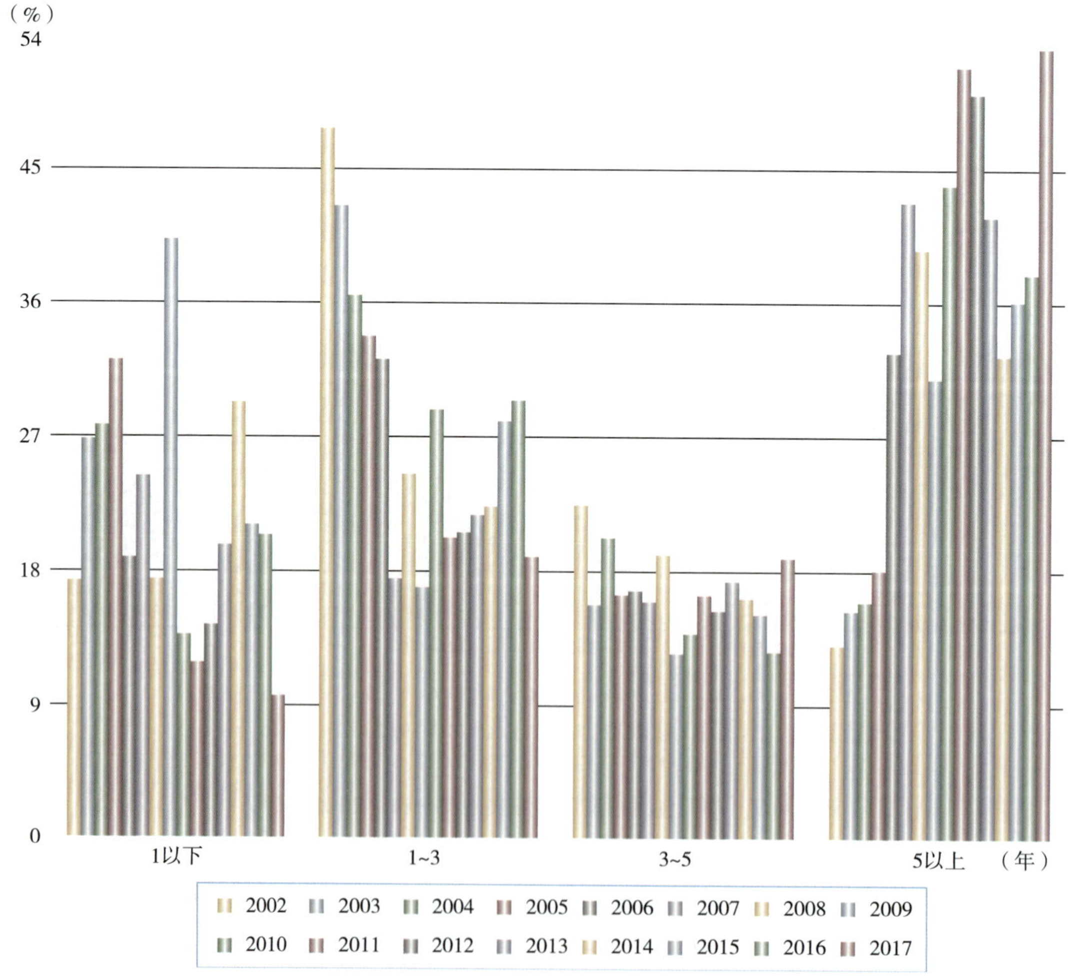

图 2-18 中国创业投资项目经营时间分布（2002~2017）

3 中国创业投资的退出

3.1 中国创业投资退出的基本情况①

2016年以来，证监会发审呈现从严监管的态势，建立了首发企业现场检查机制，严格实施IPO各环节的全过程监管，促使发行人、保荐机构、证券服务机构等各尽其责。根据市场数据显示，截至2017年12月31日，A股市场累计共有3467家企业完成IPO，2017年当年IPO项目436家，总融资额为2301.53亿元；其中，中小板市场81家，筹资额402.69亿元；创业板市场141家，筹资额521.85亿元。据科技部专项调查，2017年创业投资机构共有878个项目完成退出。其中，参与的企业中共有106个项目通过境内IPO实现退出，占全年境内IPO总量的24.3%；境外IPO退出项目14项。

2017年，中国创业投资行业披露了705个退出项目的收入分配情况，与往年相差不大，其中收入在2000万元以上的退出项目占到了31.2%，较上年度增加1.9个百分点；收入在100万元以下的退出项目占比较2016年有所下降，下降1.5个百分点（见表3–1、图3–1）。

表3–1 中国创业投资项目的退出收入分布（2009~2017） 单位：%

年份 \ 收入规模（万元）	<100	100~500	500~1000	1000~2000	>2000
2009	26.8	27.5	15.7	12.4	17.6
2010	27.3	19.7	13.7	13.7	25.7
2011	22.9	24.1	11	10.6	31.4
2012	19.2	17.1	10.5	17.4	35.8
2013	21.8	19.8	10.6	11.8	35.9
2014	15.7	24.7	14.4	12.7	32.4
2015	10.3	22.4	13.8	19.3	34.2
2016	16.8	22.3	15.3	16.2	29.3
2017	15.3	23.3	12.6	17.6	31.2

① 有效样本数为705份。

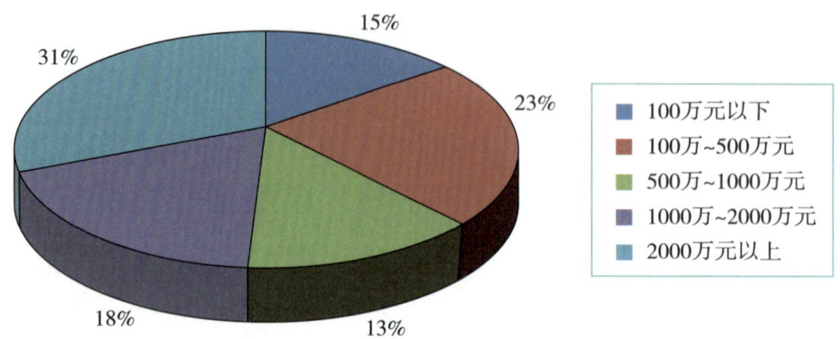

图 3-1 中国创业投资项目的退出收入分布（2017）

3.2 中国创业投资的退出方式①

3.2.1 中国创业投资的主要退出方式

根据退出渠道划分，创业投资的企业中共有 120 个项目通过 IPO 方式实现退出，占比为 13.66%，与 2016 年相比下降了 3.66 个百分点。相对而言，回购交易仍然是退出的主要渠道，退出项目数达到了 306 项，占比 34.84%；并购占比较前一年增加了近 3 个百分点；其他（含新三板）增幅较为明显，增加 5.17 个百分点（见表 3-2、图 3-2）。

表 3-2 中国创业投资的退出方式分布（2009~2017） 单位：%

年份 \ 退出方式	上市	并购	回购	清算	其他（含新三板）
2009	25.30	33.00	35.30	6.30	0.00
2010	29.80	28.63	32.82	6.87	1.91
2011	29.40	29.97	32.28	3.17	5.19
2012	29.41	15.86	45.01	6.65	3.07
2013	24.33	23.75	44.83	4.60	2.49
2014	20.72	36.02	36.02	4.83	2.41
2015	15.51	31.02	37.52	6.50	9.45
2016	17.32	29.67	40.14	8.06	4.80
2017	13.66	32.65	34.84	8.88	9.97

① 有效样本数为 732 份。

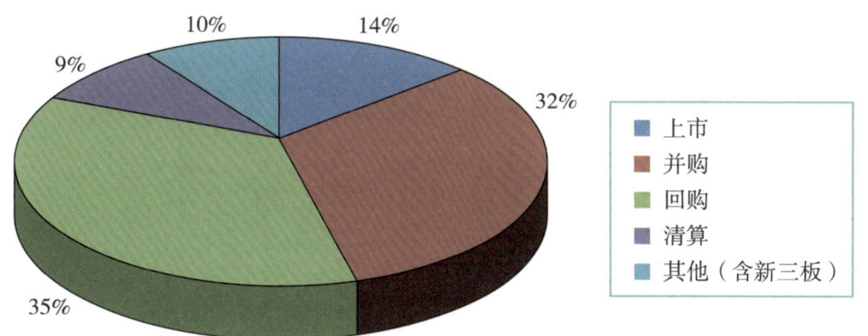

图 3-2　中国创业投资的退出方式（2017）

3.2.2　中国创业投资的 IPO 退出情况

随着我国多层次资本市场的建设，目前已形成主板、中小板、创业板以及新三板市场的构架。“沪港通”“深港通”开闸，为内地投资者投资港股开通了一条便捷的渠道，港股也逐渐成为除 A 股之外的另一个主流投资市场。据统计显示，2017 年披露项目中，共 120 个项目通过。与 2016 年不同，境内中小板市场成为退出的主要渠道，占比达到 48.48%；此外，15.15% 的企业通过境内创业板退出，31.31% 的企业通过境内主板市场退出，较 2016 年占比明显下降（见表 3-3、见图 3-3）。

表 3-3　中国创业投资退出项目的 IPO 分布（2011~2017）①　单位：%

年份	境内主板上市	境内创业板上市	境内中小板上市	境外上市
2011	14.71	30.39	49.02	5.88
2012	21.74	38.26	36.52	3.48
2013	21.26	40.94	30.71	7.09
2014	22.33	42.72	21.36	13.59
2015	48.48	28.28	16.16	7.07
2016	48.51	29.70	18.81	2.97
2017	31.31	15.15	48.48	5.05

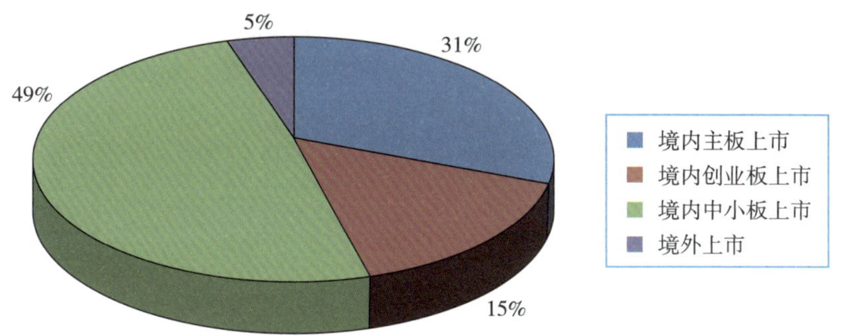

图 3-3　中国创业投资退出项目 IPO 分布（2017）

① 有效样本数为 120 份。

3.3 中国创业投资退出项目的行业分布①

从一级行业划分情况来看，2017 年，软件和信息服务业行业投资热度增加，其退出占比明显上升，上升了 2.5 个百分点，增加到 18.4%，成为实现退出最多的行业。此外，新能源和环保业、医药生物业、传播与文化娱乐行业的退出占比明显下降，计算机、通信设备制造业的退出项目占比略有上升（见表 3–4、图 3–4）。

表 3–4 中国创业投资退出项目的行业分布（2009~2017） 单位：%

行业 \ 年份	2009	2010	2011	2012	2013	2014	2015	2016	2017
软件和信息服务业②	26.7	15.9	12.9	9.4	11.5	11.6	20.3	15.9	18.4
新能源和环保业③	12.7	24.5	16.7	22.2	16.2	15.2	15.7	17.6	15.9
计算机、通信设备制造业④	18.1	14.2	14.4	10.6	14	14.2	9.9	10.9	11.2
传统制造业	12.2	7.9	11.3	14.3	17.5	12.2	9.3	8.5	8.4
医药生物业⑤	9.0	11.0	13.5	11.1	12.5	8.3	8.7	10.8	7.3
其他制造业	0.0	0.0	5.3	6.2	8.2	4.1	7.5	4.7	6.7
其他行业	9.5	11.4	5.0	6.2	3.9	8.7	7.3	12.5	11.3
农林牧副渔	1.4	4.7	6.0	6.5	3.7	4.3	3.2	3.3	2.8
金融保险业	2.7	3.1	2.2	2.2	3.9	1.8	2.9	1.6	2.4
科技服务	2.7	1.6	0.6	2.2	0.6	1.2	2.8	2.4	3.6
传播与文化娱乐	0.9	1.6	1.9	3.0	2.7	5.5	2.3	5.9	3.9
社会服务	0.0	0.0	0.6	1.6	0.8	1.4	1.5	1.6	2.4

从二级细分行业划分的情况来看，2017 年，中国创业投资实现项目退出最多的行业是其他行业，占比 11.1%。其次是传统制造业，但较 2016 年占比下滑了 0.1 个百分点。此外，医药保健、新材料工业、环保工程、网络产业，以及传播与文化娱乐产业实现项目退出的占比均出现不同程度的下降，但软件产业的退出有所增加。排名前 10 的行业合计实现退出的项目占全部退出项目的 62.5%，集中度较 2016 年下降 6.14 个百分点（见表 3–5）。

① 有效样本数为 712 份。
② 包括原有的网络产业、IT 产业、软件产业、其他 IT 产业四个细分的二级行业。
③ 包括原有的新材料工业，新能源、高效节能技术，核应用技术，环保工程四个细分的二级行业。
④ 包括原有的通信设备、半导体、计算机硬件产业、光电子与光机电一体化四个细分的二级行业。
⑤ 包括原有的医药保健、生物科技两个细分的二级行业。

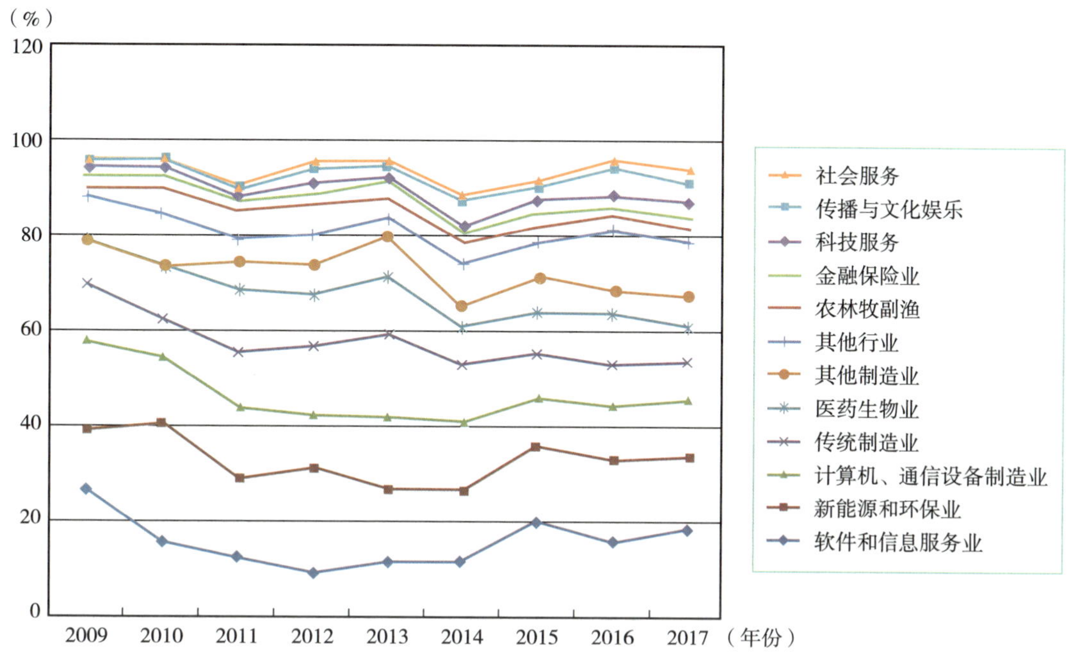

图 3-4 中国创业投资退出项目的行业分布（2009~2017）

表 3-5 中国创业投资退出项目的行业分布（2016~2017） 单位：%

行业分类	2016 年	2017 年
其他行业	12.5	11.3
传统制造业	8.5	8.4
软件产业	6.1	8.4
其他制造业	4.7	6.7
新材料工业	7.5	6.4
新能源、高效节能技术	5.2	5.3
网络产业	4.7	4.2
环保工程	4.7	4.1
传播与文化娱乐	5.9	3.9
医药保健	8.0	3.8
半导体	2.9	3.7
IT 服务业	3.5	3.6
生物科技	2.8	3.6
科技服务	2.4	3.6
通信设备	3.6	3.4
光电子与光机电一体化	2.8	3.3

续表

行业分类	2016 年	2017 年
农林牧副渔	3.3	2.8
其他 IT 产业	1.6	2.5
金融保险业	1.6	2.4
社会服务	1.6	2.4
消费产品和服务	1.9	2.0
建筑业	1.7	1.8
计算机硬件产业	1.6	1.0
交通运输、仓储和邮政业	0.3	1.0
批发和零售业	0.7	0.4

3.4 中国创业投资退出项目的地区分布①

近年来，中国创业投资退出项目的地区分布总体上未出现较大波动，其分布与创业投资机构投资分布情况较为一致，东部地区因创业投资发展相对成熟，退出项目占比较高，其中江苏、广东、浙江、北京等地区的项目退出占比长期处于领先地位。此外，2017 年广东、湖南、湖北地区的退出项目增幅较大。

2017 年，退出项目占比排名前 10 的地区合计占比 77.7%，较上一年度集中度减少了 8.1 个百分点，区域集聚效应仍然较为明显（见表 3–6、图 3–5）。

表 3–6 中国创业投资退出项目的地区分布前 10 名（2009~2017）

单位：%

2009 年	地区	江苏	广东	浙江	北京	陕西	安徽	上海	四川	湖北	天津
	比例	26.40	17.40	10.00	7.50	5.50	5.00	4.00	4.00	3.50	3.00
2010 年	地区	江苏	湖北	广东	浙江	上海	山东	北京	新疆	湖南	天津
	比例	26.60	16.70	12.40	9.00	6.40	3.40	3.00	3.00	2.60	2.60
2011 年	地区	江苏	上海	浙江	广东	天津	北京	河南	山东	湖北	福建
	比例	27.60	11.50	11.20	9.60	8.10	6.50	3.40	2.80	2.80	2.20
2012 年	地区	江苏	浙江	广东	湖北	北京	上海	河北	天津	安徽	湖南
	比例	35.60	9.80	8.40	7.60	7.30	5.40	3.80	3.80	3.80	3.50
2013 年	地区	江苏	浙江	上海	广东	北京	天津	安徽	山东	湖北	重庆
	比例	35.00	10.60	8.10	7.70	5.40	5.20	3.30	3.10	2.90	2.70

① 有效样本数为 717 份。

续表

2014 年	地区	江苏	浙江	广东	上海	北京	湖北	辽宁	湖南	山东	天津
	比例	20.40	13.50	13.30	10.20	9.80	3.80	3.30	3.10	2.90	2.70
2015 年	地区	江苏	北京	浙江	广东	上海	河南	安徽	天津	湖北	四川
	比例	24.30	13.20	10.40	8.60	5.30	4.20	4.20	4.10	3.60	3.10
2016 年	地区	江苏	浙江	北京	广东	上海	山东	天津	安徽	福建	湖南
	比例	29.70	12.70	11.80	8.00	6.10	4.30	4.00	3.50	2.90	2.80
2017 年	地区	江苏	广东	浙江	北京	上海	湖南	山东	福建	重庆	湖北
	比例	20.08	11.44	10.88	8.51	7.67	4.32	3.91	3.77	3.63	3.49

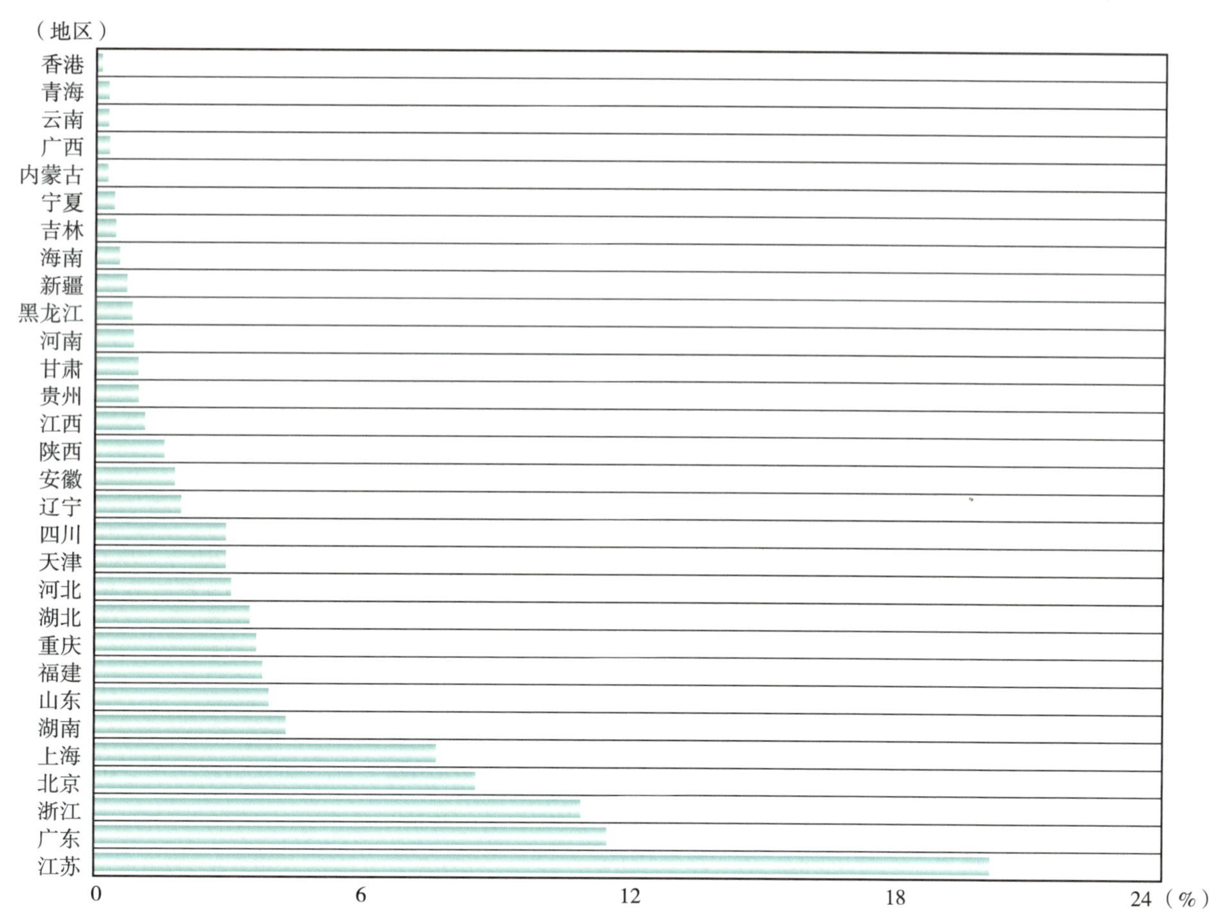

图 3–5 中国创业投资退出项目的地区分布情况（2017）

3.5 中国创业投资项目的退出绩效

3.5.1 中国创业投资退出的总体绩效表现

2017 年，资本市场总体发展较为平稳，创业投资项目退出收益率表现良好，略好于 2016 年表现，全行业的项目退出收益率达到了 243.35%。整个行业投资退出步伐略微放缓，项目平均退出时间为 4.44 年；整体行业年均收益率为 38.33%，成为除 2011 年、2012 年最高的年份（见表 3-7、图 3-6）。

表 3-7 中国创业投资退出的投资收益率（2009~2017）① 单位：%

年份	2009	2010	2011	2012	2013	2014	2015	2016	2017
总体收益率	144.89	221.87	193.71	196.35	117.70	123.04	260.18	225.73	243.35
年均收益率	19.33	37.82	45.62	44.01	13.85	23.46	32.39	29.69	38.33

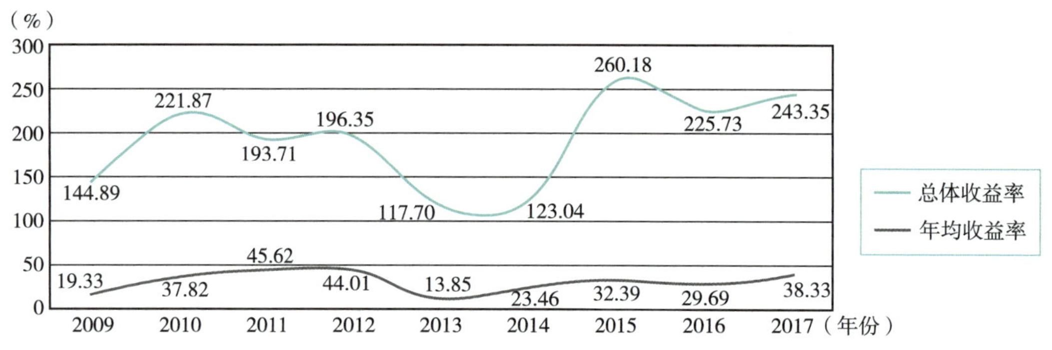

图 3-6 中国创业投资退出的投资收益率（2009~2017）

退出项目的投资收益分布趋势情况显示（见表 3-8、图 3-7）：2017 年退出项目亏损占比为 53%，较 2016 年减少 4%。此外，投资收益在 15%~20%、50%~100% 及 100% 以上阶段的项目占比高于 2016 年，收益有所增加，尤其 100% 以上增幅较大，增加 4.2 个百分点，其他阶段的收益略有下降。

表 3-8 中国创业投资退出收益率分布（2009~2017）② 单位：%

年份	亏损	0~15%	15%~20%	20%~50%	50%~100%	100% 以上
2009	63.0	4.8	3.2	10.6	4.2	14.3
2010	63.2	8.0	1.9	4.7	4.2	17.9
2011	47.9	9.9	3.0	10.6	6.5	22.1
2012	47.0	8.6	3.5	10.5	4.5	25.9

① 有效样本数为 3218 份。
② 有效样本数为 705 份。

续表

年份	亏损	0~15%	15%~20%	20%~50%	50%~100%	100% 以上
2013	67.1	2.4	2.7	8.7	2.2	16.9
2014	56.9	4.7	4.1	9.4	11.6	13.3
2015	48.9	12.1	3.5	11.8	7.4	16.2
2016	57.0	9.7	2.6	9.9	5.8	15.1
2017	53.0	7.5	3.1	9.4	7.7	19.3

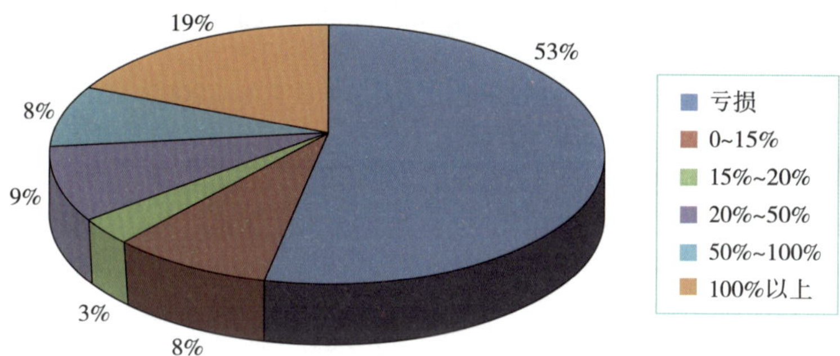

图 3-7　中国创业投资退出收益率分布（2017）

3.5.2　中国创业投资不同退出方式的绩效表现

2017 年，我国资本市场上证指数在 3052~3447 点波动，资金面临流动性压力，A 股上涨空间有限，但上市退出收益率仍然高达 1240.98%，即平均账目回报 12.4 倍，达到历史最好水平。通过并购退出的项目收益率略有下降，投资回报率达到 253.75%；清算项目亏损较为严重，项目收益损失达到了 38.91%。与 2016 年相比，新三板市场退出项目收益率出现大幅度下降，由 193.82% 下降到 51.18%（见表 3-9、图 3-8）。

表 3-9　不同渠道的创业投资退出项目总体收益率（2009~2017）①　　单位：%

年份	上市	并购	回购	清算	新三板挂牌交易
2009	327.75	4.74	−29.47	−42.66	—
2010	736.68	44.71	−21.19	−24.43	48.85
2011	799.38	41.47	−30.51	−65.37	63.19
2012	486.10	198.29	29.18	−15.34	32.48
2013	448.03	15.27	−34.28	−43.47	89.79
2014	601.66	63.55	−34.43	−34.43	27.23
2015	779.27	135.55	19.01	−15.60	16.86
2016	922.12	323.41	3.02	−43.62	193.82
2017	1240.98	253.75	−1.04	−38.91	51.18

① 有效样本数为 3218 份。

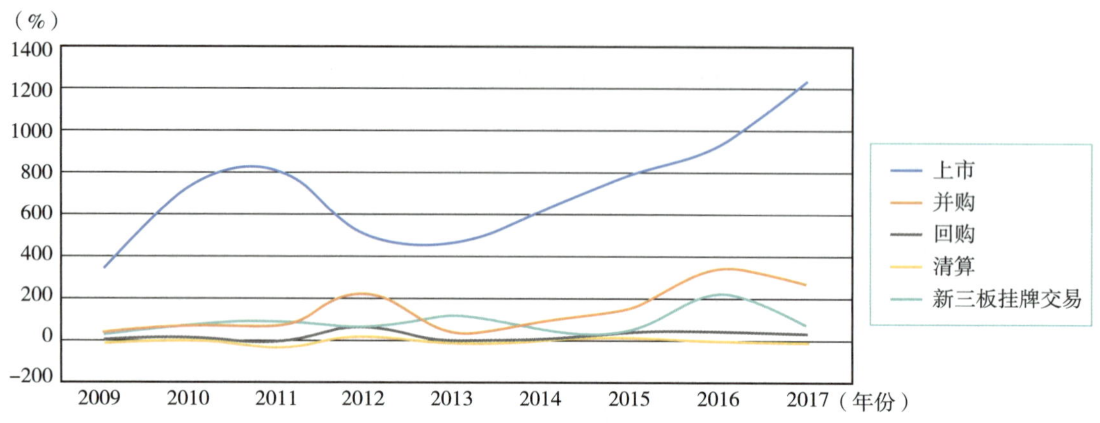

图 3-8 不同渠道的创业投资退出项目总体收益率（2009~2017）

一般而言，创业投资项目从投资到退出要经历 3~7 年时间，因此从年均收益率来看，创业投资并非一夜暴富的行业。从历年年均收益率情况来看，上市退出仍然是收益最高的退出渠道，一般年均收益率在 100% 左右，2011 年实现最高年均收益率超过 200%，2017 年实现年均收益率为 129.72%。这在一定程度上说明，尽管 2017 年上市退出实现了较高收益率，但由于通过上市退出投资周期较长，因此年度收益率并未达到历史最好水平；此外，并购退出表现良好，年均收益率达到 66.89%；新三板挂牌交易退出实现了年均收益 9.55% 的盈利水平，但与 2016 年相比大幅下降（见表 3-10、图 3-9）。

表 3-10 不同渠道的创业投资退出项目年均收益率（2009~2017）①

单位：%

年份	上市	并购	回购	清算	新三板挂牌交易
2009	113.08	-0.37	-21.02	-6.59	—
2010	187.62	5.04	-5.35	-4.83	5.64
2011	200.41	12.99	-20.71	-8.46	13.20
2012	84.62	66.4	14.86	-10.33	-4.47
2013	73.36	2.71	-19.31	-8.26	-0.90
2014	107.19	17.49	-4.22	-11.48	12.93
2015	114.38	44.45	4.05	-2.00	6.10
2016	120.35	37.58	0.38	-10.66	43.89
2017	129.72	66.89	-5.41	-9.54	9.55

① 有效样本数为 3218 份。

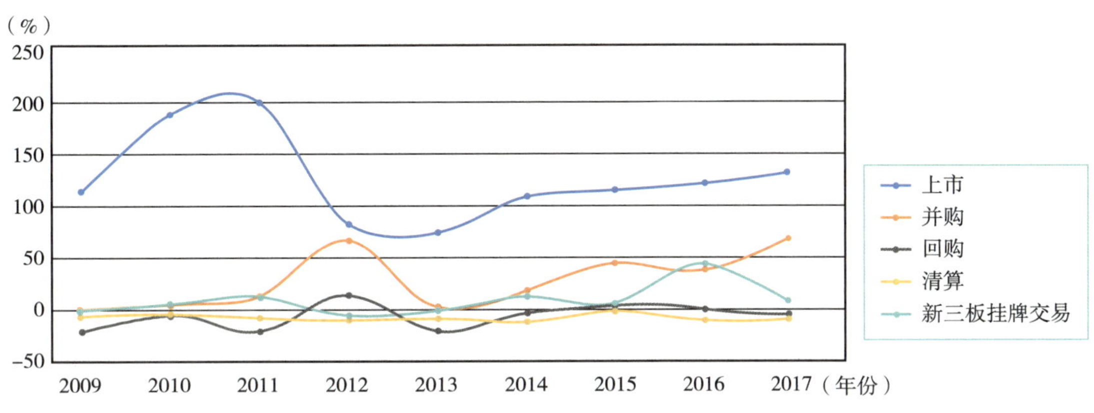

图 3-9 不同渠道的创业投资退出项目年均收益率(2009~2017)

3.5.3 中国创业投资不同行业退出的绩效表现

随着我国创业投资行业投资管理能力的逐步提升，项目的总体收益率呈现上升趋势。无论是高新技术行业还是传统行业，在经历了 2013 年的较大下滑后，项目退出的盈利水平出现回升。与 2016 年相比，2017 年项目的盈利水平均有了较大提高，尤其是传统行业创业投资退出项目，增加了 5.94 个百分点（见表 3-11、图 3-10、表 3-12、图 3-11）。

表 3-11 高新技术行业创业投资退出项目盈亏状况(2009~2017)① 单位：%

年份	2009	2010	2011	2012	2013	2014	2015	2016	2017
盈利	37.17	37.3	52.87	55.62	32.13	47.76	51.06	44.59	46.09
亏损	62.83	62.7	47.13	44.38	67.87	52.24	48.94	55.41	53.91

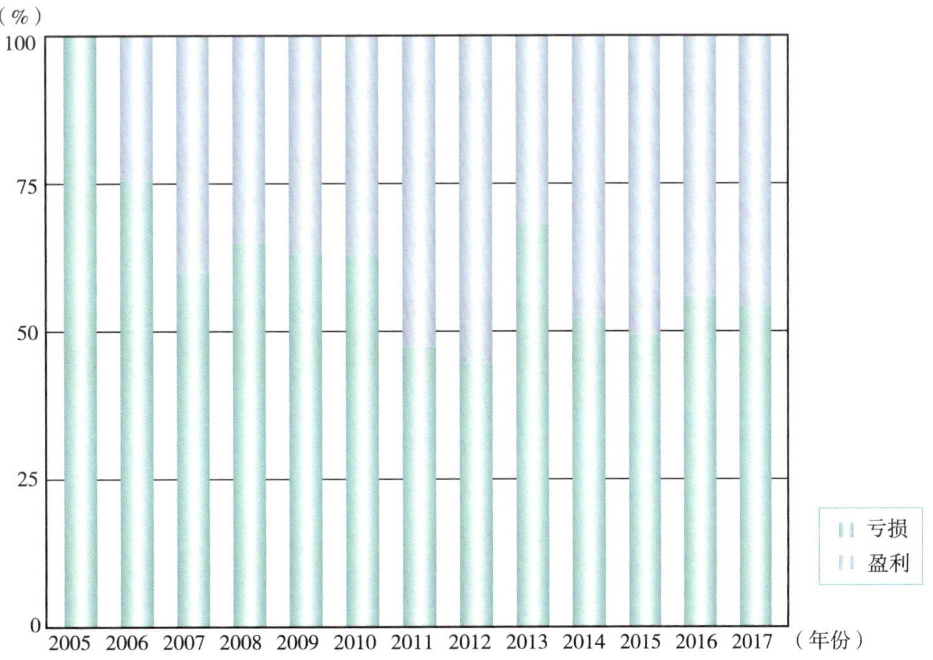

图 3-10 高新技术行业创业投资退出项目盈亏情况(2005~2017)

① 有效样本数为 384 份。

表 3-12 传统行业创业投资退出项目盈亏状况（2009~2017）① 单位：%

年份	2009	2010	2011	2012	2013	2014	2015	2016	2017
盈利	39.29	36.36	48.48	50.00	35.45	38.56	50.23	40.27	46.21
亏损	60.71	63.64	51.52	50.00	64.55	61.44	49.77	59.73	53.79

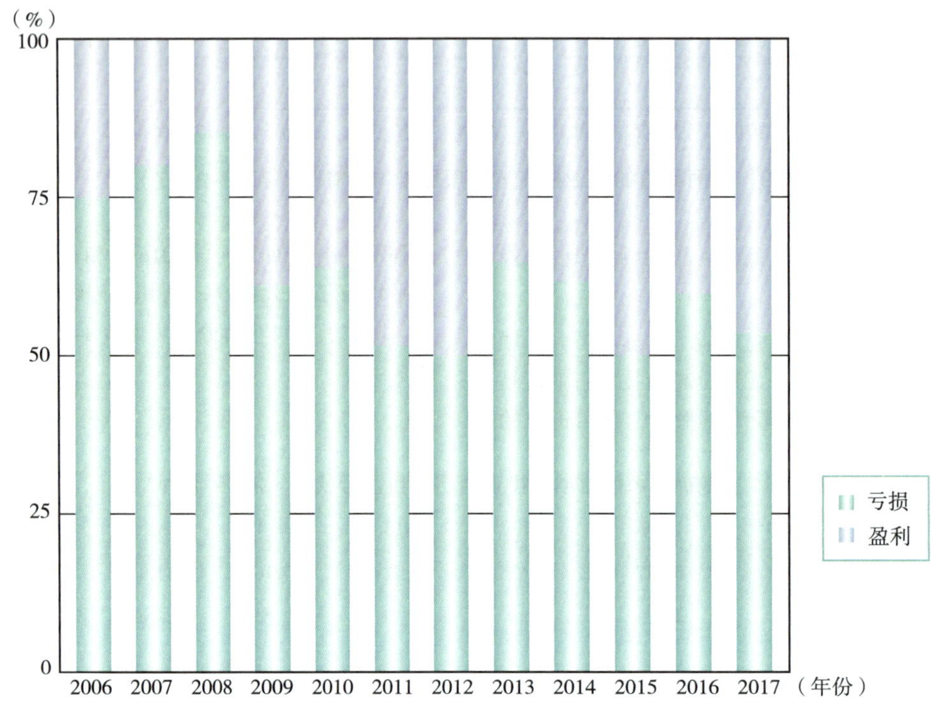

图 3-11 传统技术行业创业投资退出项目盈亏情况（2006~2017）

按细分行业划分，2017 年，半导体行业的退出平均收益水平高居榜首，达到了 20.87 倍。然后是核应用技术行业，账面回报率高达 15.31 倍。这在一程度上解释了为什么这几类行业成为新一轮的投资热点。此外，环保工程、传统制造业、网络产业，以及新能源、高效节能技术等行业的退出收益率下浮较大（见表 3-13）。

表 3-13 按细分行业划分的创业投资退出项目总体收益率（2016~2017）② 单位：%

行业	2016 年退出总体收益率	2017 年退出总体收益率
半导体	100.94	2086.59
核应用技术	—	1531.2
环保工程	207.07	174.73
传统制造业	284.38	140.64
网络产业	1351.87	123.29
新能源、高效节能技术	783.14	105.53

① 有效样本数为 290 份。
② 有效样本数为 674 份。

续表

行业	2016 年退出总体收益率	2017 年退出总体收益率
IT 服务业	76.61	93.04
其他制造业	204.14	88.8
其他 IT 产业	307.93	65.91
其他行业	138.16	40.53
光电子与光机电一体化	261.54	4.57

4 中国创业投资的绩效

4.1 创业投资机构的收入

4.1.1 投资机构的收入

2017 年，披露信息的创业投资机构[①]与投资业务相关的主营业务总收入和平均收入分别达到 196.27 亿元和 1525.02 万元，均较 2016 年有明显提高（见图 4–1）。

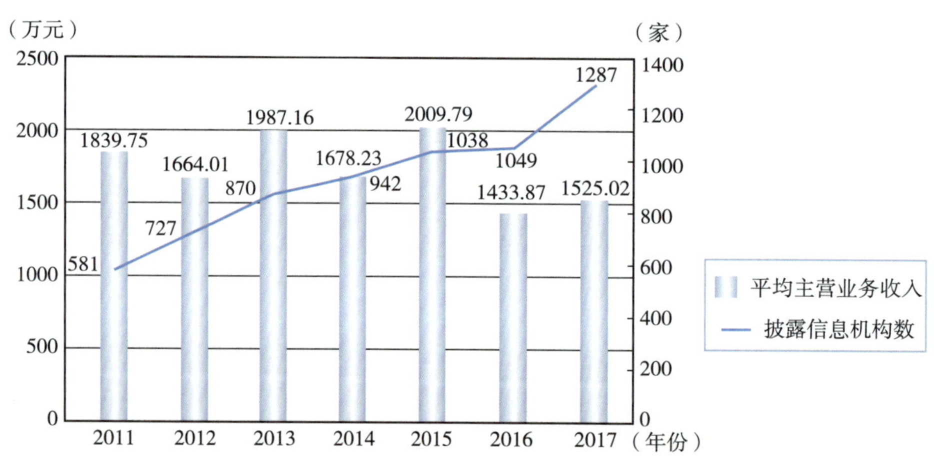

图 4–1 投资机构收入趋势 (2011~2017)

（1）机构主营业务收入权重下降。2017 年，披露收入和主营业务收入的机构数量继续增加，获得投资相关收入的机构占比下降，34.03% 的机构获得与投资相关的主营业务收入，较 2016 年大幅下降；715 家收入大于零的机构中有 438 家获得投资相关主营业务收入，占比为 61.26%。

（2）机构主营业务收入小幅增长。2017 年创业投资机构的收入规模有较大幅度提升，但主营业务收入增长不高，主营业务收入占总收入的比重则继续下降至 58.78%。

（3）基金与管理机构收入相当。分析披露信息的机构收入情况发现，403 家管理机构主营业务收入 61.12 亿元，平均每家机构为 1516.58 万元，892 家投资基金主营业务收入 135.15 亿元，平均每家机构为 1515.15 万元，基金的平均主营业务收入与管理机构相当。

（4）政府支持对机构收入的促进效应削弱。对比发现，获得政府支持的 365 家机构平均收入达到 1192.78 万元，未获得政府资金支持机构平均收入达到 1727.74 万元。

4.1.2 不同规模投资机构的收入特征[②]

按机构管理资本规模从低到高，我们将创业投资机构划分为 5 个组别，统计不同规模创业投资机构的平均收入及其占总收入比重情况，如表 4–1 所示。

① 有效样本数为 1287 份。
② 有效样本数为 1009 份。

表 4-1　不同规模投资机构的平均收入及其占比（2011~2017）

机构规模（亿元）/项目/年份	< 0.5		0.5~1		1~2		2~5		> 5	
	平均收入（万元）	占总收入比重（%）	平均收入（万元）	占总收入比重（%）	平均收入（万元）	占总收入比重（%）	平均收入（万元）	占总收入比重（%）	平均收入（万元）①	占总收入比重（%）②
2011	694.4	8.7	486.7	6.4	983.9	9.8	2777.6	28.6	5577.4	46.4
2012	916.0	10.8	593.1	7.9	1224.9	13.7	1190.6	14.8	6794.9	52.8
2013	443.4	4.7	945.4	10.1	1406.6	12.3	3150.7	31.9	7896.3	41.1
2014	319.8	4.8	1205.3	17.5	779.7	9.6	1299.7	16.5	7383.7	51.5
2015	374.6	4.6	985.9	11.0	1477.6	13.2	2049.1	18.9	9544.2	52.3
2016	417.3	8.2	1379.6	20.1	1036.8	13.0	1494.8	18.6	6090.8	40.1
2017	817.2	15.1	1006.0	12.7	433.0	5.1	1502.4	19.6	7120.4	47.5

2017 年，中国创业投资机构收入分布具有如下特征：

（1）机构规模越大平均收入越高。除管理资本 1 亿~ 2 亿元的机构，其他规模机构的平均收入与管理资本规模成正比。其中，管理资本 5000 万元以下的机构平均收入为 817.2 万元，管理资本超过 5 亿元的机构平均收入达到 7120.4 万元；大型机构收入占比保持较高水平，管理资本 5 亿元以上的机构收入占总收入的比重接近 50%，管理资本 2 亿元以上的机构收入占比达到 67.1%，而管理资本 5000 万元以下的机构收入占比仅为 15.1%。

（2）小规模机构收入有所提高。2017 年，管理资本在 5000 万元以下的机构平均收入大幅增长，甚至高于管理资本 1 亿 ~2 亿元的机构；管理资本 5000 万 ~1 亿元的机构平均收入略有下降。

（3）中等规模机构收入下滑。2017 年，管理资本 1 亿 ~2 亿元的机构平均收入下降明显，平均收入仅为 433.0 万元，占比仅为 5.1%，均是 5 个组别中最小的一组。

4.1.3　投资机构的收入来源结构

2017 年，715 家[③]创业投资机构披露了主营业务收入，其中股权转让收益占全部收入的 49.3%，分红收入占 18.4%，管理费、咨询费收入占 17.1%，其他收入占 15.2%（见图 4-2）。与 2016 年相比，股权转让收益占比降低 1.5 个百分点，分红收入占比降低 0.3 个百分点，管理费、咨询费收入占比提高 6.9 个百分点，其他收入占比降低 5.2 个百分点。

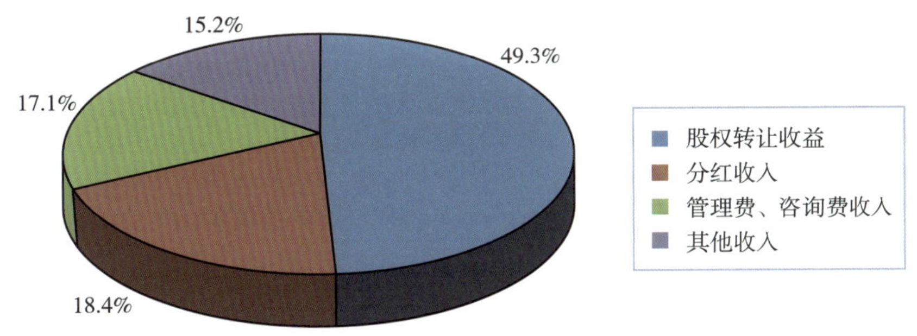

图 4-2　投资机构收入来源比例 (2017)

① 有效样本数为 1234 份。
② 有效样本数为 1234 份。
③ 仅包括收入大于 0 且各项收入占比之和等于 100% 的机构。

近年来，股权转让收益和分红收入对创业投资机构主要收入的贡献保持相对稳定的增长，2016 年以来连续两年小幅降低，管理费、咨询费收入占比明显提高。

4.1.4 投资机构当年最大收入来源①

2017 年统计调查显示，中国创业投资机构最大收入来源分布与往年相比未发生显著的结构变化。

（1）不同最大收入来源的机构分布。以股权转让为最大收入来源的机构占 22.2%，较上年降低 3.6 个百分点；以分红为最大收入来源的创业投资机构占 17.0%，较上年降低 0.6 个百分点；二者合计为 39.2%，较上年降低 4.2 个百分点。以管理费、咨询费等收入为最大收入来源的创业投资机构占比为 44.3%，再次提高 3.0 个百分点；以其他收入为最大收入来源的创业投资机构占比为 16.5%，较上年提高 1.2 个百分点（见图 4–3、表 4–2）。

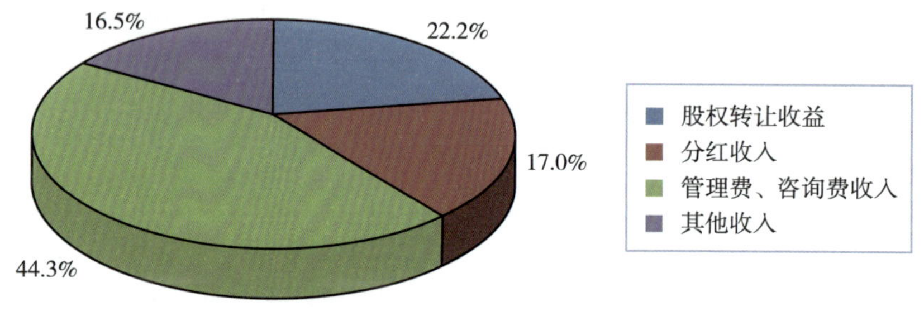

图 4–3 中国创业投资机构最大收入来源结构（2017）

表 4–2 中国创业投资机构最大收入来源结构（2008~2017） 单位：%

收入来源 / 年份	股权转让	分红	管理、咨询等	其他
2008	44.0	23.4	22.5	10.1
2009	33.8	17.4	29.8	19.0
2010	34.4	14.1	32.5	19.0
2011	36.8	15.5	30.4	17.3
2012	34.1	16.5	28.9	20.5
2013	37.1	15.0	27.4	20.5
2014	26.9	19.1	30.5	23.5
2015	27.8	18.8	35.9	17.5
2016	25.8	17.6	41.3	15.3
2017	22.2	17.0	44.3	16.5

（2）投资相关业务收入占比下降。近年来，股权转让和分红为中国创业投资机构带来了较多收益的同时，也成为更多机构的主要利润来源。2017 年，以股权转让收益和分红为第一收入来源的机构占比出现了下滑，与资本市场低迷造成市场估值下降有较大关系。

（3）最大收入来源与机构业务相关。管理公司和基金公司的主要收入来源也与其经营模式保持了高度一致，76.5% 的管理机构以管理、咨询等为最大收入来源，以管理、咨询等为最大收入来源的机构中，管理机构占比 67.6%；57.8% 的基金公司以股权转让、分红等投资直接收入为最大收入来源，比重为 71.3%，而以股权转让和分红为最大来源的机构中，基金占比分别达到 84.2% 和 86.0%。

① 有效样本数为 711 份。

4.2 创业投资项目的收益情况

2017 年调查显示，2296 家创业投资机构新增投资项目 2687 项，其中 1335 个项目披露了主营业务收入信息。

4.2.1 被投资项目的主营业务收入[①]

创业投资机构新增投资项目的主营业务收入与 2016 年相比的主要变化如下（见表 4–3、图 4–4）：

表 4–3 被投资项目的主营业务收入分布（2008~2017） 单位：%

年份 \ 收入（万元）	<100	100~500	500~1000	1000~3000	3000~5000	>5000
2008	18.8	12.1	8.1	15.1	5.6	40.3
2009	33.9	9.4	7.1	7.6	7.0	34.9
2010	29.1	6.8	5.0	12.3	4.8	41.9
2011	14.9	6.7	4.7	10.0	5.4	58.3
2012	20.3	7.7	5.5	9.8	6.7	49.9
2013	29.9	10.7	4.6	10.4	5.9	38.6
2014	54.0	5.8	3.4	8.7	4.8	23.3
2015	34.9	13.9	6.8	11.1	4.2	29.1
2016	36.8	13.3	6.5	12.2	4.7	26.5
2017	28.6	12.0	6.4	11.3	6.0	35.7

图 4–4 被投资项目的主营业务收入分布（2008~2017）

① 有效样本数为 1135 份。

（1）2017 年新增投资项目的主营业务收入仍然呈“W”形分布。与往年相比，5000 万元以上的项目占比提高，100 万元以下的项目占比降低，其他规模项目占比变化不大。

（2）按主营业务收入规模分类，大项目占比提高明显。其中 100 万元以下为 28.6%，100 万 ~3000 万元为 29.7%，3000 万元以上为 41.7%。

（3）主营业务收入 100 万元以下项目占比大幅下降。主营业务收入 100 万元以下的项目占比创 5 年新低，说明投资早前期项目的占比有所减少。

（4）主营业务收入 3000 万元以上的项目占比大幅增加。相比 2016 年，主营业务收入 3000 万元以上的项目占比大幅反弹，其中,3000 万 ~5000 万元的项目占比提高 1.3 个百分点，5000 万元以上项目占比提高 9.2 个百分点，合计提高 10.5 个百分点。

（5）中等规模项目占比略有降低。主营业务收入 100 万 ~500 万元的项目占比为 12.0%，500 万 ~1000 万元的项目占比为 6.4%，1000 万 ~ 3000 万元的项目占比为 11.3%，分别较 2016 年下降 1.3 个百分点、0.1 个百分点和 0.9 个百分点。

4.2.2 被投资项目的平均主营业务收入

2017 年，不同主营业务收入规模的中国创业投资机构投资项目的平均主营业务收入分化明显。[①]

（1）小项目收入能力不强。2017 年创业投资机构新增投资项目中，主营业务收入 100 万元以下的项目，平均主营业务收入仅为 13.9 万元，主营业务收入 100 万 ~ 500 万元的项目平均主营业务收入为 270.8 万元。这说明大部分项目的收入非常低。

（2）中型项目的收入比较平均。2017 年，主营业务收入 500 万 ~ 1000 万元、1000 万 ~ 3000 万元和 3000 万 ~ 5000 万元的项目收入分布均衡，个别组项目的平均主营业务收入处于组别的中间值。

（3）大项目收入非常高。主营业务收入 5000 万元以上的项目平均主营业务收入达到 7.5 亿元，超大项目占比较高（见表 4–4）。

表 4–4 不同规模被投资项目的平均主营业务收入（2011~2017） 单位：万元

主营业务收入（万元）/ 年份	<100	100~500	500~1000	1000~3000	3000~5000	>5000
2011	13.0	281.0	759.0	1971.0	3951.0	62777.0
2012	13.0	281.0	729.0	2170.0	4030.0	37292.0
2013	13.0	253.0	776.0	1915.0	4040.0	64047.0
2014	33.0	290.0	725.0	1871.0	4028.0	775370.0
2015	16.0	249.4	741.1	1775.4	3883.5	52008.3
2016	14.6	277.9	765.2	1824.2	3948.5	33239.5
2017	13.9	270.8	753.0	1740.0	4038.9	75334.2

4.3 创业投资项目的总体运行与趋势

4.3.1 被投资项目总体运行情况

截至 2017 年底，中国创业投资机构[②]累计投资项目达到 20674 项，其中，继续运行项目占比为 74.8%；境内外已上市项目占比为 7.3%；原股东（创业者）收购和管理层收购项目合计占比为 7.3%；被其他机构收购项目比重为 5.7%；清算的项目占比为 3.5%（见图 4–5）。

① 有效样本数为 1335 份。
② 有效样本数为 1415 份。

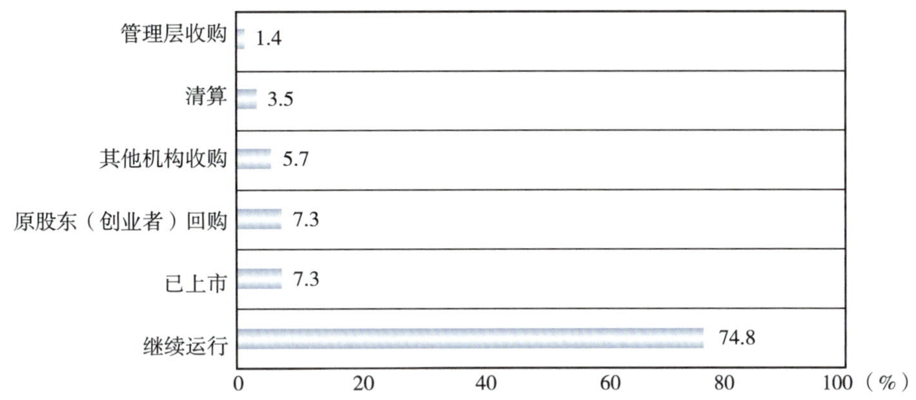

图 4–5　累计被投资项目的总体运行情况（2017）

4.3.2　被投资项目总体运行趋势

2017 年，中国创业投资机构累计投资项目的运行趋势表现出如下特征（见表 4–5）：

（1）资本市场略有回暖，上市项目比重小幅提高。2017 年，国内资本市场行情疲软，但是 IPO 进程较往年明显提速，创业板当年新增上市公司 140 家，为历史最高水平，为国内市场 IPO 创造了良好的环境；境外市场 IPO 比例虽与上年持平，但考虑到当年新增投资项目较多，境外 IPO 也为创业投资机构退出提供了良好基础。

（2）并购市场内热外冷，被投项目更受国内关注。2017 年，被境内外机构收购的项目占比为 5.7%，反映了并购市场的火热，特别是境内收购达到 5.4%，创国际金融危机以来新高。

（3）股权回购现象普遍，原股东和管理层收购略有降温。包括创业者在内的原股东、管理层收购占比达到 8.7%，其中原股东（创始人）收购占比 7.3%，管理层收购占比 1.4%，较上年一降一升。

（4）清算项目占比继续提升。2017 年清算项目比重再次提高，达到 3.5%，甚至高于国际金融危机期间的峰值。说明市场竞争日趋激烈，也从侧面反映行业的投资风险偏好发生变化。

表 4–5　累计被投资项目的总体运行状况分布（2008~2017）　单位：%

运行情况 / 年份	已上市		被收购		原股东收购	管理层收购	继续运行	清算
	境内	境外	境内收购	境外收购				
2008	1.8	1.1	3.1	2.9	6.2	0.6	82.7	1.6
2009	4.6	1.8	4.5	4.0	13.2	1.0	67.6	3.3
2010	5.9	1.7	4.7	4.1	10.6	0.9	69.6	2.5
2011	6.7	1.5	3.6	0.2	8.0	1.4	76.9	1.7
2012	6.7	1.4	3.3	0.1	7.2	1.0	78.9	1.4
2013	5.7	0.9	3.8	0.1	8.7	2.7	76.4	1.7
2014	6.0	1.6	4.4	0.3	6.6	0.7	79.0	1.4
2015	8.0	1.3	4.9	0.2	7.6	1.4	74.7	1.9
2016	6.6	0.3	4.8	0.1	7.9	1.1	76.5	2.7
2017	7.0	0.3	5.4	0.3	7.3	1.4	74.8	3.5

4.4　创业投资机构的总体运行情况评价

4.4.1　投资机构对全行业发展情况的评价①

2017 年，1613 家创业投资机构对全行业发展情况给出了评价。与 2016 年相比，中国创业投资机构对全行业的评价整体向好，乐观评价比重提高 5.7 个百分点，悲观评价比重降低 1 个百分点。认为全行业发展“非常好”和“较好”的机构比重分别提高 2.0 个百分点和 3.7 个百分点；认为“不好”和“非常不好”的机构比重分别降低 0.4 个百分点和 0.6 个百分点；认为全行业整体发展一般的机构比重从 2016 年的 45.3% 下降至 2017 年的 41.2%，对行业不确定的机构比重降低 0.6 个百分点（见表 4–6）。

表 4–6　投资机构对全行业的整体评价分布（2013~2017）　　单位：%

年份 \ 评价	非常好	较好	一般	不好	非常不好	不确定
2013	1.3	29.3	48.1	20.0	1.3	—
2014	3.4	51.5	38.0	6.7	0.4	—
2015	2.4	42.4	44.7	7.6	1.2	1.7
2016	2.7	41.9	45.3	5.9	1.1	3.1
2017	4.7	45.6	41.2	5.5	0.5	2.5

2015 年以来，中国创业投资机构对全行业的整体评价分布维持稳定。虽然对过去一年行业发展判断不置可否的比例相对波动较大，但是整体乐观评价趋势没有改变（见图 4–6）。

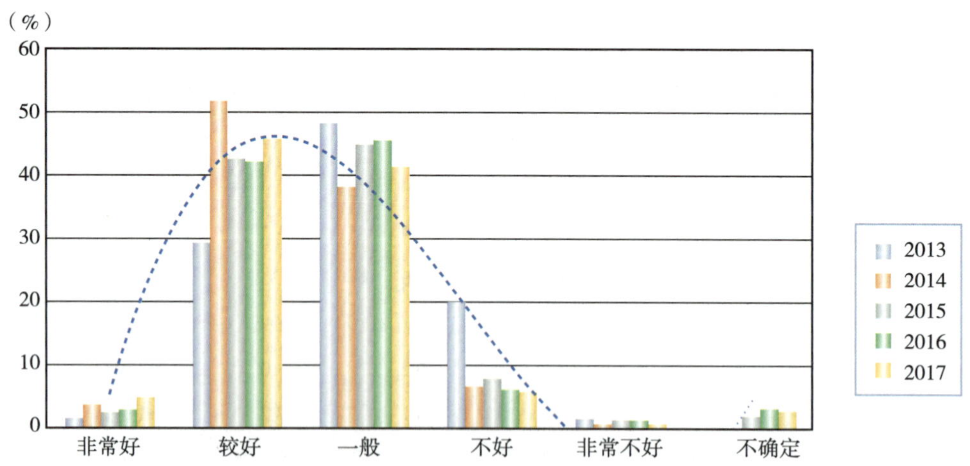

图 4–6　投资机构对全行业的整体评价分布（2013~2017）

① 有效样本数为 1613 份。

近年来，中国创业投资机构实际评价与上年预测之间始终存在较大的落差，机构上年的预测总是要比当年的实际评价更加乐观。上年预测投资前景“好”与“非常好”的比例始终高于实际评价水平，其中 2016 年预测未来投资前景“好”与“非常好”的机构比重达到 58.6%，2017 年实际评价“好”与“非常好”的机构占比为 50.3%；上年预测投资前景“不好”的机构低于实际评价悲观的比重，其中 2016 年预测未来投资前景“不好”的机构比重为 3.2%，2017 年实际评价为“不好”和“非常不好”的机构比重则达到 6.0%。

4.4.2 投资机构的投资前景预测①

对于 2018 年投资前景，中国创业投资机构整体上给出了相对乐观的预测。认为 2018 年投资前景“非常好”和“好”的机构占比分别为 7.4% 和 53.7%，合计较上年提高 2.5 个百分点，持乐观预期的机构比重连续两年提高。相应地，对 2018 年投资前景预期相对悲观的机构占比从 2017 年的 3.2% 下降至 2018 年 2.7%。对 2018 年投资前景不确定的机构比重达到 4.8%，较 2017 年进一步提高，一方面是机构对自身更早年份预期误差的修正，另一方面是对复杂国际经济局势特别是中美贸易摩擦不确定性的直接反映，80.2% 的机构认为宏观经济对行业影响较大（见表 4-7、图 4-7）。

表 4-7 投资机构投资前景的预测分布（2014~2018） 单位：%

<table>
<tr><th>整体评价
年份</th><th>非常好</th><th>好</th><th>一般</th><th>不好</th><th>非常不好</th><th>不确定</th></tr>
<tr><td>2014</td><td>2</td><td>54.6</td><td>37.9</td><td colspan="2">5.2</td><td>0.3</td></tr>
<tr><td>2015</td><td>5.6</td><td>65.2</td><td>27.7</td><td colspan="2">1.3</td><td>0.2</td></tr>
<tr><td>2016</td><td>3.7</td><td>49.3</td><td>37.8</td><td colspan="2">4.5</td><td>0.8</td></tr>
<tr><td>2017</td><td>3.6</td><td>55.0</td><td>34.1</td><td colspan="2">3.2</td><td>4.1</td></tr>
<tr><td>2018</td><td>7.4</td><td>53.7</td><td>31.3</td><td>2.4</td><td>0.3</td><td>4.8</td></tr>
</table>

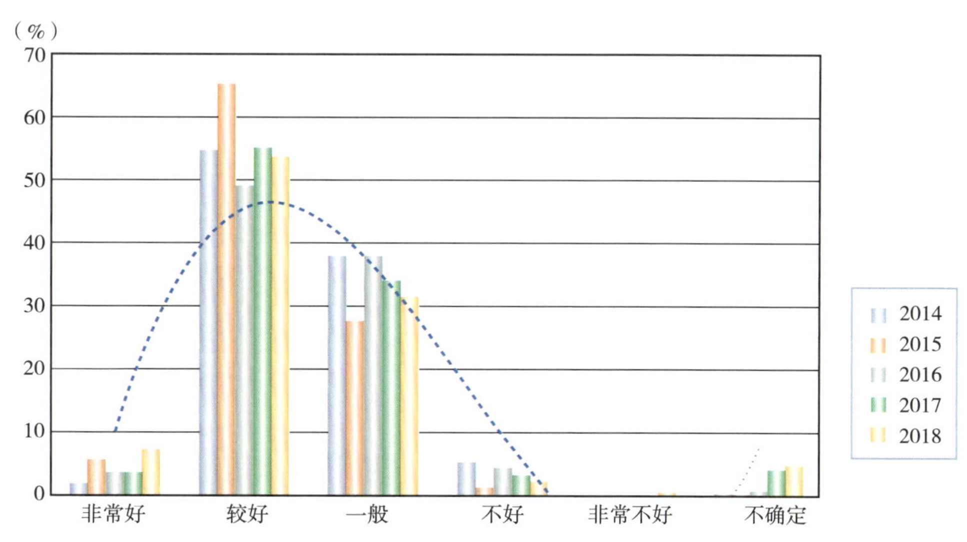

图 4-7 投资机构投资前景预测的分布（2014~2018）

① 有效样本数为 1612 份。

5 中国创业投资经营管理

5.1 中国创业投资项目来源

2017 年，中国创业投资的项目来源仍然以“政府部门推荐”“朋友介绍”和“项目中介机构”三个渠道为主①（见表 5–1、图 5–1）。三者占比较 2016 年占比有所回升，为 51.9%。此外，“股东推荐”“项目业主”“银行介绍”“媒体宣传”等信息来源占比均出现较大幅度下滑。

2015 年，统计调查首次将“众创空间”作为信息渠道之一，2016 年该渠道占比上升为 11.3%，2017 该渠道占比略有下降，为 9.1%。值得一提的是，2017 年首次将“科技金融服务平台”作为信息渠道之一，该渠道占比高达 11%。

采用“自有渠道”和“中介渠道”②划分项目来源，项目来自于自有渠道的三项之和要小于中介渠道获得项目来源。

表 5–1 创业投资机构获取项目信息来源渠道（2009~2017） 单位：%

信息渠道 / 年份	政府部门推荐	朋友介绍	项目中介机构	股东推荐	项目业主	银行介绍	媒体宣传	众创空间（孵化器）	科技金融服务平台	其他
2009	25.9	19.1	16.1	13.4	13.0	6.6	3.0	—	—	2.9
2010	26.2	17.9	18.5	13.2	11.3	7.2	2.9	—	—	2.7
2011	25.4	18.7	18.5	13.3	11.7	7.4	2.8	—	—	2.1
2012	25.2	19.2	18.6	13.2	11.5	6.9	2.2	—	—	3.2
2013	25.5	19.9	19.1	13.2	10.1	6.0	2.6	—	—	3.6
2014	24.9	17.7	17.1	14.3	11.0	7.4	3.9	—	—	3.6
2015	21.3	14.6	15.2	13.9	11.3	7.1	3.5	10.4	—	2.7
2016	20.2	15.4	15.1	14.1	11.5	6.1	3.5	11.3	—	2.7
2017	21.9	14.0	16.0	11.4	9.5	2.5	1.4	9.1	11.0	3.2

① 有效样本数为 1635 份。

② 自有渠道：朋友介绍、股东推荐、项目业主；中介渠道：政府部门推荐、项目中介机构、银行介绍、媒体宣传、众创空间（孵化器）、科技金融服务平台以及其他。

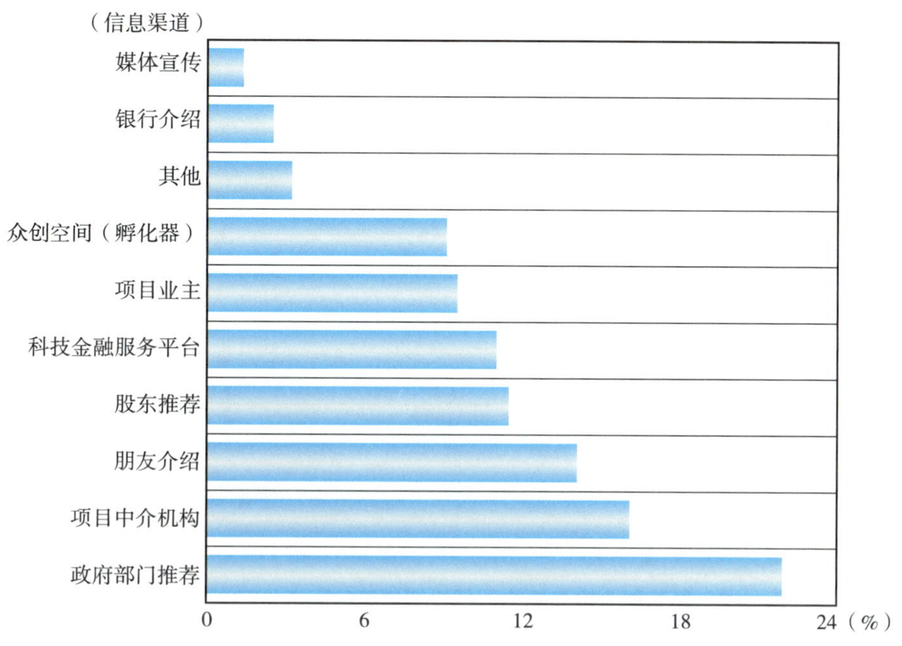

图 5–1 创业投资机构获取项目信息的渠道（2017）

5.2 中国创业投资的决策要素

2017 年调查[①]显示（见表 5–2、图 5–2）。总体来看，“市场前景”“管理团队”和“技术因素”仍然是影响创业投资机构决策的三个主要因素，且三者所占比重均较 2016 年有所上升，其中，“市场前景”上升了 12.2 个百分点，幅度最大。

同 2016 年相比，除上述三个因素比重上升，“财务状况”“盈利模式”“公司治理结构”“股权价格”“竞争对手情况”所占比重都在下降，其中，“投资地点”“中介服务质量”占比降至 1% 以下。

表 5–2 影响创业投资机构进行投资决策的因素（2013~2017） 单位：%

决策因素／年份	市场前景	管理团队	技术因素	财务状况	盈利模式	公司治理结构	股权价格	资信状况	竞争对手情况	投资地点	中介服务质量	其他
2013	24.1	22.5	12.7	9.9	12.1	5.1	4.5	3.2	2.9	2.1	0.6	0.3
2014	24.3	21.4	13.7	8.8	11.7	5.6	4.4	3.7	3.3	2.1	0.7	0.4
2015	20.3	18.2	12.7	11.0	10.8	7.2	5.8	5.1	4.7	2.6	1.1	0.6
2016	18.3	17.2	12.2	11.6	10.3	8.1	6.4	5.7	5.4	3.3	1.1	0.4
2017	30.5	24.7	17.9	9.9	8.3	2.6	2.5	1.3	1.1	0.8	0.2	0.2

① 有效样本数为 1635 份。

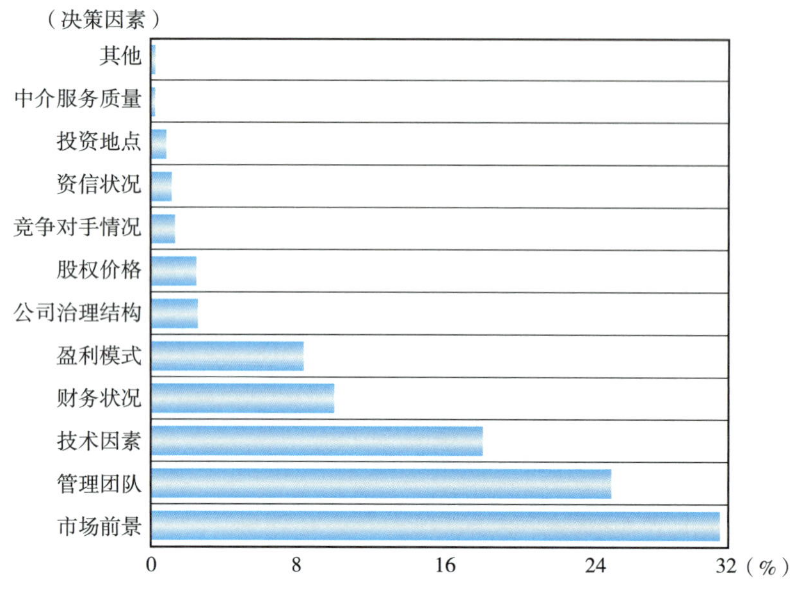

图 5-2 影响创业投资机构进行投资决策的因素（2017）

5.3 中国创业投资对被投资项目的监管方式

调查显示[①]，“董事会席位”“提供管理咨询”仍然是2017 年两个主要的监管方式，累计占比为 72.7%，较 2016 年的 74.3% 略有下降。“只限监管”所占比例达到 17.8%（见图 5-3）。

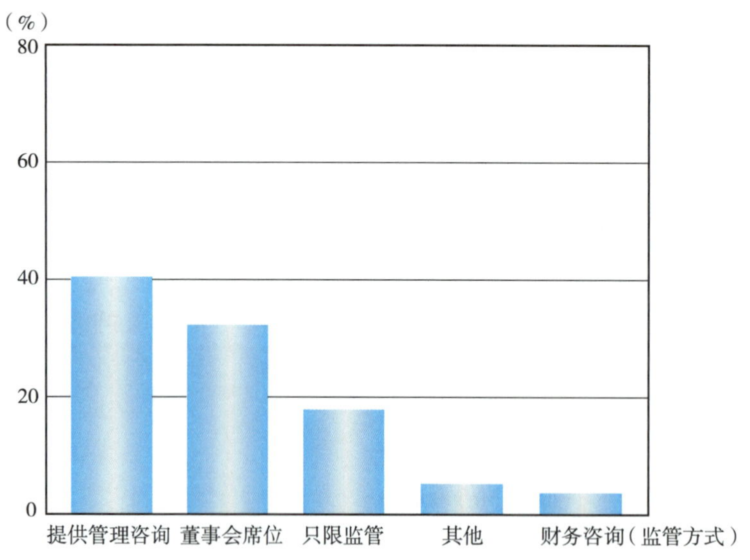

图 5-3 创业投资机构对被投资企业的监管方式（2017）

① 有效样本数为 1633 份。

与2016年相比，2017年创业投资对被投资企业的监管方式变化明显，“提供管理咨询”所占比重为40.4%，较2016年的33.9%上升了6.5个百分点。“董事会席位”监管方式所占比重从2015年的36.5%上升到2016年的40.4%，2017年又下降为32.3%，下降了8.1个百分点。“只限监管”的比重近几年持续上升，从2015年、2016年的12.3%、16%上升到2017年的17.8%。

2017年，创业投资机构依旧以“一般参股”为股权参与方式①，较2016年上升了1.2个百分点，“绝对控股”和“相对控股”的比重有所下降，“绝对控股”所占比重从2016年的3.1%下降到2017年的2.4%，“相对控股”从2016年的7.9%下降到2017年的7.4%（见表5–3、图5–4）。在一定程度上说明我国创业投资机构倾向于成为财务投资人。

表5–3 创业投资机构股权参与程度（2009~2017） 单位：%

年份 \ 股权参与程度	绝对控股	相对控股	一般参股
2009	7.7	16.1	76.3
2010	3.7	12.1	84.2
2011	4.9	8.6	86.5
2012	4.4	11.0	84.6
2013	5.2	10.2	84.6
2014	3.4	12.3	84.3
2015	3.5	7.0	89.5
2016	3.1	7.9	89.0
2017	2.4	7.4	90.2

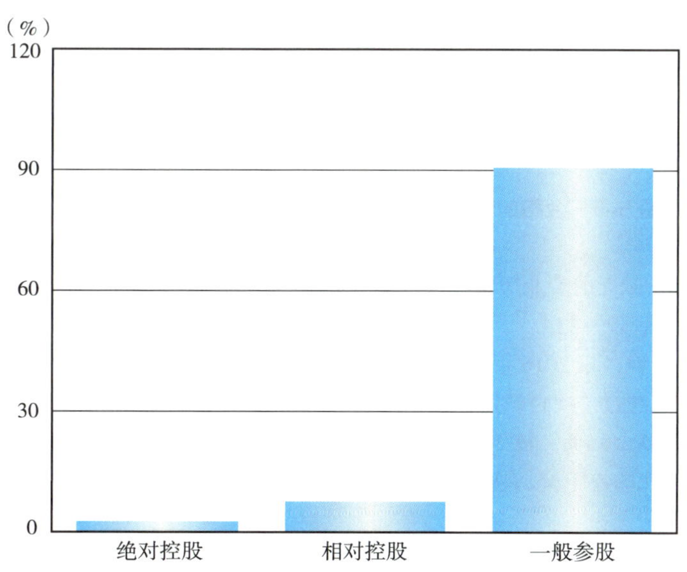

图5–4 创业投资机构的股权参与程度（2017）

① 有效样本数为2187份。

5.4 与创业投资经营管理有关的人力资源因素

对 2016 年从事创业投资人员的基本素质进行调查发现[①]（见图 5-5），“资本运作能力”和“判断力和洞察力”仍是一名合格创业投资人员最应该具备的两个素质。与 2016 年相比，两个因素所占比重都有所上升，“资本运作能力”从 20.9% 上升到至 26.0%，“判断力和洞察力”从 18.7% 上升至 20.0%。

此外，“财务管理能力”和“技术背景”所占比重有所提高，分别从 16.5%、13.9% 升至 17.0%、14.6%，“技术背景”近几年来所占比重持续上升。“商务谈判能力”和“人际关系网络和协调能力”占比分别为 12.3%、9.8%，比 2016 年分别降低了 2.5 个百分点、4.8 个百分点。

综上可知，一名合格的创业投资人应该更加注重自身的技术背景和能力，同时也应该加强资本运作能力和项目判断能力，并且对国家宏观政策高度敏感。

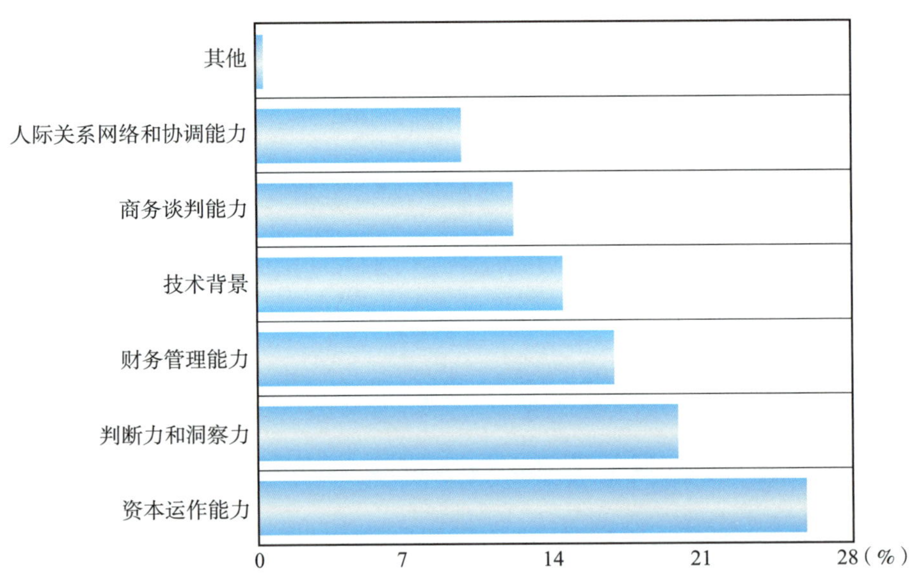

图 5-5 合格的创业风险投资人员应该具备的素质（2017）

2017 年，创业投资人员最为缺乏的专业知识包括“技术评估”“资本运作”和“企业管理”能力[②]。其中，“技术评估”成为最缺乏的专业知识，较 2016 年上升了 2.6 个百分点至 20%，“企业管理”超过“项目识别”成为第三个最缺乏的专业知识，占比为 16.1%，较 2016 年上升 2.6 个百分点。“技术背景”占比略有下降，从 2016 年的 13.0% 下将至 11.7%。“法律知识”“财务管理能力”和“商务谈判能力”的排名与 2016 年相同。但三者所占比重较 2016 年均有所下降，其中“法律知识”所占比重从 2016 年的 11.1% 下降至 9.4%，“财务管理能力”所占比重变化不大，从 2016 年的 7.9% 下降至 7.1%，“商务谈判能力”占比从 2016 年的 5.9% 下降至 4.4%（见图 5-6）。

① 有效样本数为 1629 份。
② 有效样本数为 1622 份。

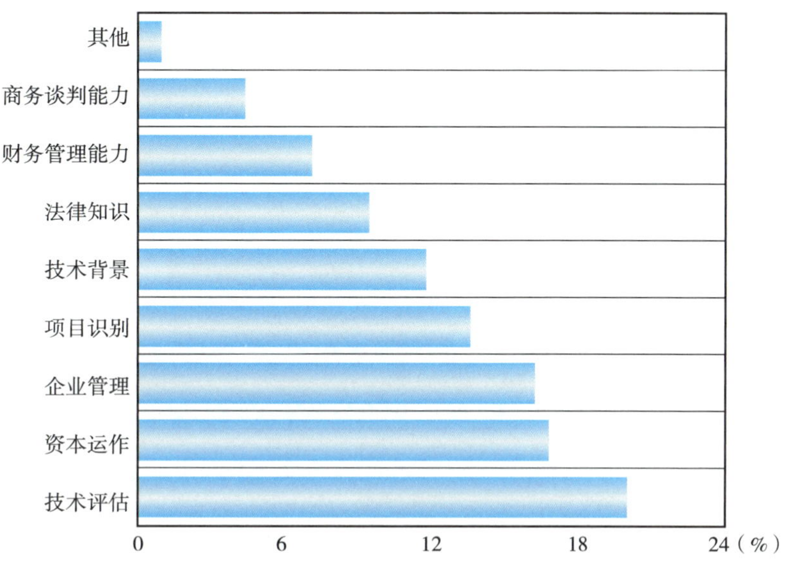

图 5-6 创业风险投资人员缺乏的专业知识（2017）

5.5 投资效果不理想的主要原因

2017 年我国创业投资效果不理想的主要原因依然集中在"退出渠道不畅""政策环境变化""市场竞争""内部管理水平有限""后续融资不力""技术不成熟"以及"缺乏诚信"等方面[①]（见表 5-4、图 5-7）。

与 2016 年相比，"退出渠道不畅""政策环境变化"所占比例有所下降，均不再延续前几年的变化态势，其中"退出渠道不畅"占比从 2016 年的 25.9% 下降至 2017 年的 18.5%，"政策环境变化"占比也从 2016 年的 23.2% 下降至 17.3%，"市场竞争"超过"政策环境变化"，占比 18.3%。这在一定程度上表明，创业投资的政策环境与退出渠道有所改善，但市场竞争不断加剧。

"内部管理水平有限""后续融资不力"和"技术不成熟"分别从 2016 年的 10.4%、9.1%、7.7% 升至 2017 年的 17.1%、11.5%、12.4%。说明投资竞争加剧，对行业内部管理提出了更高的要求。

表 5-4 创业投资机构投资效果不理想的主要原因（2013~2017）

年份 \ 原因	退出渠道不畅	政策环境变化	市场竞争	内部管理水平有限	后续融资不力	技术不成熟	其他	缺乏诚信
2013	26.6	26.7	18.2	8.4	5.7	6.8	4.6	3.1
2014	25.4	23.4	19.4	9.5	8.0	7.1	4.6	2.6
2015	26.2	23.7	17.6	10.3	8.4	6.7	4.7	2.4
2016	25.9	23.2	17.0	10.4	9.1	7.7	4.5	2.2
2017	18.5	17.3	18.3	17.1	11.5	12.4	1.0	3.9

① 有效样本数为 1597 份。

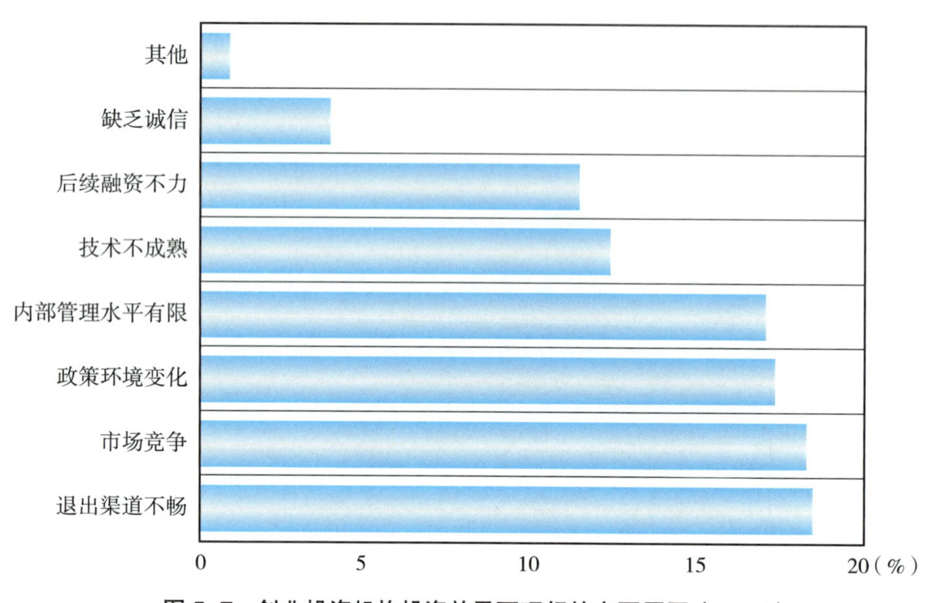

图 5-7　创业投资机构投资效果不理想的主要原因（2017）

针对于“企业退出渠道不畅”的原因，我们调查了企业在选择上市退出时的首选市场①。调查发现，企业在退出时，更愿意选择国内主板市场退出，所占比重接近一半，为 49.4%，其次是国内的创业板，占比为 23.8%，国内中小企业板和新三板分别为 12.9% 和 12.0%，海外证券市场占比最小，为 1.8%。可见，尽管中小板和创业板主要以服务科技型中小企业为主，但优秀的企业更愿意选择主板上市，难度较高（见图 5-8）。

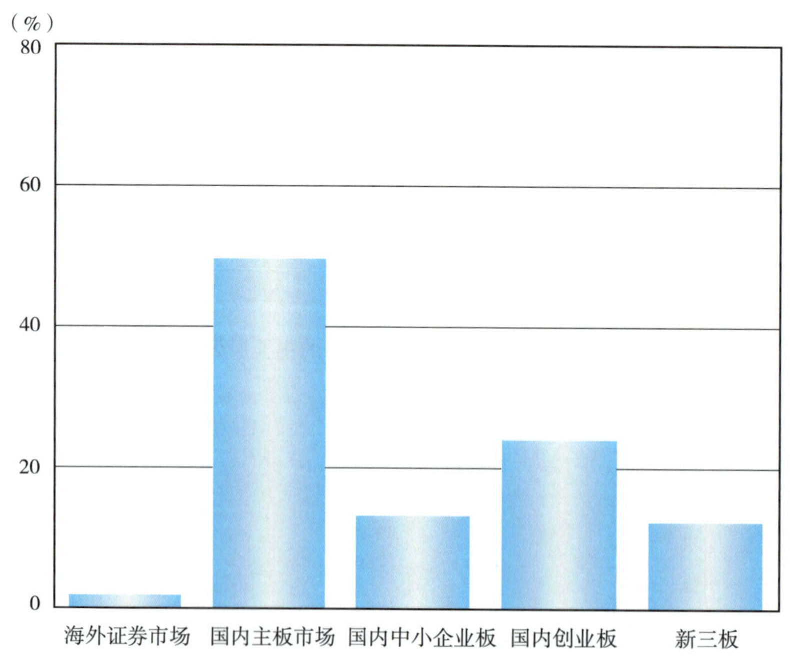

图 5-8　机构在选择上市退出时的首选

① 有效样本数为 1592 份。

5.6 创投机构最看好的投资领域

调查发现①，2018 年机构最看好的前三个投资领域分别为“计算机、通信等电子设备制造业（人工智能行业）”“新能源环保行业”和“医药与生物科技”，占比分别为 23.4%、21.9%、19.8%，总和接近所有投资领域的 2/3。随着科学技术的发展，科技在各个领域的兴起引起了投资者的关注，人工智能领域首次被作为投资者看好的领域之一，占据了 23.4% 的比重，超过其他领域位居第一。“新能源环保行业”和“医药与生物科技”占比分别提高了 8.8 个百分点、10.1 个百分点，2017 年分别达到 21.9% 和 19.8%。“金融科技（互联网金融）”和“科技服务（教育）”占比较 2016 年略有上升，分别为 5.5%、5.4%（见图 5-9）。

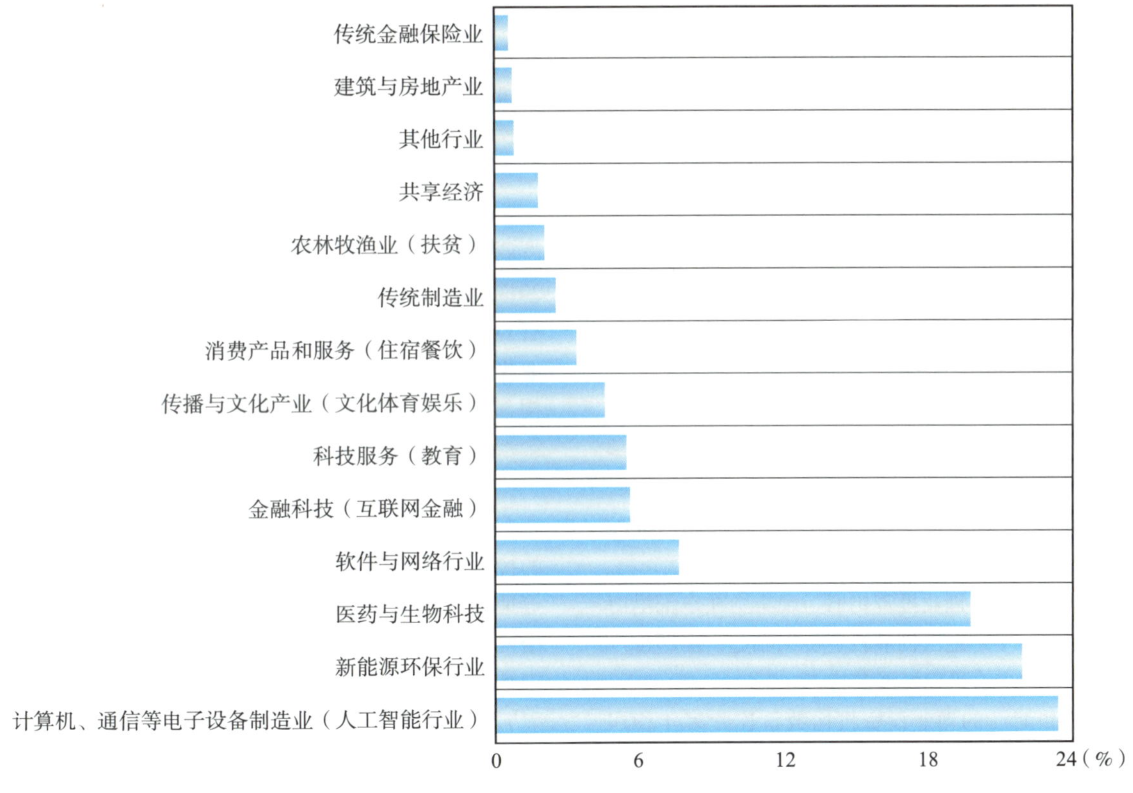

图 5-9 2018 年机构最看好的投资领域

① 有效样本数为 1608 份。

6 中国创业投资区域运行状况

6.1 创业投资机构数量地区分布

根据调查统计，2017 年全国创业投资机构总数达 2296 家，比上一年度增加 251 家，增幅达 12.3%，显示创业投资在国内持续发展。在全部 2296 家机构中，创业投资企业（基金）有 1589 家，比 2016 年增加 168 家，增幅达到 11.8%；创业投资管理机构是 707 家，比 2016 年增加 83 家。

从地域分布看，2017 年全部创业投资机构分布在全国 30 个省、直辖市和自治区，创业投资在全国的分布具有如下特点（见表 6–1、图 6–1）：

（1）创业投资在中国的发展更为广泛。目前除西藏自治区外，其余地区都有创业投资机构，说明国内绝大部分地区都认识到了创业投资对促进技术创新和经济增长、高科技产业发展的重要性，大力推动创业投资在当地的发展。

（2）整体上，中国创业投资仍旧呈现集中在东部沿海和经济发达地区，中部地区创业投资机构崛起，而西部广大地区机构数量较少、平稳发展的特点。

（3）江苏和浙江的创业投资机构数量连续多年稳居国内前两名。江苏省机构数量达 531 家，占全国总数的 24.4%，比 2016 年增加 32 家；浙江省有 423 家，占全国总数的 19.5%，比 2016 年增加 70 家。江苏和浙江的创业投资机构数量远远超过国内其他地区，其次是北京、广东的创业投资机构数量较多。江苏省和浙江省，不但创业投资机构总数保持全国领先，创投基金（公司）和创投管理机构数量也远远超过国内其他地区，江苏省的创投基金（公司）有 435 家，浙江省有 324 家，分别占全国总数的 27.4% 和 20.4%，合计约占全国半数。

（4）山东、安徽、重庆、湖南、湖北、陕西创业投资发展迅速，成为国内创业投资机构数量相对较多的地区。2017 年，山东创业投资机构有 112 家，创投基金（公司）有 86 家，双双位居全国第四名。上海、天津保持国内创业投资机构数量前列的位置，上海有 105 家创业投资机构，排名全国第五，其中创投基金（公司）有 70 家，排名第六。天津有 70 家创业投资机构，排名全国第八。

（5）西部地区和经济欠发达地区的创业投资机构虽然比东部沿海地区少很多，但是一些地区已经呈现快速增长的特点。2017 年，贵州、甘肃、新疆、山西、江西、河南等地区，创业投资机构数量比 2016 年有所提高，尤其是山西、河南、贵州和甘肃。但个别地方，如海南、青海、吉林、内蒙古、广西等，创业投资机构数量都是个位数，发展空间还很大。

（6）东北三省呈现不同状态、辽宁和黑龙江的创业投资机构数量比 2106 年增加较多，辽宁由 28 家增加到 2017 年的 47 家，黑龙江由 22 家增加到 2017 年的 40 家。但吉林省创业投资机构数量则比 2016 年有所减少。

表 6-1 中国各地区创业投资机构数量（2017） 单位：家

地区	创投机构数	创投基金数	创投管理机构数
江苏	531	435	96
浙江	423	324	99
北京	192	75	117
广东	139	95	44
山东	112	86	26
上海	105	70	35
安徽	93	76	17
湖南	79	47	32
天津	70	48	22
重庆	69	28	41
陕西	51	20	31
湖北	51	38	13
辽宁	47	28	19
福建	46	26	20
河北	41	34	7
黑龙江	40	27	13
山西	36	12	24
贵州	34	27	7
四川	32	21	11
新疆	31	19	12
河南	31	19	12
甘肃	12	12	0
云南	7	3	4
江西	5	5	0
吉林	4	4	0
宁夏	4	1	3
海南	4	2	2
广西	3	3	0
青海	3	3	0
内蒙古	1	1	0

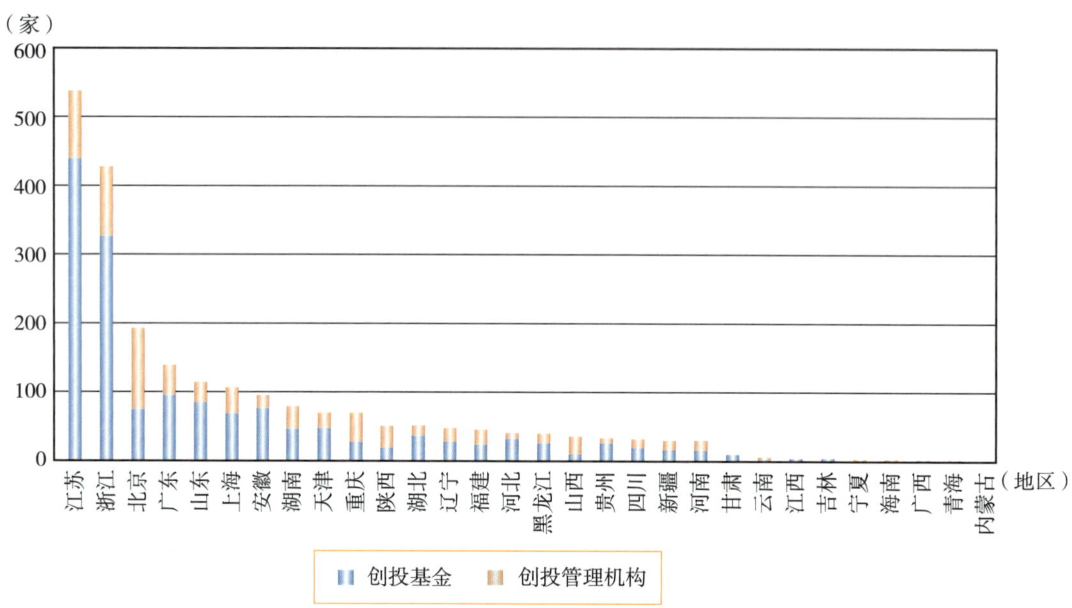

图 6-1 2017 年中国创业投资机构数

6.2 创业投资管理资本的地区分布

表 6-2 和图 6-2 显示了 2017 年我国不同地区创业投资公司的管理资本规模。

2017 年，全国创业投资公司管理资金规模达 8872.5 亿元，比 2016 年增加 595.4 亿元，增幅达 7.2%，继续保持增长势头，充分显示了国内对促进创业投资发展的重视程度。

从地区角度看，全国创业投资机构管理资金具有如下特点：

（1）整体上东西部地区创业投资管理资金规模的差距仍很明显。东部的北京、江苏的创业投资管理资金规模在千亿元以上，而西部的青海和内蒙古创业投资管理资金规模在 10 亿元以下。

（2）北京、江苏、广东和浙江的创业投资管理资本总量仍然位居全国前四名，显示这些地区创业投资资本雄厚；而且位次与 2016 年保持一致，北京创业投资资本总量仍旧位居榜首，规模达 1794.7 亿元，江苏排名第二，资本规模达 1714.51 亿元，广东以 1215.44 亿元位列第三。排名第四的浙江创业投资管理资本总量是 825.6 亿元，与北京、江苏和广东三个地区的差距相对较大。这说明浙江省内创业风险投资机构相对较小，与其机构性质是民营机构居多、有限合伙制企业数量较多有直接关系。不过与 2016 年比较，北京和江苏的创业投资管理资本总量有所减少。

（3）2017 年，安徽、陕西、山东、湖南、福建等地区的创业投资发展迅速，管理资本规模显著增加。表 6-2 显示，2017 年，安徽创业投资管理资本达 562 亿元，排名第五，比 2016 年增加 150 多亿元；重庆市创业投资管理资本达 470.31 亿元，比 2016 年增加 200 多亿元；陕西省比 2016 年增加 150 亿元，湖南增加 100 亿元，山东增加 70 亿元，福建增加 54 亿元。重要的是，安徽等地创业投资管理资本规模与浙江等地的差距在变小。

（4）部分地区创业投资管理资本虽然很少，但在 2017 年呈现增长态势。2016 年创业投资管理资本比较少的山西、江西、吉林、青海等地，2017 年创业投资管理资本都是正增长。

（5）部分地区的创业投资管理资本规模较小。2017 年，吉林、青海、海南和内蒙古创业投资管理资本总量都在 6 亿元以下，进一步发展空间很大。

表 6-2 中国创业投资管理资本地区分布（2017） 单位：亿元

地区	管理资本总额
北京	1794.70
江苏	1714.51
广东	1215.44
浙江	825.60
安徽	562.00
重庆	470.31
上海	365.02
陕西	359.91
湖南	264.15
天津	154.00
山东	151.47
河南	143.82
福建	119.00
黑龙江	106.22
新疆	98.82
湖北	95.10
山西	83.35
河北	67.26
四川	67.17
辽宁	64.91
甘肃	44.43
宁夏	29.80
云南	22.81
江西	16.68
广西	11.90
贵州	11.12
吉林	5.50
青海	4.40
海南	2.08
内蒙古	0.96
合计	8872.5

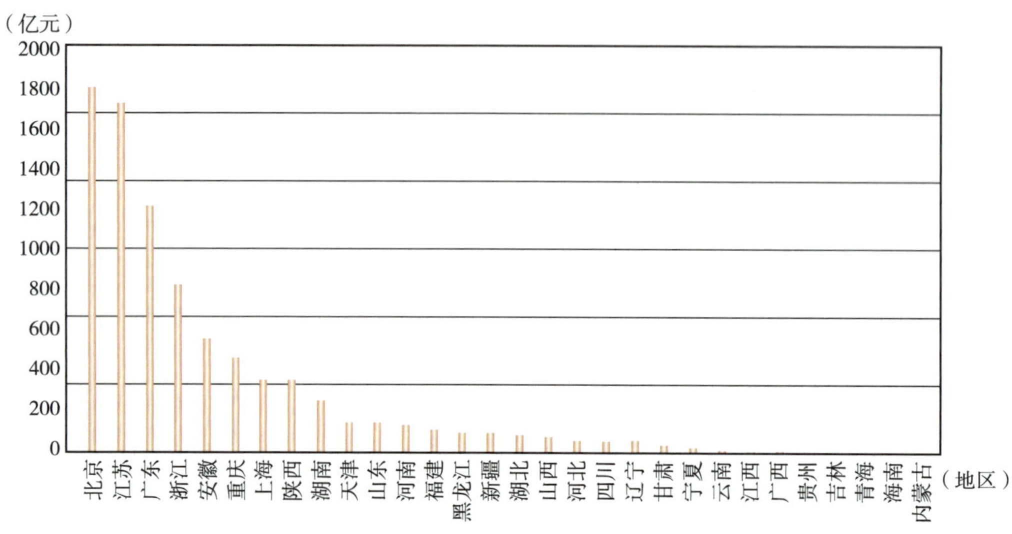

图 6-2 中国创业投资管理资本地区分布（2017）

6.3 各地区创业投资机构的规模分布

表 6-3 和图 6-3 显示了 2017 年我国不同地区创业投资管理资本的规模分布。

表 6-3 各地区创业投资机构的管理资本规模分布（2017）

单位：%

规模 地区	5000 万元以下	5000 万 ~ 1 亿元	1 亿 ~ 2 亿元	2 亿 ~ 5 亿元	5 亿元以上
湖北	8.33	19.44	27.78	36.11	8.33
四川	14.29	28.57	32.14	17.86	7.14
黑龙江	15.00	10.00	42.50	25.00	7.50
新疆	15.79	21.05	21.05	26.32	15.79
云南	16.67	—	16.67	33.33	33.33
北京	18.37	6.12	14.29	22.45	38.78
上海	18.75	7.81	25.00	29.69	18.75
贵州	21.21	36.36	30.30	9.09	3.03
安徽	21.69	9.64	21.69	26.51	20.48
山东	22.22	12.50	41.67	19.44	4.17
重庆	23.64	9.09	14.55	23.64	29.09
福建	25.64	15.38	25.64	20.51	12.82

续表

规模 地区	5000万元以下	5000万～1亿元	1亿～2亿元	2亿～5亿元	5亿元以上
陕西	27.50	5.00	22.50	35.00	10.00
江苏	28.37	17.31	23.32	22.12	8.89
河北	28.57	28.57	14.29	21.43	7.14
湖南	28.57	17.14	18.57	25.71	10.00
辽宁	28.57	21.43	33.33	11.90	4.76
河南	31.03	6.90	17.24	27.59	17.24
广西	33.33	33.33	—	—	33.33
青海	33.33	—	33.33	33.33	—
浙江	33.52	23.01	21.88	15.34	6.25
天津	36.84	15.79	24.56	15.79	7.02
广东	37.04	11.11	12.96	15.74	23.15
吉林	50.00	—	—	50.00	—
山西	56.25	12.50	3.13	21.88	6.25
海南	66.67	—	33.33	—	—
甘肃	—	9.09	9.09	36.36	45.45
内蒙古	—	100.00	—	—	—
宁夏	—	—	50.00	25.00	25.00
江西	—	—	60.00	20.00	20.00

整体上，2017年国内大部分地区创业投资机构管理资金规模分布在5000万元以下、1亿～2亿元和2亿～5亿元档次，而5000万～1亿元和5亿元以上规模的机构占比相对较小。

创业投资不发达的部分地区，其机构管理资金集中在有限几个规模水平上，包括内蒙古、青海、广西、宁夏、江西、海南、吉林等。

资本规模在5000万元以下的创业投资机构管理，有9个地区的占比超过30%，其中以不发达地区为主，分别是河南、广西、青海、吉林、山西、海南；其余3个属于经济发达地区，分别是浙江、天津、广东。浙江省的创业投资机构很多是以有限合伙形式设立的，民营性质机构居多，管理资本规模不大，因此很多机构的管理资本在5000万元以下。

管理资金规模在5亿元以上创业投资机构占比较高的地区有云南、甘肃、广西、重庆和北京，前者是经济相对不发达地区，创业投资机构大部分是由政府出资设立的，政府出资规模较大，后者是经济发达地区，地区内的创业投资机构筹集资金的能力较强（见图6–3）。

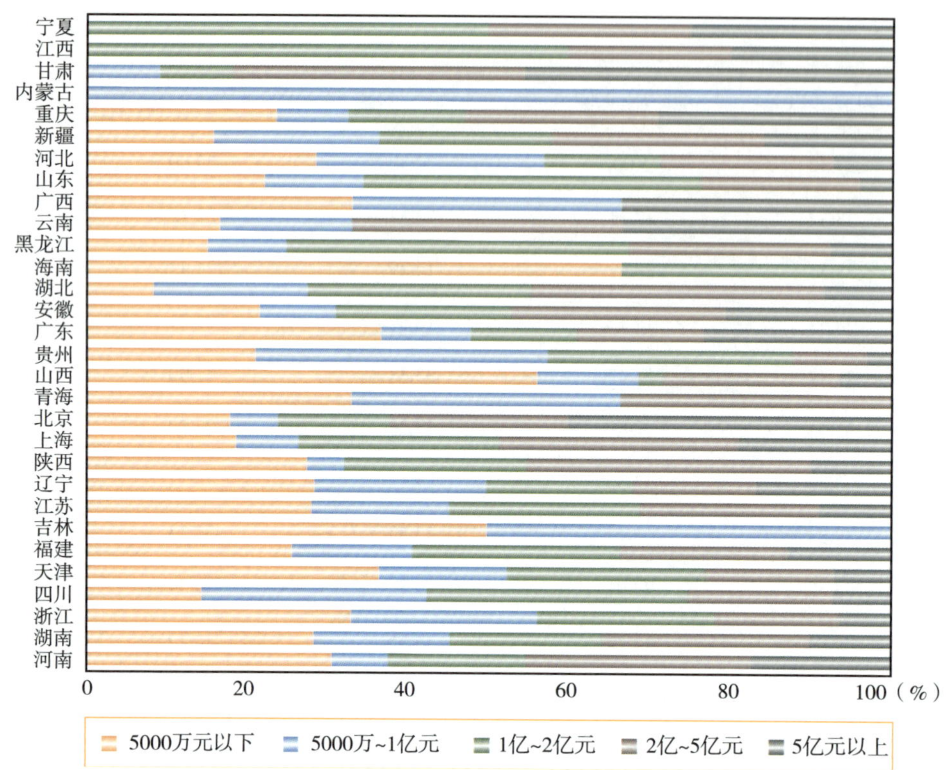

图 6-3 各地区不同规模创业风险投资机构的数量分布

6.4 各地区创业投资机构的资本来源

本部分从两个维度来分析 2017 年国内创业投资机构的资本来源。

6.4.1 政府 / 个人 / 外资

如表 6-4 所示，2017 年全国各地区创业投资机构的资本来源呈现如下典型特征：

（1）政府资金依然是国内创业投资机构的主要资金来源。

以国有独资投资机构、政府引导基金和其他政府财政资金是政府资金支持创业投资发展的三种形式。其中，有 27 个地区设有国有独资创业投资机构，而广西、湖南、贵州、江西、四川的创业投资来源主要是以国有独资形式设立投资机构；有 26 个地区设有政府引导基金，其中主要以政府引导基金方式支持创业投资的地区是宁夏、青海、甘肃、湖北、河南、黑龙江等，占比最高的宁夏达到 80.7%。

（2）民营投资机构成为很多地区创业投资机构的重要资金来源。

2017 年，除了内蒙古之外，其余地区的创业投资机构资金来源，都有民营机构参与，其中，民营投资机构资金来源占比较高的地区有北京、安徽、甘肃、海南、湖北、辽宁、山东、陕西、上海，最高的海南达到 94.2%。

民营投资机构资金来源占比很低的地区有山西、青海、广西、河南、黑龙江、吉林、江西和宁夏等，占比都在 10% 以下，其中最低的广西只有 1.8%。

（3）个人投资持续成为中国创业投资机构的重要资金来源。

在国家相关政策的引导下，个人投资者越来越乐于参与创业投资的发展。2017 年，有 26 个地区的创业投资资本来源于个人投资，其中占比较高的地区有广东、辽宁、山东、上海、四川、云南和浙江，浙江的占比最高，达28.6%。值得注意的是2017年辽宁的个人投资在创业投资的资金来源占据较高地位，达13.5%。

在甘肃、吉林、内蒙古和山西4个地区，个人投资占创业投资资本的比例是0，可能与当地个人持有者对创业投资的认同度不高有关系。

（4）部分地区混合所有制投资机构成为创业投资机构的重要资本来源。

重庆、云南、河南、陕西4个地区的混合所有制投资机构在创业投资的资本中占比较高，其中最高的河南达41.4%。

（5）外资在国内创业投资发展中起着重要作用。

有11个地区的创业投资资本中，有外资参与，其中占比最高的是北京，占比到17.3%；其次是上海，占比达3.4%。这也非常符合北京和上海的国际大都市特点。

表6-4 2017年不同地区创业投资的资本来源（一） 单位：%

地区	个人	国有独资投资机构	混合所有制投资机构	境内外资机构	民营投资机构	其他	其他政府财政资金	政府引导基金	社保基金	境外投资机构
安徽	1.3	8.4	1.6	0.2	27.6	26.7	23.6	10.1	0.4	0.0
北京	3.8	1.8	0.0	17.3	74.5	0.8	0.2	1.5	0.0	0.0
福建	7.5	6.9	9.2	0.0	19.5	41.7	7.5	7.7	0.0	0.0
甘肃	0.0	9.8	0.0	0.0	27.4	10.0	30.2	22.6	0.0	0.0
广东	16.1	7.0	2.0	0.2	20.7	40.7	7.8	5.3	0.0	0.2
广西	0.7	97.6	0.0	0.0	1.8	0.0	0.0	0.0	0.0	0.0
贵州	4.5	63.5	0.4	0.0	11.7	6.6	3.7	9.7	0.0	0.0
海南	0.5	0.0	0.0	0.0	94.2	0.5	4.9	—	0.0	0.0
河北	5.3	15.7	0.2	0.0	16.5	37.6	17.8	6.9	0.0	0.0
河南	2.7	13.5	41.4	0.1	6.4	9.9	2.9	23.1	0.0	0.0
黑龙江	6.1	29.0	1.5	0.0	6.9	13.2	18.9	24.6	0.0	0.0
湖北	9.9	11.0	4.3	0.0	27.9	14.7	4.9	27.3	0.0	0.0
湖南	9.2	50.6	3.1	0.0	8.6	17.1	1.0	10.4	0.0	0.0
吉林	0.0	0.0	0.0	0.0	6.4	0.0	93.6	0.0	0.0	0.0
江苏	9.1	12.0	4.5	0.9	11.6	51.3	4.9	4.7	0.0	1.1
江西	12.0	64.4	0.0	0.0	8.3	3.3	4.2	7.7	0.0	0.0
辽宁	13.5	26.0	0.6	1.0	23.6	4.2	26.9	4.2	0.0	0.0
内蒙古	0.0	0.0	0.0	0.0	0.0	0.0	100.0	0.0	0.0	0.0
宁夏	4.2	5.0	0.0	0.0	6.8	0.0	3.4	80.7	0.0	0.0
青海	7.6	4.3	0.0	0.0	2.9	36.3	0.0	48.8	0.0	0.0
山东	19.4	29.8	2.4	0.0	21.5	9.4	6.1	11.3	0.0	0.0
山西	0.0	11.8	0.0	0.0	2.0	69.3	0.3	16.1	0.0	0.5
陕西	1.2	9.3	27.0	0.0	49.1	9.5	1.9	2.1	0.0	0.0
上海	15.4	22.3	1.5	3.4	20.1	20.5	2.4	14.4	0.0	0.0

续表

地区	个人	国有独资投资机构	混合所有制投资机构	境内外资机构	民营投资机构	其他	其他政府财政资金	政府引导基金	社保基金	境外投资机构
四川	5.9	48.3	0.1	0.0	17.9	19.3	3.2	5.3	0.0	0.0
天津	9.9	16.9	1.9	0.1	22.8	29.8	10.1	7.9	0.0	0.5
新疆	14.0	5.5	1.3	7.2	14.0	16.8	38.3	3.0	0.0	0.0
云南	11.6	19.3	26.8	0.0	30.5	0.0	0.0	11.8	0.0	0.0
浙江	28.6	4.8	4.6	2.1	24.0	29.8	1.3	4.7	0.0	0.0
重庆	4.2	16.2	29.2	0.1	18.2	20.3	1.4	9.8	0.0	0.6

6.4.2 金融机构 / 非金融机构

从金融机构 / 非金融机构角度来看，如表 6-5 所示，2017 年中国创业投资机构的资本来源呈现如下特点：

（1）非金融资本仍旧是中国各地创业投资机构的主要资本来源。

2017 年有 22 个地区的非金融资本占创业投资机构的资本总数比例超过了 50%，其中最高的是江西和青海，占比都是 100%。广西、吉林和内蒙古的创业投资机构的资金来源中完全没有非金融资本。

（2）金融资本开始成为很多地区创业投资机构资本的重要来源。

2017 年有 10 个地区的金融资本在创业投资机构资本总数比例超过了 30%，其中山西、北京、广西、吉林、内蒙古的占比在 80% 左右，显示这些地区金融机构参与创业投资的力度很大。

（3）银行、证券和信托资金成为很多地区创业投资的资本来源。

2017 年有 22 个地区创业投资资本来源于银行，其中占比较高的地区有湖南、黑龙江、上海、四川、陕西、重庆和吉林，占比都在 10% 以上，最高的陕西达到 44.4%。

有 11 个地区创业投资资本来源于信托机构，其中河南和重庆的信托资金占创业投资资本比例较高，河南是 33%，重庆是 12.3%，其他地区的占比都相对很低。

有 14 个地区创业投资资本来源于证券机构，其中重庆的信托资金占创业投资资本比例最高，占比达 22.7%。

保险涉及创业投资的地区很少，只有 4 个地区，分别是北京、广东、江苏和陕西，但占比都很低，最高的广东占比是 3.3%。

表 6-5　2017 年不同地区创业投资的资本来源（二）　　单位：%

地区	非金融资本	其他金融资本	信托公司	银行	证券公司	保险公司
江西	100.0	0.0	0.0	0.0	0.0	0.0
青海	100.0	0.0	0.0	0.0	0.0	0.0
宁夏	99.3	0.7	0.0	0.0	0.0	0.0
甘肃	92.8	0.1	0.0	4.9	2.2	0.0
海南	92.4	2.8	0.0	4.9	0.0	0.0
安徽	89.7	8.3	0.3	1.3	0.4	0.0
新疆	89.6	6.6	1.3	0.0	2.6	0.0
江苏	82.9	13.0	1.0	2.3	0.3	0.4

续表

地区	非金融资本	其他金融资本	信托公司	银行	证券公司	保险公司
天津	82.6	15.2	0.2	2.1	0.0	0.0
浙江	80.8	16.2	0.0	3.0	0.0	0.0
辽宁	78.5	19.4	0.2	0.2	1.7	0.0
湖北	75.7	23.8	0.0	0.0	0.6	0.0
福建	74.6	15.8	0.0	0.5	9.0	0.0
湖南	70.4	14.3	0.0	15.3	0.0	0.0
黑龙江	68.3	20.8	0.0	10.9	0.0	0.0
山东	68.2	31.8	0.0	0.0	0.0	0.0
上海	67.4	22.0	0.0	10.6	0.0	0.0
四川	66.7	19.9	0.2	13.2	0.0	0.0
河北	58.1	30.9	0.0	5.3	5.7	0.0
广东	57.8	35.5	0.3	3.0	0.1	3.3
河南	54.8	9.3	33.0	1.0	1.9	0.0
贵州	50.9	48.8	0.0	0.2	0.0	0.0
云南	49.7	49.6	0.0	0.0	0.7	—
陕西	39.8	9.9	5.4	44.4	0.4	0.3
重庆	29.4	17.3	12.3	18.3	22.7	—
山西	13.8	83.2	0.0	3.0	0.0	0.0
北京	6.8	79.1	0.2	6.7	5.4	1.8
广西	0.0	95.7	0.0	4.3	0.0	0.0
吉林	0.0	87.5	0.0	12.5	0.0	0.0
内蒙古	0.0	100.0	0.0	0.0	0.0	0.0

6.5 各地区创业投资的投资特征

6.5.1 创业投资项目的地区分布

本部分从两个维度来分析 2017 年中国创业投资项目的地区分布。一个是从投资机构的注册地分析当地的创业投资机构的投资活跃状况，另一个是从投资项目所在地分析创业投资最乐于选择投资的地域。

（1）以投资机构注册地划分。

表 6-6 显示了 2017 年不同地区创业投资机构实际开展项目投资的情况。

表 6-6　2017 年已投资项目的中国创业投资机构地区分布　　单位：%

地区	投资项目占比
浙江	22.6
江苏	15.7
广东	10.2
上海	5.3
湖南	4.8
湖北	4.2
北京	4.2
陕西	3.9
重庆	3.8
安徽	3.6
黑龙江	2.9
天津	2.8
辽宁	2.5
福建	2.3
山东	2.1
河南	1.9
四川	1.7
甘肃	1.1
贵州	1.0
河北	1.0
新疆	0.9
云南	0.5
吉林	0.2
江西	0.1
广西	0.1
山西	0.1
宁夏	0.1

根据调查，2017 年全国共有 27 个地区的创业投资机构进行了项目投资，其中占据前三位的地区分别是浙江、江苏和广东。与 2016 年相比较，2016 年排名第二的浙江的创业投资机构所投资项目占比明显提高，由 15.2% 提高为 2017 年的 22.6%，2016 年排名第一的江苏省排名下降一位，占比只有 15.7%。2016 年位居第三位的北京 2017 年排名下降到与湖北并列第六，第三名则由广东替代。上海、湖南等地的创业投资机构也相对比较活跃，投资项目占比位居前列。

与 2016 年类似，2017 年广大的中西部地区，包括新疆、云南、广西、宁夏、青海、山西，创业投资机构的活跃度相对不高，投资项目很少，项目占比都低于 1%。青海和海南的创业投资机构则没有投资项目。另外，吉林和江西的创业投资也不活跃，投资项目很少（见图 6-4）。

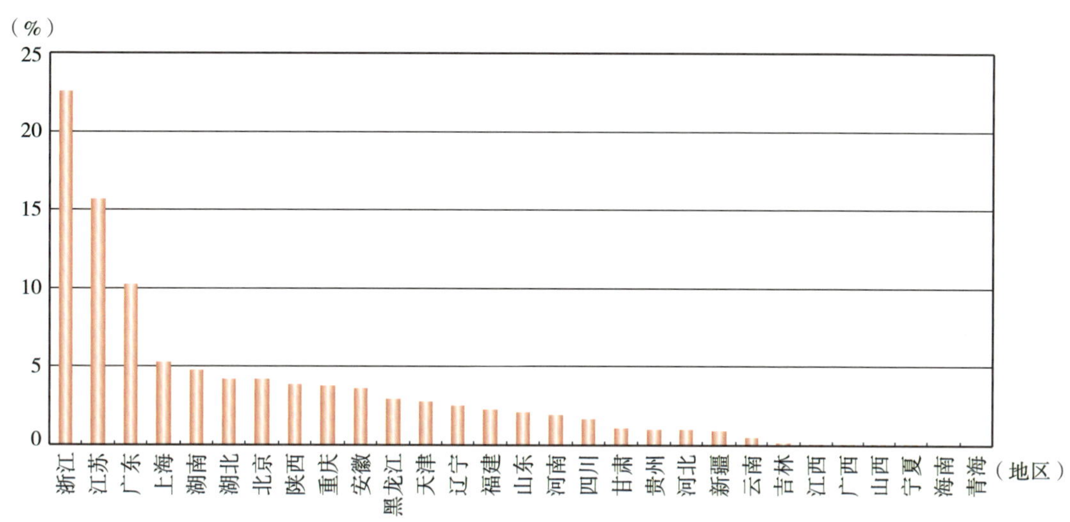

图 6-4 2017 年已开展项目投资的创业风险投资机构的地区分布

（2）以投资项目所在地划分。

表 6-7 显示 2017 年中国创业投资机构投资项目的注册地区分布。

表 6-7 2017 年中国创业投资机构所投资项目的注册地区分布

单位：%

地区	投资项目占比
浙江	15.4
江苏	15.4
北京	10.9
广东	10.7
上海	8.7
湖北	4.6
安徽	3.8
湖南	3.7
黑龙江	2.9
陕西	2.8
四川	2.4
辽宁	2.4
河南	2.3
天津	2.2
福建	2.1

续表

地区	投资项目占比
山东	2.1
重庆	1.5
贵州	1.2
甘肃	1.2
河北	0.9
新疆	0.9
云南	0.5
吉林	0.4
江西	0.2
海南	0.2
山西	0.2
内蒙古	0.2
西藏	0.1
广西	0.1
宁夏	0.1
青海	0.0

2017 年，中国创业投资机构的投资项目分布在全国 30 个地区，投资地域比 2016 年增加 2 个，基本实现了全国各地的全覆盖。与 2016 年类似，投资项目集中在东部经济和科技发达地区，江苏和浙江并列第一，项目占比最多的前五名分别是江苏、浙江、北京、广东、上海，排名与 2016 年一致，合计占全国总数的 61.1%，比 2016 年的汇总略有下降，显示这 5 个地区仍然是最受国内创业投资机构青睐的地区。

相比之下，部分地区的项目占比依旧很少，尤其是西部部分地区和东部部分地区，项目占比低于 0.5% 的地区有山西、内蒙古、西藏、广西、宁夏、青海、吉林、江西和海南，显示这些地区的投资环境有待改善。

6.5.2 各地区创业投资的投资强度

2017 年，全国 29 个地区的创业投资机构所投资项目的投资强度见表 6-8 和图 6-5。

2017 年，中国创业投资机构所投资项目的投资强度地区差距进一步扩大，最高的广西是 25300 万元 / 项，是 2016 年最高的新疆近 2 倍；最低的海南则只有 5 万元 / 项，低于 2016 年最低的吉林的 60 万元 / 项。

部分地区的创业投资机构所投资项目的平均资金非常大，广西、陕西、新疆三地投资强度都在 2 亿元以上，重庆和江西的则在 1 亿元以上，上述地区创业投资机构的投资强度远远高于经济发达地区的北京、上海、江苏、浙江和广东，可能原因是这些地区投资的行业以传统制造业居多，早期阶段的项目数量相对少。

表 6–8　各地区创业投资的投资强度（2017）

单位：万元 / 项

地区	投资强度
广西	25300.00
陕西	21392.95
新疆	20217.14
重庆	13881.92
江西	13000.00
北京	5238.75
甘肃	4934.66
广东	4257.12
河北	3388.91
河南	2696.59
云南	2609.23
安徽	2468.37
贵州	2399.42
湖南	1700.69
上海	1622.90
山西	1540.00
山东	1531.64
天津	1529.07
江苏	1241.24
黑龙江	1208.83
湖北	1114.92
浙江	1010.46
宁夏	1000.00
吉林	975.00
辽宁	828.21
福建	685.20
四川	521.38
青海	225.00
海南	5.00

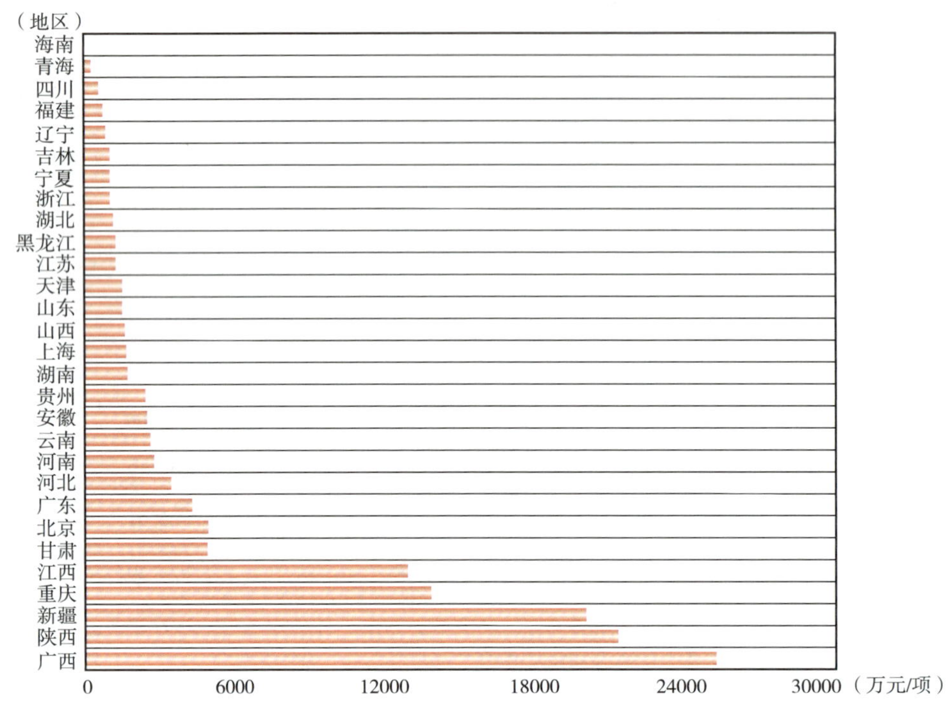

图 6-5 各地区创业投资的投资强度（2017）

6.5.3 各地区创业投资机构的项目持股结构

表 6-9 和图 6-6 表明：2017 年中国大部分地区的创业投资机构不寻求绝对控股，持股比例小于 50%的项目占全部投资总数的比例超过 90% 的地区有 25 个，远远超过 2016 年的 21 个；有 12 个地区的创业投资机构投资持股比例都在 50% 以下，远远高于 2016 年的 6 家。

贵州、新疆和安徽地区的持股比例大于 50% 投资项目较多；与 2016 年比较，2017 年持股比例大于 50% 投资项目占比最高的贵州只有 23.1%，远远低于 2016 年吉林的 100% 和宁夏的 50%。

表 6-9 2017 年中国创业投资机构所投资项目持股结构的地区分布 单位 :%

地区	持股比例≥ 50%	持股比例< 50%
贵州	23.1	76.9
新疆	18.8	81.3
安徽	13.5	86.5
重庆	8.3	91.7
福建	7.0	93.0
江苏	4.9	95.1
河北	4.2	95.8
天津	3.5	96.5
湖南	2.8	97.2
辽宁	2.4	97.6
陕西	2.4	97.6

续表

地区	持股比例≥ 50%	持股比例< 50%
广东	2.3	97.7
山东	2.2	97.8
河南	2.1	97.9
浙江	0.8	99.2
上海	0.8	99.2
广西	0	100
甘肃	0	100
山西	0	100
湖北	0	100
四川	0	100
江西	0	100
云南	0	100
北京	0	100
吉林	0	100
青海	0	100
黑龙江	0	100

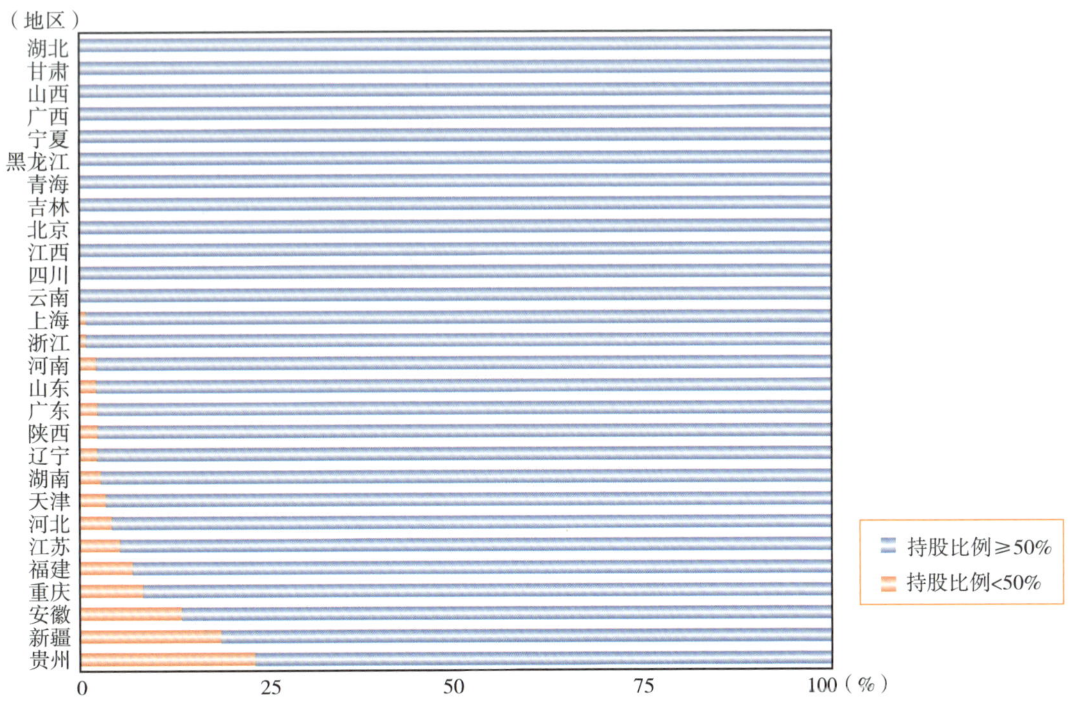

图 6-6　各地区创业风险投资机构的持股结构（2017）

6.5.4 各地区创业投资项目的所处阶段

表 6–10 和图 6–7 显示了 2017 年中国各地创业投资机构所投资项目的所处阶段。

2017 年，中国各地创业投资机构所投资项目所处阶段具有如下几个主要特点：

（1）起步期和成长（扩张）期的项目依旧是 2017 年中国大部分地区创业投资机构的投资重点。2017 年中国创业投资阶段最明显的一个特点是，有 13 个地区的创业投资机构，起步期的项目成为其投资占比最多的项目，与 2016 年的地区数量持平。

成长（扩张）期占投资项目比重最高的地区有 9 个，分别是山东、重庆、安徽、甘肃、江苏、广东、河北、山西、云南，比 2016 年增加 2 个。

（2）越来越多地区的创业投资重视种子期的项目。2017 年，有 19 个地区的种子期的项目占比超过 10%；有 16 个地区种子期的项目占比超过 15%，比 2016 年增加 3 个地区。种子期阶段项目占比最高的是海南，占比达 100%。

（3）2017 年中国创业投资在成熟（过渡）期的项目占比相对较低，除了最高的青海、江西和山东外，其他地区创业投资在成熟（过渡）期的项目占比都在 10% 以下。

（4）2017 年投资于重建期项目的地区很少，只有 6 个地区，分别是山东、湖南、江苏、浙江、云南和上海，其中最高的云南占比是 7.7%。

（5）大部分地区创业投资项目分布在企业成长的多个阶段，但是，个别地区的创业投资，投资项目集中在起步期和成长（扩张）期 2 个阶段，投资于种子期的项目为 0。

表 6–10 2017 年各地区创业投资项目的所处阶段

单位：%

地区	种子期	起步期	成长（扩张）期	成熟（过渡）期	重建期
山东	3.8	32.1	41.5	20.8	1.9
重庆	7.9	30.2	55.6	6.3	0.0
安徽	8.7	34.8	55.4	1.1	0.0
甘肃	11.5	38.5	46.2	3.8	0.0
上海	11.8	41.2	40.3	4.2	2.5
陕西	13.5	44.8	38.5	3.1	0.0
湖南	15.3	43.2	34.2	6.3	0.9
江苏	15.9	35.7	38.4	9.2	0.8
北京	16.0	44.0	36.0	4.0	0.0
福建	17.6	52.9	27.5	2.0	0.0
四川	19.0	61.9	11.9	7.1	0.0
浙江	19.6	41.1	30.8	7.7	0.8
湖北	19.6	51.4	26.2	2.8	0.0
河南	20.4	38.8	32.7	8.2	0.0
广东	21.3	21.8	53.4	3.4	0.0
黑龙江	21.6	59.5	18.9	—	0.0
辽宁	25.5	35.3	35.3	3.9	0.0
新疆	26.1	39.1	30.4	4.3	0.0
河北	30.4	13.0	52.2	4.3	0.0
天津	36.5	50.8	11.1	1.6	0.0

续表

地区	种子期	起步期	成长（扩张）期	成熟（过渡）期	重建期
贵州	42.3	34.6	23.1	0.0	0.0
海南	100.0	0.0	0.0	0.0	0.0
山西	0.0	0.0	100.0	0.0	0.0
吉林	0.0	75.0	25.0	0.0	0.0
江西	0.0	0.0	50.0	50.0	0.0
广西	0.0	50.0	50.0	0.0	0.0
云南	0.0	0.0	92.3	0.0	7.7
青海	0.0	0.0	0.0	100	0.0
宁夏	0.0	50.0	50.0	0.0	0.0

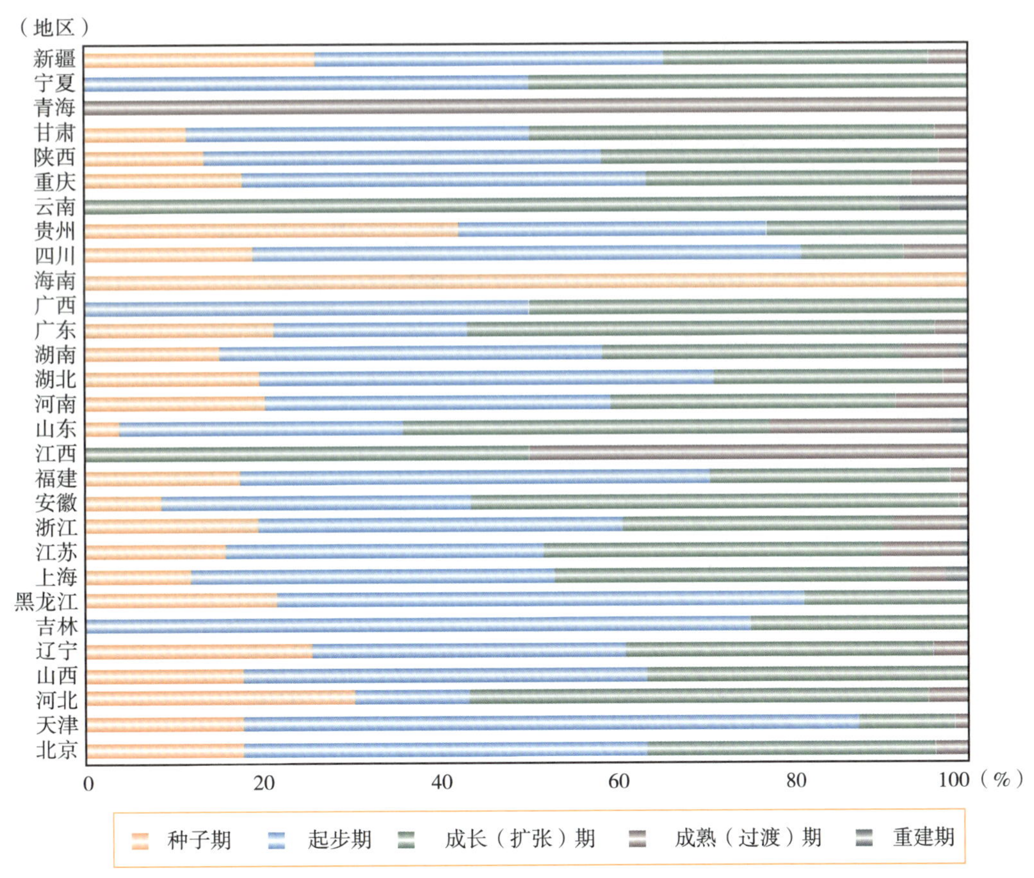

图 6-7　各地区创业投资项目所处阶段（2017）

6.6 部分地区创业投资行业投资特征

根据2017年全国创业投资调查统计，本部分对2017年中国创业投资较为活跃的地区进行重点分析，以掌握和了解这些地区投资项目的行业分布和投资资金（见表6-11~表6-20）。

2017年，北京的创业投资项目分布在18个行业，比2016年减少1个，投资领域更趋向集中；投资比例较多的行业是生物科技、网络产业、科技服务和计算机硬件产业，上述4个行业的投资项目占比超过50%。与2016年比较，生物科技成为北京市创业投资最多的行业，占比达23.2%，代替了2016年最多的网络产业，这与生物医药、人工智能高科技的快速发展相一致。网络产业则由2016年的37.5%，下降到2017年的11.6%。

至于行业投资强度，2017年北京市创业投资的行业投资强度差距加大。投资强度最高的行业是医药保健，达100925万元，远远超过2016年投资强度最高的交通、运输仓储和邮政业6.58亿元，最低的其他IT产业只有120万元，远低于2016年最低的批发和零售业的400万元。18个行业中，有10个行业的投资强度超过1000万元，比2016年减少5个（见表6-11）。

表6-11 2017年北京市创业投资的行业特点

项目数		投资强度	
行业	百分比（%）	行业	行业投资强度（万元）
生物科技	23.2	医药保健	100925.0
网络产业	11.6	传统制造业	9454.7
科技服务	8.7	其他制造业	2302.7
计算机硬件产业	7.2	农林牧副渔	2000.0
IT服务业	5.8	计算机硬件产业	1940.0
医药保健	5.8	通信设备	1600.0
新材料工业	5.8	生物科技	1588.4
其他IT产业	4.3	网络产业	1223.0
其他制造业	4.3	传播与文化娱乐	1206.6
半导体	4.3	新能源、高效节能技术	1000.0
传播与文化娱乐	4.3	新材料工业	961.7
消费产品和服务	2.9	IT服务业	800.0
通信设备	2.9	环保工程	800.0
传统制造业	2.9	科技服务	757.7
环保工程	1.4	半导体	613.3
农林牧副渔	1.4	消费产品和服务	402.5
软件产业	1.4	软件产业	288.9
新能源、高效节能技术	1.4	其他IT产业	120.0

2017年，江苏的创业投资项目分布在28个行业，比2016年增加1个，投资行业分布相对分散。其中，投资较多的行业是软件产业、制造业、网络产业、科技服务、新材料工业，上述行业占比合计44.9%。与2016年比较，江苏创业投资关注度较高的行业没有大的变化，网络产业、新材料工业、软件产业、制造业一直是江苏创业投资较多的行业。科技服务业的项目占比增幅较大，由2016年的2.8%提高到2017年的5.8%；生物科技行业占比下降幅度较大，由2016年的6.1%下降为2017年的4.7%。

至于行业投资强度，2017年江苏创业投资的行业投资强度差距增大，最高的是环保工程，达6210.1万元，高于2016年最高的批发和零售业是3250万元；最低的核应用技术只有30万元，低于2016年最低的建筑业的100万元。投资强度整体比2016年有所提高，投资强度在1000万元以上的有14个，远多于2016年的10个行业（见表6-12）。

表6-12 2017年江苏省创业投资的行业特点

项目数		投资强度	
行业	百分比(%)	行业	行业投资强度(万元)
软件产业	9.9	环保工程	6210.1
其他制造业	9.9	水、电、煤气	3858.0
传统制造业	7.2	社会服务	3546.5
网络产业	6.3	房地产业	3433.3
科技服务	5.8	交通运输、仓储和邮政业	3041.4
新材料工业	5.8	医药保健	2506.7
医药保健	5.5	其他IT产业	2000.0
光电子与光机电一体化	5.2	新能源、高效节能技术	1479.8
金融保险业	4.7	IT服务业	1400.2
生物科技	4.7	传统制造业	1348.3
IT服务业	3.9	科技服务	1302.2
其他行业	3.9	通信设备	1299.7
新能源、高效节能技术	3.3	光电子与光机电一体化	1290.5
消费产品和服务	2.8	软件产业	1142.2
半导体	2.8	网络产业	999.2
农林牧副渔	2.8	新材料工业	953.3
批发和零售业	2.8	其他制造业	911.2
交通运输、仓储和邮政业	2.2	半导体	907.4
环保工程	1.7	金融保险业	892.2
社会服务	1.7	计算机硬件产业	872.0
通信设备	1.7	批发和零售业	824.7
传播与文化娱乐	1.7	农林牧副渔	777.5
计算机硬件产业	1.4	消费产品和服务	765.6
建筑业	1.1	传播与文化娱乐	750.0

续表

项目数		投资强度	
行业	百分比 (%)	行业	行业投资强度 (万元)
房地产业	0.8	建筑业	612.0
其他 IT 产业	0.3	生物科技	399.2
水、电、煤气	0.3	其他行业	384.9
核应用技术	0.3	核应用技术	30.0

2017 年，浙江的创业投资项目分布在 27 个行业，比 2016 年增加 1 个；投资较多的行业是 IT 服务业、科技服务、软件产业、传播与文化娱乐、消费产品和服务、其他行业、网络产业，合计占 56.8%。与 2016 不同的是，IT 服务业代替了网络产业，成为 2017 年投资最多的行业，占比是 10.5%。与 2016 年一样，传播与文化娱乐、IT 服务业、科技服务、软件产业、网络产业也是浙江创业投资比较青睐的行业。

2017 年，浙江创业投资行业投资强度最高的是采掘业，达 6645.7 万元，最低的是社会服务业，只有 559.3 万元。与 2016 年比较，2017 年浙江创业投资的行业投资强度比 2016 年提高较大，最高的采掘业比 2016 年最高的硬件产业多 2774.9 万元，最低的社会服务业也比 2016 年最低的批发和零售业多 447.2 万元。投资强度在 1000 万元以上的行业有 14 个，多于 2016 年的 11 个行业（见表 6–13）。

表 6–13　2017 年浙江省创业投资的行业特点

项目数		投资强度	
行业	百分比 (%)	行业	行业投资强度 (万元)
IT 服务业	10.5	采掘业	6645.7
科技服务	9.6	建筑业	2330.0
软件产业	9.4	新材料工业	2186.1
传播与文化娱乐	7.9	交通运输、仓储和邮政业	1984.0
消费产品和服务	7.2	新能源、高效节能技术	1549.0
其他行业	6.3	网络产业	1490.8
网络产业	5.9	水、电、煤气	1450.0
医药保健	4.2	计算机硬件产业	1330.6
其他制造业	3.7	半导体	1311.8
传统制造业	3.5	金融保险业	1160.2
社会服务	3.5	生物科技	1120.6
生物科技	3.3	软件产业	1096.4
环保工程	3.3	IT 服务业	1034.9
金融保险业	3.1	通信设备	1018.6
新材料工业	2.6	医药保健	927.8
新能源、高效节能技术	2.6	传统制造业	909.0

续表

项目数		投资强度	
行业	百分比 (%)	行业	行业投资强度 (万元)
批发和零售业	2.0	消费产品和服务	831.1
交通运输、仓储和邮政业	1.8	其他行业	787.1
通信设备	1.7	环保工程	784.0
其他 IT 产业	1.5	其他制造业	752.8
计算机硬件产业	1.3	光电子与光机电一体化	741.7
建筑业	1.3	科技服务	678.7
光电子与光机电一体化	1.1	批发和零售业	638.3
半导体	0.7	其他 IT 产业	583.9
农林牧副渔	0.7	农林牧副渔	576.0
水、电、煤气	0.6	传播与文化娱乐	562.7
采掘业	0.6	社会服务	559.3

2017 年，广东的创业投资项目分布在 23 个行业，比 2016 年增加 3 个；投资较多的行业有其他行业、医药保健、其他制造业、消费产品和服务和生物科技，另外软件产业和新材料工业的投资项目也相对较多。与 2016 年比较，其他行业和新材料工业一直是广东创业投资较多的行业，医药保健、其他制造业、消费产品和服务成为创业投资新的投资热点。2016 年投资较多的科技服务占比下降幅度较大，由 2016 年的 16.7% 下降为 2017 年的 3.5%。

至于行业投资强度，与 2016 年比较，2017 年广东创业投资行业投资强度大幅度提高，最高的建筑业竟然达到 100000 万元，排名第二的是生物科技，投资强度达 38316.3 万元，都远远高于 2016 年最高行业传播与文化娱乐行业的 8400 万元；最低的行业是半导体，投资强度达 567.2 万元，也远高于 2016 年最低行业——光电子与光机电一体化的 120 万元。投资强度在 1000 万元以上的行业有 16 个，比 2016 年增加 3 个（见表 6–14）。

表 6–14　2017 年广东省创业投资的行业特点

项目数		投资强度	
行业	百分比 (%)	行业	行业投资强度 (万元)
其他行业	18.5	建筑业	100000.0
医药保健	10.0	生物科技	38316.3
其他制造业	9.0	医药保健	4687.6
消费产品和服务	8.0	其他行业	3367.0
生物科技	6.5	环保工程	3291.4
软件产业	5.5	新能源、高效节能技术	3128.6
新材料工业	5.0	光电子与光机电一体化	3105.6
半导体	4.0	传统制造业	2683.6
计算机硬件产业	3.5	传播与文化娱乐	2145.0

续表

项目数		投资强度	
行业	百分比 (%)	行业	行业投资强度 (万元)
新能源、高效节能技术	3.5	计算机硬件产业	2045.1
金融保险业	3.5	新材料工业	1971.4
科技服务	3.5	网络产业	1746.5
光电子与光机电一体化	3.0	农林牧副渔	1565.0
IT 服务业	3.0	社会服务	1500.0
传播与文化娱乐	3.0	其他制造业	1492.3
网络产业	3.0	消费产品和服务	1179.0
环保工程	2.5	软件产业	809.5
传统制造业	1.5	IT 服务业	717.5
其他 IT 产业	1.5	通信设备	700.0
农林牧副渔	0.5	金融保险业	658.6
通信设备	0.5	其他 IT 产业	616.8
建筑业	0.5	科技服务	572.4
社会服务	0.5	半导体	567.2

2017 年，上海的创业投资项目分布在 23 个行业，整体上投资集中在新兴高科技行业，投资最多的前五名行业有生物科技，新能源、高效节能技术，环保工程，其他行业，医药保健，合计占比是 52.9%，其中最高的是生物科技，占比是 12.2%。

至于行业投资强度，2017 年上海创业投资的行业投资强度与北京、广东等地方明显不同，不同行业之间的投资强度差距不是很大，大部分集中在 1000 万 ~ 4500 万元，23 个行业中，投资强度超过 1000 万元的行业有 17 个，占比是 78.3%。最高的行业是金融保险业，投资强度达 4489 万元，最低的社会服务行业是 125 万元（见表 6–15）。

表 6–15　2017 年上海市创业投资的行业特点

项目数		投资强度	
行业	百分比 (%)	行业	行业投资强度 (万元)
生物科技	12.2	金融保险业	4489.0
新能源、高效节能技术	10.6	批发和零售业	4000.0
其他行业	10.6	消费产品和服务	3285.7
环保工程	10.6	光电子与光机电一体化	3100.0
医药保健	8.9	其他行业	2865.8
其他制造业	5.7	传统制造业	2568.6
消费产品和服务	5.7	网络产业	2125.0
新材料工业	4.1	环保工程	1887.7
IT 服务业	4.1	新能源、高效节能技术	1727.8
半导体	4.1	计算机硬件产业	1560.0

续表

项目数		投资强度	
行业	百分比 (%)	行业	行业投资强度（万元）
其他 IT 产业	3.3	医药保健	1504.4
金融保险业	3.3	半导体	1398.0
软件产业	3.3	IT 服务业	1363.0
传播与文化娱乐	2.4	其他制造业	1255.2
科技服务	2.4	交通运输、仓储和邮政业	1200.0
传统制造业	1.6	新材料工业	1080.0
网络产业	1.6	生物科技	1039.3
计算机硬件产业	1.6	农林牧副渔	980.0
光电子与光机电一体化	0.8	其他 IT 产业	930.0
交通运输、仓储和邮政业	0.8	传播与文化娱乐	811.3
批发和零售业	0.8	科技服务	571.8
农林牧副渔	0.8	软件产业	288.0
社会服务	0.8	社会服务	125.0

2017 年，安徽的创业投资项目分布在 23 个行业，比 2016 年减少 1 个，投资集中在其他行业、制造业、医药保健、科技服务、半导体行业。与 2016 年比较，其他制造业、科技服务是安徽创业机构一直投资较多的行业，医药保健成为 2017 年安徽创业投资青睐的新领域。

至于行业投资强度，2017 年安徽创业投资的行业投资强度差距很大，最高的社会服务高达 30000 万元，排名第二的通信设备也超过 1 亿元，最低的金融保险业则只有 120 万元。与 2016 年比较，2017 年安徽创业投资的行业投资强度远远超过 2016 年，最高的社会服务行业比 2016 年最高的其他 IT 产业多 1 亿元，排名第二的通信设备超出 5000 多万元，第三名的建筑业也比 2016 年的社会服务多 6700 万元。投资强度在 1000 万元以上的有 15 个行业，超过 2016 年 2 个（见表 6–16）。

表 6–16　2017 年安徽省创业投资的行业特点

项目数		投资强度	
行业	百分比 (%)	行业	行业投资强度（万元）
其他行业	22.0	社会服务	30000.0
其他制造业	12.1	通信设备	10320.9
医药保健	9.9	建筑业	9266.7
科技服务	9.9	其他制造业	3887.3
传统制造业	5.5	交通运输、仓储和邮政业	3000.0
半导体	5.5	其他行业	2680.6
新材料工业	4.4	水、电、煤气	2661.1
生物科技	3.3	新能源、高效节能技术	2000.0
建筑业	3.3	IT 服务业	1635.0

续表

项目数		投资强度	
行业	百分比(%)	行业	行业投资强度(万元)
光电子与光机电一体化	3.3	传统制造业	1618.0
计算机硬件产业	2.2	医药保健	1572.2
IT 服务业	2.2	新材料工业	1224.8
新能源、高效节能技术	2.2	光电子与光机电一体化	1100.0
传播与文化娱乐	2.2	环保工程	1050.0
环保工程	2.2	软件产业	1040.0
水、电、煤气	2.2	半导体	860.0
交通运输、仓储和邮政业	1.1	生物科技	753.0
金融保险业	1.1	计算机硬件产业	600.0
农林牧副渔	1.1	消费产品和服务	500.0
社会服务	1.1	科技服务	405.6
通信设备	1.1	农林牧副渔	396.0
消费产品和服务	1.1	传播与文化娱乐	299.9
软件产业	1.1	金融保险业	120.0

2017 年，湖北的创业投资项目分布于 20 个行业，比 2016 年减少 3 个行业，投资较多的行业是其他制造业、医药保健、软件产业、其他行业、传播与文化娱乐。与 2016 年比较，医药保健、传播与文化娱乐及其他制造业一直是湖北创业投资机构青睐的行业，软件产业受到投资机构的追捧，投资项目占比由 2016 年的 6.3% 提高到 10.6%；2016 年投资最多的新材料工业下降幅度很大，由 2016 年的 11.5%下降为 2017 年的 1.9%。

整体上看，2017 年湖北创业投资的行业投资强度呈现明显分化特征，9 个行业的投资强度在 1000 万元以上，11 个行业的投资强度在 1000 万元以下，金融保险业、计算机硬件产业平均投资只有 100 多万元。与 2016 年比较，2017 年湖北创业投资的行业投资强度有所下降，2017 最高的传统制造业是 2628.4 万元，低于 2016 年最高的新能源、高效节能技术的 3941.3 万元，2017 年最低的行业是计算机硬件产业，只有 141.6 万元，也低于 2016 年最低行业光电子与光机电一体化的 200 万元；投资强度在 1000 万元以上只有 9 个行业，也远远低于 2016 年的 16 个行业（见表 6–17）。

表 6–17 2017 年湖北省创业投资的行业特点

项目数		投资强度	
行业	百分比(%)	行业	行业投资强度(万元)
其他制造业	13.5	传统制造业	2628.4
医药保健	11.5	农林牧副渔	2000.0
软件产业	10.6	社会服务	1996.0
其他行业	9.6	新能源、高效节能技术	1851.3

续表

项目数		投资强度	
行业	百分比(%)	行业	行业投资强度(万元)
传播与文化娱乐	7.7	软件产业	1550.9
消费产品和服务	6.7	传播与文化娱乐	1115.9
IT 服务业	6.7	IT 服务业	1070.9
通信设备	4.8	医药保健	1037.4
科技服务	3.8	科技服务	1009.5
新能源、高效节能技术	3.8	消费产品和服务	996.9
传统制造业	3.8	其他行业	969.9
网络产业	2.9	其他制造业	819.0
环保工程	2.9	交通运输、仓储和邮政业	650.0
农林牧副渔	1.9	网络产业	627.3
交通运输、仓储和邮政业	1.9	通信设备	599.2
生物科技	1.9	新材料工业	550.0
金融保险业	1.9	环保工程	466.4
新材料工业	1.9	生物科技	325.0
社会服务	1.0	金融保险业	150.0
计算机硬件产业	1.0	计算机硬件产业	141.6

2017 年，湖南的创业投资项目分布在 22 个行业，比 2016 年增加 3 个行业，投资领域更加广泛；投资项目较多的行业是新材料工业、金融保险业、其他行业、传统制造业、其他制造业、软件产业、计算机硬件产业，投资最多的新材料工业占比高达 10.3%。与 2016 年比较，其他制造业、金融保险业一直是湖南创业投资机构青睐的行业。新材料工业、软件产业、计算机硬件产业、传统制造业成为 2017 年湖南创业投资机构最关注的行业，其中新材料工业占比增幅最多，由 2016 年的 4.6% 上升至 2017 年的 10.3%。而 2016 年投资最多的网络产业，则下降为 4.3%。

2017 年，湖南创业投资的行业投资强度比 2016 年明显提高。金融保险业仍旧是湖南创业投资强度最高的行业，高达 6226.5 万元，比 2016 年增加 2000 多万元，排名第二的 IT 服务业是 5483.2 万元，远远超过 2016 年 IT 服务业的 641.8 万元，最低的计算机硬件产业是 164.1 万元，也高于 2016 年最低科技服务的 70 万元。投资强度在 1000 万元以上的行业有 14 个，远远多于 2016 年的 7 个行业（见表 6–18）。

表 6–18　2017 年湖南省创业投资的行业特点

项目数		投资强度	
行业	百分比(%)	行业	行业投资强度(万元)
新材料工业	10.3	金融保险业	6226.5
金融保险业	8.6	IT 服务业	5483.2
其他行业	8.6	传统制造业	3611.5
传统制造业	7.8	新能源、高效节能技术	2210.0

续表

项目数		投资强度	
行业	百分比 (%)	行业	行业投资强度（万元）
其他制造业	6.9	建筑业	1552.0
软件产业	6.9	新材料工业	1533.7
计算机硬件产业	6.0	批发和零售业	1428.0
生物科技	5.2	采掘业	1292.0
医药保健	5.2	医药保健	1233.3
传播与文化娱乐	5.2	其他 IT 产业	1192.8
网络产业	4.3	其他行业	1168.1
农林牧副渔	4.3	环保工程	1165.9
环保工程	3.4	农林牧副渔	1112.6
其他 IT 产业	3.4	其他制造业	1004.8
新能源、高效节能技术	2.6	软件产业	855.3
IT 服务业	2.6	传播与文化娱乐	836.2
建筑业	2.6	交通运输、仓储和邮政业	800.0
科技服务	1.7	生物科技	617.0
消费产品和服务	1.7	科技服务	370.0
交通运输、仓储和邮政业	0.9	网络产业	320.0
采掘业	0.9	消费产品和服务	170.0
批发和零售业	0.9	计算机硬件产业	164.1

2017 年，重庆的创业投资分布在 16 个行业，比 2016 年减少 7 个行业，投资领域相对集中；投资较多的行业是其他制造业、建筑业、消费产品和服务、其他行业、医药保健，合计占比达 67.6%。与 2016 年比较，医药保健、消费产品和服务一直是重庆创业投资机构青睐的行业，而建筑业成为重庆创业投资的新热门行业；2016 年投资热点的新材料工业，在 2017 年却没有涉及。

至于投资强度，2017 年重庆创业投资强度差距进一步加大，投资最高的是社会服务，高达 100000 万元，最低的批发和零售业只有 400 万元；而 2016 年最高的行业是建筑业，只有 18963 万元。整体上，2017 年重庆创业投资的行业投资强度呈现大幅度的提高，有 6 个行业的投资强度都在 1 亿元以上，远远超过 2016 年的 2 个行业，有 12 个行业的投资强度超过 1000 万元（见表 6–19）。

表 6–19　2017 年重庆市创业投资项目的行业特点

项目数		投资强度	
行业	百分比 (%)	行业	行业投资强度（万元）
其他制造业	16.2	社会服务	100000.0
建筑业	14.7	建筑业	60800.0
消费产品和服务	13.2	农林牧副渔	42833.3

续表

项目数		投资强度	
行业	百分比 (%)	行业	行业投资强度（万元）
其他行业	13.2	金融保险业	30961.8
医药保健	10.3	其他行业	12677.8
金融保险业	7.4	消费产品和服务	12072.2
传播与文化娱乐	4.4	传播与文化娱乐	7276.2
农林牧副渔	4.4	交通运输、仓储和邮政业	5300.0
交通运输、仓储和邮政业	2.9	医药保健	3544.3
新能源、高效节能技术	2.9	新能源、高效节能技术	3250.0
传统制造业	2.9	其他制造业	2213.6
通信设备	1.5	软件产业	1000.0
社会服务	1.5	传统制造业	898.8
软件产业	1.5	通信设备	888.6
其他 IT 产业	1.5	其他 IT 产业	500.0
批发和零售业	1.5	批发和零售业	400.0

2017 年，陕西省创业投资项目分布在 20 个行业，明显集中在半导体，其他行业，新材料工业，新能源、高效节能技术，生物科技，半导体领域投资最多，占比达 26.3%，呈现较高的行业集中度。

至于投资强度，2017 年陕西省创业投资行业的投资强度呈现两极分化，最高的是采掘业，达 375687.5 万元，社会服务行业的投资强度也非常高，达 15500 万元，显示陕西省创业投资在传统行业的投资力度很大；最低的是网络产业，只有 120 万元（见表 6–20）。

表 6–20　2017 年陕西省创业投资项目的行业特点

项目数		投资强度	
行业	百分比 (%)	行业	行业投资强度（万元）
半导体	26.3	采掘业	375687.5
其他行业	15.8	社会服务	15500.0
新材料工业	11.6	其他行业	3856.7
新能源、高效节能技术	6.3	光电子与光机电一体化	2250.0
生物科技	6.3	其他制造业	2194.7
通信设备	4.2	软件产业	2075.0
网络产业	4.2	医药保健	2000.0
采掘业	4.2	新能源、高效节能技术	1605.8
其他制造业	3.2	新材料工业	1520.0
软件产业	2.1	消费产品和服务	1200.0

续表

项目数		投资强度	
行业	百分比 (%)	行业	行业投资强度 (万元)
传统制造业	2.1	计算机硬件产业	1029.5
光电子与光机电一体化	2.1	环保工程	1000.0
计算机硬件产业	2.1	半导体	811.4
社会服务	2.1	农林牧副渔	800.0
环保工程	2.1	通信设备	793.0
农林牧副渔	1.1	生物科技	598.8
消费产品和服务	1.1	科技服务	300.0
IT 服务业	1.1	传统制造业	275.0
科技服务	1.1	IT 服务业	250.0
医药保健	1.1	网络产业	120.0

6.7 各经济区域创业投资活动情况

本部分从经济区域角度来比较、分析 2017 年我国创业投资的运行状况，尤其在当前中国经济发展进入新常态的情况下，通过比较经济发达、有特色的地区与经济相对不发达、创投活动不活跃地区之间的差异，一定程度上揭示创业投资对促进地区经济发展的重要作用，为我国创业投资今后的发展起到指南针作用。

本部分的区域划分，是根据经济发展的联系紧密程度以及发展特色，并参照国家现有的经济区域划分，本着研究的连续性来划分的。当前我国最为关注的几个经济区域增长带是珠三角地区、长三角地区，以及围绕北京、天津这样的大型城市、具有知识高密度的京津冀等地区，同时还有正在重新振兴的东北三省老工业基地。故本部分按照之前的划分分为以下几个区域：

（1）京津冀地区（包括北京、天津、河北）。

（2）长三角地区（包括浙江、上海、江苏）。

（3）珠三角地区：广东（深圳）。

（4）东北三省地区（包括辽宁、吉林、黑龙江）。

（5）其他地区（福建省放在这个部分统计）。

6.7.1 我国创业投资机构项目的区域分布

表 6–21 显示了 2017 年中国不同区域创业投资机构所投资项目的占比。与 2016 年一样，长三角地区仍然是国内创业投资最活跃的区域，投资项目占比是 39.5%，比 2016 年增加 0.4 个百分点。京津冀、珠三角地区和东北三省地区创业投资机构所投资项目数量占比都比 2016 年有所增加，京津冀的占比增加 1.3 个百分点，而珠三角地区占比幅度较大，比 2016 年增加 4.9 个百分点，东北三省的占比则增加 1.4 个百分点。相比之下，其他地区创业投资机构所投资项目数量占比却减少了 7.9 个百分点。

表 6–21 2017 年中国创业投资项目的区域分布

单位：%

区域	长三角	京津冀	珠三角	东北三省	其他地区
项目占比	39.5	14.1	10.7	5.8	30.0

6.7.2 我国不同区域创业投资的投资强度

表 6–22 和图 6–8 显示：除了其他地区外，2017 年珠三角地区创业投资的投资强度最高，达 4257.1 万元，比 2016 年增加 2300 多万元。京津冀地区创业投资的投资强度是 3702.8 万元，比 2016 年呈现大幅度下降，平均减少 4590 万元。长三角地区和东北三省创业投资的投资强度相比 2016 年都有一定程度的增加。其他地区创业投资的投资强度，也比 2016 年呈现大幅度的上涨，平均增加 4000 多万元。因此，2017 年，除了京津冀地区之外，其余区域创业投资的投资强度都呈现增加的态势。

表 6–22　2017 年中国创业投资强度的区域分布　单位：万元 / 项

区域	珠三角	京津冀	长三角	东北三省	其他地区
投资强度	4257.1	3702.8	1167.8	1032.1	6167.0

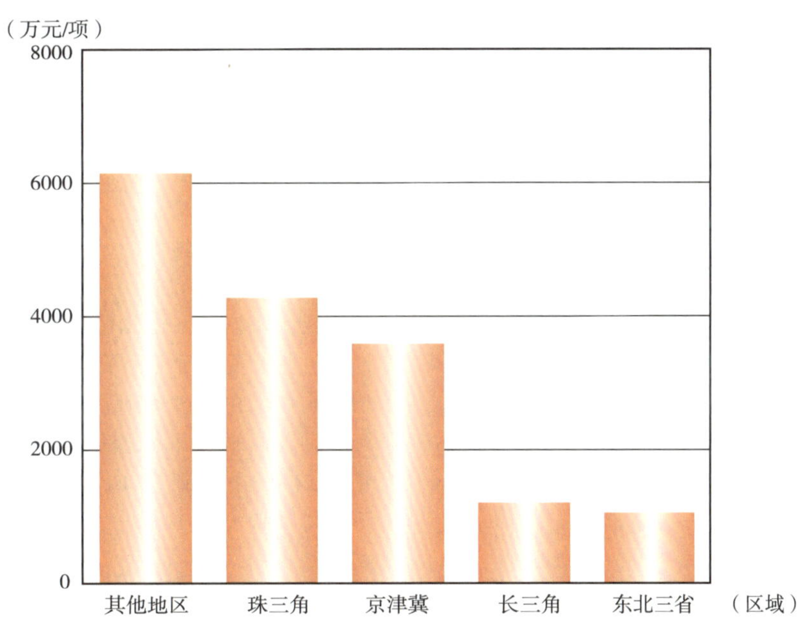

图 6–8　2017 年中国创业投资强度的区域分布

6.7.3 不同区域创业投资的持股结构

表 6–23 与图 6–9 显示：整体上各个区域的创业投资追求绝对控股的比例在减少，除了长三角地区与 2016 年持平之外，2017 年其余区域的创业投资持股比例≥ 50% 的项目占比都在减少，其中以东北三省和京津冀地区尤为明显，东北三省持股比例≥ 50% 的项目占比由 2016 年的 7.5% 下降到 2017 年的 0.9%。京津冀由 2016 年的 3.1% 下降为 2017 年的 1.9%。

表 6–23　2017 年各经济区域创业投资的持股结构　单位：%

区域	东北三省	京津冀	长三角	珠三角	其他地区
持股比例≥ 50%	0.9	1.9	2.1	2.3	5.2
持股比例< 50%	99.1	98.1	97.9	97.7	94.8

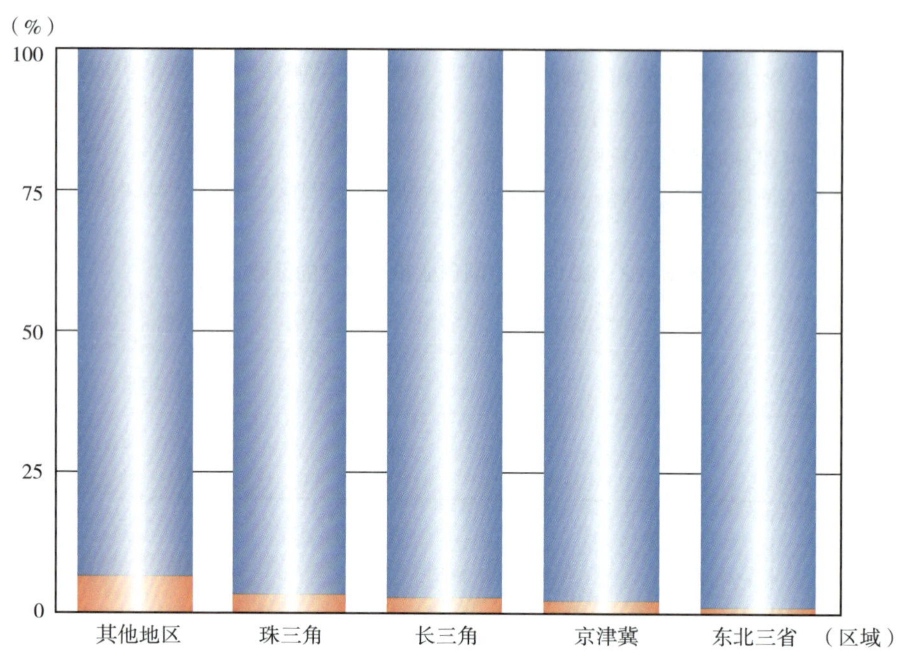

图 6-9 2017 年各经济区域创业投资的持股结构

6.7.4 不同经济区域创业投资项目所处阶段

表 6-24 和图 6-10 显示了 2017 年京津冀、东北三省和珠三角三个地区创业投资更加关注种子期的项目。京津冀地区处在种子期的项目占比最高，超过 1/4，种子期和起步期的项目占比合计达 68.3%，显示该地区创业投资很重视早期阶段的企业培育。东北三省创业投资在种子期项目占比排名第二，比 2016 年提高近 5 个百分点；珠三角地区创业投资更重视种子期的项目，投资占比比 2016 年增加 6.4 个百分点。相反，长三角地区和其他地区创业投资在种子期的项目占比都有所下降，长三角地区由 2016 年的 21.7% 下降到 17.2%，其他地区由 2016 年的 18.3% 下降到 2017 年的 14.9%。

表 6-24 2017 年各经济区域创业投资项目所处阶段

单位：%

所处阶段 / 区域	种子期	起步期	成长（扩张）期	成熟（过渡）期	重建期
京津冀	26.1	42.2	28.6	3.1	0.0
东北三省	22.5	50.4	25.6	1.6	0.0
珠三角	21.3	21.8	53.4	3.4	0.0
长三角	17.2	39.1	34.8	7.9	1.0
其他地区	14.9	41.4	37.9	5.4	0.4

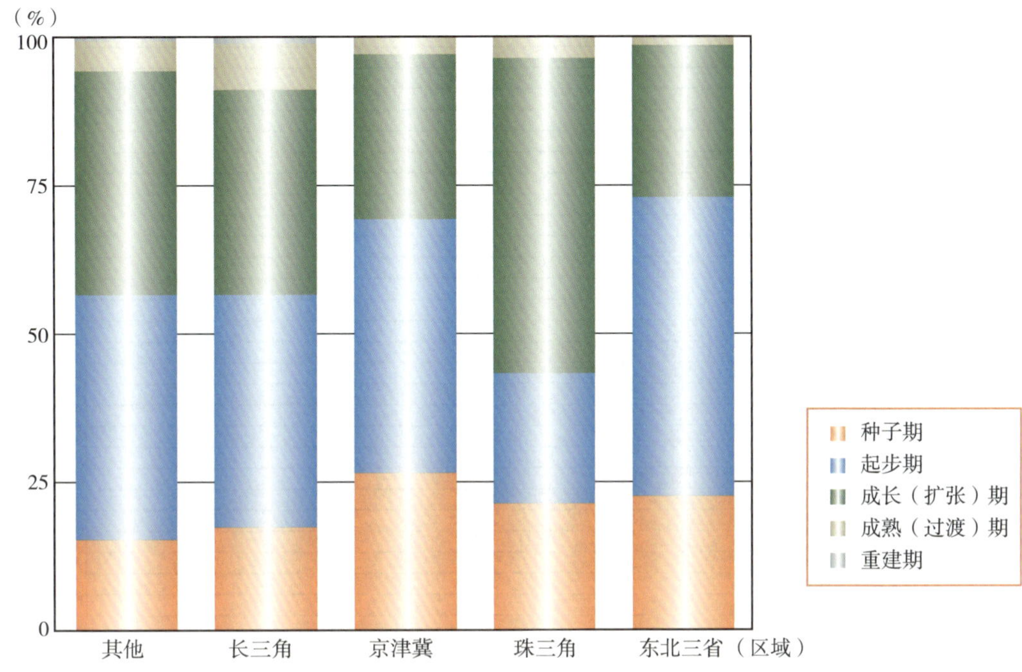

图 6-10 2017 年各经济区域创业投资项目所处阶段

6.7.5 各经济区域创业投资项目的行业分布

图 6-11 至 图 6-15 分别显示了 2017 年我国不同经济区域创业投资的行业分布。

图 6-11 表明：2017 年长三角地区创业投资分布在 29 个行业，比 2016 年多 1 个。长三角地区的创业投资所投资的行业相对分散，投资最多的是软件产业，占比是 8.8%，其次是 IT 服务业、科技服务。与 2016 年比较，前几年一直高居投资榜首的网络产业则被软件产业代替，而 IT 服务业一直则是长三角地区创业投资比较青睐的行业。

图 6-12 显示：2017 年京津冀地区创业投资分布在 23 个行业，与 2016 年持平，投资项目较多的是生物科技、医药保健、其他制造业、传统制造业、科技服务和网络产业。与 2016 年不同的是，生物科技成为 2017 年京津冀地区创业投资最关注的行业，投资占比最高达 14.9%，明显高于排名第二位的医药保健行业。2016 年投资最多的网络产业，2017 年的项目占比明显减少，由 2016 年的近 1/3，下降到 2017 年的 5.8%。

图 6-13 显示：2017 年珠三角地区创业投资分布在 23 个行业，比 2016 年增加 3 个，投资领域有所扩展，投资较多的行业是其他行业、医药保健、其他制造业、消费产品和服务、生物科技和软件产业。与 2016 年比较，2016 年投资较多的科技服务和新材料工业，项目占比下降明显，科技服务由 16.7% 下降为 2017 年的 3.5%，新材料工业由 8.9% 下降为 5%。医药保健、其他制造业、消费产品和服务成为 2017 年珠三角地区创业投资的关注重点。

图 6-14 显示：2017 年东北三省创业投资分布在 20 个行业，与 2016 年持平，投资最多的是传播与文化娱乐、软件产业、其他行业，传统制造业和新材料工业的项目也相对较多。2017 年，东北三省的创业投资相对集中，传播与文化娱乐、软件产业、其他行业分别占比是 15.7%，明显高于 2016 年投资占比最高的软件产业的 11.4%。与 2016 年比较，东北三省的创业投资重点基本没变，传播与文化娱乐和软件产业一直都是东北三省的创业投资高度关注的行业。

图 6-15 显示：2017 年其他地区创业投资分布在 27 个行业，比 2016 年减少 1 个。2017 年其他地区的创业投资的行业变化是：2016 年创业投资靠前的网络产业和软件产业，被制造业和医药保健代替。

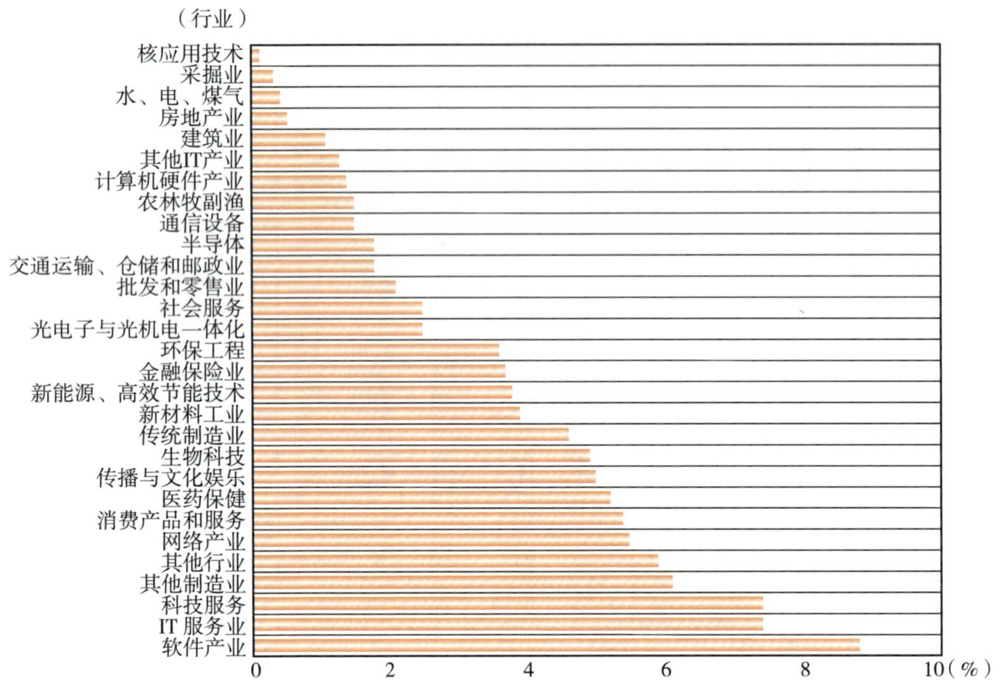

图 6-11 长三角地区创业风险投资项目的行业分布（2017）

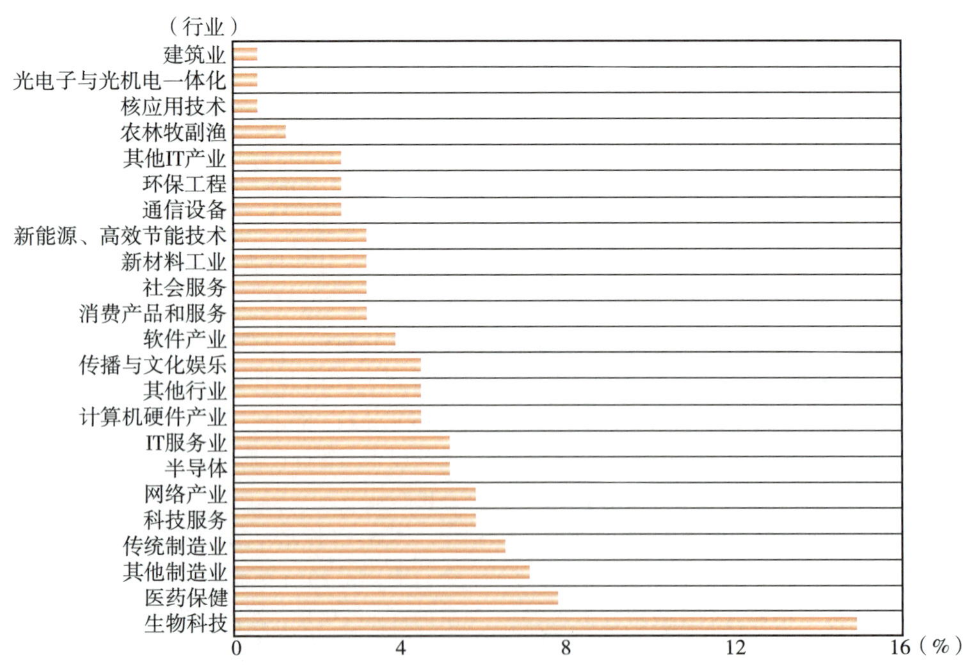

图 6-12 京津冀地区创业风险投资项目的行业分布（2017）

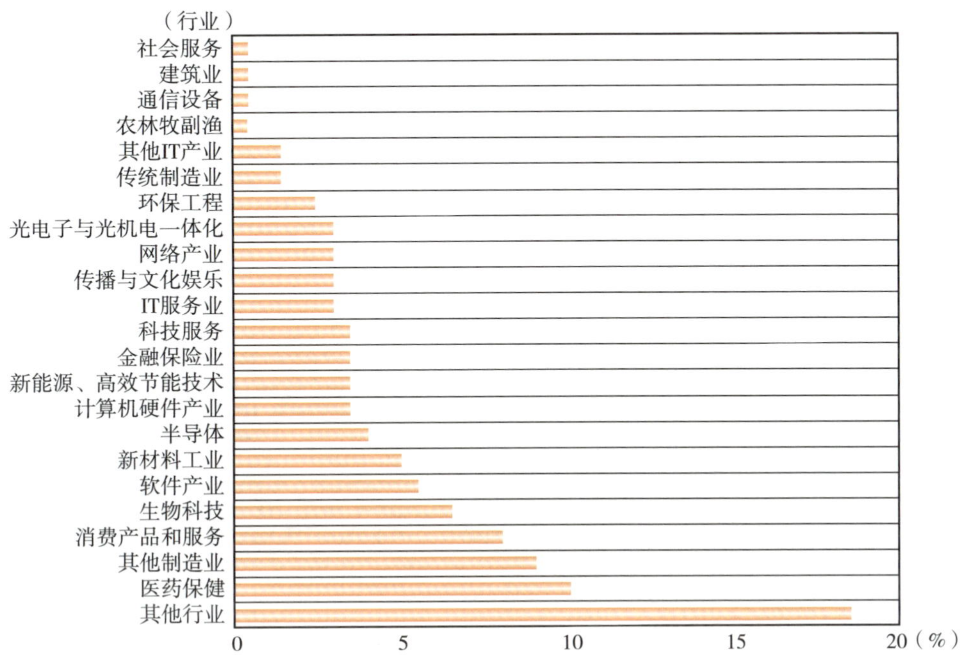

图 6-13 珠三角地区创业风险投资项目的行业分布（2017）

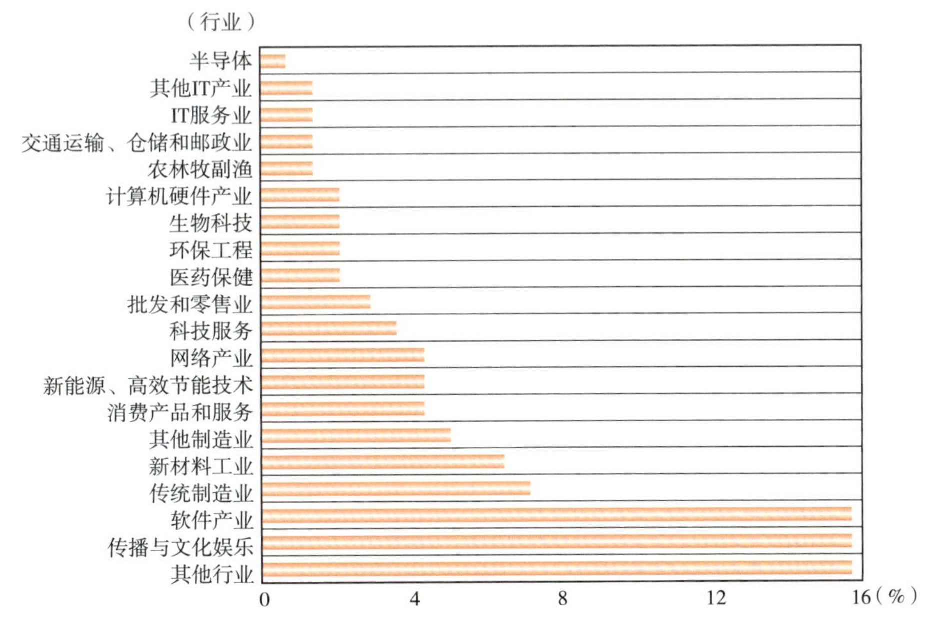

图 6-14 东北三省地区创业风险投资项目的行业分布（2017）

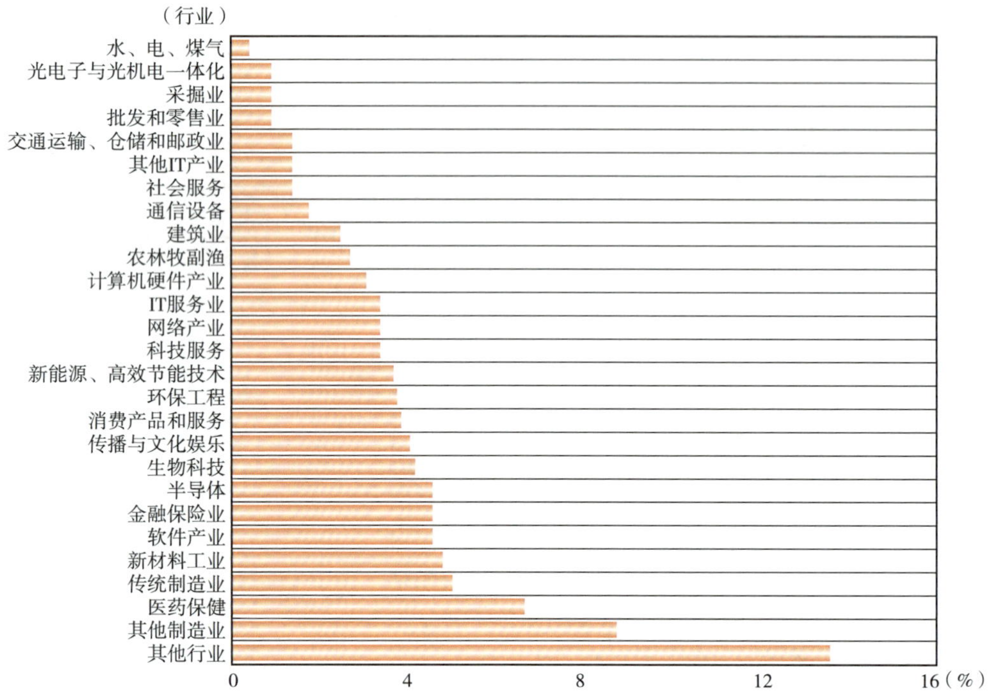

图 6-15 其他地区创业风险投资项目的行业分布（2017）

7 外资创业投资机构的运行状况

7.1 外资创业投资项目的行业分布

通过对2017年外资创业投资机构总体情况调查发现，[①]投资项目主要集中在6个行业（见表7–1），分别是其他行业，软件产业，医药保健，新能源、高效节能技术，生物科技，半导体领域。与2016年相比，“医药保健”“软件产业”仍然是外资关注的重点领域，但“网络产业”等不再是外资投资的关注点。

表7–1 外资创业投资项目的行业分布：投资金额与投资项目（2017） 单位：%

投资行业	投资金额占比	投资项目占比
其他行业	25.78	22.22
软件产业	21.71	22.22
医药保健	20.73	11.11
新能源、高效节能技术	16.28	22.22
生物科技	13.57	11.11
半导体	1.93	11.11

按投资金额划分（见图7–1），2017年外资投资项目金额较2016年更为集中，其中“其他行业”“软件行业”和“医药保健”投资金额占比都超过20%，共占比68.22%，“新能源、高效节能技术”作为2017年新增投资行业，投资金额和投资项目占比分别为16.28%和22.22%。

2017年外资创业投资项目数量则较为集中（见图7–2）。其中，“软件行业”“新能源、高效节能技术”以及“其他行业”占比都为22.22%，其次是“生物科技”“医药保健”和“半导体”，占比都为11.11%。

表7–2给出了2017年在投资金额和投资项目项下，按外资创业投资“投资金额”排序的外资和内资的行为特征。总体而言，无论从投资金额还是投资项目占比情况看，外资机构投资领域相较内资机构投资都更为集中。

从投资金额看，2017年外资机构投资金额前三个行业之和共占比68.22%，内资机构投资金额最高的三个行业则分别是采掘业（20.2%）、建筑业（14.4%）以及医药保健（9%）。与2016年相比，无论外资和内资机构都将资金更多地投向与网络相关产业，而2017年关注领域有了明显差异，“网络产业”投资金额占比陡然下降，内资投资金额从33.8%下降至2%，而外资并没有在“网络产业”投资。2017年，内资和外资机构在“医药保健”领域的投资金额占比都有了大幅提升，外资机构投资金额占比从11.7%上升至20.7%，内资占比从3.5%上升至9%。从投资金额看，相较于外资，内资机构更倾向于传统行业，而且投资领域更为分散。

①2017年，根据各地方填报数据情况看，我国境内共有外资创业风险投资机构共35家，以下章节涉及内容是根据不同机构披露信息情况进行统计的结果。

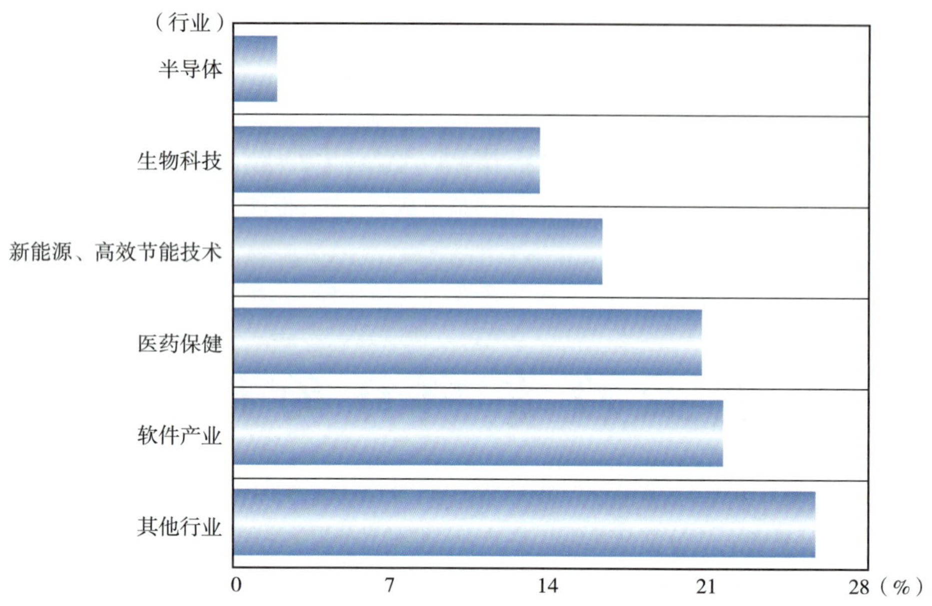

图 7–1　外资创业投资项目的行业分布：按投资金额（2017）

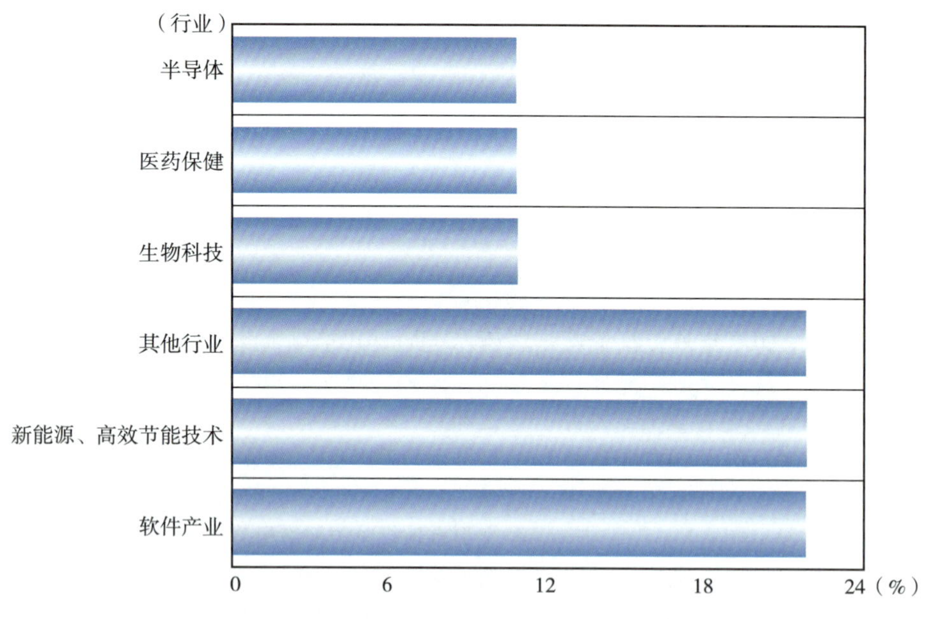

图 7–2　外资创业投资项目的行业分布：按投资项目（2017）

按投资项目看，2017 年外资投资项目前三个行业之和共占比66.6%，内资机构前三个行业分别是“其他行业”（10.4%）、“软件产业”（7.1%）和“医药保健”（6.1%），占比合计 23.6%。

2017 年，外资机构投资项目比内资机构更为集中。与 2016 年相比，新增“新能源、高效节能技术”的投资，占比分别为 22.2% 和 3.7%，而外资和内资机构投资于半导体的投资项目也有所上升，比例分别从 1.8% 和 1.3% 上升至 11.1% 和 3.1%，上升了 9.3 个和 1.8 个百分点。从这一比例看，创业投资机构已经意识到将资金过度集中在商业模式创新并不是长久之计，尽管技术创新的投资回报率相对较低、时间较长，但也逐渐获得资本关注。

表 7–2 外资、内资创业投资项目前六大行业分布：投资金额和投资项目（2017） 单位：%

投资行业	投资金额		投资项目	
	外资	内资	外资	内资
其他行业	25.8	7.5	22.2	10.4
软件产业	21.7	2.1	22.2	7.1
医药保健	20.7	9.0	11.1	6.1
新能源、高效节能技术	16.3	2.0	22.2	3.7
生物科技	13.6	8.0	11.1	5.2
半导体	1.9	0.8	11.1	3.1

注：按外资创业投资“投资金额”占比排序。

7.2 外资创业投资项目所处阶段

通过对 2017 年外资创业投资项目所处阶段的调查发现（见图 7–3），外资机构的投资金额和投资项目主要集中在“起步期”和“成长（扩张）期”。相较于 2016 年，没有机构投资的项目处于“种子期”；投资于“起步期”所占比例分别上升了 39.3% 和 25.1%，上升至 62.3% 和 63.6%；“成长（扩张）期”所占比例略有下降，分别从 67.6% 和 36.2% 下降至 36.2% 和 27.3%。

对比 2017 年外资和内资机构投资项目所处阶段（见表 7–3）可以发现：从投资金额看，与 2016 年外资和内资机构将投资重点放在“成长（扩张）期”不同，2017 年外

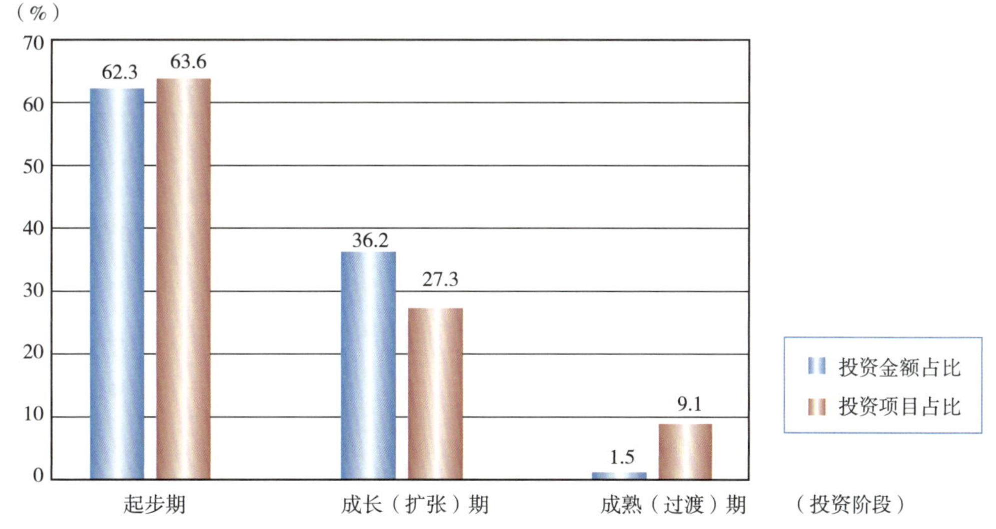

图 7–3 外资创业投资项目所处阶段（2017）

资机构将更多资金放在“起步期”，占比由2016年的23%上升至2017年的62.3%；投资于“成长（扩张）期”的投资金额则从2016年的67.6%下降至36.2%；新增投资于“成熟（过渡）期”的投资金额，占比为1.5%。相比之下，内资机构仍然将投资金额重点放在“成长（扩张）期”，占比由2016年的38.1%上升至2017年的44.7%。

从投资项目看，外资机构也将“起步期”的项目作为投资重点，占比由2016年的38.5%上升至2017年的63.6%；与2016年明显不同的是2017年外资机构没有投在“种子期”的项目，而这一数据在2016年为24.9%。相比内资，“起步期”也是内资机构投资重点，占比较2016年略上升了1个百分点，由38.4%上升至39.4%。

表 7-3　外资、内资创业投资项目所处阶段（2017）　　单位：%

投资阶段	投资金额		投资项目	
	外资	内资	外资	内资
种子期	—	4.5	—	17.9
起步期	62.3	20.7	63.6	39.4
成长（扩张）期	36.2	44.7	27.3	36.3
成熟（过渡）期	1.5	29.9	9.1	5.9
重建期	—	0.2	—	0.6

7.3　外资创业投资项目情况

2017年，外资创业投资单项投资金额分布与2016年及以前年份存在较大差异（见表7-4、图7-4）：

（1）单笔投资金额在500万~2000万元的项目占比累计为85.1%。

表 7-4　外资创业投资单项投资金额的规模分布（2011~2017）　　单位：%

年份 \ 投资额分布（万元）	<100	100~300	300~500	500~1000	1000~2000	＞2000
2011	0.0	0.2	0.3	3.3	13.9	82.3
2012	0.4	0.4	1.4	9.7	24.5	63.7
2013	0.0	0.1	1.3	4.2	16.1	78.2
2014	0.1	0.4	0.9	5.3	18.1	75.2
2015	0.0	1.0	0.7	2.4	9.3	86.5
2016	0.6	4.1	2.1	13.3	18.5	61.5
2017	2.9	3.6	8.5	38.3	46.8	0.0

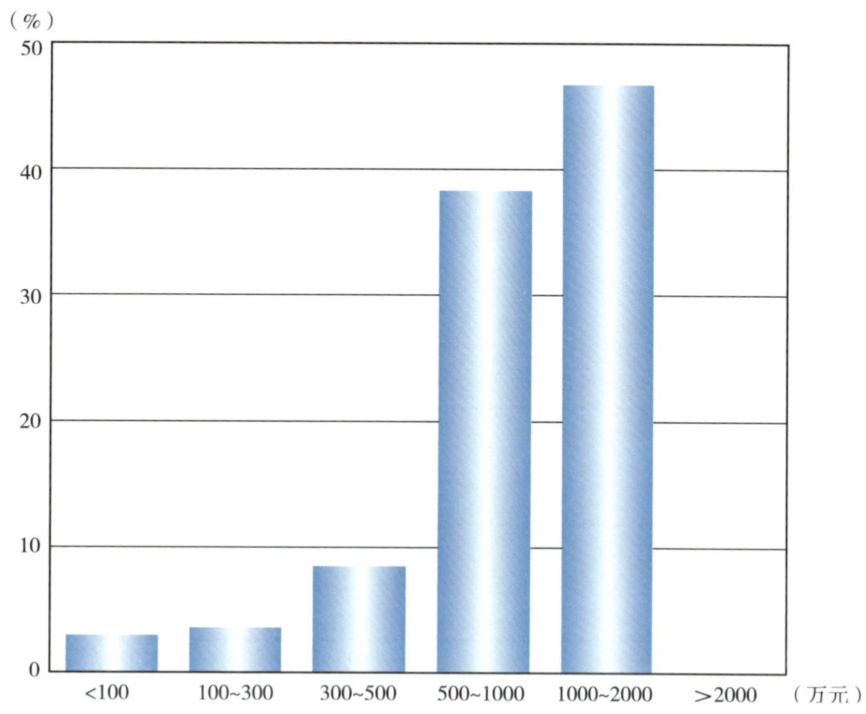

图 7-4 外资创业投资单项投资金额的规模分布（2017）

（2）首次没有单笔在 2000 万元以上的大额投资。

（3）单笔投资金额在“100 万元以下”“300 万 ~500 万元”“500 万 ~1000 万元”和“1000 万 ~2000 万元”项目占比自 2011 年以来最高，分别比 2016 年提高了 2.3 个、6.4 个、25 个和 28.3 个百分点。

针对上述数据的分析，再一次证明 2017 年外资投资机构的投资倾向，即相比过去，2017 年外资机构都明显减少和降低了对成长期项目的关注和投资，逐渐回归创业投资属性。

通过对比外资和内资风险投资单项投资金额的规模分布（见表 7-5、图 7-5）可以发现，2017 年外资与内资差异最大的部门是投资金额在“2000 万元以上”占比情况：2017 年内资机构仍然延续 2016 年特征，“2000 万元及以上”仍然占主要份额，从 2016 年的 78.7% 上升至 2017 年的 82.8%。受此影响，外资与内资机构单项投资金额在 2000 万元以下的占比差异也较往年更为明显。

表 7-5 外资、内资创业投资单项投资金额的规模分布（2017） 单位：%

投资金额（万元）	<100	100~300	300~500	500~1000	1000~2000	> 2000
外资	2.9	3.6	8.5	38.3	46.8	0.0
内资	0.2	1.2	2.3	5.1	8.4	82.8

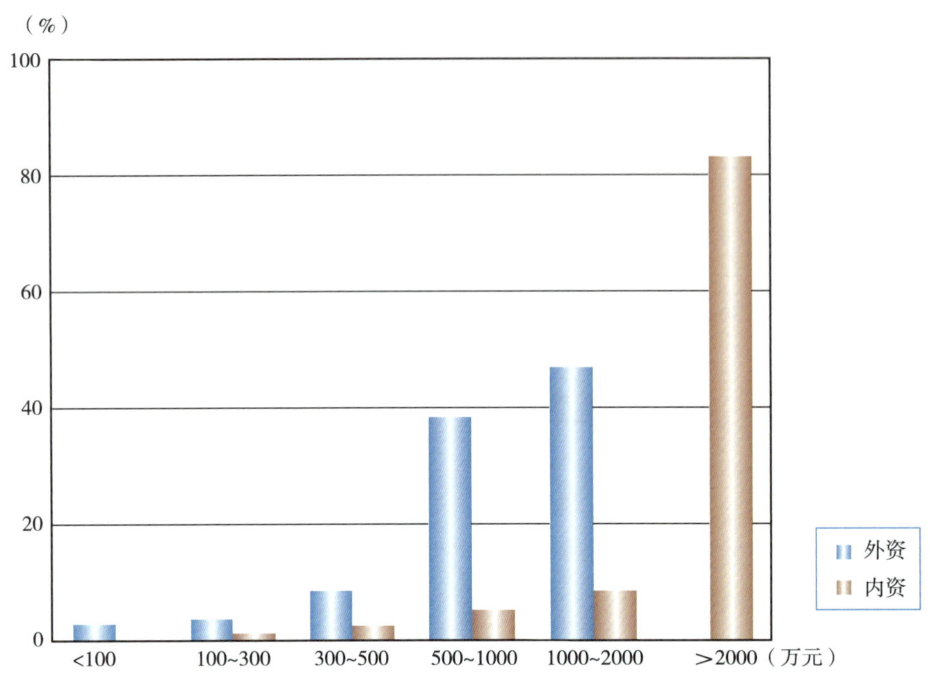

图 7-5 外资、内资创业投资单项投资金额的规模分布（2017）

7.4 外资创业投资项目雇员情况

调查显示（见表 7-6、图 7-6），2017 年外资创业投资项目的雇员依然延续了 2016 年特征，人数主要规模集中在 100 人以下。其中，“10 人以下”“10 ~50 人”和“50 ~100 人”各自所占比重分别为 20%、60% 和 20%。

表 7-6 外资创业投资项目雇员人数分布（2011~2017） 单位：%

年份	10 人以下	10 ~50 人	50 ~100 人	100 ~150 人	150 ~200 人	200 人以上
2011	3.6	13.4	8.9	14.3	13.4	46.4
2012	8.3	17.9	9.5	21.4	10.7	32.1
2013	13.3	13.3	16.7	10	6.7	40.0
2014	10.5	19.7	10.5	15.8	6.6	36.8
2015	14.3	28.6	14.3	0.0	14.3	28.6
2016	36.8	31.6	31.6	—	—	—
2017	20.0	60.0	20.0	—	—	—

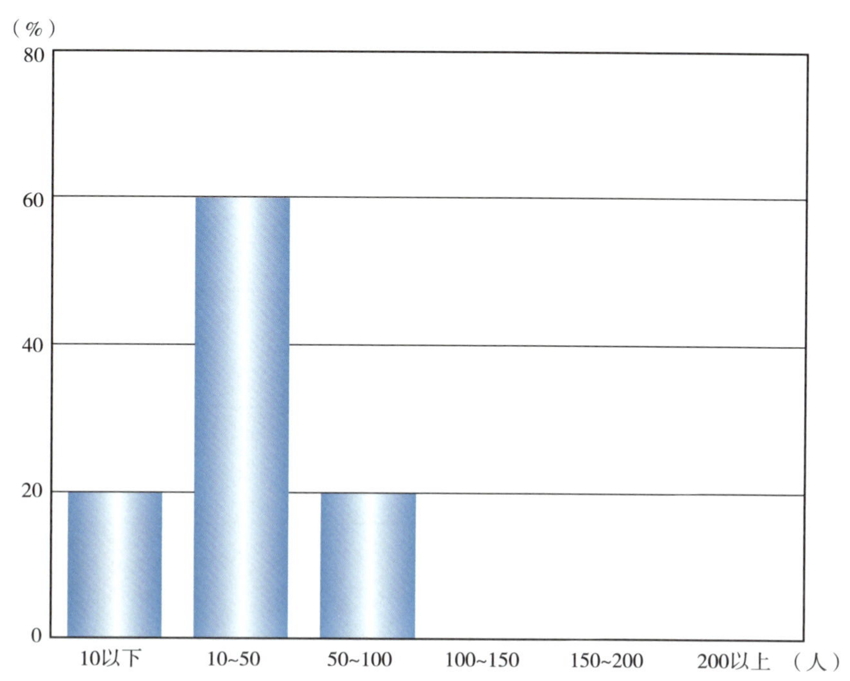

图 7-6　外资创业投资项目雇员人数分布（2017）

表 7-7 和图 7-7 给出了 2017 年外资与内资创业投资项目雇员人数分布情况。对比内外资投资项目雇员情况，2017 年，外资机构投资项目雇员数量相较内资机构投资项目雇员数量而言更为集中。其中，内资和外资机构投资项目雇员在“10 ~50 人”的较为集中，占比分别为 60% 和 32.8%，较 2016 年增长了 28.4% 和降低了 5.2%。此外，内资机构投资项目雇员人数在 100 人以上的所占比重也较外资机构有较明显差异，累计占比为 33.2%，较 2016 年增长了 26.7%。

表 7-7　外资与内资创业投资项目雇员人数分布（2017）

单位：%

分布比例	10 人以下	10 ~50 人	50 ~100 人	100 ~150 人	150 ~200 人	200 人以上
外资	20.0	60.0	20.0	0.0	0.0	0.0
内资	17.6	32.8	16.4	7.3	5.8	20.1

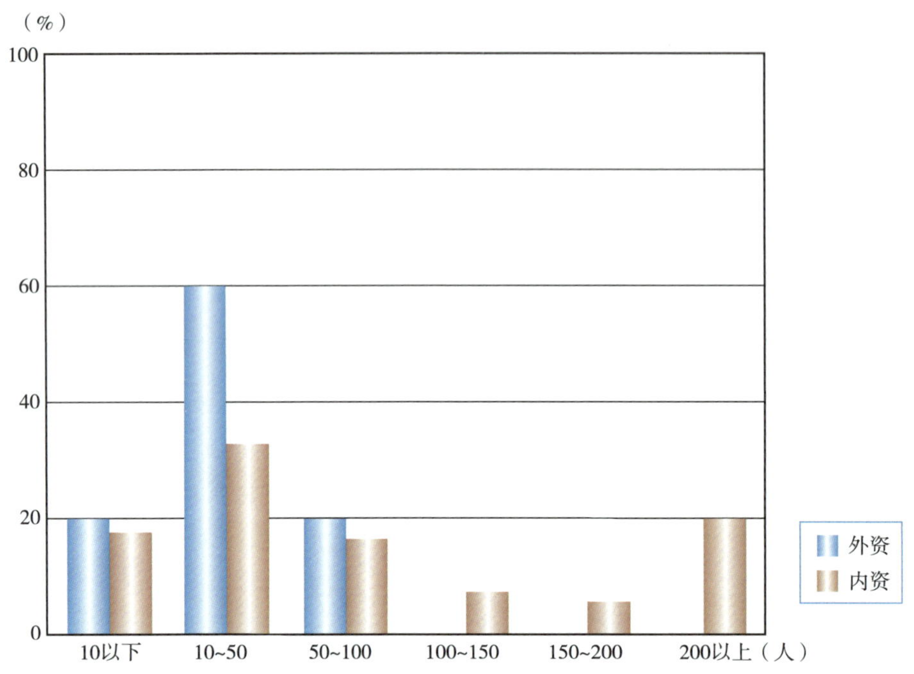

图 7-7 外资与内资创业投资项目雇员人数分布（2017）

7.5 外资创业投资项目总体运作情况

表 7-8、图 7-8 给出了 2012~2017 年外资创业投资项目运行的基本情况。通过调查发现，2017 年外资创业投资的整体投资周期仍然较长，74.6% 的项目仍然处于继续运行中，较 2016 年下降了 14.9%，从侧面反映出外资创业投资机构对早前期的投资项目还在持续关注。

2017 年，我国政府一方面防控金融风险是金融工作的根本性任务，另一方面还要发挥金融服务实体经济作用。所以 2017 年，外资机构投资项目"已上市"所占比例较 2016 年上升了 2.3 个百分点，且全部集中在"境内上市"部分。"被其他机构收购"所占比例较 2016 年增加了 2.6 个百分点，其中被"境内上市公司收购"和"境外收购"各占 7.6% 和 1.6%。"原股东（创业者）回购"所占比例为三年最高，较 2016 年增长了 7.1 个百分点。"继续运行"所占比例则较 2016 年下降了 14.9 个百分点。

表 7-8 外资创业投资项目的运行情况（2012~2017） 单位：%

年份 \ 运作情况 \ 投资项目	已上市		准备上市		被其他机构收购			原股东（创业者）回购	管理层收购	继续运行	清算
	境内上市	境外上市	境内上市	境外上市	境内上市公司收购	境内非上市公司或自然人收购	境外收购				
2012	10.7		6.2		6			6.5	0.7	68.8	1.1
	7.6	3.1	5.1	1.1	1.1	4.9	0				
2013	10.8		7		5.1			10	14	52	1.1
	7.4	3.4	6.5	0.5	0.8	4.1	0.2				

续表

<table>
<tr><th rowspan="2">投资项目
运作
情况
年份</th><th colspan="2">已上市</th><th colspan="2">准备上市</th><th colspan="3">被其他机构收购</th><th rowspan="2">原股东（创业者）回购</th><th rowspan="2">管理层收购</th><th rowspan="2">继续运行</th><th rowspan="2">清算</th></tr>
<tr><th>境内上市</th><th>境外上市</th><th>境内上市</th><th>境外上市</th><th>境内上市公司收购</th><th>境内非上市公司或自然人收购</th><th>境外收购</th></tr>
<tr><td rowspan="2">2014</td><td colspan="2">4.5</td><td colspan="2">15</td><td colspan="3">9.8</td><td rowspan="2">4</td><td rowspan="2">0</td><td rowspan="2">70.6</td><td rowspan="2">0.9</td></tr>
<tr><td>3.3</td><td>1.2</td><td>9.5</td><td>5.5</td><td>0.5</td><td>5.5</td><td>3.8</td></tr>
<tr><td rowspan="2">2015</td><td colspan="2">15.5</td><td colspan="2">0</td><td colspan="3">8.8</td><td rowspan="2">11.8</td><td rowspan="2">0.2</td><td rowspan="2">61.1</td><td rowspan="2">2.6</td></tr>
<tr><td>13.7</td><td>1.8</td><td>0</td><td>0</td><td>7.2</td><td>0</td><td>1.6</td></tr>
<tr><td rowspan="2">2016</td><td colspan="2">1.5</td><td colspan="2">0</td><td colspan="3">6.6</td><td rowspan="2">2.1</td><td rowspan="2">1.7</td><td rowspan="2">89.5</td><td rowspan="2">1.7</td></tr>
<tr><td>1.1</td><td>0.4</td><td>0.0</td><td>0.0</td><td>6.6</td><td>0.0</td><td>0.0</td></tr>
<tr><td rowspan="2">2017</td><td colspan="2">3.8</td><td colspan="2">0</td><td colspan="3">9.2</td><td rowspan="2">9.2</td><td rowspan="2">1.6</td><td rowspan="2">74.6</td><td rowspan="2">1.6</td></tr>
<tr><td>3.8</td><td>0.0</td><td>0</td><td>0</td><td>7.6</td><td>0.0</td><td>1.6</td></tr>
</table>

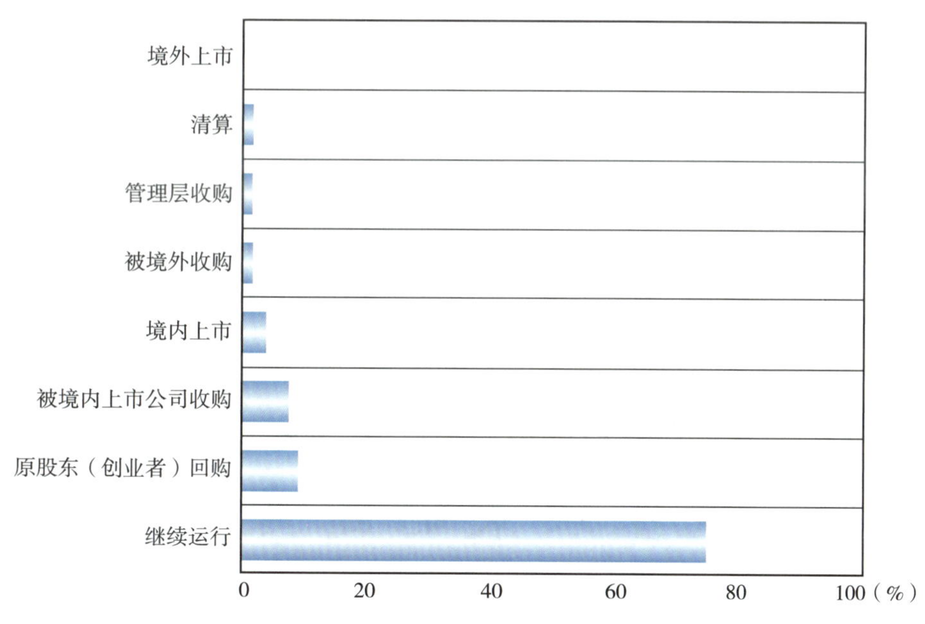

图 7-8 外资创业投资项目的运行情况（2017）

表 7-9、图 7-9 给出了 2017 年外资与内资创业投资项目运作情况的对比。从表 7-9 中可以看出内资机构和外资机构的投资项目运作情况并没有明显的结构性差异，“继续运行”仍然是外资和内资机构投资项目的主要运行状态，内资机构投资项目“已上市”较外资机构投资项目所占比例高了 3.5 个百分点。

表 7-9 外资与内资创业投资项目的运作情况（2017） 单位：%

运作情况	继续运行	其他机构收购	已上市	原股东（创业者）回购	管理层收购	清算	准备上市
外资	74.6	9.2	3.8	9.2	1.6	1.6	—
内资	74.8	5.6	7.3	7.3	1.4	3.5	—

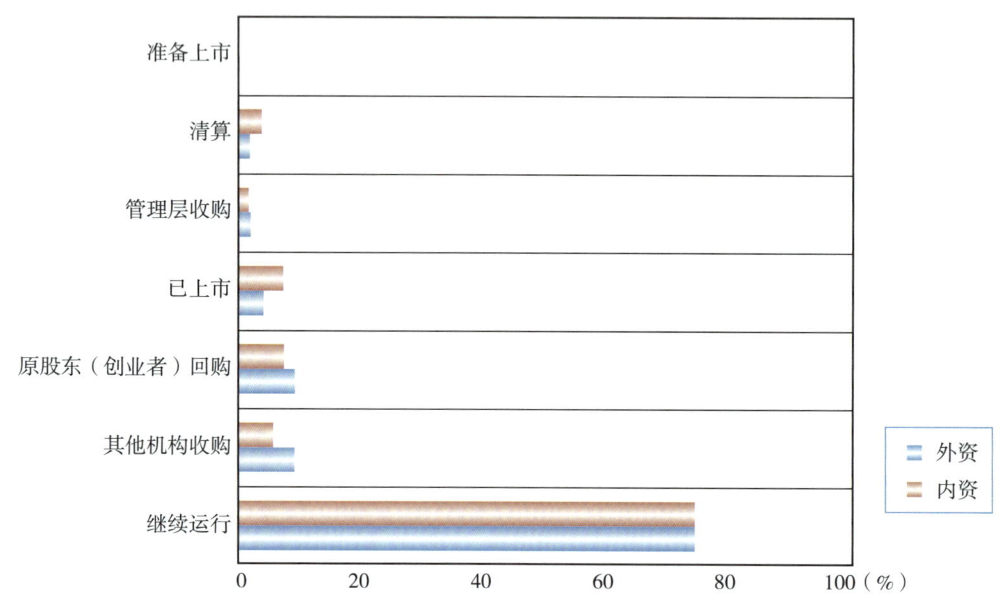

图 7-9 外资与内资创业投资项目的运作情况（2017）

7.6 影响外资创业投资机构投资决策的因素

2017 年影响外资创业投资机构的前三个主要原因分别是“市场前景”“管理团队”和“技术因素”（见图 7-10），占比分别为 31.1%、25.6% 和 18.9%。与 2016 年相比，“技术因素”和“财务状况”所占比重超过“盈利模式”成为影响外资机构投资决策的第三个因素。

对比 2017 年外资和内资创业投资机构决策因素可以发现，“市场前景”“管理团队”“技术因素”“财务状况”以及“盈利模式”是影响内资和外资投资决策的前五个共同要素，累计所占比重分别为 91.3% 和 92.3%，较 2016 年分别降低 21.5 个百分点和 27.9 个百分点。

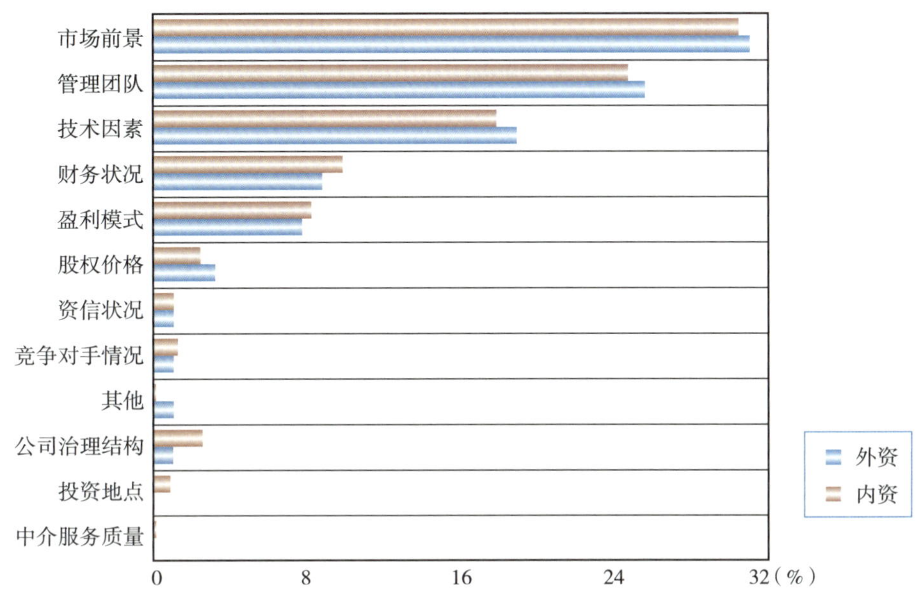

图 7-10　影响外资与内资创业投资机构投资决策的因素（2017）

7.7　外资创业投资机构获取信息的主要渠道

通过对内资和外资创业投资获取信息渠道的调查发现（见图 7-11），获取信息的主要渠道与 2016 年相比没有明

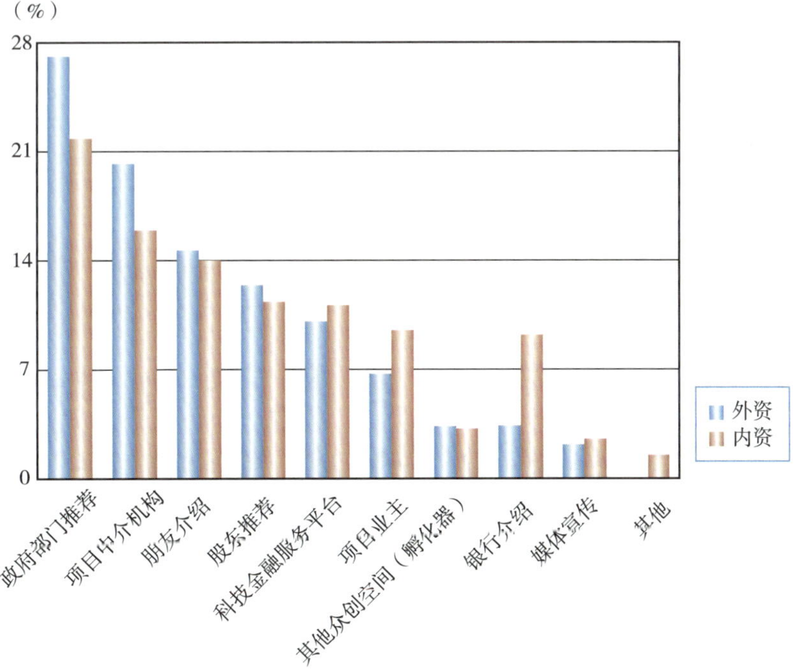

图 7-11　外资与内资创业投资机构获取信息的主要渠道（2017）

显变化。

“政府部门推荐”成为外资和内资获取信息的最主要渠道，占比分别由 2016 年的 19.1% 和 20.2% 提升至 27% 和 21.8%；“项目中介机构”“朋友介绍”以及“股东推荐”分别排名第二、第三、第四位；与 2016 年相比，新增渠道来源“科技金融服务平台”，外资和内资占比分别为 10.1% 和 11.1%。

7.8 外资创业投资项目的监管模式

2017 年，外资创业投资的监管模式主要集中在“提供管理咨询”“董事会席位”和“其他”，分别占比 43.8%、31.3% 和 12.5%；对比内资机构，“只限监管”超过“其他”成为第三个监管模式，前三个监管模式分别为“提供管理咨询”“董事会席位”以及“只限监管”，所占比重分别为 40.3%、32.4% 以及 17.9%。2017 年，外资与内资“财务咨询”所占比例分别为 3.1% 和 3.8%（见图 7-12）。

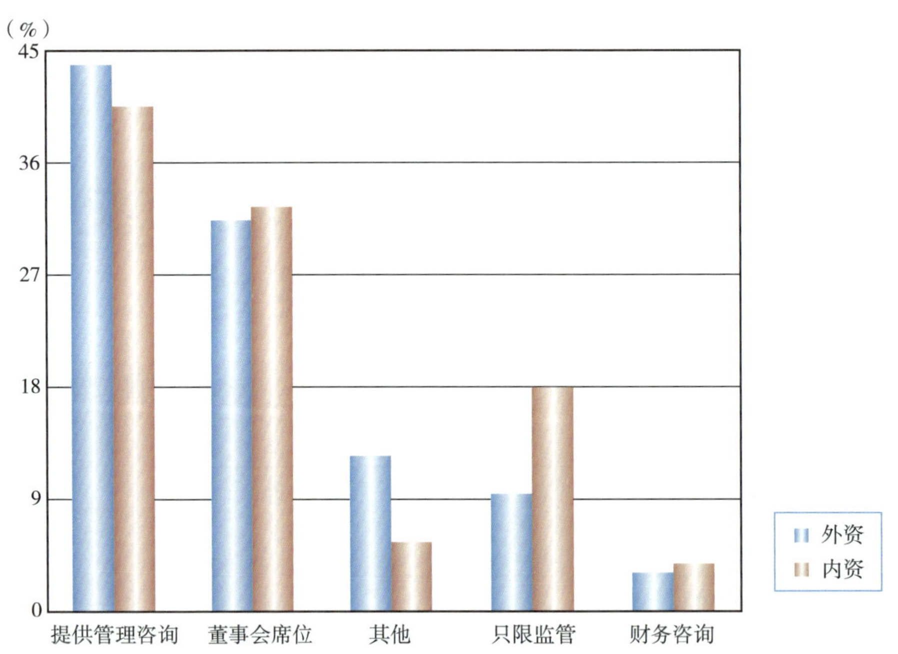

图 7-12 外资与内资创业投资项目的监管模式（2017）

7.9 与外资创业投资机构经营有关的人力资源因素

通过调查外资和内资创业投资机构对创业投资从业人员基本素质要求发现（见图 7-13），2017 年外资机构对合格创业人员从业素质要求略有变化，但就整体而言，外资与内资机构都认为合格的创业投资人员应该具备多种素质。

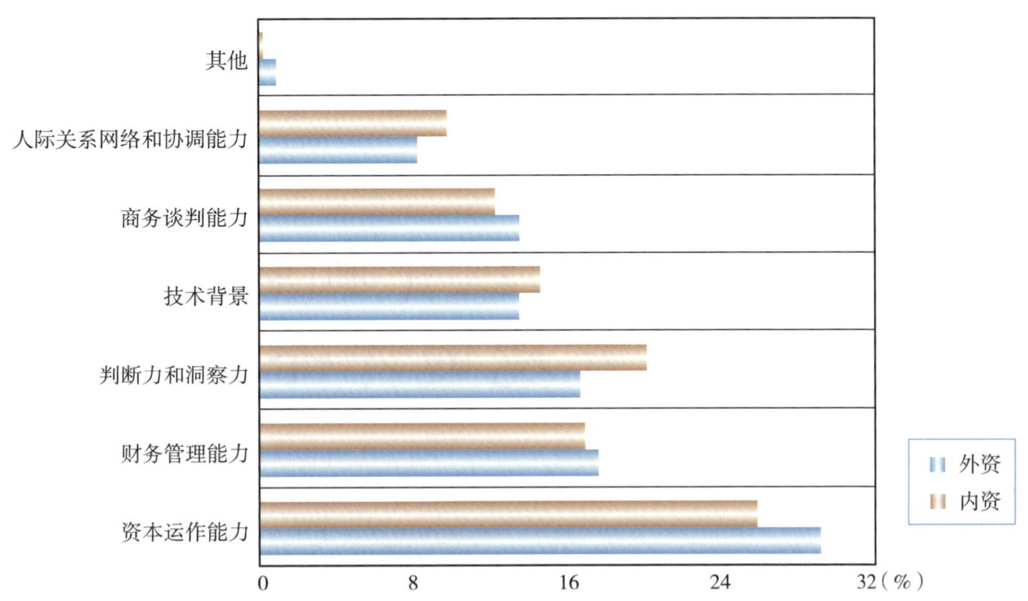

图 7-13　外资与内资创业投资机构对合格创业投资人员素质要求（2017）

与 2016 年相比，“资本运作能力”替代“判断力和洞察力”成为外资机构最看重的因素，二者占比分别为 29.2% 和 16.7%；“财务管理能力”由 2016 年的第四位上升至 2017 年的第二位，所占比重为 17.7%；“人际关系网络和协调能力”连续三年占比都较为靠后，占比 8.3%。

对比外资、内资机构，内资机构更看重合格创业投资人员具备“资本运作能力”“判断力和洞察力”以及“财务管理能力”，所占比重分别为 25.9%、20.1% 以及 16.9%。

调查显示（见图 7-14），2017 年外资机构认为“企业管理”“技术评估”以及“资本运作”是我国创业投资

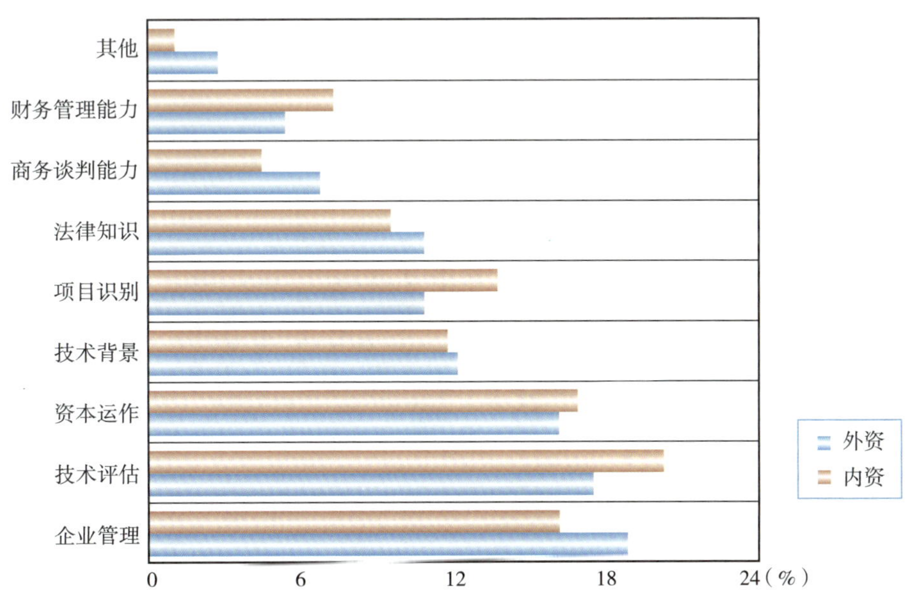

图 7-14　外资与内资创业投资机构认为我国创业投资从业人员缺乏的专业知识（2017）

从业人员最缺乏的三项专业知识，占比分别为 18.7%、17.3% 和 16%，“企业管理”由 2016 年的第四位上升至 2017 年的第一位。

对比外资创业投资机构对于人才的要求，2017 年内资创业投资机构认为从业人员最缺乏的知识依然是“技术评估”“资本运作”以及“企业管理”，所占比例分别是 20.1%、16.7% 以及 16%。

7.10 外资创业投资机构对总体发展环境的评价

根据对外资创业投资机构关于投资效果是否理想的调查（见图 7–15），2017 年，“退出渠道不畅”“政策环境变化”以及“内部管理水平有限”成为外资机构认为投资效果不理想的前三个因素，所占比例分别为 24.6%、20% 以及 20%；“市场竞争”所占比例由 2016 年的第二位下降至 2017 年的第五位，所占比例由 2016 年的 19.4% 下降至 2017 年的 12.3%。

对比内、外资创投机构可以发现，二者对政策环境的评价稍微存在差异。内资创业投资机构认为“市场竞争”是导致投资效果不理想的最主要因素，“退出渠道不畅”是内资机构认为影响投资效果的第二重要因素，所占比重分别为 18.5% 和 18.4%；“政策环境变化”则被内资机构认为是导致效果不佳的第三个因素，占比 17.3%。

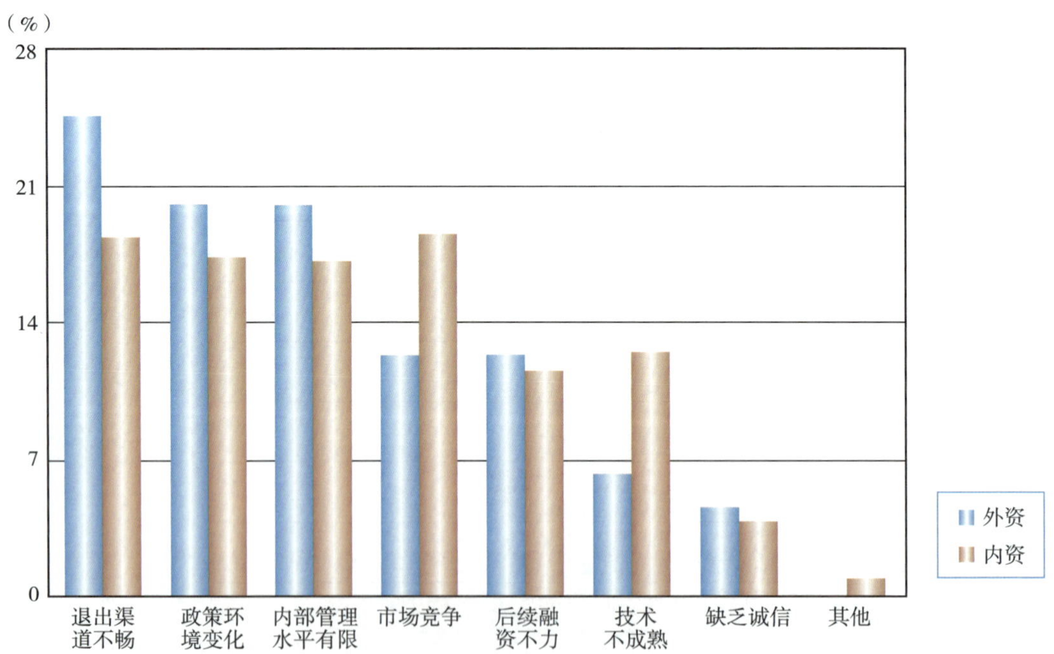

图 7–15 外资与内资创业投资机构认为投资效果不理想的原因（2017）

8 中国创业投资发展环境

8.1 中国创业投资机构的政策环境

近年来，我国中央政府和地方各级政府在建立风险投资发展所需的内外部环境方面发挥了积极的作用，出台了一系列适宜风险投资的税收政策和相关法律法规，完善了风险投资机构监管体系，推动了创业投资行业的健康成长。本部分将重点阐述2017年我国创业投资机构所处的政策环境，分析国家科技计划与创业投资项目对接的关键因素，并总结中国近年来促进创业投资发展的主要政策。

8.1.1 中国创业投资机构可以享受的政府扶持政策

图8-1列示了2017年我国创业投资机构能够享受的政府扶持政策情况①。其中，政府提供的信息交流方面的扶持政策居于首位，28.9%的创业投资机构获得了相关信息交流服务，比2016年略微下降（2016年数据为29.2%）；其次是各级政府的所得税减免政策，得到该项扶持的创业投资企业占比为22.3%，较2016年有所提升（2016年数据为20.3%）；政府的资金直接支持位居第三，能够享受此项政策的创业投资机构占18.6%，与2016年相比进一步降低（2016年数据为17.6%）；13.7%的创业投资机构在人员培训上获得了政府支持，比2016年的14.5%下降了0.8个百分点；10.8%的创业投资机构享受

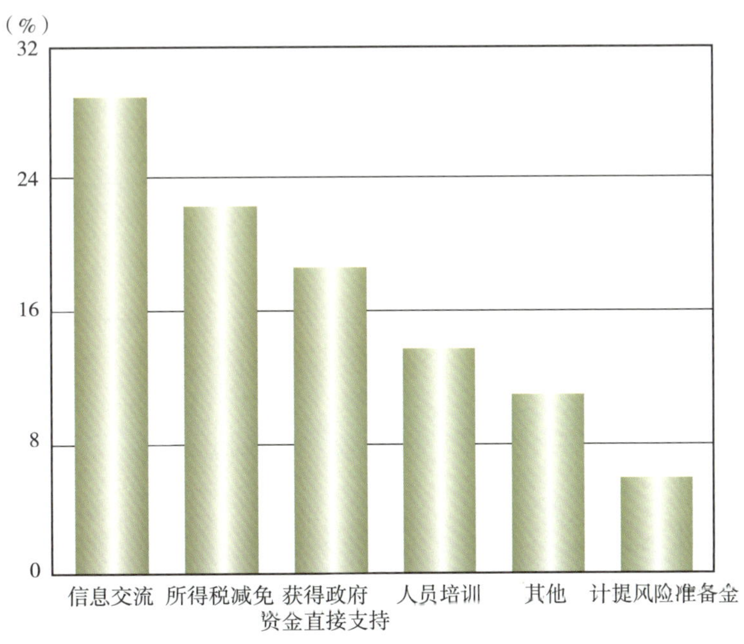

图8-1 创业投资机构可以享受的政府扶持政策占比（2017）

① 有效样本数为1547份。

了其他扶持政策，较 2016 年降低 2 个百分点。总体来看，2017 年我国创业投资机构从政府获得的扶持以间接服务和税收优惠为主。

图 8-2①、图 8-3② 按照政府层级对 2017 年我国创业投资机构能够享受的扶持政策情况做了进一步划分。在中央政府扶持政策中（见图 8-2），创业投资机构享受的信息交流服务与所得税减免分列前两位，占比分别为 29.2% 和 22.4%；获得政府资金直接支持则排在第三位，占比

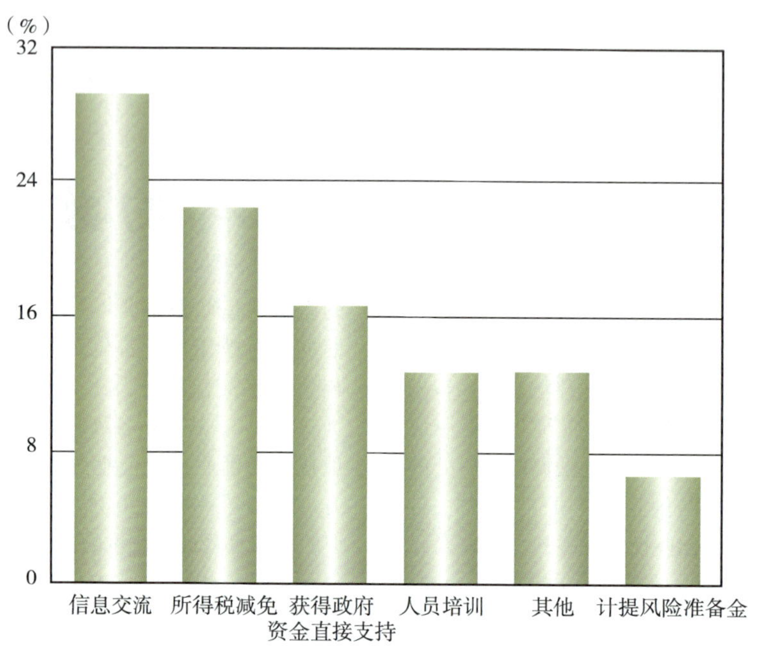

图 8-2 创业投资机构可以享受的中央政府扶持政策占比（2017）

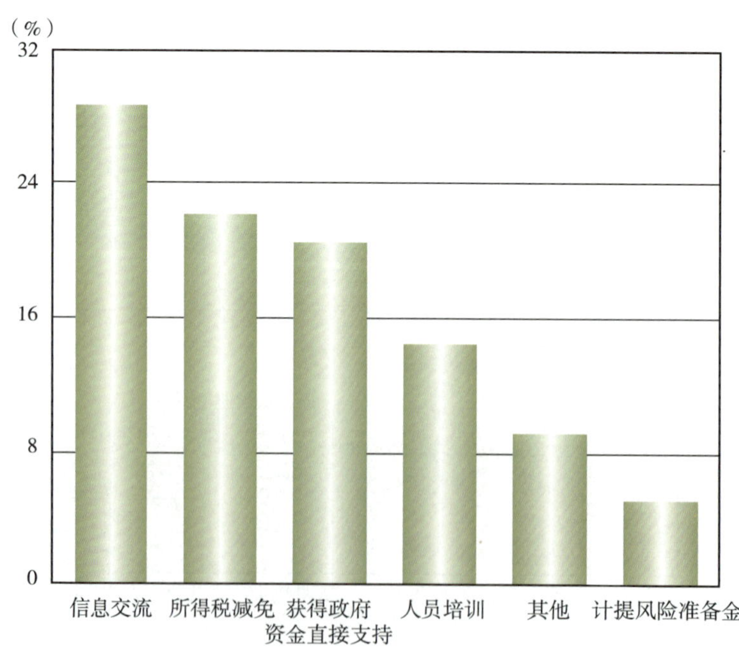

图 8-3 创业投资机构可以享受的地方政府扶持政策占比（2017）

① 有效样本数为 1471 份。
② 有效样本数为 1531 份。

16.5%。在地方层面（见图 8-3），28.7% 的创业投资企业得到了地方政府的信息交流支持，22.2% 的创业投资企业享受了地方政府的税收优惠；获得地方政府资金直接支持的创业投资机构占 20.5%。通过图 8-2 与图 8-3 的对比，不难发现，2017 年中央政府与地方政府在促进创业投资发展的政策导向上存在一定差异，与中央政府相比，地方政府对创业投资机构更倾向于采用直接资金扶持的方式。

按地域划分，2017 年我国创业投资机构享受政府扶持政策情况如图 8-4 所示①。可以看出，2017 年各地创业投资机构获得的各类型扶持政策并不均衡。重庆、浙江、江苏、山东、北京、广东等是创业投资较为活跃的地区，创业投资机构可以享受的各项政策相对平均，甘肃、内蒙古、广西、青海等地的创业投资企业获得的政策扶持相对单一。信息交流服务和所得税减免是各地创业投资机构享受的主要政策形式。其中，安徽、福建、甘肃、广西等 22 个地区的创业投资企业得到信息交流支持的比例超过了 25%，安徽、广东、广西、贵州等 20 个地区超过 20% 的创业投资机构获得了所得税优惠。吉林、内蒙古、青海、四川等地区的创业投资机构获得政府资金直接支持的比例均超过了 30%，内蒙古、青海、海南等地的创业投资企业主要通过计提风险准备金降低投资风险和投资成本。

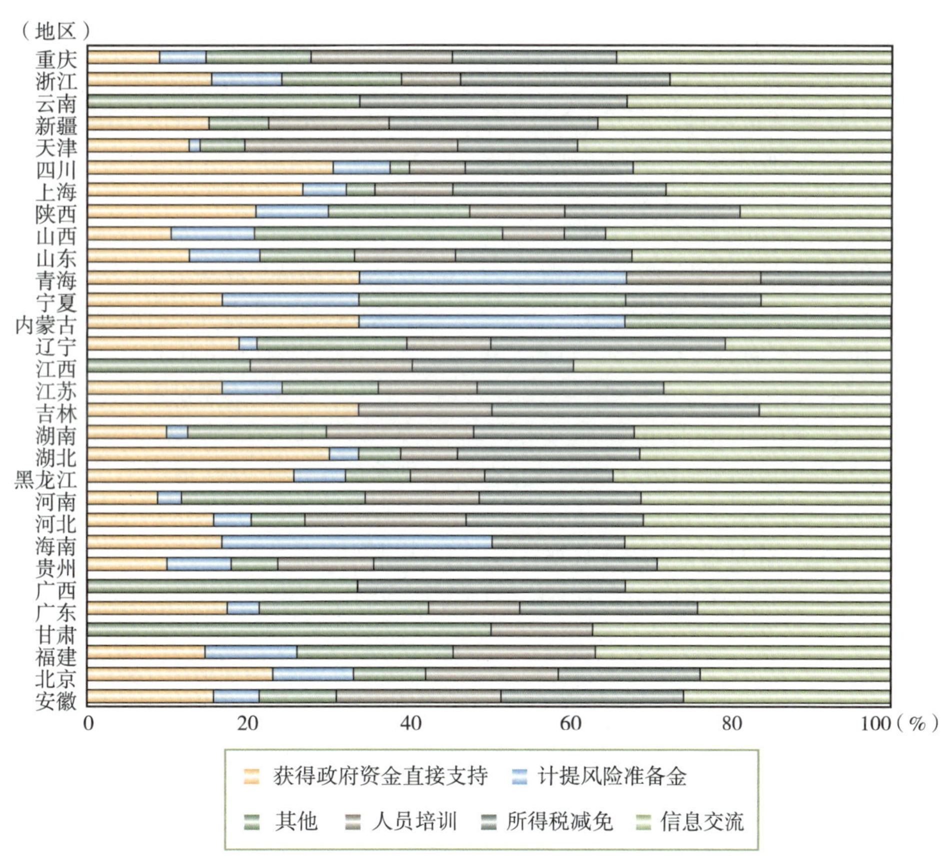

图 8-4 各地创业投资机构可以享受的政府扶持政策占比（2017）

8.1.2 中国创业投资机构享受的主要税收政策及缴税情况②

2007 年 2 月，财政部、国家税务总局出台《关于促进创业投资企业发展有关税收政策的通知》（财税〔2007〕31 号），明确对创业投资机构实行税收优惠政策。2009 年 4 月，《国家税务总局关于实施创业投资企业所得税优惠问题的通知》（国税发〔2009〕87 号）就创业投资企业所得税优惠的有关问题做了具体规定。2015 年 10 月，《财政

① 有效样本数为 1471 份。

② 有效样本数为 1321 份。

部 国家税务总局关于将国家自主创新示范区有关税收试点政策推广到全国范围实施的通知》(财税〔2015〕116 号)对有限合伙制创业投资企业法人合伙人企业所得税优惠政策进行了具体说明。2016 年 9 月，财政部、国家税务总局联合发布《关于完善股权激励和技术入股有关所得税政策的通知》(财税〔2016〕101 号)指出："对符合条件的非上市公司股票期权、股权期权、限制性股票和股权奖励实行递延纳税政策，员工在取得股权激励时可暂不纳税，递延至转让该股权时纳税，税率降低为 20%；对上市公司股票期权、限制性股票和股权奖励延长纳税期限，个人可自股票期权行权、限制性股票解禁或取得股权奖励之日起，在不超过 12 个月的期限内缴纳个人所得税；对技术成果投资入股实施选择性税收优惠政策。"2017 年 4 月，财政部、国家税务总局联合发布《关于创业投资企业和天使投资个人有关税收试点政策的通知》(财税〔2017〕38 号)，从税收试点政策、相关政策条件、管理事项及管理要求、执行时间及试点地区四个方面做了具体说明。

2017 年统计数据显示，国内披露缴税情况的创业投资机构 1321 家(2016 年为 1054 家)，合计缴税金额逾 23.78 亿元(2016 年为 17.89 亿元)；其中，享受投资中小高新技术企业所得税减免的创业投资机构共 56 家，可享受减免的额度合计超过 4.32 亿元。

8.1.3 中国创业投资机构的政策需求①

图 8-5 列示了 2017 年中国创业投资机构最希望出台的政府激励政策，主要类型如下：

(1)完善创业投资税收优惠政策。统计数据显示，2017 年中国创业投资机构最希望出台的政府激励政策是税收优惠类，占比为 31%。与往年相比，创业投资企业的税收政策诉求有所下降(2016 年数据为 43%)。

(2)设立政策性基金。16.6% 的创业投资企业希望设立政策性基金，并通过市场化的运作方式支持创业投资发展，与 2016 年相比，这一数据有所上升(2016 年数据为 13.1%)。

(3)加快注册制改革，建立转板机制。希望政府继续推动资本市场注册制改革，加快建立场内外市场之间的转板机制的创业投资企业占 16.2%。与 2016 年相比，该项诉求提升了 1.4 个百分点(2016 年数据为 14.8%)。

(4)发展众创空间等新型孵化器。11% 的创业投资机构希望政府加大众创空间等新型孵化器的扶持力度，进一步加快推进大众创新创业，该数据较 2016 年亦有较大提升(2016 年数据为 6%)。

(5)完善和落实相关法律。根据调查统计，9.5% 的创业投资机构希望政府能够完善和落实创业投资的相关法律，营造规范的制度环境(2016 年数据为 6%)。

(6)鼓励科研人员创新创业。数据显示，9.2% 的创业投资机构认为政府应当出台鼓励科研人员创新创业的相关政策，进一步激发创新创业热情，促进科技成果转化。这一数据相比往年上升较多(2016 年数据为 5.6%)。

(7)理顺国有创投管理体制。6% 的创业投资机构认为，应当健全符合创业投资行业特点和发展规律的国有创业投资管理体制，激发国有创投活力，提高国有创投运行效率。该项诉求较 2016 年有所下降(2016 年数据为 10.4%)。

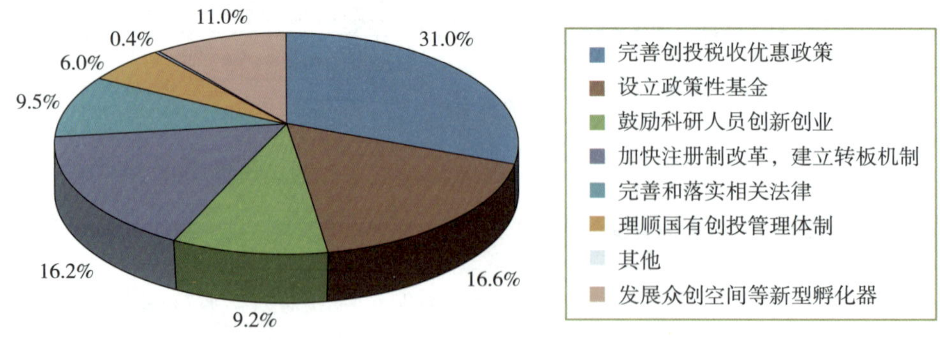

图 8-5 创业投资机构希望的政府激励政策占比(2017)

① 有效样本数为 1592 份。

8.2 国家科技计划支撑创业投资发展

2017 年，对“国家科技计划与创业投资项目对接的关键因素”的调查问题统计显示①，26.1% 的创业投资机构认为加大基础、应用和开发投入是国家科技计划与创业投资项目对接的首要因素。与 2016 年相比，这一比例有所下降（2016 年数据为 32.9%）；21.1% 的创业投资机构认为应当尽快设立科技型中小企业上市的绿色通道，低于 2016 年的 25.7%；18.8% 的创业投资机构认为需要直接资助创业投资项目，低于 2016 年的 22%；13.9% 的创业投资机构认为应鼓励、资助创业投资机构与孵化器之间的合作，比 2016 年的 11.4% 略高；11.8% 的创业投资机构要求加大科技项目信息的公开度，这一比例与 2016 年相比有较大幅度的提升（2016 年数据为 4.9%）；仅有 7.9% 的创业投资机构认为应当对科技类投资项目提供培训、管理咨询，比 2016 年的 2.7% 亦有较大幅度提升（见图 8-6）。

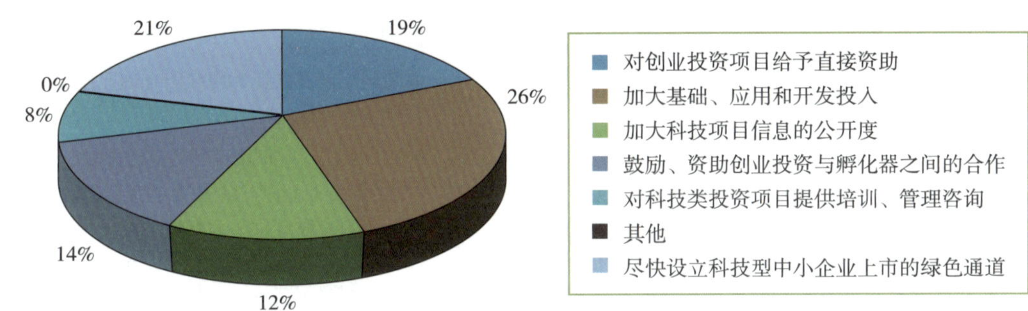

图 8-6 国家科技计划与创业投资良好对接的关键因素占比（2017）

8.3 中国促进创业投资发展主要政策

政府部门的政策支持是创业投资发展的直接助推器。自 1999 年国务院办公厅转发科技部等七部门联合出台的《关于建立风险投资机制的若干意见》开始，我国各有关部门相继出台了一系列支持创业投资发展的政策，涉及外商投资、监督管理、税收优惠、商事制度、国有股转持、引导基金等方面，有效推动了我国创业投资事业的前进。本部分将对近五年来国家层面出台的促进中国创业投资发展的相关文件进行梳理（见表 8-1）。

表 8-1 近五年来中国促进创业投资发展主要政策文件

文件名称	发布时间	发布机构	主要内容（或主要目标）
《全国中小企业股份转让系统有限责任公司管理暂行办法》	2013 年	证监会	进一步完善多层次资本市场建设，有利于创业风险投资机构股权退出
《中小企业发展专项资金管理办法》	2014 年	财政部、工业和信息化部、科技部、商务部	进一步完善科技型中小企业创业投资引导基金管理模式和支持方式
《私募投资基金监督管理暂行办法》	2014 年	证监会	将创投等以私募性质募集资金的投资基金纳入备案监管

① 有效样本数为 1594 份。

续表

文件名称	发布时间	发布机构	主要内容（或主要目标）
《基金从业资格考试管理办法（试行）》	2015 年	证监会	加强基金从业人员资格考试管理工作，完善基金从业资格考试管理流程
《关于推广中关村国家自主创新示范区税收试点有关问题的通知》	2015 年	财政部、国家税务总局	将中关村关于股权奖励个人所得税政策、有限合伙制创业投资企业法人合伙人企业所得税政策等推广到国家自创区
《关于将国家自主创新示范区有关税收试点政策推广到全国范围实施的通知》	2015 年	财政部、国家税务总局	进一步推广国家自主创新示范区关于创业投资的优惠政策
《关于印发〈国家科技成果转化引导基金贷款风险补偿管理暂行办法〉的通知》	2015 年	科技部、财政部	规范国家科技成果转化引导基金贷款风险补偿工作
《国务院关于取消和调整一批行政审批项目等事项的决定》	2015 年	国务院	豁免国有创业投资机构和国有创业投资引导基金国有股转持义务审核
《关于取消豁免国有创业投资机构和国有创业投资引导基金国有股转持义务审批事项后有关管理工作的通知》	2015 年	财政部	《国务院关于取消和调整一批行政审批项目等事项的决定》（国发〔2015〕11 号）要求，对豁免创投机构和引导基金国有股转持义务事项不再进行审批。为加强后续监管，确保该政策顺利实施，并避免对国有股转持政策造成不利影响，从资质条件、办理程序、国有股回拨和监督管理有关事项做了详细规定
《政府投资基金暂行管理办法》	2015 年	财政部	明确政府应当设立投资基金支持创新创业，增加创业投资资本供给
《关于财政资金注资政府投资基金支持产业发展的指导意见》	2015 年	财政部	对创业投资引导基金支持战略性新兴产业等新兴产业及中小企业提出指导意见
《私募投资基金募集行为管理办法》	2016 年	证监会	加强对基金募集行为的规范管理
《国家创新驱动发展战略纲要》	2016 年	中共中央、国务院	对实施创新驱动发展战略、推进新时期创新工作做出顶层设计和系统谋划。鼓励拓展多层次资本市场支持创新功能，积极发展天使投资，壮大创业投资规模
《关于做好国家新兴产业创业投资引导基金参股基金推荐工作的通知》	2016 年	国家发改委、财政部	按照国务院批复的《国家新兴产业创业投资引导基金设立方案》有关要求，为加快推进国家新兴产业创业投资引导基金设立及运行工作，推荐一批国家新兴产业创业投资引导基金参股基金方案
《关于促进创业投资持续健康发展的若干意见》	2016 年	国务院	对创业投资的投资主体、资金来源、政策扶持、法律法规、退出机制、市场环境、双向开放及行业自律与服务等提出指导性意见
《关于完善股权激励和技术入股有关所得税政策的通知》	2016 年	财政部、国家税务总局	调整股权激励和技术入股税收政策，从税率和纳税时点两方面进一步降低股权激励税收负担
《政府出资产业投资基金管理暂行办法》	2016 年	国家发改委	明确政府出资产业投资基金募集和登记管理、投资运作和终止、绩效评价、行业信用建设、监督管理等事宜

续表

文件名称	发布时间	发布机构	主要内容（或主要目标）
《关于创业投资企业和天使投资个人有关税收试点政策的通知》	2017 年	财政部、国家税务总局	从税收试点政策、相关政策条件、管理事项及管理要求、执行时间及试点地区四个方面作了具体说明
《关于建设第二批大众创业万众创新示范基地的实施意见》	2017 年	国务院	从总体目标、政策举措、步骤安排三个方面作了详细说明
《关于推广支持创新相关改革举措的通知》	2017 年	国务院	提出推广改革的主要内容，其中涉及科技金融创新方面 3 项，创新创业政策环境方面 5 项，外籍人才引进方面 2 项，军民融合创新方面 3 项
《私募投资基金管理暂行条例（征求意见稿）》	2017 年	国务院、证监会	对私募基金管理人的登记、私募基金产品的备案等方面进行了规范
《关于规范金融机构资产管理业务的指导意见》	2018 年	中国人民银行、中国银行保险监督管理委员会、中国证券监督管理委员会、国家外汇管理局	统一投资范围、杠杆约束、信息披露等要求；强化金融机构的勤勉尽责和信息披露义务；明确资产管理业务不得承诺保本保收益，打破刚性兑付；严格非标准化债权类资产投资要求；分类统一负债和分级杠杆要求；加强监管协调，强化宏观审慎管理和功能监管

2016~2018 年，国家深入实施创新驱动发展战略，加大推动供给侧结构性改革，针对创新创业密集出台了多部系统性、高级别和纲领性的政策文件。

2016 年 9 月 20 日，国务院印发《关于促进创业投资持续健康发展的若干意见》（以下简称《意见》），从投资主体、资金来源、政策扶持、法律法规、退出机制、市场环境、双向开放及行业自律与服务八个方面提出进一步促进创业投资持续健康发展的指导性意见；《意见》是迄今为止针对创业投资发展的最为全面系统的纲领性文件，是创业投资领域的顶层设计和新里程碑。《意见》的出台为我国创业投资行业健康发展和制定具体政策提供了基本遵循，为进一步扩大创业投资规模，促进创业投资企业做大、做强、做优提供了坚实的制度保障。

为进一步鼓励和支持创业投资沿着健康的轨道蓬勃发展，2017 年 4 月 19 日，国务院常务会议作出决定，在京津冀、上海、广东、安徽、四川、武汉、西安、沈阳 8 个全面创新改革试验地区和苏州工业园区开展创业投资企业和天使投资个人税收政策试点。4 月 28 日，财政部和国家税务总局根据国务院决定，联合出台了有关创业投资企业与天使投资个人投资种子期、初创期科技型企业（以下简称初创科技型企业）投资抵扣的税收优惠政策，即《关于创业投资企业和天使投资个人有关税收试点政策的通知》（以下简称《通知》）。为了使纳税人更好地理解和把握《通知》中的政策规定，规范各地税务机关政策执行口径，保证相关税收优惠政策精准落地，2017 年 6 月 1 日，国家税务总局发布了《国家税务总局关于创业投资企业和天使投资个人税收试点政策有关问题的公告》。总体而言，上述文件旨在进一步细化 2016 年出台的《意见》中所提到的“按照税收中性、税收公平原则和税制改革方向与要求，统筹研究鼓励创业投资企业和天使投资人投资种子期、初创期等科技型企业的税收支持政策，进一步完善创业投资企业投资抵扣税收优惠政策，研究开展天使投资人个人所得税试点工作”。

2017 年 8 月 30 日，《私募投资基金管理暂行条例（征求意见稿）》（以下简称《私募暂行条例》）出台，由国务院法制办、证监会共同起草，征求意见截止日为 2017 年 9 月 30 日。《私募暂行条例》共十一章五十八条，首次对私募基金概念及投资活动范围、管理人、托管人、资金募集、投资运作、信息提供、行业自律、监督管理、法律责任作出系统性规定，并设专章就创业投资基金做出特别规定。《私募暂行条例》将之前散布于“一法三规五办法三指引”的各项基础性规范统一置于一部法律文件中，使之相互衔接，提纲挈领，自成体系。可以预见，《私募暂行条例》的发布将成为国内私募投资基金行业发展的新纪元。

2018 年 4 月 27 日，《关于规范金融机构资产管理业务的指导意见》正式发布。按照产品类型统一监管标准，从募集方式和投资性质两个维度对资产管理产品进行分类，分别统一投资范围、杠杆约束、信息披露等要求。坚持产品和投资者匹配原则，加强投资者适当性管理，强化金融机构的勤勉尽责和信息披露义务。明确资产管理业务不得承诺保本保收益，打破刚性兑付。严格非标准化债权类资产投资要求，禁止资金池，防范影子银行风险和流动性风险。分类统一负债和分级杠杆要求，消除多层嵌套，抑制通道业务。加强监管协调，强化宏观审慎管理和功能监管。《关于规范金融机构资产管理业务的指导意见》紧扣近年涌现的新问题，在资管行业这一新兴领域及时补充了金融安全的微观机制基础；迈出了以监管协同和宏观审慎监管预防风险的新步伐，避免单独依靠货币政策托底，也反映出我国金融服务实体经济的方向不会动摇。

9 中国创业投资引导基金发展情况

9.1 创业投资引导基金支持创业投资发展概况

近年来，国家推动“大众创业、万众创新”，加快供给侧结构性改革，通过发展引导基金，优化创业投资环境。通过带动社会资本流向创业投资领域，引导基金支持了一大批创业投资机构和优质创业创新项目。

本项调查结果显示，截至 2017 年底，全国创业投资引导基金共计 483 只，增幅 7.8%；累计出资 620.9 亿元，引导带动创业投资机构管理资金规模合计 2913.2 亿元。

2017 年调查结果显示，获得引导基金支持的创业投资机构平均管理资本规模达到 43469.5 万元，比 2016 年的 56358.1 万元减少了 29.65%。未获得引导基金支持的创业投资机构平均管理资本规模为 39302.2 万元，比 2016 年的 60988 万元减少了 35.56%（见图 9–1）[①]。由此可见，无论是否获得引导基金支持，与 2016 年相比，2017 年的创业投资机构平均管理资本规模都有所下降，且引导基金的平均管理资本高于未获得政府引导基金的公司。

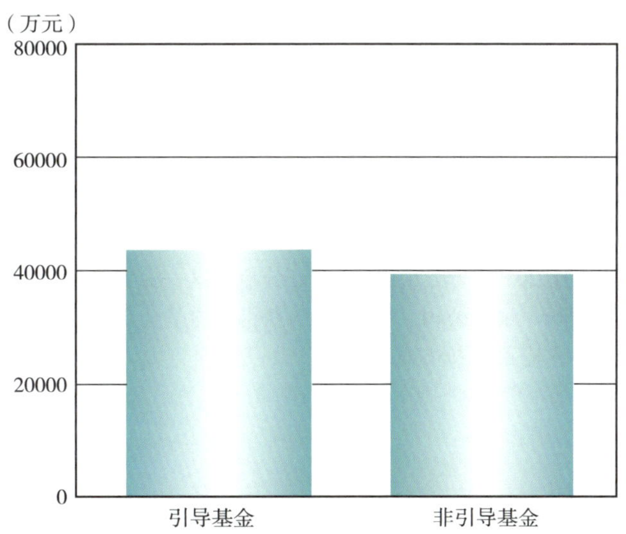

图 9–1 创业投资机构平均管理资本规模比较（2017）

① 有效样本数：获得引导基金支持创投为 386 份、未获得引导基金支持创投为 1341 份。

本章对 2017 年创业投资机构的资金来源进行了分类。

按机构所有制性质进行划分（见图 9–2），2017 年数据显示，在获得引导基金支持的创业投资机构资本构成中，其他类型资本居于首位，占比高达 43.3%，较 2016 年比重出现大幅上涨；其次是民营投资机构的资金支持，占比为 14.7%，较 2016 年的 19.6% 下降了 4.9 个百分点；政府引导基金位列第三位，占比达 11.8%。未获得引导基金支持的创业投资机构资本构成中，民营投资机构占比达到 31.4%，从 2016 年的第三位跃居首位；其次是其他，占比为 22.3%，比 2016 年的 33.1% 下降了 10.8 个百分点。总体来看，不论是否获得引导基金支持，民营投资机构超过政府部门成为当前我国创业投资企业发展的重要推动力量。

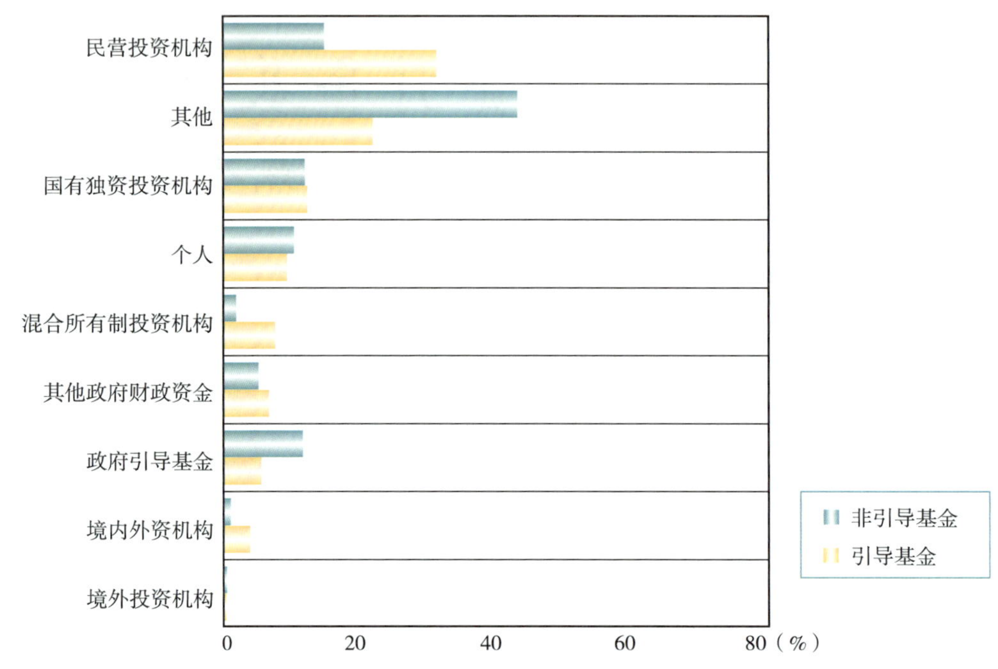

图 9–2　2017 年创业投资机构的资本构成比较（分类一）

按金融资本属性进行划分（见图 9–3），2017 年数据显示，获得引导基金参与的创业投资机构资本构成中，非金融资本居于首位，占比 72.5%，较 2016 年的 79.9% 下降了 7.4 个百分点；其他金融资本占比 20.8%，较 2016 年的 17.6% 增加了 3.2 个百分点，而银行、证券公司、信托公司、保险公司等金融资本占比微乎其微。未获得引导基金参与的创业投资机构资本构成中，非金融资本占比 55.9%，较 2016 年的 68.5% 降低了 12.6 个百分点；其他金融资本占比 30.3%，较 2016 年的 24.1% 上升了 6.2 个百分点。这一分布态势与 2016 年一致，非金融资本更看重获得引导基金支持的创业投资机构。

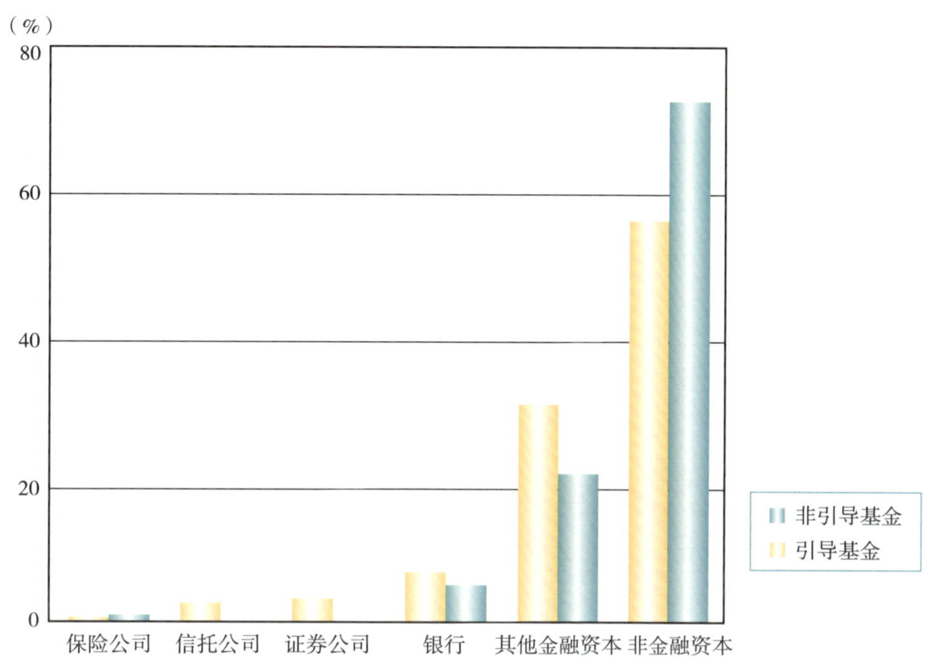

图 9-3 2017 年创业投资机构的资本构成比较（分类二）

9.2 中国创业投资引导基金投资项目的行业分布①

总体来看，本书通过与未获得引导基金支持创业投资机构的投资项目行业分布情况进行对比（见图 9-4）②，结果显示：

2017 年获得引导基金支持的创业投资机构倾向于其他行业、其他制造业、医药保健、生物科技、软件产业、IT 服务业领域，这六个行业合计投资的项目数占比达到 48.1%；未获得引导基金支持的创业投资机构倾向于其他行业、软件产业、科技服务、其他制造业、医药保健、传播与文化娱乐等领域，这六个行业合计投资的项目数占比达到 40.2%。

具体到按照项目的投资金额和投资项目数的分类标准来看，2017 年引导基金支持的创业投资机构的行业分布情况如下：

按照项目的投资金额进行统计（见图 9-5），2017 年，引导基金支持的创业投资机构，其投资资金主要集中在生物科技、医药保健、其他行业、其他制造业、金融保险业，这五个行业合计投资金额占比达到 64.3%。

按照投资项目数进行统计（见图 9-6），2017 年引导基金支持的创业投资机构投资项目主要集中在其他行业、其他制造业、医药保健、生物科技、软件产业等，上述行业集中了当年 42.3% 以上的项目。

总体上看，与投资金额分布相比，获得引导基金支持的创业投资机构在投资项目数量上更加分散。

① 2017 年有效样本数为 727 份，2016 年有效样本数为 710 份，2015 年有效样本数为 1076 份。
② 有效样本数：获得引导基金支持创投为 727 份、未获得引导基金支持创投为 1572 份。

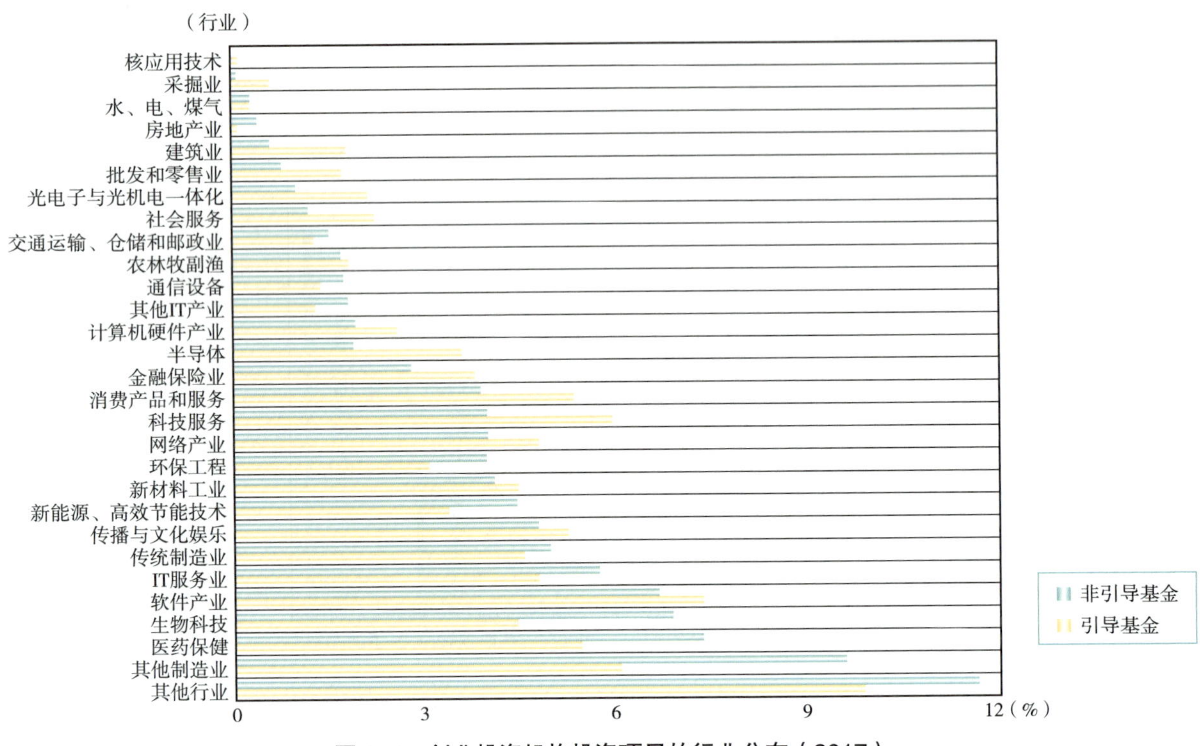

图 9-4　创业投资机构投资项目的行业分布（2017）

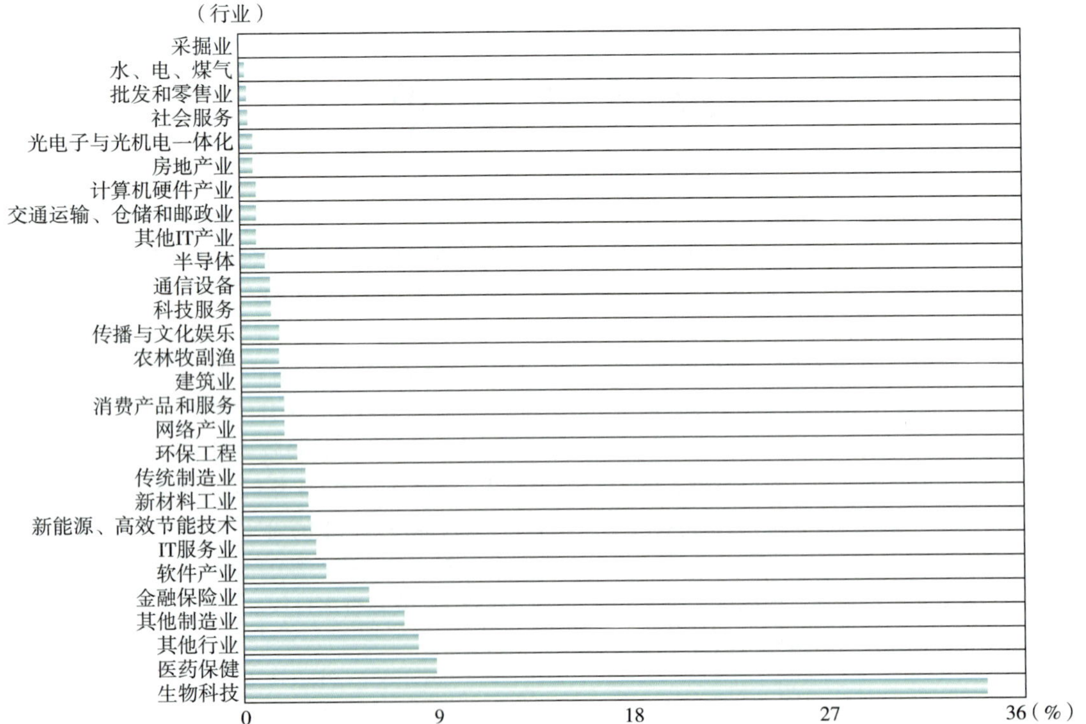

图 9-5　获得引导基金支持创业投资企业投资项目按投资金额的行业分布（2017）

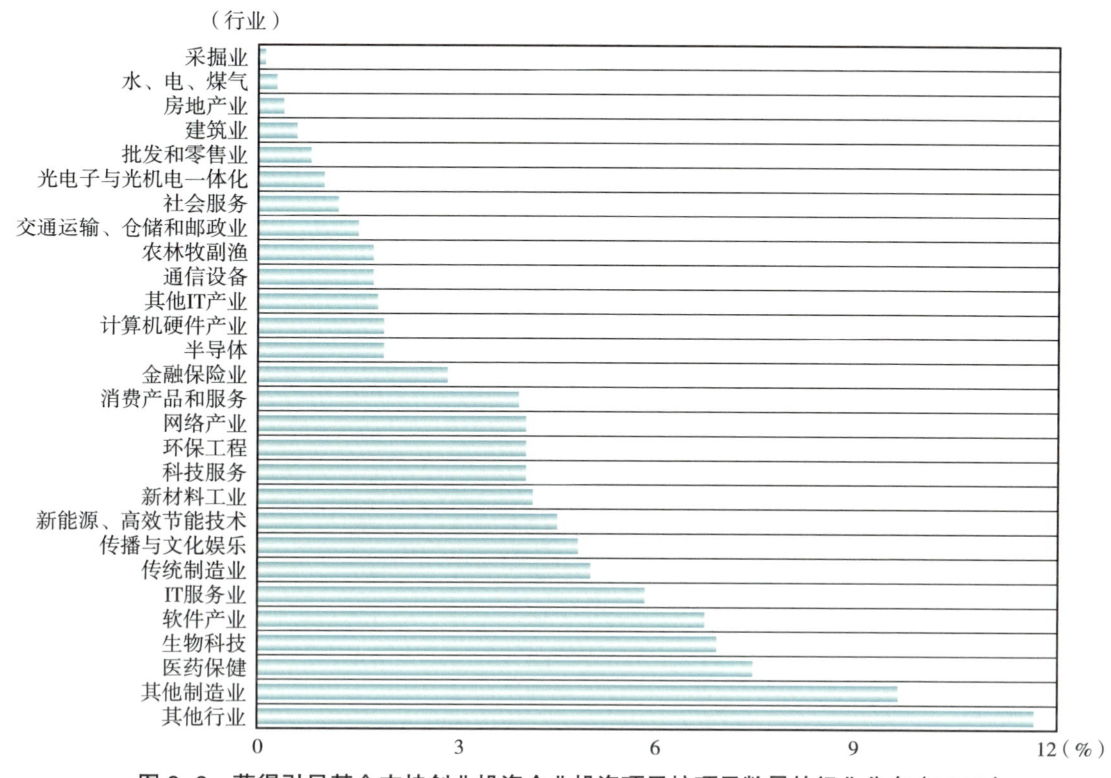

图 9-6　获得引导基金支持创业投资企业投资项目按项目数量的行业分布（2017）

按投资项目的趋势进行统计，表 9-1 列示了 2015~2017 年获得引导基金支持创业投资机构的投资项目行业分布情况。与 2016 年相比，2017 年获得引导基金支持创业投资机构在生物科技、其他制造业、金融保险业投资金额上有了大幅度提升；投向生物科技，其他制造业，新能源、高效节能技术的项目数量明显增加；医药保健、新材料工业、环保工程、网络产业、传播与文化娱乐、科技服务则在投资金额和项目数量上均出现了回落。综合近三年行业变化趋势来看，生物科技的占比大幅上升，医药保健、其他制造业、软件产业始终是热门的投资领域，而传统制造业受关注程度则持续下滑。

表 9-1　获得引导基金支持创业投资企业的投资项目行业分布（2015~2017）①　　单位：%

投资行业	投资金额			投资项目		
	2017 年	2016 年	2015 年	2017 年	2016 年	2015 年
生物科技	34.2	4.4	3.0	6.9	5.6	3.8
医药保健	8.9	8.3	5.2	7.4	8.3	4.6
其他行业	8.0	30.1	9.2	11.7	11.4	9.3
其他制造业	7.4	2.8	5.4	9.6	3.8	5.3
金融保险业	5.8	3.5	5.4	2.8	2.8	3.4
软件产业	3.8	4.2	4.9	6.7	6.5	7.4
IT 服务业	3.4	3.3	3.8	5.8	5.9	6.0

① 行业分类在国家统计局颁布的国民经济行业分类标准（GB/T 4754−2011）基础上适度调整，按照 2017 年投资金额比例由高到低列示。

续表

投资行业	投资金额			投资项目		
	2017 年	2016 年	2015 年	2017 年	2016 年	2015 年
新能源、高效节能技术	3.1	3.1	5.6	4.5	3.8	5.1
新材料工业	3.0	5.4	12.3	4.1	4.8	6.3
传统制造业	2.9	4.5	2.7	5.0	4.9	2.3
环保工程	2.5	4.3	4.6	4.0	4.4	4.5
消费产品和服务	1.9	3.6	9.1	3.9	4.2	3.2
网络产业	1.9	3.6	9.1	4.0	7.6	16.1
建筑业	1.8	0.8	0.2	0.6	0.4	0.2
农林牧副渔	1.7	0.4	1.9	1.7	1.3	1.0
传播与文化娱乐	1.7	6.5	4.2	4.8	6.9	4.7
科技服务	1.4	3.1	2.4	4.0	5.6	3.5
通信设备	1.3	1.9	3.0	1.7	3.0	2.3
半导体	1.1	0.5	1.3	1.9	1.0	1.5
交通运输、仓储和邮政业	0.7	0.7	0.3	1.8	1.1	1.0
其他 IT 产业	0.7	0.7	0.3	1.8	1.1	1.0
计算机硬件产业	0.7	2.3	0.5	1.9	1.7	1.0
房地产业	0.6	—	—	0.4	—	—
光电子与光机电一体化	0.6	1.2	1.3	1.0	1.5	1.9
社会服务	0.4	1.2	2.5	1.2	2.0	3.1
批发和零售业	0.3	0.3	0.1	0.8	0.4	0.2
水、电、煤气	0.2	—	—	0.3	—	—
采掘业	0.1	—	—	0.1	—	—

9.3 中国创业投资引导基金投资项目所处阶段①

从投资金额上来看，统计数据显示，与未获得引导基金支持的创业投资机构相比，2017 年获得引导基金支持的创业投资机构更加倾向于投资成长（扩张）期等企业，其投资金额占比达到 59.3%，投资金额占比明显高于未获得引导基金支持的创业投资机构的 40.7%（见图 9–7）。

① 有效样本数：获得引导基金支持创投为 713 份、未获非引导基金支持创投为 1504 份。

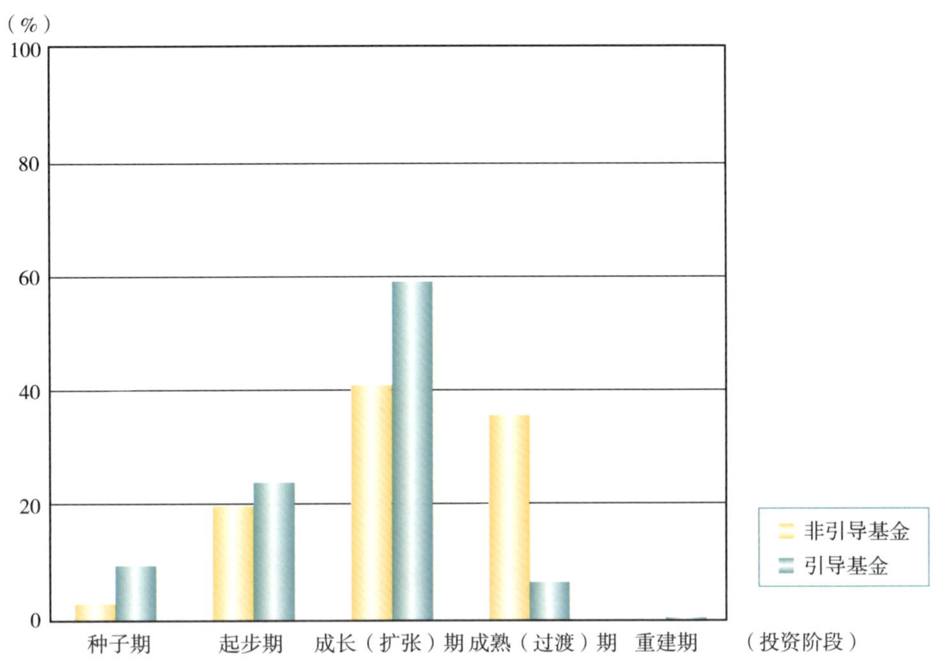

图 9-7 创业投资机构投资项目按投资金额计算的所处阶段分布对比（2017）

2017 年获得引导基金支持创业投资机构的投资项目所处阶段分布情况如表 9-2、图 9-8 所示：2017 年，获得引导基金支持的创业投资机构主要投资处于起步期和成长（扩张）期项目，投资金额分别占 24% 和 59.3%，合计 83.3%；种子期、起步期和成长（扩张）期的投资金额占比分布态势与 2016 年基本一致，其中投资于成长（扩张）期的项目金额占比增加了 21.1 个百分点。种子期和起步期投资项目数量占比分别为 16.4% 和 38.8%，合计 55.2%，与 2016 年相比，二者占比合计小幅增加。这在一定程度上说明，2017 年获得引导基金支持的创业投资机构投资于创业早期的项目单笔金额同比有所增加。

表 9-2 获得引导基金支持创业投资机构的投资项目所处阶段分布（2017） 单位：%

成长阶段	种子期	起步期	成长（扩张）期	成熟（过渡）期	重建期
投资金额	9.7	24.0	59.3	6.6	0.4
投资项目	16.4	38.8	37.3	6.9	0.6

上述统计数据表明：近年来引导基金倾向于投资起步期和成长（扩张）期等投资项目，引导投资资金流向初创企业，支持创业投资机构更多地投资于处于起步阶段的成长空间大、市场前景较好的企业。

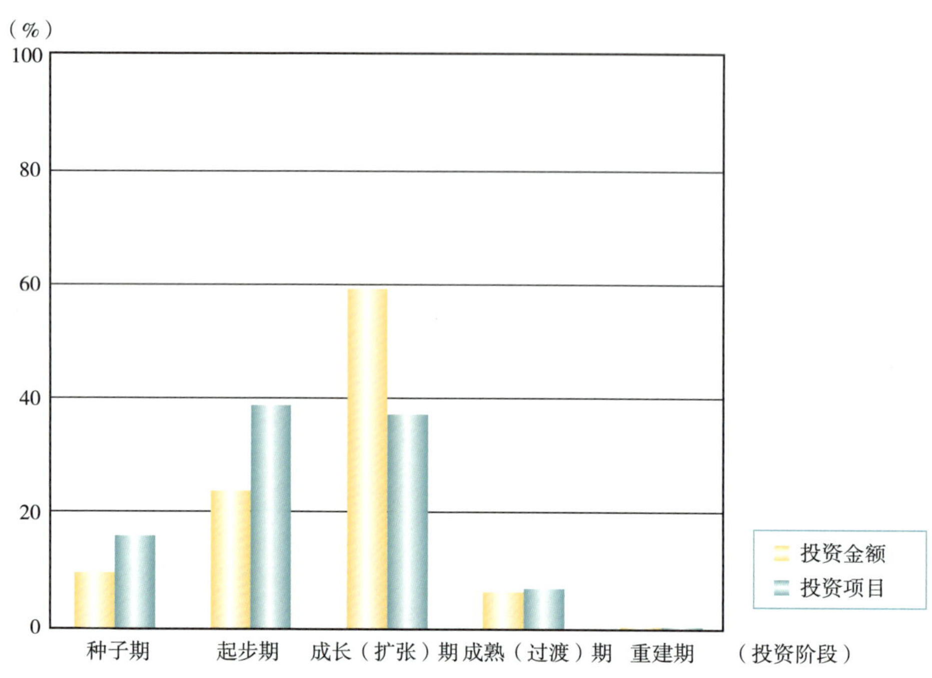

图 9-8 获得引导基金支持创业投资机构的投资项目所处阶段分布（2017）

9.4 中国创业投资引导基金投资项目运作情况

2017 年，获得引导基金支持的创业投资机构在单项投资金额上的分布情况如表 9-3 所示①。数据显示，单笔投资金额在 1000 万元以上的项目所占比重达到 86.3%，较 2016 年有小幅上升。在总体分布态势上，2017 年较 2016 年差异不大。

表 9-3 获得引导基金支持的创业投资机构的单项投资金额（2016~2017） 单位：%

单项投资金额（万元）/ 年份	<100	100~300	300~500	500~1000	1000~2000	>2000
2016	0.3	2.4	4.0	11.1	19.2	63.0
2017	0.2	1.4	3.5	8.6	17.5	68.8

2017 年，获得引导基金支持的创业投资机构与未获得引导基金支持的创业投资机构在投资强度上存在一定差异。相比于获得引导基金支持的创业投资机构，未获得引导基金支持的创业投资机构单项投资金额在 1000 万元以

① 2017 年有效样本数为 762 份，2016 年有效样本数为 794 份。

上的比重更高，达到 92.3%。对于在 500 万 ~1000 万元的单项投资，获得引导基金支持的创业投资机构较未获得引导基金支持的创业投资机构高出 4.3 个百分点。这在一定程度上说明，获得引导基金支持创业投资企业的单项投资金额更小，更倾向于投资前期项目（见图 9–9）。

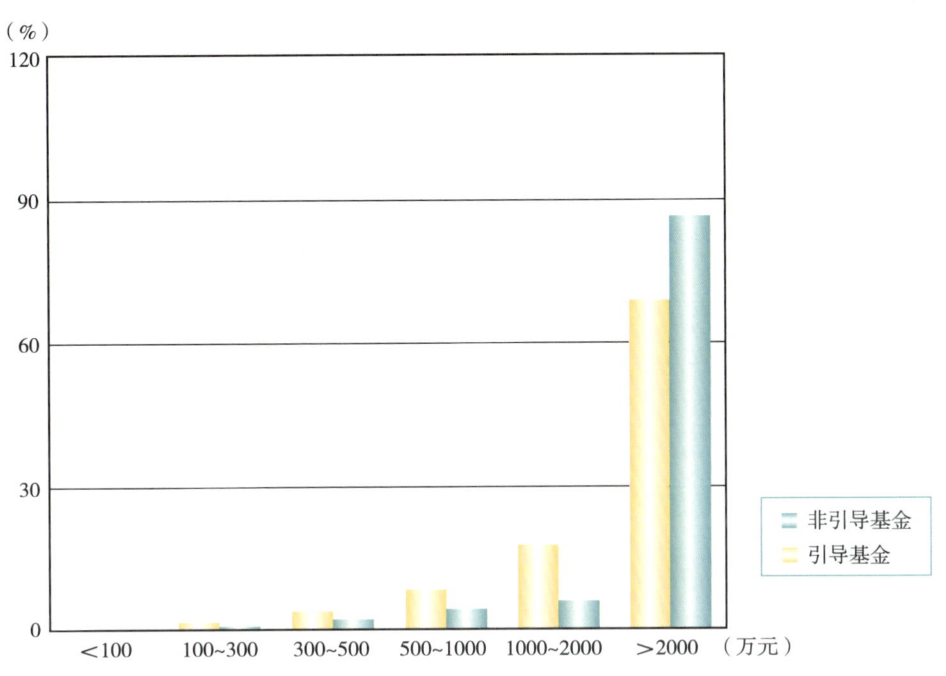

图 9–9　创业投资机构单项投资金额分布比较（2017）

统计数据显示，2017 年获得引导基金支持的创业投资机构共计投资了 298 家高新技术企业，占总投资项目数的 39.1%；未获得引导基金支持的创业投资机构共计投资了 414 家高新技术企业，占总投资项目数的 23.1%。可以看出，获得引导基金支持的创业投资机构更倾向于选择高新技术企业进行投资。与 2016 年相比，获得引导基金支持的创业投资机构投资于高新技术企业的项目数占比和平均投资金额均有所上升（见表 9–4）①。

表 9-4　创业投资机构项目中投资高新技术企业情况（2016~2017）

企业分类	投资高新技术企业数量（家）		投资高新技术企业项目数占比（%）		平均投资金额（万元）	
	2017 年	2016 年	2017 年	2016 年	2017 年	2016 年
非引导基金	414	271	23.1	17	1760.8	1241.4
引导基金	298	198	39.1	24.9	1786.3	1550.4

表 9–5、图 9–10 对比了 2017 年获得引导基金支持创业投资机构和未获得引导基金支持创业投资机构的项目运作状况②。结果显示，获得引导基金支持创业投资机构的投资项目中，境内上市、原股东（创业者）回购、被境内上市公司收购的比例相对较高，未获得引导基金支持的企业投资项目中清算的比例相对较高。同时，不论是否获得引导基金支持，继续运行仍然是 2017 年创业投资机构的主要选择，与 2016 年相比，所占比例有所提高。

① 有效样本数：获得引导基金支持创投为 298 份、未获得引导基金支持创投为 414 份。
② 有效样本数：引导基金为 372 份、非引导基金 1199 份。

表 9-5 创业投资机构项目运作状况（2017）

单位：%

运作情况	继续运行	境内上市	原股东（创业者）回购	被境内上市公司收购	管理层收购	清算	被境外机构收购	境外上市
引导基金	76.8	7.3	7.0	4.6	1.9	1.7	0.5	0.1
非引导基金	74	6.9	7.4	5.6	1.2	4.2	0.2	0.3

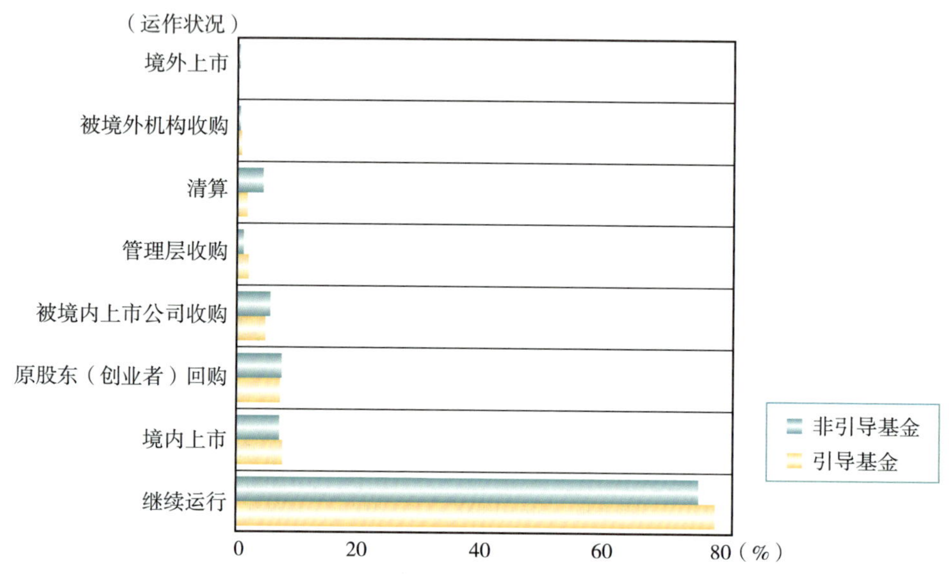

图 9-10 创业投资项目运作状况（2017）

从总体上看（见图 9-11[①]），无论是否获得引导基金支持，影响创业投资机构投资决策的因素中，市场前景、管理团队、技术因素、财务状况、盈利模式的占比相对较高，没有明显差异。

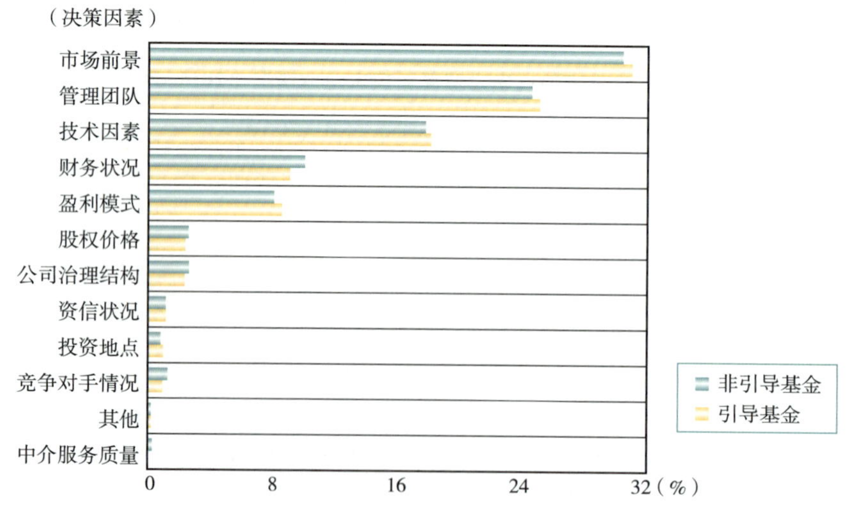

图 9-11 影响有引导基金参与的创投企业投资与无引导基金参与的机构投资决策的因素

① 有效样本数：引导基金为 375 份、非引导基金为 1260 份。

附录 1　2017 年美国创业投资综述

一、总体概括

2017 年，美国创业投资 (VC) 行业活跃的创投企业与管理资产额持续增长。数据显示，截至 2017 年底，美国有 970 家创业投资管理机构，管理着 1722 家创投基金，管理资本 3590 亿美元。

美国产业的发展与创业需求的增加，导致了美国创投行业连续四年的投资额超过 700 亿美元。在 2015 年投资达到高峰后，2016 年投资趋于往年水平，但 2017 年再次加速，达到了至网络时代以来的最高水平。然而，投资金额的增加主要缘于独角兽公司获得了大量的投资——这掩盖了创投企业减少的趋势。

募资和退出对美国创投生态系统的健康发展也具有重要的影响。2017 年，创投募集的资金来源依然强劲，连续四年超过 300 亿美元。尽管 2017 年由于独角兽企业的退出创下历史新高，但退出企业数量相对减少的趋势对于行业的投资生命周期而言仍具有非常重要的影响。

2017 年，加利福尼亚州、马萨诸塞州和纽约州的创投管理资本合计占全美总额的 83.6 %，高于 2016 年的 82.8 %。截至 2017 年底，22 个州的创投管理资本额达到或超过 10 亿美元。两极分化效应加剧，管理资本在 10 亿美元以上的企业数从 2016 年的 68 家增加到 2017 年的 83 家。与此同时，管理资本在 2500 万美元以下的企业数从 2016 年的 241 家增加到 2017 年的 427 家，占总量的 1/3 以上。

二、行业资源

2017 年，美国创投实现了持续四年的全面增长。截至 2017 年底，共有 970 家创投企业管理着 1722 只创投基金，管理资金规模约为 3590 亿美元。尽管募资与 2016 年相比，下降了约 18 %。但自 2014 年以来，募资一直保持着强劲的增长态势，规模均超过 300 亿美元；这使得该行业的平均管理资本额保持了自 2007 年以来年均 4% 的增长速度（见附表 1–1）。

附表 1–1　美国创业投资（VC）总体情况统计

指标	2005 年	2011 年	2017 年
现存 VC 企业数量（家）	912	814	970
现存 VC 基金数量（只）	1651	1303	1722
首次募集 VC 基金数量（只）	50	18	36
当年募集资金 VC 基金数量（只）	168	147	214
当年募集的资本额（十亿美元）	23.5	25.3	32.8
VC 管理资本金额（十亿美元）	177.5	266.5	192.5
平均 VC 管理资本额（百万美元）	127.8	235.5	192.7
截至目前 VC 基金平均规模（百万美元）	119.1	134.8	135.9
当年新增 VC 基金平均规模（百万美元）	147.0	185.9	154.7
VC 管理机构管理资金规模中位值（百万美元）	180.0	200.9	126.6
截至目前 VC 基金规模中位值（百万美元）	52.0	55.0	50.0
当年 VC 基金规模中位值（百万美元）	63.0	46.0	60.1
截至目前最大 VC 基金募集额（百万美元）	2322.0	3000.0	3300.0

从全球范围来看，美国的创投规模一直在全球占据主导地位，但近年来的比重有所下滑。2017 年，美国创业投资额在全球的占比为 54%，自 2004 年以来下滑了 20 个百分点（见附表 1-2、附表 1-3、附表 1-4）。

附表 1-2 美国创投募资在全球的占比情况（2004~2017）

指标 年份	全球募资资金（十亿美元）	美国募资资金（十亿美元）	全球募资项目（项）	美国募资项目（项）	美国募资资金占全球比重（%）	美国募资项目数占全球比重（%）
2004	22.88	17.50	235	157	76	67
2005	32.46	23.52	282	168	72	60
2006	48.11	34.78	396	190	72	48
2007	54.89	35.03	400	183	64	46
2008	50.99	30.05	428	185	59	43
2009	22.52	12.02	325	119	53	37
2010	38.07	20.06	373	154	53	41
2011	46.12	25.29	415	147	55	35
2012	38.20	23.73	400	186	62	47
2013	31.61	20.78	358	201	66	56
2014	48.56	35.35	434	276	73	64
2015	56.60	35.17	424	261	62	62
2016	65.32	40.16	436	283	61	65
2017	49.84	32.79	324	214	66	66

附表 1-3 美国创投交易量在全球的占比情况（2005~2017）

指标 年份	全球交易值（十亿美元）	美国交易值（十亿美元）	全球交易数（项）	美国交易数（项）	美国占全球交易值的百分比（%）	美国占全球交易数的百分比（%）
2005	29.18	23.55	4052	2949	81	73
2006	36.42	29.4	4824	3314	81	69
2007	46.08	35.64	6308	4292	77	68
2008	49.1	36.94	6966	4693	75	67
2009	35.08	26.7	6679	4438	76	66
2010	46.4	31.67	8509	5357	68	63
2011	63.52	43.97	10870	6711	69	62
2012	59.78	41.27	12970	7842	69	60
2013	66.24	45.31	15786	9176	68	58
2014	110	69.89	18505	10420	64	56
2015	143.37	79.73	19191	10468	56	55
2016	137.49	72.37	16324	8665	53	53
2017	157.91	84.97	13890	8295	54	60

附表 1–4　美国创投退出在全球的占比情况（2005~2017）

指标 / 年份	全球退出值（十亿美元）	美国退出值（十亿美元）	全球退出数（项）	美国退出数（项）	美国占全球退出值的百分比（%）	美国占全球退出数的百分比（%）
2005	28.84	18.33	703	443	64	63
2006	34.87	24.18	860	529	69	62
2007	60.47	41.62	1053	622	69	59
2008	24.09	16.45	810	485	68	60
2009	24.9	15.7	769	479	63	62
2010	47.07	31.61	1162	697	67	60
2011	51.34	34.42	1224	739	67	60
2012	64.84	55.53	1384	865	86	63
2013	62.79	37.21	1504	890	59	59
2014	114.74	80.35	1878	1065	70	57
2015	79.22	49.58	1830	1002	63	55
2016	84.26	52.94	1599	865	63	54
2017	79.35	55.49	1446	809	70	56

三、资金募集

2017 年，美国创投募资情况并不比 2016 年的情况更好，在募集资金的金额与募集基金的数量方面，分别下滑了 18%、24%。然而，考虑到创投行业的属性，这种下滑并不令人意外。尽管如此，2017 年仍有 214 家创投基金获得了 328 亿美元融资，这是连续第四年募集资金总额超过 300 亿美元，使得自 2014 年以来的募资总金额达到了 430 亿美元。此外，2017 年首次进行融资的基金共 36 只，融资额达到了 34 亿美元（见附图 1–1）。

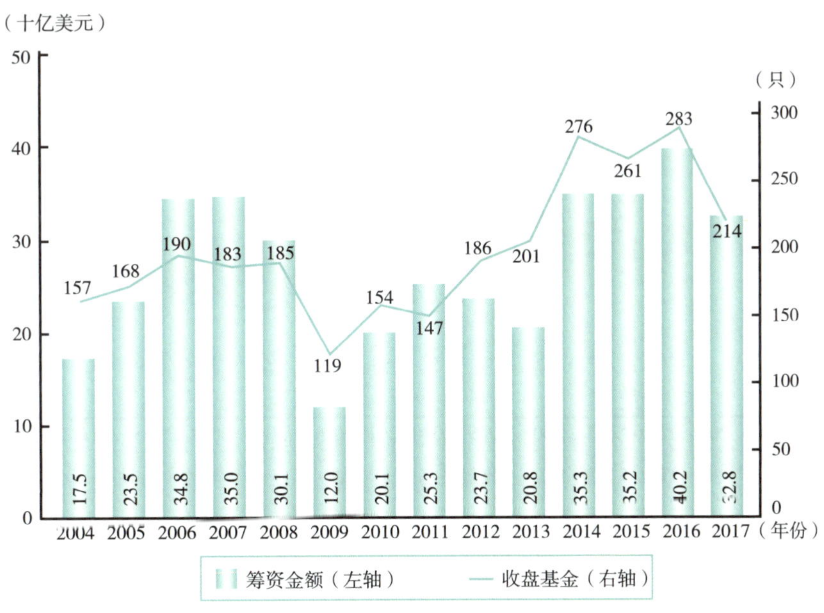

附图 1–1　美国创业投资基金募集情况（2004~2017）

2016 年的募资大幅上涨主要源于一些大的基金，特别是有 7 只基金的募资规模超过了 10 亿美元。相比之下，2017 年仅有 3 只新募基金规模超过 10 亿美元，包括恩颐投资公司的第 16 期基金，该基金融资规模 33 亿美元，是迄今为止募资最高的创投基金（见附表 1–5）。

附表 1–5　2017 年美国募集的十大创投基金

投资者	基金名称	基金规模（百万美元）	募资完成日	基金所在州
恩颐投资公司	恩颐投资公司 16 号基金	3300.00	2017–06–19	加利福尼亚州
TPG 增长基金	增长基金	2000.00	2017–10–04	哥伦比亚特区
IVP	机构风险合伙公司 XVI 号基金	1500.00	2017–09–26	加利福尼亚州
克拉斯企业	克拉斯企业Ⅳ号基金	910.00	2017–07–18	马萨诸塞州
迈特里资本管理公司	迈特里Ⅱ号基金	850.00	2017–01–19	加利福尼亚州
迦南创投	迦南 XI 号基金	800.00	2017–07–25	加利福尼亚州
顶峰投资	顶峰投资Ⅳ号风险基金	730.00	2017–04–04	马萨诸塞州
旗舰先锋	旗舰先锋Ⅵ号基金	618.00	2017–12–20	马萨诸塞州
星火投资	星火投资Ⅱ号增长基金	612.85	2017–03–15	马萨诸塞州
Oak HC/FT	Oak HC/FT 创投Ⅱ基金	600.00	2017–04–17	康涅狄格州

四、投资活动

2017 年美国风险投资公司的投资活动呈现出两种趋势。一方面，当年投入资金达到 850 亿美元，是自网络时代以来的最好水平。另一方面，被投资公司数量仅为 8031 家，是自 2012 年以来的最低水平，而 2012 年投入的资金额却不到 2017 年的一半（见附图 1–2、附表 1–6）。这主要缘于对独角兽企业的投资（即价值 10 亿美元或以上的企业）提振了 2017 年的总投资额，这些企业吸引了 190 亿美元的投资金额，占总投资的 23 %，但交易企业数量却不足 2016 年的 1 %（见附图 1–3）。

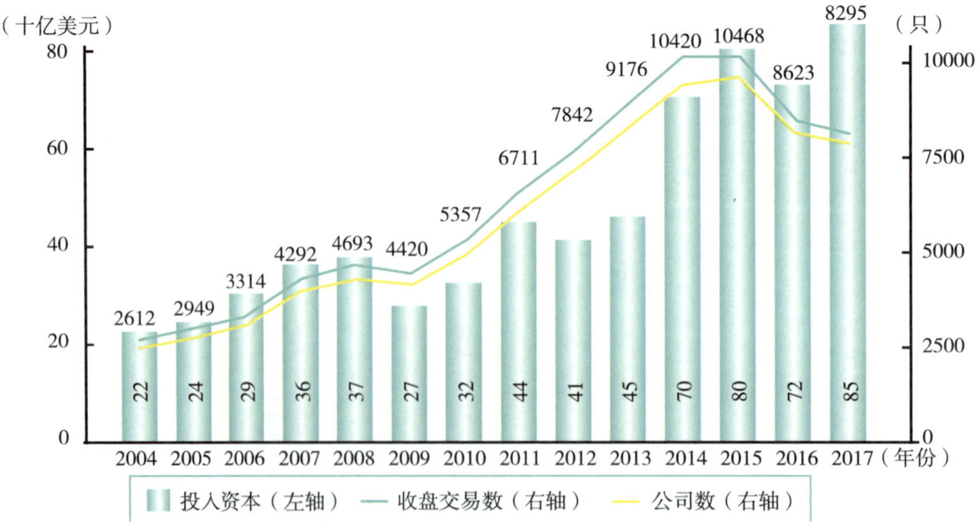

附图 1–2　美国风险投资公司当年投资情况（2004~2016）

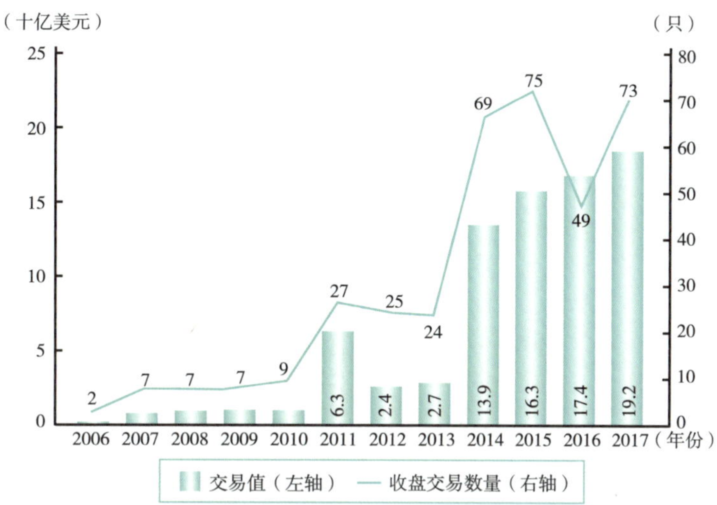

附图 1–3　美国创业投资的独角兽企业情况（2006~2017）

附表 1–6　2017 年美国创业投资的十大交易情况

公司名称	投资时间	交易规模（百万美元）	投资阶段	投资行业	投资地区
WeWork	2017–08–24	3000.00	后期 VC	商业产品和服务（B2B）	纽约
Lyft	2017–12–05	1500.00	后期 VC	信息技术	加利福尼亚州
Grail (Biotechnology)	2017–11–22	1211.66	前期 VC	医疗保健	加利福尼亚州
Airbnb	2017–03–09	1003.31	后期 VC	消费产品和服务（B2C）	加利福尼亚州
Faraday Future	2017–12–22	1000.00	前期 VC	消费产品和服务（B2C）	加利福尼亚州
Intarcia Therapeutics	2017–08–03	615.00	后期 VC	医疗保健	马萨诸塞州
Lyft	2017–05–10	600.00	后期 VC	信息技术	加利福尼亚州
Planet	2017–10–27	575.00	后期 VC	商业产品和服务（B2B）	加利福尼亚州
Compass	2017–12–07	550.00	后期 VC	消费产品和服务（B2C）	纽约州
Outcome Health	2017–06–06	509.88	后期 VC	医疗保健	伊利诺伊州

（一）投资行业

2017 年，软件行业吸引了最多的创投资金，共 3154 项投资项目，吸引了 300 亿美元的资金，行业交易数量与投资金额分别占总量的 38%、35 %。例如，按需打车软件平台“Lyft”吸引了年度最大的投资额，软件行业内排名前两位的投资共计 210 万美元。其他大的项目包括，5 亿美元投资于电子商务平台 Wish，4.13 亿美元投资于交付 APP Instacart，4 亿美元投资于 VR 游戏开发者 Unity 等。

此外，生命科学公司引起了投资者很大的关注，并成为主流趋势。在 Pharma & Biotech 的带领下，1071 家生命科学公司吸引了 180 亿美元的创投资金，创下 14 年来的新高，占投资总额的 21 %，完成交易总额的 14 %。事实上，2017 年有两家生命科学公司——癌症筛查公司 Grail 和药物治疗公司 Intarcia Therapeutics，其投资额进入年度前六名。主要投资行业分类如附表 1–7 所示。

附表 1-7 按行业分类统计的投资状况（2016~2017） 单位：十亿美元

行业分类	2016 年	2017 年
软件	32.98	30.16
制药与生物技术	7.79	12.93
医疗设备和用品	3.86	4.85
商业服务	3.46	4.55
医疗服务和系统	3.32	3.97
IT 硬件	2.52	2.71
消费品与娱乐	2.13	2.77
媒体	1.42	1.62
能源	1.35	1.09
其他行业	10.27	20.34

（二）投资阶段

2017 年创业投资交易数量与金额整体下滑主要缘于天使 / 种子阶段的投资项目数减少到了近 3900 笔（仅占上年的 47 %），这是自 2012 年以来的最低水平。对天使 / 种子阶段的投资放缓始于 2016 年，并持续到 2017 年，恢复到 2014 年以前的常态（见附表 1-8、附图 1-4）。

附表 1-8 美国创业投资的阶段分布（按交易数量）（2005~2017）

阶段＼年份	2005	2006	2007	2008	2009	2010	2011	2012	2013	2014	2015	2016	2017
天使 / 种子期	317	451	766	903	1200	1704	2579	3511	4598	5430	5679	4372	3898
早期	1585	1750	2120	2254	1829	2090	2434	2584	2730	3025	2937	2673	2734
后期	1047	1113	1406	1536	1409	1563	1698	1747	1848	1965	1852	1620	1663

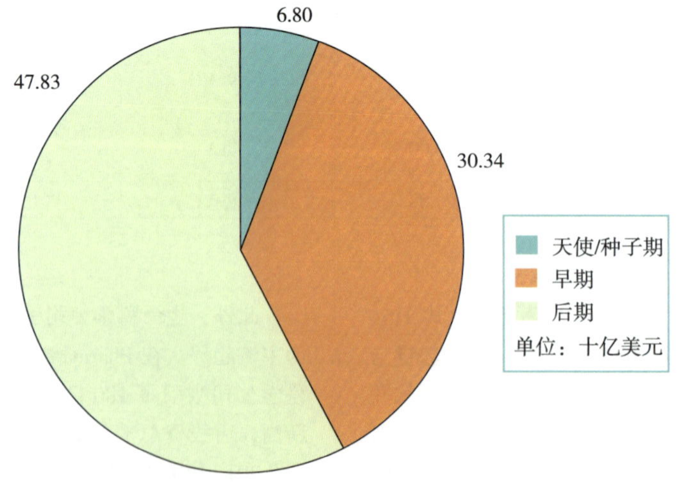

附图 1-4 2017 年美国创业投资的阶段分布（按交易金额）

（三）投资轮次

2017 年，创业投资项目首轮融资企业数继续下降到 2425 家公司，这是 2011 年以来最少的，投资金额为 78 亿美元（见附图 1-5、附图 1-6）。就获得首轮投资的项目数而言，各个投资行业均出现下滑；然而，从获得的资金量而言，生命科学行业的投资再次成为亮点。2017 年，218 家生命科学公司获得了首轮融资，共吸引了 22 亿美元资金，较 2016 年增长了 36 %，创下了 14 年新高。

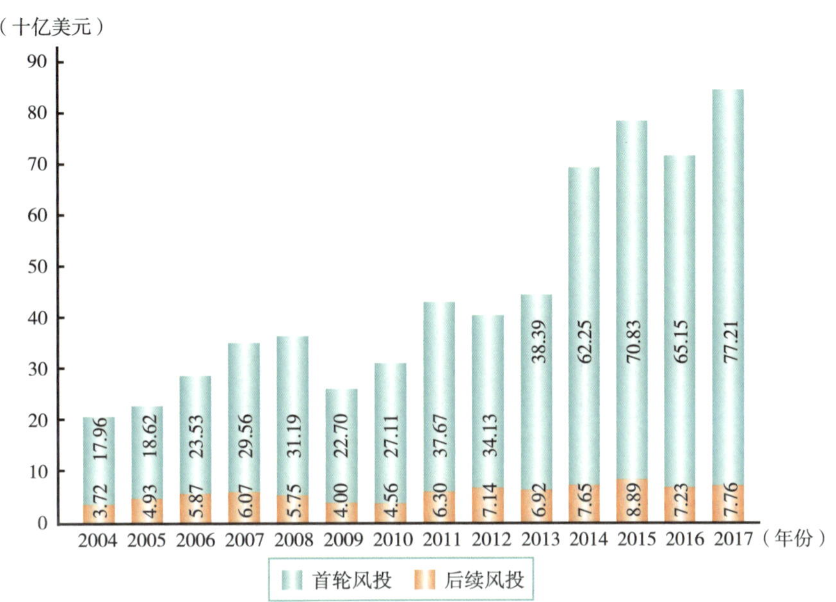

附图 1-5 美国创业投资的首轮投资与后续投资（2004~2017）（按交易金额）

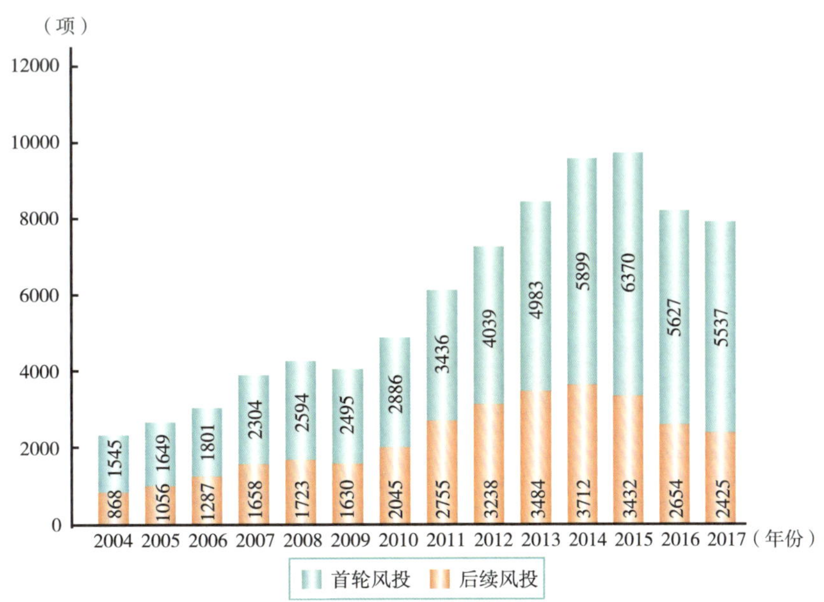

附图 1-6 美国创业投资的首轮投资与后续投资（2004~2017）（按交易数量）

（四）投资地区

2017 年，美国创业投资地区覆盖了全美 50 个州和哥伦比亚特区、213 个都市统计区域和 366 个国会选区。加利福尼亚州、马萨诸塞州和纽约州的投资规模继续占据主导地位，投资总额与项目数合计分别占比 76%、53%，均比 2016 年略有下降。2017 年交易数量同比大幅增加的州主要包括：怀俄明州、新墨西哥州、爱荷华州、康涅狄格州、堪萨斯州、阿肯色州、北卡罗来纳州和科罗拉多州（见附表 1–9）。

附表 1–9 主要地区投资情况（2017）

地区	机构数（家）	投资项目数（笔）	投资额（百万美元）
加利福尼亚州	2749	2843	43360.69
纽约州	925	958	12265.25
马萨诸塞州	555	573	8972.81
伊利诺伊州	218	228	1948.13
得克萨斯州	396	399	1811.04
华盛顿州	314	330	1762.18
佛罗里达州	226	229	1515.31
科罗拉多州	276	285	1220.47
格鲁吉亚州	126	127	1197.11
犹他州	106	112	1050.24

（五）企业创投（CVC）

2017 年，参与创投的企业继续增长。全年共有 1355 笔创投交易涉及企业参与，连续 5 年参与的交易数超过 1000 笔。2017 年，企业创投的交易占比增加到 16 %。在这 1355 笔交易中，至少有一家企业投资者参与的交易总额达到了 390 亿美元，创下了 14 年来的新高。其中，最活跃的企业创投集团包括：GV、英特尔资本、Salesforce 创投、康卡斯特创投、高通创投、微软创投和 Bloomberg Beta，它们都参与了 20 多项投资交易（见附表 1–10）。

附表 1–10 企业创业投资情况（2017）

指标 \ 年份	2011	2012	2013	2014	2015	2016	2017
所有 VC 交易总数（笔）	6741	7871	2013	10485	10547	8737	8376
有 CVC 参与的交易总数（笔）	732	854	1082	1334	1447	1324	1355
有 CVC 参与的交易数占比（%）	11	11	12	13	14	15	16
平均交易值（VC，百万美元）	7.5	6	5.8	7.8	8.8	9.6	11.2
平均交易值（CVC，百万美元）	19	15.4	15.2	22.2	27.6	28.6	31
交易值中位数（VC，百万美元）	1.7	1.5	1.5	1.5	1.8	2	2.7
交易值中位数（CVC，百万美元）	8.3	8	6.7	8	10	10	11
平均后期估值（VC，百万美元）	161.8	60.8	59.7	112.8	124.2	134.4	128.3
平均后期估值（CVC，百万美元）	157	114.3	120.2	220.3	343.8	278.2	244.9
后期估价中位数（所有 VC，百万美元）	17.5	16.3	16.4	18	19.7	21	24.9
后期估价中位数（CVC，百万美元）	41.6	39.6	40	45.6	54.8	50	50
VC 资本增长（百万美元）	44736.80	41669.20	46723.60	71440.90	81538.60	75036.10	85687.90
CVC 资本增长（百万美元）	13066.70	12111.60	15060.20	27375.40	36588.30	34455.30	38658.20
有 CVC 参与的交易额占比（%）	29	29	32	38	45	46	45

五、投资退出

一旦成功的初创企业发展成熟，创投通常会通过首次公开募股（IPO）或出售给其他企业（通过收购、合并或交易出售）或金融买家（如私募股权买家），退出它们在这些公司中的股份。退出使创投机构获得收益并分配给投资者，为未来的投资筹措资金。2017 年，美国创投退出的基本情况见附图 1-7 所示。

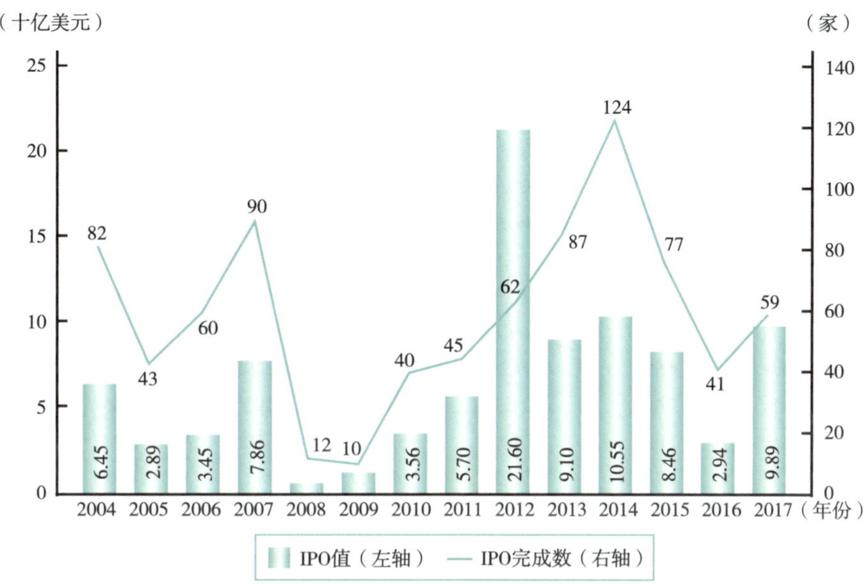

附图 1-7 美国创投支持企业 IPO 情况（2004~2017）

IT 行业在 2017 年的 IPO 企业中占据主导地位，移动相机应用程序开发公司——Snap 持有年度最大的股本。神经退行性疾病治疗开发公司 Denali Treatory 是 IPO 十强中唯一一家生命科学风险公司，但在 2017 年的 IPO 中，生命科学领域仍占据主导地位，共计 29 家企业完成 IPO（见附表 1-11）。

附表 1-11 2017 年美国创投企业投资的 IPO 前十强

公司名称	IPO 筹资额（百万美元）	行业领域	地区
Snap	3400.00	信息技术	加利福尼亚州
Blue Apron	586.50	消费产品和服务	纽约
Switch (Nevada)	531.25	信息技术	内华达
Razer	528.73	信息技术	加利福尼亚州
Roku	252.26	信息技术	加利福尼亚州
Denali Therapeutics	250.00	医疗保健	加利福尼亚州
Cloudera	225.00	信息技术	加利福尼亚州
MuleSoft	221.00	信息技术	加利福尼亚州
MongoDB	192.00	信息技术	纽约
Okta	187.00	信息技术	加利福尼亚州

纵观近十年情况，创投的退出（IPOs 和 M&A）自 2014 年达到顶峰以来一直在下降。尽管 2017 年是以 IPO 同期增长结束的，但许多人预期的复苏从未完全实现。2017 年创投退出的 59 家 IPO 企业在 IPO 前筹集了 95 亿美元的资金，在 IPO 时筹集了 99 亿美元，总价值超过 580 亿美元。从首次 VC 融资到 IPO 的时间由 2016 年的 8.3 年略微缩短到 2017 年的 7.1 年（见附表 1-12）。

附表 1-12 美国创业投资企业的 IPO 价值及特征（2005~2017）

年份	IPO 数量（只）	交易值（百万美元）	交易值中位数（百万美元）	平均交易值（百万美元）	IPO 后价值（百万美元）	IPO 后价值中位数（百万美元）	IPO 后价值平均数（百万美元）	从首次 VC 到退出的时间中位值（年）	从首次 VC 到退出的平均时间（年）
2005	43	2890.7	55.0	74.1	8622.4	200.3	233.0	4.83	4.58
2006	60	3446.2	54.0	62.7	13840.8	219.8	251.7	4.96	5.20
2007	90	7859.9	75.0	94.7	34151.2	331.9	416.5	5.17	5.57
2008	12	626.2	71.4	78.3	2773.4	237.0	396.2	5.59	5.38
2009	10	1255.0	86.6	125.5	4824.2	342.1	536.0	7.32	7.50
2010	40	3564.4	75.0	89.1	15506.4	284.5	387.7	6.56	7.18
2011	45	5704.0	86.7	135.8	43326.7	421.3	1056.7	5.74	6.66
2012	62	21595.9	79.0	372.3	115517.6	360.1	2100.3	7.05	7.43
2013	87	9103.7	75.0	109.7	52757.4	320.7	635.6	6.72	7.26
2014	124	10554.4	65.1	87.2	51932.8	249.4	436.4	6.91	7.04
2015	77	8459.8	76.9	111.3	42803.8	302.5	586.4	6.94	6.51
2016	41	2938.5	70.3	73.5	16113.4	250.0	402.8	8.27	7.57
2017	59	9889.7	77.0	173.5	58303.9	411.2	1100.1	7.08	6.83

美国创业投资企业公开并购交易数自 2014 年以来继续稳步下滑，但在 2017 年实现退出的 809 次交易中占比达到了 93 %，共产生了 456 亿美元的公开退出价值。2017 年，创投首次融资至 IPO 退出的时间中位数缩短，而并购时间则相反，从 2016 年的 4.7 年增加到 2017 年的 5.4 年（见附图 1-8、附表 1-13）。

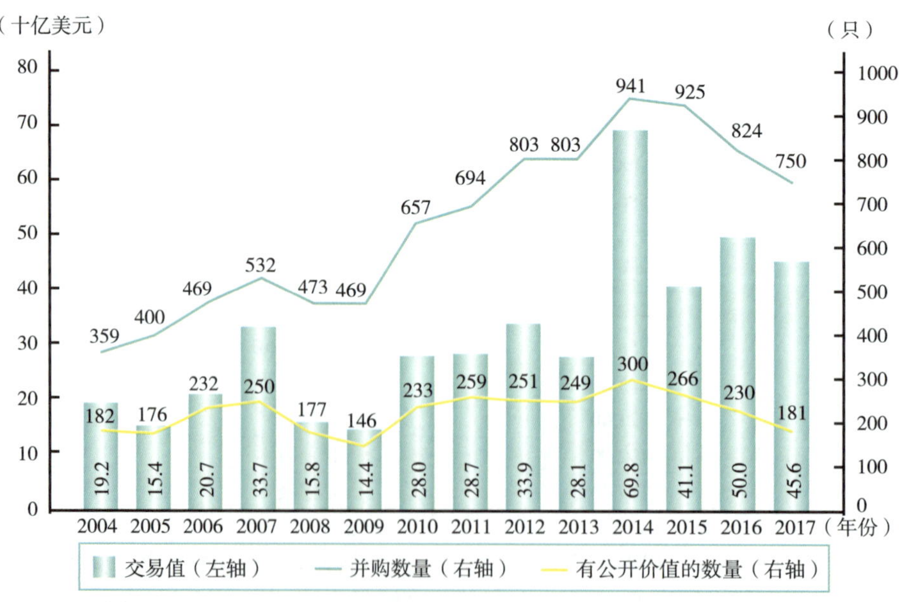

附图 1-8 美国创投支持企业并购（M&A）情况（2004~2017）

附表 1–13 美国创业投资企业并购退出情况及特征（2005~2017）

指标 年份	并购数量（家）	披露并购数（家）	交易值（百万美元）	平均交易值（百万美元）	交易值中位数（百万美元）	从首次投资到退出时间的中位值（年）	从首次投资到退出的平均时间（年）
2005	400	176	15436.5	87.7	40.8	4.74	4.57
2006	469	232	20735.2	89.4	42.3	4.75	4.70
2007	532	250	33760.2	135.0	50.0	4.68	4.86
2008	473	177	15826.5	89.4	36.0	4.79	4.96
2009	469	146	14443.8	98.9	25.0	4.38	4.93
2010	657	233	28040.8	120.3	38.0	4.36	5.03
2011	694	259	28717.1	110.9	49.0	4.25	4.94
2012	803	251	33936.3	135.2	46.0	4.53	5.03
2013	803	249	28105.4	112.9	37.0	3.96	5.07
2014	941	300	69794.7	232.6	50.1	4.51	5.34
2015	925	266	41124.5	154.6	46.3	4.38	5.51
2016	824	230	49997.5	217.4	73.9	4.67	5.86
2017	750	181	45603.5	252.0	91.0	5.39	6.33

2017 年美国创业投资企业中最大的两次并购发生在上半年：商业应用软件提供商 AppDynamics 1 月向 Cisco 出售了 40 亿美元，宠物食品零售商 Chewy 5 月向 PetSmart 出售了 34 亿美元。软件公司继续吸引了最多的并购数量和并购估值，2017 年十大并购交易中占据了四个，然后是生命科学领域（见附表 1–14）。2017 年既是独角兽企业的投资年，也是退出年。全年 21 家独角兽企业完成退出（14 家通过 IPO，7 家通过并购），这是有记录以来年度交易总量最高的一年，交易总额为 220 亿美元。

附表 1–14 2017 年美国创业投资企业并购前十强

公司名称	交易规模（百万美元）	行业领域	地区
AppDynamics	4032.80	信息技术	加利福尼亚州
Chewy	3350.00	消费产品和服务	佛罗里达州
IFM Therapeutics	2320.00	医疗保健	马萨诸塞州
Naurex	1721.70	医疗保健	伊利诺伊州
Bai	1700.00	消费产品和服务	新泽西州
NeoTract	1100.00	医疗保健	加利福尼亚州
Altor BioScience	1080.00	医疗保健	佛罗里达州
Musical.ly	1000.00	信息技术	加利福尼亚州
ServiceMax	915.00	信息技术	加利福尼亚州
Moat	850.00	信息技术	纽约州

资料来源：美国风险投资协会（National Venture Capital Association）提供。

附录 2 2017 年欧洲创业投资回顾

2017 年，欧洲私募股权基金超过 1250 多家，其中，89% 的企业披露了管理资本，达到 6400 亿欧元。总体情况如附图 2–1 所示。

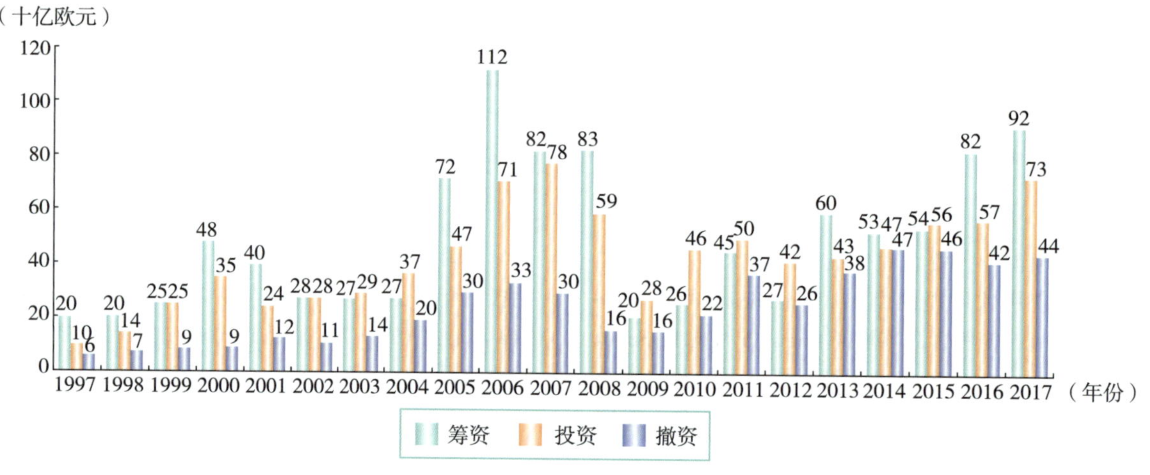

附图 2–1 欧洲私募股权基金总体情况一览（1997~2017）

一、资金募集

2017 年，欧洲整个私募股权投资市场募资总额达到 919 亿欧元，为 2006 年以来的最好水平，同比增长 12%。新增募资基金 542 只，增长 15 %(见附表 2–1、附图 2–2)。按资金来源划分，养老基金占募集资本的 29%，其次是基金（20%）、家庭办公室和个人（15%）、主权财富基金（9%）和保险公司（8%）。欧洲以外的机构投资者的贡献超过 40%，其中，亚洲投资者贡献最大，占 15%（见附图 2–3）。

2017 年，欧洲创投行业募资达到 77 亿欧元，略低于 2016 年的 82 亿欧元。新募基金 50 只，其中 15 只基金的募集资本超过 1 亿欧元，占总额的 80 %。按照资金来源划分，政府机构出资占资金总额的 29 %，其次是家庭办公室和个人 (23 %)、基金和其他资产管理公司的基金 (18 %)，以及公司投资者 (8 %) (见附图 2–3)。

附表 2–1 欧洲私募股权投资市场募资主要特征（2017）

	所有私募股权基金	创投基金	并购基金	成长基金
新募基金额（亿欧元）	919	77	651	68
新募基金数（只）	542	163	119	113

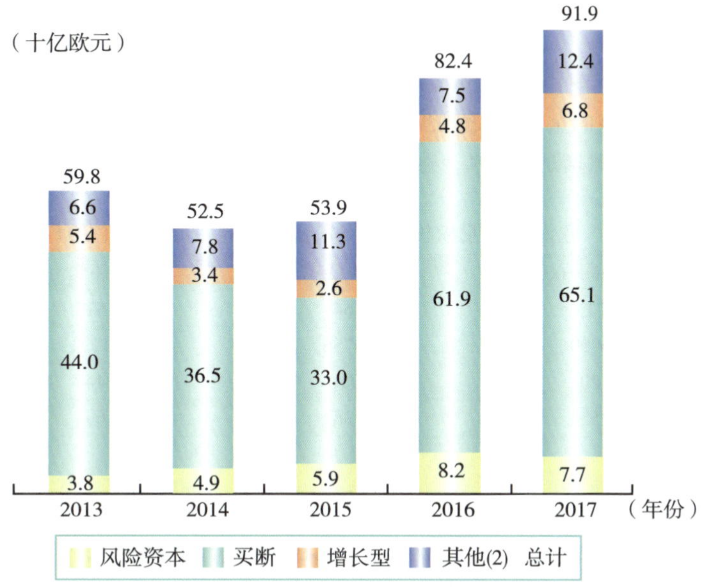

附图 2-2 欧洲私募股权基金募资情况（2013~2017）

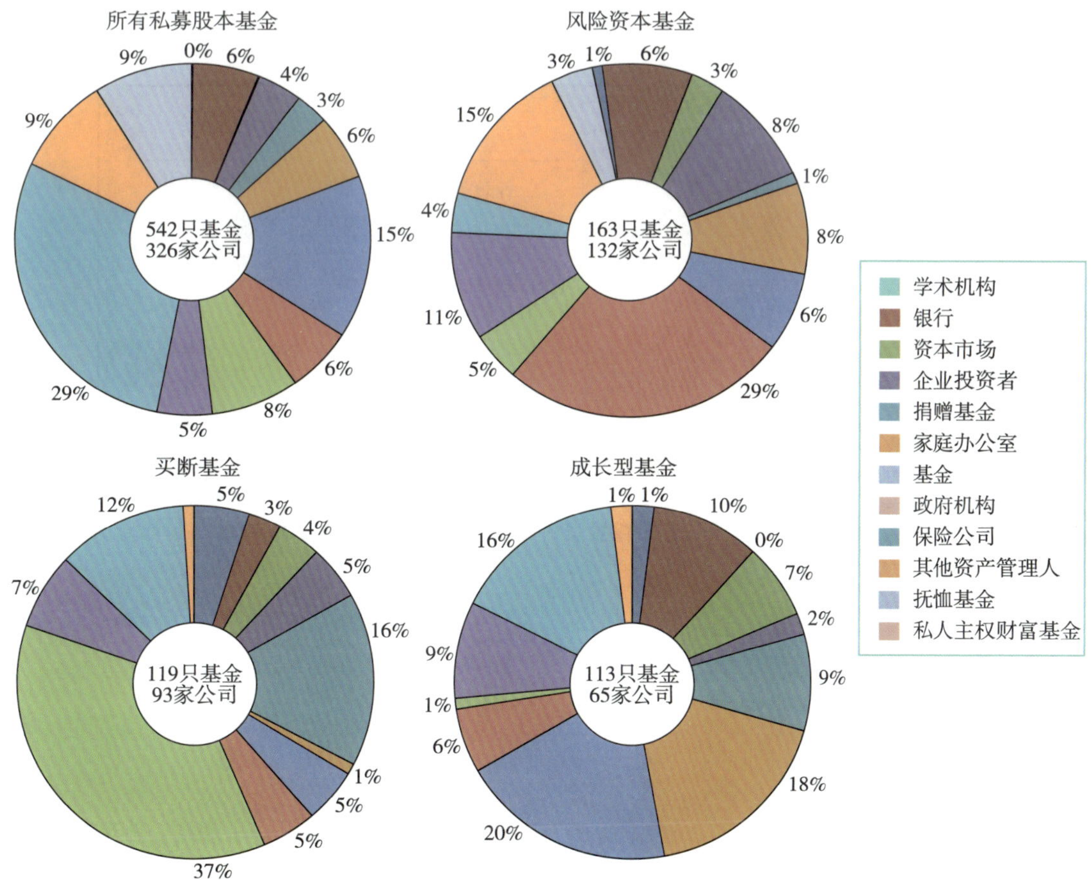

附图 2-3 欧洲私募股权基金募资来源（2017）

二、投资活动

2017 年，欧洲私募股权投资金额同比增长 29%，增至 717 亿欧元，是有记录以来第二高的金额，仅比 2007 年的峰值低 4%。获得投资的公司数量增加了 7 %，达到近 7000 家，其中 87% 是中小企业（见附表 2-2）。

另外，创业投资增长 34 %，达到 64 亿欧元，是十年来的新高，超过 2008 年的 13%。近 3800 家公司获得了创投支持，增长了 8%。

附表 2-2 欧洲私募股权投资市场投资活动的主要特征（2017）

	所有私募股权投资	创投资本	并购	成长资本
投资金额（亿欧元）	717	64	512	115
投资公司数（家）	6999	3756	1171	2107
投资企业数（家）	1204	710	447	465
涉及的基金数（只）	2523	1361	691	1122

长期来看，2000 年至今，整个欧洲私募股权投资市场投资金额占 GDP 的比重为 0.2%~0.6%。2017 年，欧洲股权投资市场投资金额占 GDP 的比重为 0.45%，较 2016 年上升了 0.09 个百分点。其中，创业投资的投资金额占 GDP 的比重为 0.039%，卢森堡创业风险投资占 GDP 的比重排在第一，达到 0.182%（见附图 2-4、附图 2-5）。

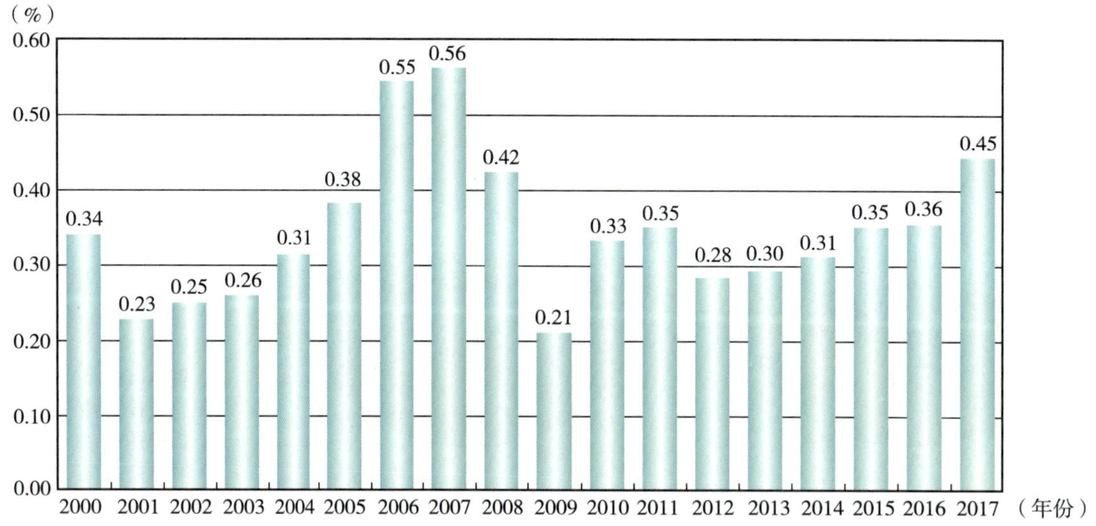

附图 2-4 欧洲私募股权投资占 GDP 的比重（2000~2017）

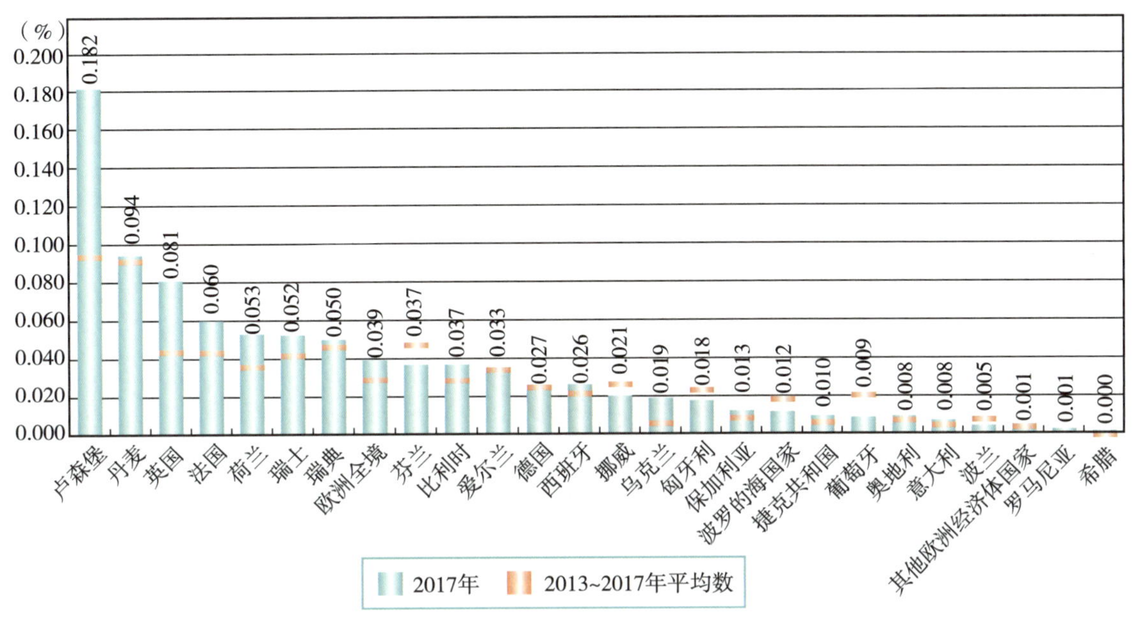

附图 2-5 欧洲主要国家创业投资占 GDP 的比重（2017）

（一）投资阶段

2017 年，欧洲地区创业投资金额共计 64 亿欧元，较 2016 年大幅增长。其中，投资于种子期和起步期的资金增长近 50%，分别达到 6.49 亿欧元和 35 亿欧元；投资于后期阶段的资金增长 17 %，达到 23 亿欧元，是 2008 年以来的最高水平（其投资阶段占比见附图 2-6、附图 2-7）。

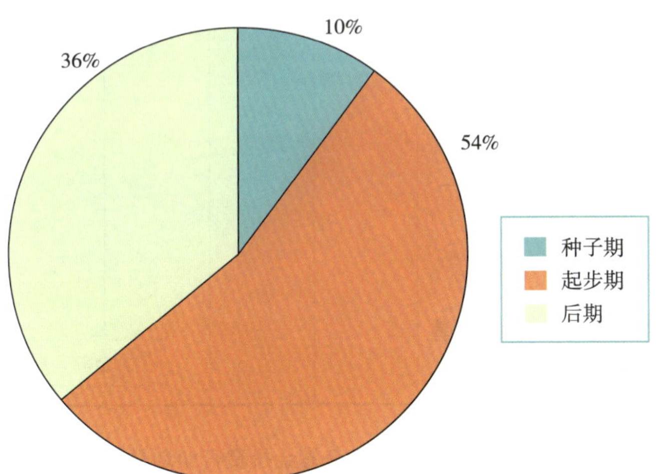

附图 2-6 欧洲创业投资的投资阶段（按投资金额）（2017）

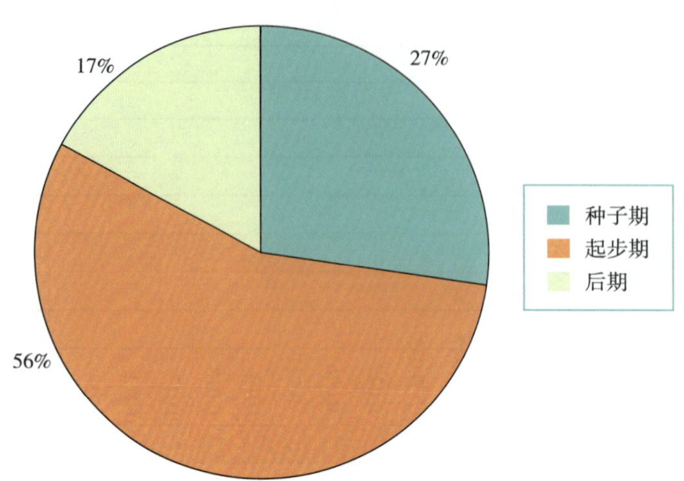

附图 2-7 欧洲创业投资的投资阶段（按投资项目）（2017）

（二）投资行业分布

按行业划分，从整个欧洲私募股权市场来看，消费产品和服务行业是投资最多的领域，投资金额占比 24.4%；其次是商业产品和服务业，投资金额占比 23.5%（见附图 2-8）。

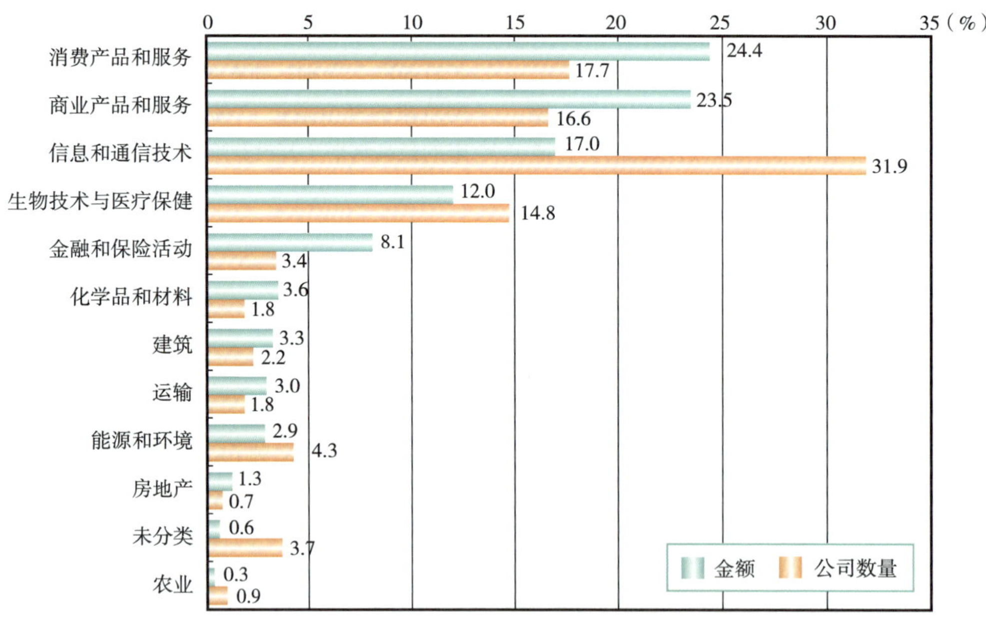

附图 2-8 欧洲私募股权投资基金投资行业划分（2017）

从创业投资的行业来看，主要集中在信息和通信技术领域（资金占比 45%），其次是生物技术和医疗保健（资金占比 23%）以及消费产品和服务（8%）（见附图 2-9、附图 2-10）。

（三）投资轮次

从投资轮次分布来看，2015 年以前，欧洲股权投资市场的首轮投资与后续投资占比大致保持一致。2016年以后，首轮投资占比持续下滑，2017 年，首轮投资占比仅为 26%（见附图 2-11）。

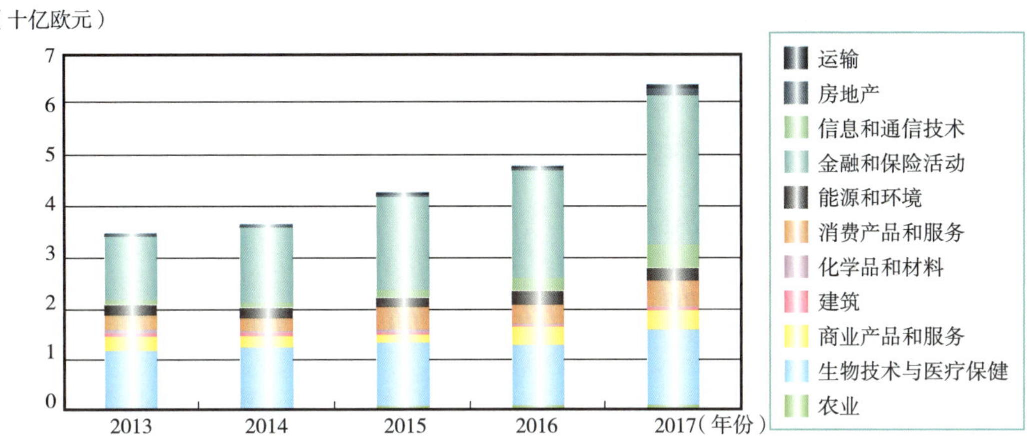

附图 2-9　欧洲创业投资基金投资的行业分布（按投资金额）（2013~2017）

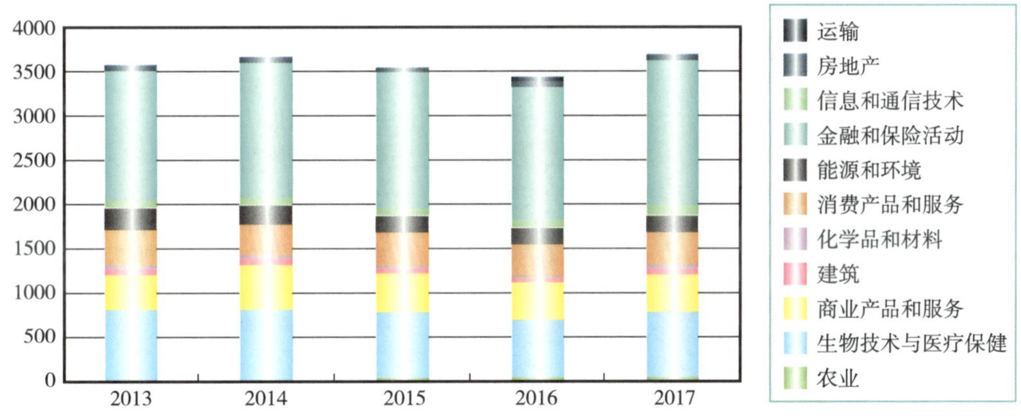

附图 2-10　欧洲创业投资基金投资的行业分布（按投资项目）（2013~2017）

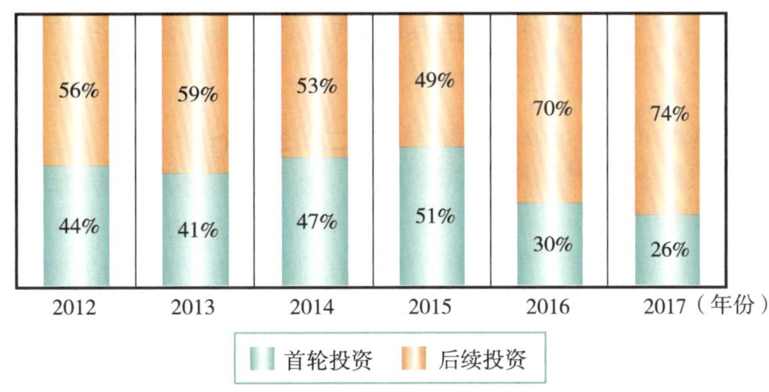

附图 2-11　欧洲股权投资的首轮投资与后续投资（2012~2017）

三、退出活动

2017 年，大约有 3800 家欧洲私募股权投资项目实现退出，与2016年相似。按以往股权投资额(以成本价撤资)计算，总值为 427 亿欧元，同比增长 7 %，是过去十年的第三高水平（见附表 2–3）。

附表 2–3 欧洲私募股权市场退出活动概况（2017）

	所有私募股权	创业投资	并购	成长资本
退出金额（亿欧元）	427	21	326	57
退出项目数量（家）	3752	1159	879	1435
涉及的企业数（家）	751	357	345	299
涉及的基金数量（只）	2018	733	609	784

（一）退出方式

2017 年，欧洲创业投资退出金额达到 21 亿欧元。按退出的金额划分，主要退出方式依次为贸易出售（占比 42%），较 2016 年大幅上升了 15 个百分点；清算（占比 18%）；IPO（占比 13%）；出售给其他 PE 公司（占比 9%）等（见附图 2–12）。

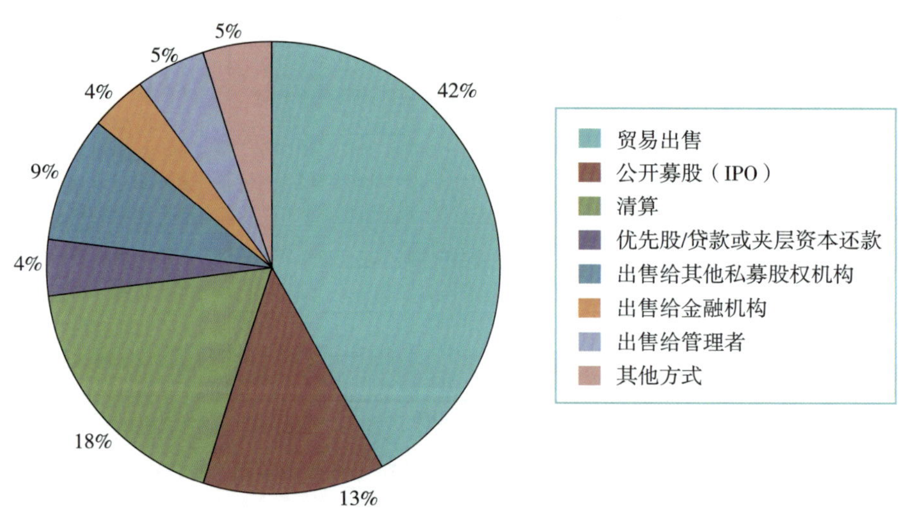

附图 2–12 欧洲创业投资的主要退出方式（按金额划分）（2017）

2017 年，欧洲创业投资实现退出项目 1159 家公司，较 2016 年略有减少。按退出项目划分，主要退出方式依次为优先股还款（占比 31%）、贸易出售（占比 19%）、清算（占比 17%）、出售给管理层（占比 9%）；全年通过 IPO 退出的占比 9%（见附图 2–13）。

（二）退出行业

按照行业划分，2017 年欧洲创投项目退出最多的行业依然是信息和通信技术行业，实现退出金额占比 31%，项目占比 34%。其次是生物技术和医疗保健（资金占比 26%，项目占比 17%）、消费产品和服务（资金占比 21%，项目占比 13%）、商业产品和服务（资金占比 14%，项目占比 22%）、能源和环境（资金占比 5%，项目占比 6%）等（见附图 2–14）。

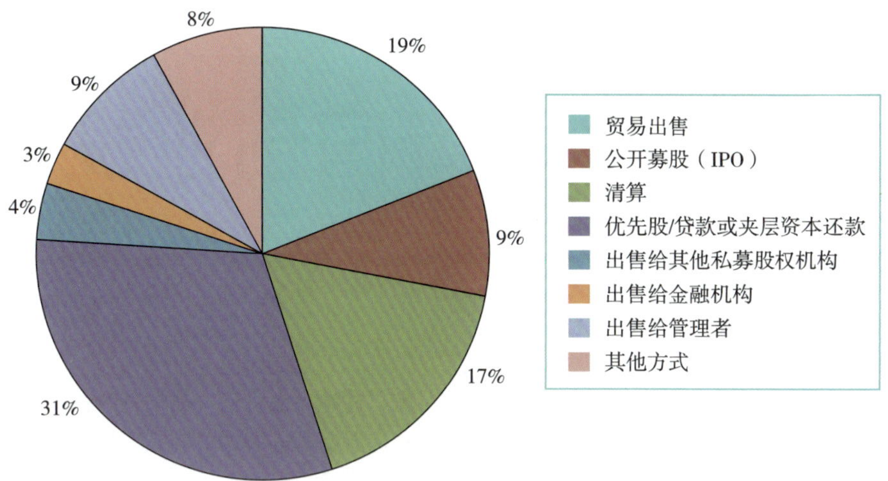

附图 2-13 欧洲创业投资的主要退出方式（按项目划分）（2017）

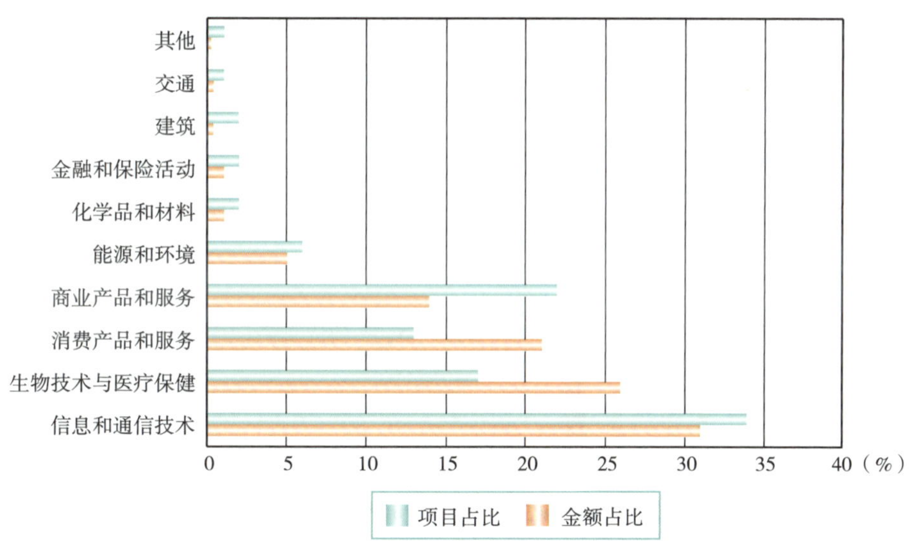

附图 2-14 欧洲创业投资退出项目的行业划分（2017）

资料来源：欧洲风险投资协会（Europe Venture Capital Association）提供。

附录 3　2017 年韩国创业投资回顾

一、韩国创业投资市场概况

2017 年，韩国创业投资稳定发展，新增创投机构 5 家，注销 4 家机构，当年公司存量与 2016 年持平，累计注册资本达 15228 亿韩元（见附表 3-1）。

附表 3-1　韩国创业投资基本情况（2007~2017）

指标＼年份	2007	2008	2009	2010	2011	2012	2013	2014	2015	2016	2017
当年新注册数（注销数）	7（10）	5（9）	12（9）	13（10）	9（7）	6（6）	3（7）	6（4）	14（2）	13（8）	5（4）
当年公司存量（家）	101	97	100	103	105	105	101	103	115	120	120
累计注册资本（十亿韩元）	1555.8	1457.8	1360.8	1383.8	1398.5	1445.5	1394.7	1418.5	1484.3	1502.6	1522.8

截至 2017 年，共有 120 家创业投资企业管理着 718 只基金（见附表 3-1、附表 3-2、附图 3-1），其中当年新注册基金 120 只，与 2016 年新增数量相同；注销基金 51 只，较 2016 年有所上升；创业投资企业累计金额 20141.7 亿韩元。

附表 3-2　韩国创业投资总体情况（2007~2017）

指标＼年份	2007	2008	2009	2010	2011	2012	2013	2014	2015	2016	2017
当年新注册数（只）	67	51	74	66	66	41	54	82	108	120	120
金额（十亿韩元）	1126.9	963.3	1404.3	1574.6	2148.3	906.5	1664.9	2619.5	2634.6	3462.5	4443.0
当年注销数（只）	90	49	54	53	45	46	31	37	26	44	51
金额（十亿韩元）	942.0	416.4	566.2	576.8	454.0	858.6	527.2	832.9	570.9	827.4	1114.3
当年存量（只）	328	328	350	363	384	379	402	447	529	605	718
累计金额（十亿韩元）	5062.4	5611.8	6449.9	7447.7	9142.0	9189.0	10327.6	12114.2	14177.9	16813.0	20141.7

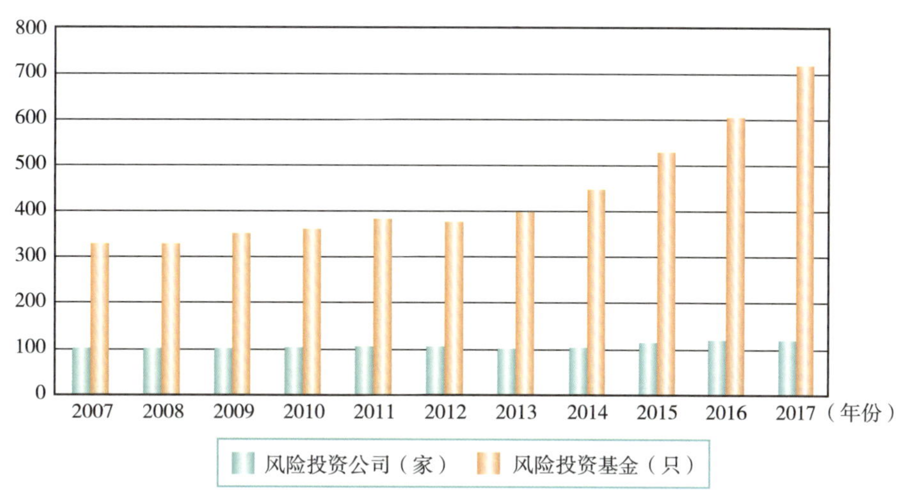

附图 3-1　韩国创业投资市场概况（2007~2017）

二、韩国创业投资活动

2017 年，韩国创业投资企业共投资项目 1266 项，投资金额为 23803 亿韩元，投资强度较 2016 年有所提升，为 1.88 十亿韩元 / 项（见附表 3-3）。

附表 3-3　韩国创业投资项目数及金额（2007~2017）

指标＼年份	2007	2008	2009	2010	2011	2012	2013	2014	2015	2016	2017
新投资项目数（项）	615	991.7	496	560	613	688	755	901	1045	1191	1266
新投资金额数（十亿韩元）	991.7	724.7	867.1	1091.0	1260.8	1233.3	1384.5	1639.3	2085.8	2150.3	2380.3
投资强度（十亿韩元 / 项）	1.61	1.46	1.65	1.95	2.06	1.79	1.83	1.82	1.44	1.81	1.88

三、韩国创业投资行业分布

2017 年，从投资金额看，ICT 服务、零售 / 服务、生物 / 医药分别集中了大量资金，其中生物 / 医药行业投资金额较 2016 年有所下降，投资金额由 2016 年的 4686 亿韩元下降到 3788 亿韩元，零售 / 服务投资金额则较 2016 年上涨了 67.88%。从投资项目看，排名前三的分别是 ICT 服务、图像 / 性能 / 储存和零售 / 服务（见附表 3-4、附图 3-2）。

附表 3-4　韩国创业投资行业分布（2017）

指标＼行业	ICT 制造	ICT 服务	电子 / 机器 / 设备	化工 / 材料	生物 / 医药	图像 / 性能 / 存储	游戏	零售 / 服务	其他	总量
金额（十亿韩元）	156.6	515.9	240.7	127.0	378.8	287.4	126.9	418.7	128.3	2380.3
项目（项）	96	283	121	54	137	260	76	178	64	1266

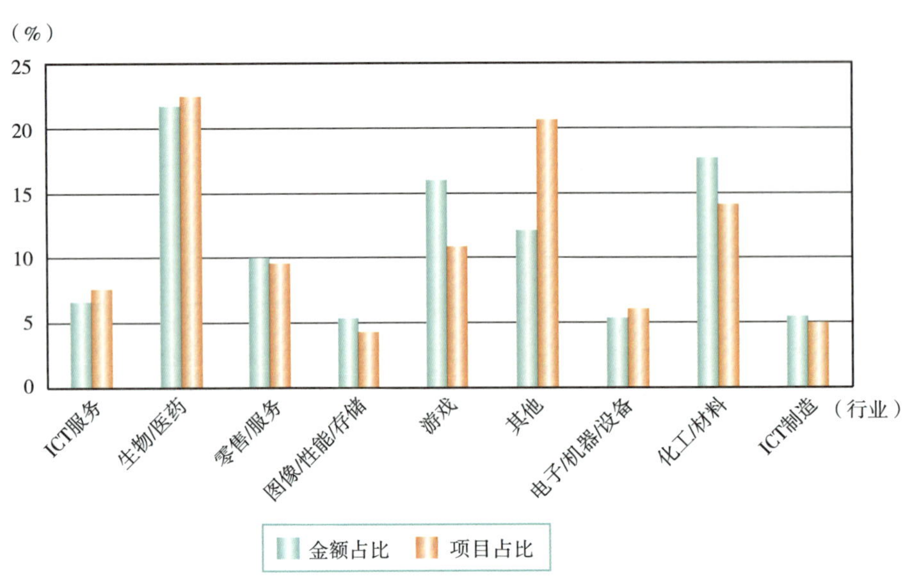

附图 3-2 韩国创业投资行业分布（2017）

四、韩国创业投资项目阶段分布

2017 年韩国创业投资项目仍然主要集中在早期阶段，与 2016 年韩国创业投资各阶段特征基本保持一致。从投资金额看，投资于早期、创建期和扩展期的差距较 2015 年有所缩小，分别占比 32.75%、27.90% 和 39.35%；而投资项目则多集中于早期，占比 45.02%（见附表 3-5、附图 3-3、附图 3-4）。

附表 3-5 韩国创业投资阶段分布（2017）

阶段	早期	创建期	扩展期	总量
金额（十亿韩元）	779.6	664.1	936.6	2380.3
项目（项）	570	363	373	1266

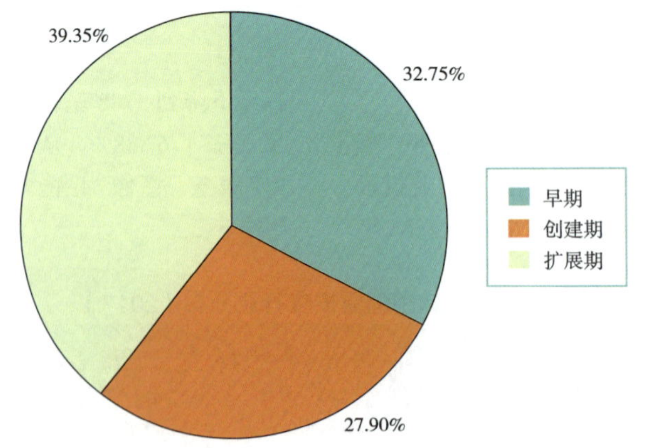

附图 3-3 韩国创业投资阶段分布（按金额划分）（2017）

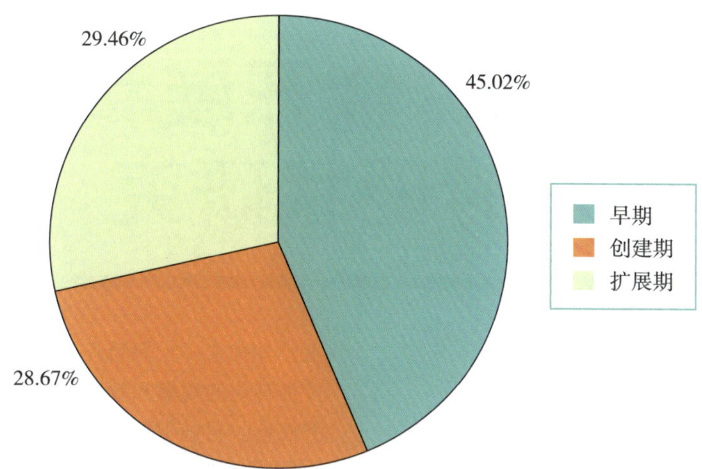

附图 3-4　韩国创业投资阶段分布（按项目划分）（2017）

资料来源：韩国风险投资协会（Korean Venture Capital Association）提供。

附录 4 保险资金开展私募股权投资的现状研究

一、保险资金运用的现状分析

（一）保险资金运用的整体情况

过去 10 年，保险业发展非常迅速，截至 2018 年 4 月末，保险业总资产规模达到 17.34 万亿元，是 10 年前的 7.68 倍，保险资金运用余额达到 15.4 万亿元，是 10 年前的 7.5 倍，按照保险业“十三五”的规划目标，到 2020 年保险业总资产管理规模将超 25 万亿元。

保险资金运用范围广泛，不仅包括银行存款、债券、股票、基金、银行理财、资产支持证券、券商的资产管理计划、信托等，还包括保险资产管理机构发行的基础设施投资计划、不动产投资计划、股权投资计划等，可投资产品范围覆盖了从传统到另类，从公募到私募，从国内到海外等全投资领域。

自 2006 年以来，保险资金作为长期投资者，通过债权计划、股权计划、私募基金等多种形式投资实体经济超过 4 万亿元，有力支持国家“一带一路”倡议以及国家区域发展战略，而且保险资金作为中国资本市场最重要的机构投资者之一，越发成为中国资本市场的稳定器和减震器。

（二）保险资金投资私募股权的整体情况

截至 2018 年 4 月末，保险资金进行长期股权投资的规模为 1.59 万亿元，比年初增长 7.46%，资产占比达到 10.3%，比年初提高了 0.41 个百分点。保险资金的股权投资主要由四部分构成，包括未上市股权、上市股权、私募股权基金和股权投资计划。从历年情况看，保险机构的股权资产占比稳步增加，在各类资产中，其收益率水平位居前列。

二、保险资金开展私募股权投资的现实意义

（一）国家经济发展的需要

保险是金融市场的重要组成部分，是社会资金融通的主要方式之一。保险资金投资私募股权，可以提高储蓄向投资转化的规模和效率，提升直接融资比例，降低国民经济杠杆。目前保险总资产规模超过 16 万亿元，按 10% 的比例算，保险资金可投入股权市场的规模不低于 1.6 万亿元，有充足的资本实力对国民经济起到巨大的推动作用。

保险资金的可投资范围可以扩展到其符合国家政策和产业政策的相关企业，对促进经济转型和产业结构升级具有巨大的引领作用。并且，股权投资作为一种新兴的服务业，重视长期收益，关注企业价值的增长潜力，有足够的利益驱动和丰富经验去实现人才、组织和资金等资源的最大化合理配置。

（二）保险资产负债匹配的需要

随着保险业务的快速发展，保险业资产规模快速提升，保险资金的运用压力明显增大。保险资金具有长期性和负债成本确定性，需要相应的资产来匹配。股权投资与保险资金性质具有高度的契合性，保险资金青睐资产的长期配置，这与股权投资的长期性非常匹配。

近年来随着资本回报率的下降，适当进行股权投资有利于提高保险资金的整体收益率水平。据统计，截至 2016 年底，保险资金以长期股权投资的方式运用，余额的比例不到 10%，贡献了占比超过 20% 的投资收益。

三、保险资金开展股权投资的历程

（一）股权投资的主要类型

私募股权投资按照被投资企业发展阶段划分，股权投资可分为创业投资（Venture Capital，VC）、成长资本投资（Development Capital）、并购资本、Pre-IPO 投资以及上市后私募投资。

从市场参与主体来看，主要有国家以及地方政府的引导基金、国内直投的法人机构、个人投资者以及国内外股权投资基金。

从投资方式上来看，分为直接投资和间接投资两种方式。其中间接投资不直接投资标的股权，通常作为有限合伙人（Limited Partner，LP）投资其他基金，政府的引导基金通常属于此类基金。

（二）海外主要国家保险资金股权投资的发展情况

目前美国是全世界最重要的保险市场，具有巨大的保险资产管理规模，早在2002年美国的保费收入已经高达1万亿美元，占全世界保费市场的38%，占其GDP的10%左右。美国是股权投资的先驱者，美国股权投资的资本主要来源于机构投资者，其中养老基金是美国股权投资最重要的资金来源，然后是基金会和捐赠基金，最后是银行和保险公司。在美国保险公司的资金运用中，股权投资越来越重要，其投资占比在逐渐升高。1992~2002年，股权投资在美国保险公司资产份额中的比例以年均15.2%的速度增长。

欧洲在股权投资方面，是美国的追随者。在美国股权投资市场已经成熟的时候，欧洲的股权投资才刚刚开始出现，并且通常欧洲的早期股权投资基金是由美国的投资公司发起设立的。20世纪70年代，欧洲各国相继放松对股权投资的管制，保险公司等机构开始进入股权投资行业。根据欧洲创业投资协会的数据，1998~2002年，银行、养老基金、保险在股权基金的资金来源所占比重分别为24%、22%、12%。

日本的股权投资发展历程呈现周期性起伏，自20世纪70年代，大约每十年出现一次股权投资的浪潮，但在日本以银行为主导的金融体制下，保险公司在股权投资市场的比重一直不高，2004年保险资金占风险资本融资规模的2.9%，远低于银行的28.6%。

（三）我国保险资金开展股权投资的历程

我国保险资金投资私募股权的发展历程，大致可以分为试点、扩大试点以及常态化三个阶段。

2007年12月之前是保险资金股权投资的试点阶段。2006年6月，国务院颁布了《关于保险业改革发展的若干意见》，明确提出“扩大保险资金投资资产证券化产品的规模和品种，开展保险资金投资不动产和创业投资企业试点，支持保险资金参股商业银行”，标志着保险资金参与私募股权投资的正式开始。同年，中国保监会出台了《关于保险机构投资商业银行股权的通知》，旨在拓宽保险资金的运用范围，该政策将股权投资分为一般投资和重大投资。投资商业银行股本5%以内为一般投资，5%以上为重大投资，并对投资10%以上的其他重大投资进行例外管理。

2008年1月至2010年8月为保险资金投资股权的扩大试点阶段。2008年10月，国务院批准保险资金可以投资未上市优质企业股权。根据《保险法》第一百零六条规定，2010年8月，中国保监会发布了《保险资金运用管理暂行办法》。该项政策对投资范围和投资比例作出了规定，即实现控股的股权投资限于保险类企业、非保险类金融企业以及与保险业务相关企业。投资未上市企业股权的账户余额，不高于本公司上季度度末总资产的5%；相关金融产品的账面余额，不高于本公司上季度末总资产的4%，两项合计不高于本公司上季度末总资产的5%。

自2010年9月以来，是保险资金开展股权投资的常态化阶段。期间，中国保监会颁布了《保险资金投资股权暂行办法》和《关于保险资金投资股权和不动产有关问题的通知》。《保险资金投资股权暂行办法》对以前的政策进行进一步细化，扩大了投资范围，提高了投资比例，进一步放松了部分限制，同时强化了风控要求。2014年9月中国保险资产管理协会成立，2017年保险资产管理协会建立了股权投资监管报送系统，对保险公司以及受托保险资金的私募股权投资机构要求上报股权投资情况，进一步强化了监控和监管。

1994年以来，保险行业投资股权业务已有初步探索，但规模占比较小，并以直接股权投资为主，投资范围主要

附表4-1 历年保险资金直接股权投资账面余额

年份	账面余额（亿元）	占比（%）	笔数
1994	224.00	12.22	1
2006	550.02	30.01	4
2008	14.38	0.78	6
2009	72.44	3.95	5

续表

年份	账面余额（亿元）	占比（%）	笔数
2010	119.59	6.53	2
2011	56.00	3.06	1
2012	796.23	43.45	8
合计	1832.66	100.00	27

资料来源：中国保监会。

为金融业及基础设施行业。附表 4–1 是历年保险资金直接股权投资账面余额情况，可以看出保险资金股权投资的笔数仍然较少。

四、保险资金进行私募股权投资的主要形式

（一）直接投资模式

直接投资模式是一种保险机构通过设立专业的股权投资团队直接投资标的公司股权的模式。该模式对保险公司的要求相对较高，需要拥有一支经验丰富的股权投资团队，团队职能包含投前项目线索发掘、尽职调查、投中风控、投后管理等多种职能，同时保险公司需要具备完善的风控机制和激励机制。大型的保险公司或者保险资产管理公司通常都设有专业的另类投资部门，负责股权投资。

直接股权投资的形式通常有两种类型，第一种是保险公司直接持有公司股权，比如中国人寿投资广发银行的案例。第二种是保险公司或者保险资产管理公司通过投资工具投资标的公司股权，此类通常设立股权投资计划、有限合伙企业或者契约型基金等方式，比如平安牵头设立的京沪高铁股权投资计划等。

（二）间接投资模式

间接投资模式也称为委托投资模式。通常保险公司不直接投资标的公司股权，而是以出资人身份参与由一般合伙人（General Partner，GP）设立的基金，借由股权投资基金投资标的公司，而对标的公司的投后管理以及退出均由 GP 来操作管理，保险公司不参与基金的具体运作。

相比较直接投资，保险资产委托给专业的投资管理机构，有利于降低保险公司的资产管理成本，使其专注保险主业；有利于充分利用专业机构的知识和经验，改善投资收益水平；有利于提高保险资产管理的监管水平，保险资产的专业化管理为监管创造了有利条件。

（三）其他创新模式

随着保险资产管理机构的能力建设的不断提高，在 2014 年“国十条”文件中提出允许专业保险机构设立夹层基金、并购基金、不动产基金等私募基金。2015 年 9 月保监会发布《关于设立保险私募基金的有关事项的通知》。截至目前，保监会正式核准的保险私募基金公司 10 家，设立私募基金 12 只，规模近 600 亿元。保险私募基金的模式有利于保险资管机构的私募基金业务专业化运作，隔离风险，有利于保险私募基金与市场优秀投资主体的合作。

五、保险资金股权投资面临的问题和挑战以及应对

（一）保险资金股权投资面临的问题和挑战

保险资金的股权投资能力虽然经过多年的发展已经有显著提升，但与股权投资业务的复杂性之间仍存在矛盾。总体而言，保险资金投资仍然以固定收益为主，在股权投资领域的人才储备、投资理念、投资经验与市场上其他的机构仍有差距。此外股权投资，交易复杂，除了面临常规的金融投资风险，还面临较高的道德风险，存在利益输送的动机和空间。

保险资金的稳定收益特性与股权投资收益不确定性之间存在矛盾。股权投资收益具有明显的“J 曲线效应”，股权投资的现金流难以预测，通常被投资项目退出后，才产生收益，给保险资金的资产负债匹配增加了难度。由于收益风险特征的不匹配，保险资金开展股权投资业务还面临较高的不确定性风险。

（二）保险资金股权投资问题的应对

1. 加强保险资金股权投资能力建设

股权投资业务的开展需要与自身股权投资能力相匹

配，因此保险机构应持续加强股权投资能力建设，包括股权投资人才的培养、市场的培育、加强与市场上其他具有优秀实力机构的合作。

2. 支持保险私募基金健康持续的发展

保险私募基金是保险资金走向股权投资专业化运作的有效方式，特别是母基金的形式，有助于保险资金分散配置，遴选优秀的基金管理人，平滑收益波动，提高收益率，抵御投资风险。

3. 加强行业监管和行业自律

自中国保险资产管理协会设立以来，协会通过信息技术手段，构建了“J博士股权投资报送系统”，已经形成了股权投资的定期报送制度，强化了股权投资的信息报送和信息披露，增强了保险资金股权投资的透明度，确保监管要求落实到位。通过协会的纽带作用，搭建了行业沟通交流平台，为政策解读、经验分享、信息沟通提供有效渠道。

参考文献

［1］陈文辉 . 保险资金股权投资问题研究［M］. 中国金融出版社，2014.

［2］陈成，程磊 . 保险资金开展私募股权投资的相关研究［J］. 中国保险，2009（2）.

（本文由马国超提供）

附录 5 关于创业投资企业和天使投资个人有关税收政策的通知

（财税〔2018〕55 号）

各省、自治区、直辖市、计划单列市财政厅（局）、国家税务局、地方税务局，新疆生产建设兵团财政局：

为进一步支持创业投资发展，现就创业投资企业和天使投资个人有关税收政策问题通知如下：

一、税收政策内容

（一）公司制创业投资企业采取股权投资方式直接投资于种子期、初创期科技型企业（以下简称初创科技型企业）满 2 年（24 个月，下同）的，可以按照投资额的 70% 在股权持有满 2 年的当年抵扣该公司制创业投资企业的应纳税所得额；当年不足抵扣的，可以在以后纳税年度结转抵扣。

（二）有限合伙制创业投资企业（以下简称合伙创投企业）采取股权投资方式直接投资于初创科技型企业满 2 年的，该合伙创投企业的合伙人分别按以下方式处理：

1. 法人合伙人可以按照对初创科技型企业投资额的 70% 抵扣法人合伙人从合伙创投企业分得的所得；当年不足抵扣的，可以在以后纳税年度结转抵扣。

2. 个人合伙人可以按照对初创科技型企业投资额的 70% 抵扣个人合伙人从合伙创投企业分得的经营所得；当年不足抵扣的，可以在以后纳税年度结转抵扣。

（三）天使投资个人采取股权投资方式直接投资于初创科技型企业满 2 年的，可以按照投资额的 70% 抵扣转让该初创科技型企业股权取得的应纳税所得额；当期不足抵扣的，可以在以后取得转让该初创科技型企业股权的应纳税所得额时结转抵扣。

天使投资个人投资多个初创科技型企业的，对其中办理注销清算的初创科技型企业，天使投资个人对其投资额的 70% 尚未抵扣完的，可自注销清算之日起 36 个月内抵扣天使投资个人转让其他初创科技型企业股权取得的应纳税所得额。

二、相关政策条件

（一）本通知所称初创科技型企业，应同时符合以下条件：

1. 在中国境内（不包括港、澳、台地区）注册成立、实行查账征收的居民企业；

2. 接受投资时，从业人数不超过 200 人，其中具有大学本科以上学历的从业人数不低于 30%；资产总额和年销售收入均不超过 3000 万元；

3. 接受投资时设立时间不超过 5 年（60 个月）；

4. 接受投资时以及接受投资后 2 年内未在境内外证券交易所上市；

5. 接受投资当年及下一纳税年度，研发费用总额占成本费用支出的比例不低于 20%。

（二）享受本通知规定税收政策的创业投资企业，应同时符合以下条件。

1. 在中国境内（不含港、澳、台地区）注册成立、实行查账征收的居民企业或合伙创投企业，且不属于被投资初创科技型企业的发起人；

2. 符合《创业投资企业管理暂行办法》（发展改革委等 10 部门令第 39 号）规定或者《私募投资基金监督管理暂行办法》（证监会令第 105 号）关于创业投资基金的特别规定，按照上述规定完成备案且规范运作；

3. 投资后 2 年内，创业投资企业及其关联方持有被投资初创科技型企业的股权比例合计应低于 50%。

（三）享受本通知规定的税收政策的天使投资个人，应同时符合以下条件：

1. 不属于被投资初创科技型企业的发起人、雇员或其亲属（包括配偶、父母、子女、祖父母、外祖父母、孙子女、外孙子女、兄弟姐妹，下同），且与被投资初创科技型企业不存在劳务派遣等关系；

2. 投资后 2 年内，本人及其亲属持有被投资初创科技型企业股权比例合计应低于 50%。

（四）享受本通知规定的税收政策的投资，仅限于通过向被投资初创科技型企业直接支付现金方式取得的股权投资，不包括受让其他股东的存量股权。

三、管理事项及管理要求

（一）本通知所称研发费用口径，按照《财政部　国家税务总局　科技部关于完善研究开发费用税前加计扣除政策的通知》（财税〔2015〕119 号）等规定执行。

（二）本通知所称从业人数，包括与企业建立劳动关系的职工人员及企业接受的劳务派遣人员。从业人数和资产总额指标，按照企业接受投资前连续 12 个月的平均数计算，不足 12 个月的，按实际月数平均计算。

本通知所称销售收入，包括主营业务收入与其他业务收入；年销售收入指标，按照企业接受投资前连续 12 个月的累计数计算，不足 12 个月的，按实际月数累计计算。

本通知所称成本费用，包括主营业务成本、其他业务成本、销售费用、管理费用、财务费用。

（三）本通知所称投资额，按照创业投资企业或天使投资个人对初创科技型企业的实缴投资额确定。

合伙创投企业的合伙人对初创科技型企业的投资额，按照合伙创投企业对初创科技型企业的实缴投资额和合伙协议约定的合伙人占合伙创投企业的出资比例计算确定。合伙人从合伙创投企业分得的所得，按照《财政部　国家税务总局关于合伙企业合伙人所得税问题的通知》（财税〔2008〕159 号）规定计算。

（四）天使投资个人、公司制创业投资企业、合伙创投企业、合伙创投企业法人合伙人、被投资初创科技型企业应按规定办理优惠手续。

（五）初创科技型企业接受天使投资个人投资满 2 年，在上海证券交易所、深圳证券交易所上市的，天使投资个人转让该企业股票时，按照现行限售股有关规定执行，其尚未抵扣的投资额，在税款清算时一并计算抵扣。

（六）享受本通知规定的税收政策的纳税人，其主管税务机关对被投资企业是否符合初创科技型企业条件有异议的，可以转请被投资企业主管税务机关提供相关材料。对纳税人提供虚假资料，违规享受税收政策的，应按税收征管法相关规定处理，并将其列入失信纳税人名单，按规定实施联合惩戒措施。

四、执行时间

本通知规定的天使投资个人所得税政策自 2018 年 7 月 1 日起执行，其他各项政策自 2018 年 1 月 1 日起执行。执行日期前 2 年内发生的投资，在执行日期后投资满 2 年，且符合本通知规定的其他条件的，可以适用本通知规定的税收政策。

《财政部　国家税务总局关于创业投资企业和天使投资个人有关税收试点政策的通知》（财税〔2017〕38 号）自 2018 年 7 月 1 日起废止，符合试点政策条件的投资额可按本通知的规定继续抵扣。

财政部　国家税务总局

2018 年 5 月 14 日

附录 6 私募投资基金监督管理暂行办法

（中国证券监督管理委员会令第 105 号）

《私募投资基金监督管理暂行办法》已经 2014 年 6 月 30 日中国证券监督管理委员会第 51 次主席办公会议审议通过，现予公布，自公布之日起施行。

第一章 总则

第一条 为了规范私募投资基金活动，保护投资者及相关当事人的合法权益，促进私募投资基金行业健康发展，根据《证券投资基金法》、《国务院关于进一步促进资本市场健康发展的若干意见》，制定本办法。

第二条 本办法所称私募投资基金（以下简称私募基金），是指在中华人民共和国境内，以非公开方式向投资者募集资金设立的投资基金。

私募基金财产的投资包括买卖股票、股权、债券、期货、期权、基金份额及投资合同约定的其他投资标的。

非公开募集资金，以进行投资活动为目的设立的公司或者合伙企业，资产由基金管理人或者普通合伙人管理的，其登记备案、资金募集和投资运作适用本办法。

证券公司、基金管理公司、期货公司及其子公司从事私募基金业务适用本办法，其他法律法规和中国证券监督管理委员会（以下简称中国证监会）有关规定对上述机构从事私募基金业务另有规定的，适用其规定。

第三条 从事私募基金业务，应当遵循自愿、公平、诚实信用原则，维护投资者合法权益，不得损害国家利益和社会公共利益。

第四条 私募基金管理人和从事私募基金托管业务的机构（以下简称私募基金托管人）管理、运用私募基金财产，从事私募基金销售业务的机构（以下简称私募基金销售机构）及其他私募服务机构从事私募基金服务活动，应当恪尽职守，履行诚实信用、谨慎勤勉的义务。

私募基金从业人员应当遵守法律、行政法规，恪守职业道德和行为规范。

第五条 中国证监会及其派出机构依照《证券投资基金法》、本办法和中国证监会的其他有关规定，对私募基金业务活动实施监督管理。

设立私募基金管理机构和发行私募基金不设行政审批，允许各类发行主体在依法合规的基础上，向累计不超过法律规定数量的投资者发行私募基金。建立健全私募基金发行监管制度，切实强化事中事后监管，依法严厉打击以私募基金为名的各类非法集资活动。

建立促进经营机构规范开展私募基金业务的风险控制和自律管理制度，以及各类私募基金的统一监测系统。

第六条 中国证券投资基金业协会（以下简称基金业协会）依照《证券投资基金法》、本办法、中国证监会其他有关规定和基金业协会自律规则，对私募基金业开展行业自律，协调行业关系，提供行业服务，促进行业发展。

第二章 登记备案

第七条 各类私募基金管理人应当根据基金业协会的规定，向基金业协会申请登记，报送以下基本信息：

（一）工商登记和营业执照正副本复印件；

（二）公司章 程或者合伙协议；

（三）主要股东或者合伙人名单；

（四）高级管理人员的基本信息；

（五）基金业协会规定的其他信息。

基金业协会应当在私募基金管理人登记材料齐备后的 20 个工作日内，通过网站公告私募基金管理人名单及其基本情况的方式，为私募基金管理人办结登记手续。

第八条 各类私募基金募集完毕，私募基金管理人应当根据基金业协会的规定，办理基金备案手续，报送以下基本信息：

（一）主要投资方向及根据主要投资方向注明的基金类别；

（二）基金合同、公司章 程或者合伙协议。资金募集过程中向投资者提供基金招募说明书的，应当报送基金招募说明书。以公司、合伙等企业形式设立的私募基金，还应当报送工商登记和营业执照正副本复印件；

（三）采取委托管理方式的，应当报送委托管理协议。委托托管机构托管基金财产的，还应当报送托管协议；

（四）基金业协会规定的其他信息。

基金业协会应当在私募基金备案材料齐备后的 20 个工作日内，通过网站公告私募基金名单及其基本情况的方式，为私募基金办结备案手续。

第九条　基金业协会为私募基金管理人和私募基金办理登记备案不构成对私募基金管理人投资能力、持续合规情况的认可；不作为对基金财产安全的保证。

第十条　私募基金管理人依法解散、被依法撤销、或者被依法宣告破产的，其法定代表人或者普通合伙人应当在 20 个工作日内向基金业协会报告，基金业协会应当及时注销基金管理人登记并通过网站公告。

第三章　合格投资者

第十一条　私募基金应当向合格投资者募集，单只私募基金的投资者人数累计不得超过《证券投资基金法》、《公司法》、《合伙企业法》等法律规定的特定数量。投资者转让基金份额的，受让人应当为合格投资者且基金份额受让后投资者人数应当符合前款规定。

第十二条　私募基金的合格投资者是指具备相应风险识别能力和风险承担能力，投资于单只私募基金的金额不低于 100 万元且符合下列相关标准的单位和个人：

（一）净资产不低于 1000 万元的单位；

（二）金融资产不低于 300 万元或者最近三年个人年均收入不低于 50 万元的个人。

前款所称金融资产包括银行存款、股票、债券、基金份额、资产管理计划、银行理财产品、信托计划、保险产品、期货权益等。

第十三条　下列投资者视为合格投资者：

（一）社会保障基金、企业年金等养老基金，慈善基金等社会公益基金；

（二）依法设立并在基金业协会备案的投资计划；

（三）投资于所管理私募基金的私募基金管理人及其从业人员；

（四）中国证监会规定的其他投资者。

以合伙企业、契约等非法人形式，通过汇集多数投资者的资金直接或者间接投资于私募基金的，私募基金管理人或者私募基金销售机构应当穿透核查最终投资者是否为合格投资者，并合并计算投资者人数。但是，符合本条第（一）、（二）、（四）项规定的投资者投资私募基金的，不再穿透核查最终投资者是否为合格投资者和合并计算投资者人数。

第四章　资金募集

第十四条　私募基金管理人、私募基金销售机构不得向合格投资者之外的单位和个人募集资金，不得通过报刊、电台、电视、互联网等公众传播媒体或者讲座、报告会、分析会和布告、传单、手机短信、微信、博客和电子邮件等方式，向不特定对象宣传推介。

第十五条　私募基金管理人、私募基金销售机构不得向投资者承诺投资本金不受损失或者承诺最低收益。

第十六条　私募基金管理人自行销售私募基金的，应当采取问卷调查等方式，对投资者的风险识别能力和风险承担能力进行评估，由投资者书面承诺符合合格投资者条件；应当制作风险揭示书，由投资者签字确认。

私募基金管理人委托销售机构销售私募基金的，私募基金销售机构应当采取前款规定的评估、确认等措施。

投资者风险识别能力和承担能力问卷及风险揭示书的内容与格式指引，由基金业协会按照不同类别私募基金的特点制定。

第十七条　私募基金管理人自行销售或者委托销售机构销售私募基金，应当自行或者委托第三方机构对私募基金进行风险评级，向风险识别能力和风险承担能力相匹配的投资者推介私募基金。

第十八条　投资者应当如实填写风险识别能力和承担能力问卷，如实承诺资产或者收入情况，并对其真实性、准确性和完整性负责。填写虚假信息或者提供虚假承诺文件的，应当承担相应责任。

第十九条　投资者应当确保投资资金来源合法，不得非法汇集他人资金投资私募基金。

第五章 投资运作

第二十条 募集私募证券基金，应当制定并签订基金合同、公司章程或者合伙协议(以下统称基金合同)。基金合同应当符合《证券投资基金法》第九十三条、第九十四条规定。募集其他种类私募基金，基金合同应当参照《证券投资基金法》第九十三条、第九十四条规定，明确约定各方当事人的权利、义务和相关事宜。

第二十一条 除基金合同另有约定外，私募基金应当由基金托管人托管。

基金合同约定私募基金不进行托管的，应当在基金合同中明确保障私募基金财产安全的制度措施和纠纷解决机制。

第二十二条 同一私募基金管理人管理不同类别私募基金的，应当坚持专业化管理原则；管理可能导致利益输送或者利益冲突的不同私募基金的，应当建立防范利益输送和利益冲突的机制。

第二十三条 私募基金管理人、私募基金托管人、私募基金销售机构及其他私募服务机构及其从业人员从事私募基金业务，不得有以下行为：

(一)将其固有财产或者他人财产混同于基金财产从事投资活动；

(二)不公平地对待其管理的不同基金财产；

(三)利用基金财产或者职务之便，为本人或者投资者以外的人牟取利益，进行利益输送；

(四)侵占、挪用基金财产；

(五)泄露因职务便利获取的未公开信息，利用该信息从事或者明示、暗示他人从事相关的交易活动；

(六)从事损害基金财产和投资者利益的投资活动；

(七)玩忽职守，不按照规定履行职责；

(八)从事内幕交易、操纵交易价格及其他不正当交易活动；

(九)法律、行政法规和中国证监会规定禁止的其他行为。

第二十四条 私募基金管理人、私募基金托管人应当按照合同约定，如实向投资者披露基金投资、资产负债、投资收益分配、基金承担的费用和业绩报酬、可能存在的利益冲突情况以及可能影响投资者合法权益的其他重大信息，不得隐瞒或者提供虚假信息。信息披露规则由基金业协会另行制定。

第二十五条 私募基金管理人应当根据基金业协会的规定，及时填报并定期更新管理人及其从业人员的有关信息、所管理私募基金的投资运作情况和杠杆运用情况，保证所填报内容真实、准确、完整。发生重大事项的，应当在 10 个工作日内向基金业协会报告。

私募基金管理人应当于每个会计年度结束后的 4 个月内，向基金业协会报送经会计师事务所审计的年度财务报告和所管理私募基金年度投资运作基本情况。

第二十六条 私募基金管理人、私募基金托管人及私募基金销售机构应当妥善保存私募基金投资决策、交易和投资者适当性管理等方面的记录及其他相关资料，保存期限自基金清算终止之日起不得少于 10 年。

第六章 行业自律

第二十七条 基金业协会应当建立私募基金管理人登记、私募基金备案管理信息系统。

基金业协会应当对私募基金管理人和私募基金信息严格保密。除法律法规另有规定外，不得对外披露。

第二十八条 基金业协会应当建立与中国证监会及其派出机构和其他相关机构的信息共享机制，定期汇总分析私募基金情况，及时提供私募基金相关信息。

第二十九条 基金业协会应当制定和实施私募基金行业自律规则，监督、检查会员及其从业人员的执业行为。

会员及其从业人员违反法律、行政法规、本办法规定和基金业协会自律规则的，基金业协会可以视情节轻重，采取自律管理措施，并通过网站公开相关违法违规信息。会员及其从业人员涉嫌违法违规的，基金业协会应当及时报告中国证监会。

第三十条 基金业协会应当建立投诉处理机制，受理投资者投诉，进行纠纷调解。

第七章 监督管理

第三十一条 中国证监会及其派出机构依法对私募基金管理人、私募基金托管人、私募基金销售机构及其他私募服务机构开展私募基金业务情况进行统计监测和检查，依照《证券投资基金法》第一百一十四条规定采取有关措施。

第三十二条 中国证监会将私募基金管理人、私募基金托管人、私募基金销售机构及其他私募服务机构及其从业人员诚信信息记入证券期货市场诚信档案数据库；根据私募基金管理人的信用状况，实施差异化监管。

第三十三条　私募基金管理人、私募基金托管人、私募基金销售机构及其他私募服务机构及其从业人员违反法律、行政法规及本办法规定，中国证监会及其派出机构可以对其采取责令改正、监管谈话、出具警示函、公开谴责等行政监管措施。

第八章　关于创业投资基金的特别规定

第三十四条　本办法所称创业投资基金，是指主要投资于未上市创业企业普通股或者依法可转换为普通股的优先股、可转换债券等权益的股权投资基金。

第三十五条　鼓励和引导创业投资基金投资创业早期的小微企业。

享受国家财政税收扶持政策的创业投资基金，其投资范围应当符合国家相关规定。

第三十六条　基金业协会在基金管理人登记、基金备案、投资情况报告要求和会员管理等环节，对创业投资基金采取区别于其他私募基金的差异化行业自律，并提供差异化会员服务。

第三十七条　中国证监会及其派出机构对创业投资基金在投资方向检查等环节，采取区别于其他私募基金的差异化监督管理；在账户开立、发行交易和投资退出等方面，为创业投资基金提供便利服务。

第九章　法律责任

第三十八条　私募基金管理人、私募基金托管人、私募基金销售机构及其他私募服务机构及其从业人员违反本办法第七条、第八条、第十一条、第十四条至第十七条、第二十四条至第二十六条规定的，以及有本办法第二十三条第一项至第七项和第九项所列行为之一的，责令改正，给予警告并处三万元以下罚款；对直接负责的主管人员和其他直接责任人员，给予警告并处三万元以下罚款；有本办法第二十三条第八项行为的，按照《证券法》和《期货交易管理条例》的有关规定处罚；构成犯罪的，依法移交司法机关追究刑事责任。

第三十九条　私募基金管理人、私募基金托管人、私募基金销售机构及其他私募服务机构及其从业人员违反法律法规和本办法规定，情节严重的，中国证监会可以依法对有关责任人员采取市场禁入措施。

第四十条　私募证券基金管理人及其从业人员违反《证券投资基金法》有关规定的，按照《证券投资基金法》有关规定处罚。

第十章　附则

第四十一条

本办法自公布之日起施行。

附录 7 关于规范金融机构资产管理业务的指导意见

（银发〔2018〕106 号）

近年来，我国资产管理业务快速发展，在满足居民和企业投融资需求、改善社会融资结构等方面发挥了积极作用，但也存在部分业务发展不规范、多层嵌套、刚性兑付、规避金融监管和宏观调控等问题。按照党中央、国务院决策部署，为规范金融机构资产管理业务，统一同类资产管理产品监管标准，有效防控金融风险，引导社会资金流向实体经济，更好地支持经济结构调整和转型升级，经国务院同意，现提出以下意见：

一、规范金融机构资产管理业务主要遵循以下原则：

（一）坚持严控风险的底线思维。把防范和化解资产管理业务风险放到更加重要的位置，减少存量风险，严防增量风险。

（二）坚持服务实体经济的根本目标。既充分发挥资产管理业务功能，切实服务实体经济投融资需求，又严格规范引导，避免资金脱实向虚在金融体系内部自我循环，防止产品过于复杂，加剧风险跨行业、跨市场、跨区域传递。

（三）坚持宏观审慎管理与微观审慎监管相结合、机构监管与功能监管相结合的监管理念。实现对各类机构开展资产管理业务的全面、统一覆盖，采取有效监管措施，加强金融消费者权益保护。

（四）坚持有的放矢的问题导向。重点针对资产管理业务的多层嵌套、杠杆不清、套利严重、投机频繁等问题，设定统一的标准规制，同时对金融创新坚持趋利避害、一分为二，留出发展空间。

（五）坚持积极稳妥审慎推进。正确处理改革、发展、稳定关系，坚持防范风险与有序规范相结合，在下决心处置风险的同时，充分考虑市场承受能力，合理设置过渡期，把握好工作的次序、节奏、力度，加强市场沟通，有效引导市场预期。

二、资产管理业务是指银行、信托、证券、基金、期货、保险资产管理机构、金融资产投资公司等金融机构接受投资者委托，对受托的投资者财产进行投资和管理的金融服务。金融机构为委托人利益履行诚实信用、勤勉尽责义务并收取相应的管理费用，委托人自担投资风险并获得收益。金融机构可以与委托人在合同中事先约定收取合理的业绩报酬，业绩报酬计入管理费，须与产品一一对应并逐个结算，不同产品之间不得相互串用。

资产管理业务是金融机构的表外业务，金融机构开展资产管理业务时不得承诺保本保收益。出现兑付困难时，金融机构不得以任何形式垫资兑付。金融机构不得在表内开展资产管理业务。

私募投资基金适用私募投资基金专门法律、行政法规，私募投资基金专门法律、行政法规中没有明确规定的适用本意见，创业投资基金、政府出资产业投资基金的相关规定另行制定。

三、资产管理产品包括但不限于人民币或外币形式的银行非保本理财产品，资金信托，证券公司、证券公司子公司、基金管理公司、基金管理子公司、期货公司、期货公司子公司、保险资产管理机构、金融资产投资公司发行的资产管理产品等。依据金融管理部门颁布规则开展的资产证券化业务，依据人力资源社会保障部门颁布规则发行的养老金产品，不适用本意见。

四、资产管理产品按照募集方式的不同，分为公募产品和私募产品。公募产品面向不特定社会公众公开发行。公开发行的认定标准依照《中华人民共和国证券法》执行。私募产品面向合格投资者通过非公开方式发行。

资产管理产品按照投资性质的不同，分为固定收益类产品、权益类产品、商品及金融衍生品类产品和混合类产品。固定收益类产品投资于存款、债券等债权类资产的比例不低于80%，权益类产品投资于股票、未上市企业股权等权益类资产的比例不低于80%，商品及金融衍生品类产品投资于商品及金融衍生品的比例不低于80%，混合类产品投资于债权类资产、权益类资产、商品及金融衍生品类资产且任一资产的投资比例未达到前三类产品标准。非因金融机构主观因素导致突破前述比例限制的，金融机构应当在流动性受限资产可出售、可转让或者恢复交易的15个交易日内调整至符合要求。

金融机构在发行资产管理产品时，应当按照上述分类标准向投资者明示资产管理产品的类型，并按照确定的产品性质进行投资。在产品成立后至到期日前，不得擅自改变产品类型。混合类产品投资债权类资产、权益类资产和商品及金融衍生品类资产的比例范围应当在发行产品时予以确定并向投资者明示，在产品成立后至到期日前不得擅自改变。产品的实际投向不得违反合同约定，如有改变，除高风险类型的产品超出比例范围投资较低风险资产外，应当先行取得投资者书面同意，并履行登记备案等法律法规以及金融监督管理部门规定的程序。

五、资产管理产品的投资者分为不特定社会公众和合格投资者两大类。合格投资者是指具备相应风险识别能力和风险承担能力，投资于单只资产管理产品不低于一定金额且符合下列条件的自然人和法人或者其他组织。

（一）具有2年以上投资经历，且满足以下条件之一：家庭金融净资产不低于300万元，家庭金融资产不低于500万元，或者近3年本人年均收入不低于40万元。

（二）最近1年末净资产不低于1000万元的法人单位。

（三）金融管理部门视为合格投资者的其他情形。

合格投资者投资于单只固定收益类产品的金额不低于30万元，投资于单只混合类产品的金额不低于40万元，投资于单只权益类产品、单只商品及金融衍生品类产品的金额不低于100万元。

投资者不得使用贷款、发行债券等筹集的非自有资金投资资产管理产品。

六、金融机构发行和销售资产管理产品，应当坚持“了解产品”和“了解客户”的经营理念，加强投资者适当性管理，向投资者销售与其风险识别能力和风险承担能力相适应的资产管理产品。禁止欺诈或者误导投资者购买与其风险承担能力不匹配的资产管理产品。金融机构不得通过拆分资产管理产品的方式，向风险识别能力和风险承担能力低于产品风险等级的投资者销售资产管理产品。

金融机构应当加强投资者教育，不断提高投资者的金融知识水平和风险意识，向投资者传递“卖者尽责、买者自负”的理念，打破刚性兑付。

七、金融机构开展资产管理业务，应当具备与资产管理业务发展相适应的管理体系和管理制度，公司治理良好，风险管理、内部控制和问责机制健全。

金融机构应当建立健全资产管理业务人员的资格认定、培训、考核评价和问责制度，确保从事资产管理业务的人员具备必要的专业知识、行业经验和管理能力，充分了解相关法律法规、监管规定以及资产管理产品的法律关系、交易结构、主要风险和风险管控方式，遵守行为准则和职业道德标准。

对于违反相关法律法规以及本意见规定的金融机构资产管理业务从业人员，依法采取处罚措施直至取消从业资格，禁止其在其他类型金融机构从事资产管理业务。

八、金融机构运用受托资金进行投资，应当遵守审慎经营规则，制定科学合理的投资策略和风险管理制度，有效防范和控制风险。

金融机构应当履行以下管理人职责：

（一）依法募集资金，办理产品份额的发售和登记事宜。

（二）办理产品登记备案或者注册手续。

（三）对所管理的不同产品受托财产分别管理、分别记账，进行投资。

（四）按照产品合同的约定确定收益分配方案，及时向投资者分配收益。

（五）进行产品会计核算并编制产品财务会计报告。

（六）依法计算并披露产品净值或者投资收益情况，确定申购、赎回价格。

（七）办理与受托财产管理业务活动有关的信息披露事项。

（八）保存受托财产管理业务活动的记录、账册、报表和其他相关资料。

（九）以管理人名义，代表投资者利益行使诉讼权利或者实施其他法律行为。

（十）在兑付受托资金及收益时，金融机构应当保证受托资金及收益返回委托人的原账户、同名账户或者合同约定的受益人账户。

（十一）金融监督管理部门规定的其他职责。

金融机构未按照诚实信用、勤勉尽责原则切实履行受托管理职责，造成投资者损失的，应当依法向投资者承担赔偿责任。

九、金融机构代理销售其他金融机构发行的资产管理产品，应当符合金融监督管理部门规定的资质条件。未经金融监督管理部门许可，任何非金融机构和个人不得代理销售资产管理产品。

金融机构应当建立资产管理产品的销售授权管理体系，明确代理销售机构的准入标准和程序，明确界定双方的权利与义务，明确相关风险的承担责任和转移方式。

金融机构代理销售资产管理产品，应当建立相应的内部审批和风险控制程序，对发行或者管理机构的信用状况、经营管理能力、市场投资能力、风险处置能力等开展尽职调查，要求发行或者管理机构提供详细的产品介绍、相关市场分析和风险收益测算报告，进行充分的信息验证和风险审查，确保代理销售的产品符合本意见规定并承担相应责任。

十、公募产品主要投资标准化债权类资产以及上市交易的股票，除法律法规和金融管理部门另有规定外，不得投资未上市企业股权。公募产品可以投资商品及金融衍生品，但应当符合法律法规以及金融管理部门的相关规定。

私募产品的投资范围由合同约定，可以投资债权类资产、上市或挂牌交易的股票、未上市企业股权（含债转股）和受（收）益权以及符合法律法规规定的其他资产，并严格遵守投资者适当性管理要求。鼓励充分运用私募产品支持市场化、法治化债转股。

十一、资产管理产品进行投资应当符合以下规定：

（一）标准化债权类资产应当同时符合以下条件：

1. 等分化，可交易。

2. 信息披露充分。

3. 集中登记，独立托管。

4. 公允定价，流动性机制完善。

5. 在银行间市场、证券交易所市场等经国务院同意设立的交易市场交易。

标准化债权类资产的具体认定规则由中国人民银行会同金融监督管理部门另行制定。

标准化债权类资产之外的债权类资产均为非标准化债权类资产。金融机构发行资产管理产品投资于非标准化债权类资产的，应当遵守金融监督管理部门制定的有关限额管理、流动性管理等监管标准。金融监督管理部门未制定相关监管标准的，由中国人民银行督促根据本意见要求制定监管标准并予以执行。

金融机构不得将资产管理产品资金直接投资于商业银行信贷资产。商业银行信贷资产受（收）益权的投资限制由金融管理部门另行制定。

（二）资产管理产品不得直接或者间接投资法律法规和国家政策禁止进行债权或股权投资的行业和领域。

（三）鼓励金融机构在依法合规、商业可持续的前提下，通过发行资产管理产品募集资金投向符合国家战略和产业政策要求、符合国家供给侧结构性改革政策要求的领域。鼓励金融机构通过发行资产管理产品募集资金支持经济结构转型，支持市场化、法治化债转股，降低企业杠杆率。

（四）跨境资产管理产品及业务参照本意见执行，并应当符合跨境人民币和外汇管理有关规定。

十二、金融机构应当向投资者主动、真实、准确、完整、及时披露资产管理产品募集信息、资金投向、杠杆水平、收益分配、托管安排、投资账户信息和主要投资风险等内容。国家法律法规另有规定的，从其规定。

对于公募产品，金融机构应当建立严格的信息披露管理制度，明确定期报告、临时报告、重大事项公告、投资风险披露要求以及具体内容、格式。在本机构官方网站或者通过投资者便于获取的方式披露产品净值或者投资收益情况，并定期披露其他重要信息：开放式产品按照开放频率披露，封闭式产品至少每周披露一次。

对于私募产品，其信息披露方式、内容、频率由产品合同约定，但金融机构应当至少每季度向投资者披露产品净值和其他重要信息。

对于固定收益类产品，金融机构应当通过醒目方式向投资者充分披露和提示产品的投资风险，包括但不限于产品投资债券面临的利率、汇率变化等市场风险以及债券价格波动情况，产品投资每笔非标准化债权类资产的融资客户、项目名称、剩余融资期限、到期收益分配、交易结构、风险状况等。

对于权益类产品，金融机构应当通过醒目方式向投资者充分披露和提示产品的投资风险，包括产品投资股票面临的风险以及股票价格波动情况等。

对于商品及金融衍生品类产品，金融机构应当通过醒目方式向投资者充分披露产品的挂钩资产、持仓风险、控制措施以及衍生品公允价值变化等。

对于混合类产品，金融机构应当通过醒目方式向投资者清晰披露产品的投资资产组合情况，并根据固定收益类、权益类、商品及金融衍生品类资产投资比例充分披露和提示相应的投资风险。

十三、主营业务不包括资产管理业务的金融机构应当设立具有独立法人地位的资产管理子公司开展资产管理业务，强化法人风险隔离，暂不具备条件的可以设立专门的资产管理业务经营部门开展业务。

金融机构不得为资产管理产品投资的非标准化债权类资产或者股权类资产提供任何直接或间接、显性或隐性的担保、回购等代为承担风险的承诺。

金融机构开展资产管理业务，应当确保资产管理业务与其他业务相分离，资产管理产品与其代销的金融产品相分离，资产管理产品之间相分离，资产管理业务操作与其他业务操作相分离。

十四、本意见发布后，金融机构发行的资产管理产品资产应当由具有托管资质的第三方机构独立托管，法律、行政法规另有规定的除外。

过渡期内，具有证券投资基金托管业务资质的商业银行可以托管本行理财产品，但应当为每只产品单独开立托管账户，确保资产隔离。过渡期后，具有证券投资基金托管业务资质的商业银行应当设立具有独立法人地位的子公司开展资产管理业务，该商业银行可以托管子公司发行的资产管理产品，但应当实现实质性的独立托管。独立托管有名无实的，由金融监督管理部门进行纠正和处罚。

十五、金融机构应当做到每只资产管理产品的资金单独管理、单独建账、单独核算，不得开展或者参与具有滚动发行、集合运作、分离定价特征的资金池业务。

金融机构应当合理确定资产管理产品所投资资产的期限，加强对期限错配的流动性风险管理，金融监督管理部门应当制定流动性风险管理规定。

为降低期限错配风险，金融机构应当强化资产管理产品久期管理，封闭式资产管理产品期限不得低于 90 天。资产管理产品直接或者间接投资于非标准化债权类资产的，非标准化债权类资产的终止日不得晚于封闭式资产管理产品的到期日或者开放式资产管理产品的最近一次开放日。

资产管理产品直接或者间接投资于未上市企业股权及其受（收）益权的，应当为封闭式资产管理产品，并明确股权及其受（收）益权的退出安排。未上市企业股权及其受（收）益权的退出日不得晚于封闭式资产管理产品的到期日。

金融机构不得违反金融监督管理部门的规定，通过为单一融资项目设立多只资产管理产品的方式，变相突破投资人数限制或者其他监管要求。同一金融机构发行多只资产管理产品投资同一资产的，为防止同一资产发生风险波及多只资产管理产品，多只资产管理产品投资该资产的资金总规模合计不得超过 300 亿元。如果超出该限额，需经相关金融监督管理部门批准。

十六、金融机构应当做到每只资产管理产品所投资资产的风险等级与投资者的风险承担能力相匹配，做到每只产品所投资资产构成清晰，风险可识别。

金融机构应当控制资产管理产品所投资资产的集中度：

（一）单只公募资产管理产品投资单只证券或者单只证券投资基金的市值不得超过该资产管理产品净资产的 10%。

（二）同一金融机构发行的全部公募资产管理产品投资单只证券或者单只证券投资基金的市值不得超过该证券市值或者证券投资基金市值的 30%。其中，同一金融机构全部开放式公募资产管理产品投资单一上市公司发行的股票不得超过该上市公司可流通股票的 15%。

（三）同一金融机构全部资产管理产品投资单一上市公司发行的股票不得超过该上市公司可流通股票的 30%。

金融监督管理部门另有规定的除外。

非因金融机构主观因素导致突破前述比例限制的，金融机构应当在流动性受限资产可出售、可转让或者恢复交易的 10 个交易日内调整至符合相关要求。

十七、金融机构应当按照资产管理产品管理费收入的 10% 计提风险准备金，或者按照规定计量操作风险资本或相应风险资本准备。风险准备金余额达到产品余额的 1% 时可以不再提取。风险准备金主要用于弥补因金融机构违法违规、违反资产管理产品协议、操作错误或者技术故障等给资产管理产品财产或者投资者造成的损失。金融机构应当定期将风险准备金的使用情况报告金融管理部门。

十八、金融机构对资产管理产品应当实行净值化管理，净值生成应当符合企业会计准则规定，及时反映基础金融资产的收益和风险，由托管机构进行核算并定期提供报告，由外部审计机构进行审计确认，被审计金融机构应当披露审计结果并同时报送金融管理部门。

金融资产坚持公允价值计量原则，鼓励使用市值计量。符合以下条件之一的，可按照企业会计准则以摊余成本进行计量：

（一）资产管理产品为封闭式产品，且所投金融资产以收取合同现金流量为目的并持有到期。

（二）资产管理产品为封闭式产品，且所投金融资产暂不具备活跃交易市场，或者在活跃市场中没有报价、也不能采用估值技术可靠计量公允价值。

金融机构以摊余成本计量金融资产净值，应当采用适当的风险控制手段，对金融资产净值的公允性进行评估。当以摊余成本计量已不能真实公允反映金融资产净值时，托管机构应当督促金融机构调整会计核算和估值方法。金融机构前期以摊余成本计量的金融资产的加权平均价格与资产管理产品实际兑付时金融资产的价值的偏离度不得达到 5% 或以上，如果偏离 5% 或以上的产品数超过所发行产品总数的 5%，金融机构不得再发行以摊余成本计量金融资产的资产管理产品。

十九、经金融管理部门认定，存在以下行为的视为刚性兑付：

（一）资产管理产品的发行人或者管理人违反真实公允确定净值原则，对产品进行保本保收益。

（二）采取滚动发行等方式，使得资产管理产品的本金、收益、风险在不同投资者之间发生转移，实现产品保本保收益。

（三）资产管理产品不能如期兑付或者兑付困难时，发行或者管理该产品的金融机构自行筹集资金偿付或者委托其他机构代为偿付。

（四）金融管理部门认定的其他情形。

经认定存在刚性兑付行为的，区分以下两类机构进行惩处：

（一）存款类金融机构发生刚性兑付的，认定为利用具有存款本质特征的资产管理产品进行监管套利，由国务院银行保险监督管理机构和中国人民银行按照存款业务予以规范，足额补缴存款准备金和存款保险保费，并予以行政处罚。

（二）非存款类持牌金融机构发生刚性兑付的，认定为违规经营，由金融监督管理部门和中国人民银行依法纠正并予以处罚。

任何单位和个人发现金融机构存在刚性兑付行为的，可以向金融管理部门举报，查证属实且举报内容未被相关部门掌握的，给予适当奖励。

外部审计机构在对金融机构进行审计时，如果发现金融机构存在刚性兑付行为的，应当及时报告金融管理部门。外部审计机构在审计过程中未能勤勉尽责，依法追究相应责任或依法依规给予行政处罚，并将相关信息纳入全国信用信息共享平台，建立联合惩戒机制。

二十、资产管理产品应当设定负债比例（总资产 / 净资产）上限，同类产品适用统一的负债比例上限。每只开放式公募产品的总资产不得超过该产品净资产的 140%，每只封闭式公募产品、每只私募产品的总资产不得超过该产品净资产的 200%。计算单只产品的总资产时应当按照穿透原则合并计算所投资资产管理产品的总资产。

金融机构不得以受托管理的资产管理产品份额进行质押融资，放大杠杆。

二十一、公募产品和开放式私募产品不得进行份额分级。

分级私募产品的总资产不得超过该产品净资产的 140%。分级私募产品应当根据所投资资产的风险程度设定分级比例（优先级份额 / 劣后级份额，中间级份额计入优先级份额）。固定收益类产品的分级比例不得超过 3∶1，权益类产品的分级比例不得超过 1∶1，商品及金融衍生品类产品、混合类产品的分级比例不得超过 2∶1。发行分级资产管理产品的金融机构应当对该资产管理产品进行自主管理，不得转委托给劣后级投资者。

分级资产管理产品不得直接或者间接对优先级份额认购者提供保本保收益安排。

本条所称分级资产管理产品是指存在一级份额以上的份额为其他级份额提供一定的风险补偿，收益分配不按份额比例计算，由资产管理合同另行约定的产品。

二十二、金融机构不得为其他金融机构的资产管理产品提供规避投资范围、杠杆约束等监管要求的通道服务。

资产管理产品可以再投资一层资产管理产品，但所投资的资产管理产品不得再投资公募证券投资基金以外的资产管理产品。

金融机构将资产管理产品投资于其他机构发行的资产管理产品，从而将本机构的资产管理产品资金委托给其他机构进行投资的，该受托机构应当为具有专业投资能力和资质的受金融监督管理部门监管的机构。公募资产管理产品的受托机构应当为金融机构，私募资产管理产品的受托机构可以为私募基金管理人。受托机构应当切实履行主动管理职责，不得进行转委托，不得再投资公募证券投资基金以外的资产管理产品。委托机构应当对受托机构开展尽职调查，实行名单制管理，明确规定受托机构的准入标准和程序、责任和义务、存续期管理、利益冲突防范机制、信息披露义务以及退出机制。委托机构不得因委托其他机构投资而免除自身应当承担的责任。

金融机构可以聘请具有专业资质的受金融监督管理部门监管的机构作为投资顾问。投资顾问提供投资建议指导委托机构操作。

金融监督管理部门和国家有关部门应当对各类金融机构开展资产管理业务实行平等准入、给予公平待遇。资产管理产品应当在账户开立、产权登记、法律诉讼等方面享有平等的地位。金融监督管理部门基于风险防控考虑，确实需要对其他行业金融机构发行的资产管理产品采取限制措施的，应当充分征求相关部门意见并达成一致。

二十三、运用人工智能技术开展投资顾问业务应当取得投资顾问资质，非金融机构不得借助智能投资顾问超范围经营或者变相开展资产管理业务。

金融机构运用人工智能技术开展资产管理业务应当严格遵守本意见有关投资者适当性、投资范围、信息披露、风险隔离等一般性规定，不得借助人工智能业务夸大宣传资产管理产品或者误导投资者。金融机构应当向金融监督管理部门报备人工智能模型的主要参数以及资产配置的主要逻辑，为投资者单独设立智能管理账户，充分提示人工智能算法的固有缺陷和使用风险，明晰交易流程，强化留痕管理，严格监控智能管理账户的交易头寸、风险限额、交易种类、价格权限等。金融机构因违法违规或者管理不当造成投资者损失的，应当依法承担损害赔偿责任。

金融机构应当根据不同产品投资策略研发对应的人工智能算法或者程序化交易，避免算法同质化加剧投资行为的顺周期性，并针对由此可能引发的市场波动风险制定应对预案。因算法同质化、编程设计错误、对数据利用深度不够等人工智能算法模型缺陷或者系统异常，导致羊群效应、影响金融市场稳定运行的，金融机构应当及时采取人工干预措施，强制调整或者终止人工智能业务。

二十四、金融机构不得以资产管理产品的资金与关联方进行不正当交易、利益输送、内幕交易和操纵市场，包括但不限于投资于关联方虚假项目、与关联方共同收购上市公司、向本机构注资等。

金融机构的资产管理产品投资本机构、托管机构及其控股股东、实际控制人或者与其有其他重大利害关系的公司发行或者承销的证券，或者从事其他重大关联交易的，应当建立健全内部审批机制和评估机制，并向投资者充分披露信息。

二十五、建立资产管理产品统一报告制度。中国人民银行负责统筹资产管理产品的数据编码和综合统计工作，会同金融监督管理部门拟定资产管理产品统计制度，建立资产管理产品信息系统，规范和统一产品标准、信息分类、代码、数据格式，逐只产品统计基本信息、募集信息、资产负债信息和终止信息。中国人民银行和金融监督管理部门加强资产管理产品的统计信息共享。金融机构应当将含债权投资的资产管理产品信息报送至金融信用信息基础数据库。

金融机构于每只资产管理产品成立后 5 个工作日内，向中国人民银行和金融监督管理部门同时报送产品基本信息和起始募集信息；于每月 10 日前报送存续期募集信息、资产负债信息，于产品终止后 5 个工作日内报送终止信息。

中央国债登记结算有限责任公司、中国证券登记结算有限公司、银行间市场清算所股份有限公司、上海票据交易所股份有限公司、上海黄金交易所、上海保险交易所股份有限公司、中保保险资产登记交易系统有限公司于每月 10 日前向中国人民银行和金融监督管理部门同时报送资产管理产品持有其登记托管的金融工具的信息。

在资产管理产品信息系统正式运行前，中国人民银行会同金融监督管理部门依据统计制度拟定统一的过渡期数据报送模板；各金融监督管理部门对本行业金融机构发行的资产管理产品，于每月 10 日前按照数据报送模板向中国人民银行提供数据，及时沟通跨行业、跨市场的重大风险信息和事项。

中国人民银行对金融机构资产管理产品统计工作进行监督检查。资产管理产品统计的具体制度由中国人民银行会同相关部门另行制定。

二十六、中国人民银行负责对资产管理业务实施宏观审慎管理，会同金融监督管理部门制定资产管理业务的标准规制。金融监督管理部门实施资产管理业务的市场准入和日常监管，加强投资者保护，依照本意见会同中国人民银行制定出台各自监管领域的实施细则。

本意见正式实施后，中国人民银行会同金融监督管理部门建立工作机制，持续监测资产管理业务的发展和风险状况，定期评估标准规制的有效性和市场影响，及时修订完善，推动资产管理行业持续健康发展。

二十七、对资产管理业务实施监管遵循以下原则：

（一）机构监管与功能监管相结合，按照产品类型而不是机构类型实施功能监管，同一类型的资产管理产品适用同一监管标准，减少监管真空和套利。

（二）实行穿透式监管，对于多层嵌套资产管理产品，向上识别产品的最终投资者，向下识别产品的底层资产（公募证券投资基金除外）。

（三）强化宏观审慎管理，建立资产管理业务的宏观审慎政策框架，完善政策工具，从宏观、逆周期、跨市场的角度加强监测、评估和调节。

（四）实现实时监管，对资产管理产品的发行销售、投资、兑付等各环节进行全面动态监管，建立综合统计制度。

二十八、金融监督管理部门应当根据本意见规定，对违规行为制定和完善处罚规则，依法实施处罚，并确保处罚标准一致。资产管理业务违反宏观审慎管理要求的，由中国人民银行按照法律法规实施处罚。

二十九、本意见实施后，金融监督管理部门在本意见框架内研究制定配套细则，配套细则之间应当相互衔接，避免产生新的监管套利和不公平竞争。按照"新老划断"原则设置过渡期，确保平稳过渡。过渡期为本意见发布之日起至 2020 年底，对提前完成整改的机构，给予适当监管激励。过渡期内，金融机构发行新产品应当符合本意见的规定；为接续存量产品所投资的未到期资产，维持必要的流动性和市场稳定，金融机构可以发行老产品对接，但应当严格控制在存量产品整体规模内，并有序压缩递减，防止过渡期结束时出现断崖效应。金融机构应当制定过渡期内的资产管理业务整改计划，明确时间进度安排，并报送相关金融监督管理部门，由其认可并监督实施，同时报备中国人民银行。过渡期结束后，金融机构的资产管理产品按照本意见进行全面规范（因子公司尚未成立而达不到第三方独立托管要求的情形除外），金融机构不得再发行或存续违反本意见规定的资产管理产品。

三十、资产管理业务作为金融业务，属于特许经营行业，必须纳入金融监管。非金融机构不得发行、销售资产管理产品，国家另有规定的除外。

非金融机构违反上述规定，为扩大投资者范围、降低投资门槛，利用互联网平台等公开宣传、分拆销售具有投资门槛的投资标的、过度强调增信措施掩盖产品风险、设立产品二级交易市场等行为，按照国家规定进行规范清理，构成非法集资、非法吸收公众存款、非法发行证券的，依法追究法律责任。非金融机构违法违规开展资产管理业务的，依法予以处罚；同时承诺或进行刚性兑付的，依法从重处罚。

三十一、本意见自发布之日起施行。

本意见所称"金融管理部门"是指中国人民银行、国务院银行保险监督管理机构、国务院证券监督管理机构和国家外汇管理局。"发行"是指通过公开或者非公开方式向资产管理产品的投资者发出认购邀约，进行资金募集的活动。"销售"是指向投资者宣传推介资产管理产品，办理产品申购、赎回的活动。"代理销售"是指接受合作机构的委托，在本机构渠道向投资者宣传推介、销售合作机构依法发行的资产管理产品的活动。

附录 8 国务院办公厅关于推广支持创新相关改革举措的通知

国办发〔2017〕80 号

各省、自治区、直辖市人民政府，国务院各部委、各直属机构：

为深入实施创新驱动发展战略，党中央、国务院确定在京津冀、上海、广东（珠三角）、安徽（合芜蚌）、四川（成德绵）、湖北武汉、陕西西安、辽宁沈阳 8 个区域开展全面创新改革试验，推进相关改革举措先行先试，着力破除制约创新发展的体制机制障碍。有关地区和部门认真落实党中央、国务院决策部署，在深化科技体制改革、提升自主创新能力、优化创新创业环境等方面进行了大胆探索，形成了一批支持创新的相关改革举措。为进一步加大支持创新的力度，营造有利于大众创业、万众创新的制度环境和公平竞争市场环境，为创新发展提供更加优质的服务，经国务院批准，将有关改革举措在全国或 8 个改革试验区域内推广。现就有关事项通知如下：

一、推广改革举措的主要内容

（一）科技金融创新方面 3 项："以关联企业从产业链核心龙头企业获得的应收账款为质押的融资服务""面向中小企业的一站式投融资信息服务""贷款、保险、财政风险补偿捆绑的专利权质押融资服务"。

（二）创新创业政策环境方面 5 项："专利快速审查、确权、维权一站式服务""强化创新导向的国有企业考核与激励""事业单位可采取年薪制、协议工资制、项目工资等灵活多样的分配形式引进紧缺或高层次人才""事业单位编制省内统筹使用""国税地税联合办税"。

（三）外籍人才引进方面 2 项："鼓励引导优秀外国留学生在华就业创业，符合条件的外国留学生可直接申请工作许可和居留许可""积极引进外籍高层次人才，简化来华工作手续办理流程，新增工作居留向永久居留转换的申请渠道"。

（四）军民融合创新方面 3 项："军民大型国防科研仪器设备整合共享""以股权为纽带的军民两用技术联盟创新合作""民口企业配套核心军品的认定和准入标准"。

二、高度重视推广工作

各地区、各部门要深入实施创新驱动发展战略，深刻认识推广支持创新相关改革举措的重大意义，将其作为深入贯彻落实创新、协调、绿色、开放、共享发展理念和推进供给侧结构性改革的重要抓手。要着力推动政策制度创新，深化简政放权、放管结合、优化服务改革，加快政府职能转变，提高政府管理水平，推进构建与创新驱动发展要求相适应的新体制、新模式，持续释放改革红利，激发全社会的创新创造活力，加快培育壮大经济发展新动能。

三、切实做好组织实施

各省（区、市）人民政府要将支持创新相关改革举措推广工作列为本地区重点工作，结合实际情况，积极创造条件、扎实推进，确保改革举措落地生根、产生实效。国务院各有关部门要结合工作职能，积极协调、指导推进推广工作。国家发展改革委和科技部要适时督促检查推广工作进展情况及效果，重大问题及时向国务院报告。

附件：支持创新相关改革举措推广清单

国务院办公厅
2017 年 9 月 7 日
（此件公开发布）

支持创新相关改革举措推广清单

序号	改革举措	主要内容	责任部门	推广范围
1	专利快速审查、确权、维权一站式服务	在专利密集型产业集聚区，依托知识产权快速维权中心，开展集专利快速审查、快速确权、快速维权于一体的一站式综合服务	国家知识产权局	全国
2	以关联企业从产业链核心龙头企业获得的应收账款为质押的融资服务	以从核心龙头企业获得的应收账款作为质押，为关联产业链大企业、供应商中小微企业提供融资服务	人民银行、工业和信息化部	全国
3	面向中小企业的一站式投融资信息服务	构建物理载体和信息载体，通过政府引导、民间参与、市场化运作，搭建债权融资服务、股权融资服务、增值服务三大信息服务体系，加强科技与金融融合，为中小企业提供全方位、一站式投融资信息服务	人民银行、银监会、证监会	全国
4	贷款、保险、财政风险补偿捆绑的专利权质押融资服务	金融机构、地方政府等依法按市场化方式自主选择建立“贷款＋保险保障＋财政风险补偿”的专利权质押融资新模式，为中小企业专利贷款提供保证保险服务	人民银行、国家知识产权局、银监会、保监会	全国
5	强化创新导向的国有企业考核与激励	完善对地方国有企业重大创新工程和项目的容错机制，引入领导人员任期激励等创新导向的中长期激励方式	国务院、国资委	全国
6	事业单位可采取年薪制、协议工资制、项目工资等灵活多样的分配形式引进紧缺或高层次人才	高校和科研院所采取年薪制、协议工资制或项目工资等灵活多样的形式引进紧缺或高层次人才	人力资源和社会保障部、财政部、教育部、中科院	全国
7	事业单位编制省内统筹使用	建立“动态调整、周转使用”的事业单位编制省内统筹调剂使用制度，形成需求引领、基数不变、存量整合、动态供给的编制管理新模式	中央编办、人力资源和社会保障部、教育部、财政部	全国
8	国税地税联合办税	国税、地税合作共建办税服务厅，统筹整合双方办税资源，实现“进一家门、办两家事”的目标	税务总局	全国
9	军民大型国防科研仪器设备整合共享	建立共享服务平台，整合一定区域内大型国防科研设施与高校、科研院所仪器设备，逐步实现开放共享	国家国防科工局、中央军委装备发展部、财政部	全国
10	以股权为纽带的军民两用技术联盟创新合作	联盟成员单位通过股权合作，构建紧密的组织形式和成果分享机制，提升军民两用技术的联合研发创新能力，促进科技成果转化	国家国防科工局、中央军委装备发展部	全国
11	民口企业配套核心军品的认定和准入标准	在军工企业中确定可面向民口企业配套核心军品的认定、准入标准，形成军工企业与民口企业分工协作的合作模式	国家国防科工局、中央军委装备发展部	全国
12	鼓励引导优秀外国留学生在华就业创业，符合条件的外国留学生可直接申请工作许可和居留许可	外国留学生凭国内高校毕业证书、创业计划书，可申请加注“创业”的私人事务类居留许可；注册企业的，凭国内高校毕业证书和企业注册证明等材料，可申请工作许可和工作类居留许可	人力资源和社会保障部、教育部、公安部、国家外专局	全国
		获得硕士及以上学位的外国留学生，符合一定条件的，可直接申请外国人来华工作许可和工作类居留许可	国家外专局、人力资源和社会保障部、教育部、公安部	全国
13	积极引进外籍高层次人才，简化来华工作手续办理流程，新增工作居留向永久居留转换的申请渠道	整合外国专家来华工作许可和外国人入境就业许可，实行一个窗口办理发放外国人来华工作许可证	国家外专局、人力资源和社会保障部	全国
		在原有永久居留政策基础上，新增与工资和税收挂钩的市场化渠道，外籍人员达到工资、缴税、工作年限等方面规定标准后，即可申请永久居留	公安部、国家外专局、人力资源和社会保障部	8 个改革试验区域

附录 9 中国创业投资机构名录

公司名称	成立时间	网址	电话
安丰创业投资有限公司	2008-02-28	—	0571-87633580
安徽爱众筹投资管理股份有限公司	2014-10-10	—	0551-65346666
安徽安元投资基金有限公司	2015-07-17	—	0551-63894124
安徽大学资产经营有限公司	2009-10-13	www.zcgs.ahu.cn	0551-65329875
安徽鼎信创业投资有限公司	2012-06-05	—	0551-65319112
安徽丰创生物技术产业创业投资有限公司	2013-04-02	—	0551-65182095
安徽高科创业投资有限公司	2010-01-28	www.ahgoco.com	0551-65319112
安徽高新金通安益二期创业投资基金（有限合伙）	2015-12-24	—	—
安徽高新金通安益股权投资基金（有限合伙）	2015-03-23	—	0551-66103790
安徽高新同华创业投资基金（有限合伙）	2015-03-25	—	—
安徽高新招商致远股权投资基金（有限合伙）	2015-03-23	—	—
安徽国安创业投资有限公司	2010-09-15	—	0551-65732844
安徽国耀创业投资有限公司	2013-11-28	—	—
安徽国元创投有限责任公司	2010-06-13	www.ahgyct.com	0551-63699700
安徽合信投资有限公司	2002-12-30	—	—
安徽恒兴创业投资有限管理有限公司	2002-04-26	—	—
安徽红土创业投资有限公司	2010-08-10	www.szvc.com.cn	0551-65666025
安徽华文创业投资管理有限公司	2003-06-04	—	0551-63533281
安徽徽商产业投资基金管理有限公司	2008-03-18	www.hygcapital.com	0551-5844598
安徽汇智富创业投资有限公司	2013-03-26	—	0551-65383158
安徽火花科技创业投资有限公司	2013-06-25	—	—
安徽昆冈创业股权投资合伙企业（有限合伙）	2010-08-17	—	0553-3887132
安徽联华盈创投资管理有限公司	2013-09-05	—	0551-65367321
安徽启光能源科技研究院有限公司	2012-10-31	www.qiguang.org	0553-3021991
安徽庆余投资管理有限公司	2012-07-23	—	—
安徽省安庆发展投资（集团）有限公司	2004-07-19	www.aqfztz.com	0556-5595212

公司名称	成立时间	网址	电话
安徽省创投资本基金有限公司	2010-07-27	—	0551-67131875
安徽省创业投资有限公司	2008-07-09	—	0551-63677211
安徽省高新创业投资有限责任公司	2009-12-23	—	—
安徽省高新技术产业投资有限公司	2014-12-16	www.ahinv.com	0551-63677211
安徽省科创投资管理咨询有限责任公司	2000-10-31	—	0551-66195765
安徽省科技产业投资有限公司	1999-07	www.ahkjtz.com.cn	0551-66195708
安徽省闽商投资控股有限公司	2010-06-22	—	—
安徽西格玛壹号投资合伙企业（有限合伙）	2013-05-24	—	—
安徽新安金融集团股份有限公司	2003-07-22	—	—
安徽兴皖创业投资有限公司	2010-08-20	—	0551-65732843
安徽亿诚融资理财信息服务有限公司	2012-08-29	www.ahycrzlc.com	0556-5275508
安徽益明投资理财咨询服务有限公司	2013-09-04	www.ahymlc.com	0556-5696657
安徽智鼎创业投资有限公司	2009-11	www.qyzyw.com	—
安庆百科实业有限公司	2004-02-09	—	0556-5323811
安庆发投创业投资有限公司	2012-09-28	—	—
安阳惠通高创新材料创业投资合伙企业（有限合伙）	2012-07-25	—	0371-86615676
白银科键创新创业投资基金合伙企业（有限合伙）	2016-11-04	—	—
白银兰白大健康产业创业投资基金（有限合伙）	2017-02-15	—	—
蚌埠大学生创业园天使基金	2010-02-10	—	—
蚌埠市科技创业投资有限公司	2008-06-26	—	0552-3186802
蚌埠市天使投资基金（有限合伙）	2016-10-20	—	0552-3183818
蚌埠市远大创新创业投资有限公司	2010-09-28	—	0551-63186678
蚌埠皖北金牛创业投资有限公司	2011-05-17	—	0552-4129773
蚌埠中城创业投资有限公司	2009-03-16	—	0552-3183818
保定城典股权投资基金管理有限公司	2014-05-04	—	0312-6775367
保定市创元科技风险投资有限公司	2008-12-22	—	0312-6775532
保定市科锐特创业投资有限公司	2006-02-27	www.krtvc.com	0312-3371336
保定市长城创业投资有限公司	2004-04-14	—	—
北国华盖（辽宁）投资管理有限公司	2016-07-06	—	024-22699248
北极光创投	2005-12-15	www.nlvc.com	010-59696185
北极光创业投资企业	2009	—	010-59696185
北京安芙兰创业投资有限公司	2009-06-11	www.vcpe.hk	010-66416805
北京安芙兰投资中心（有限合伙）	2012-01-11	—	010-66416805
北京澳银资本投资管理有限公司	2012-07-26	—	010-88825637

公司名称	成立时间	网址	电话
北京北科迅达科技投资有限公司	2014-12-19	www.boomfun.cn	010-62607133
北京春晓汇商股权投资管理有限公司	2015-05-05	www.chunxiao.cn	—
北京芳晟投资管理中心（有限合伙）	2011-04-21	—	010-65035588
北京宏福博奥科技孵化器有限公司	—	—	—
北京厚持投资管理有限责任公司	2011-12-12	www.holchcapital.com	010-81399901
北京华创嘉成投资管理有限公司	2013-06-26	—	—
北京嘉华汇金投资管理有限公司	2011-02-24	—	010-64685181
北京开物昌盛投资管理有限公司	2012-12	—	—
北京科创文华投资管理有限公司	2013-06-26	—	—
北京老鹰投资基金管理有限公司	2015-07-21	www.eaglesfund.com	010-62680865
北京南车创业投资有限公司	2011-09	—	010-52608040
北京诺善同创投资管理中心（有限合伙）	2016-02-29	—	010-62988017
北京青山同创投资有限公司	2011-11-18	www.hwazing.com	010-85910317
北京上古新泰投资管理有限公司	2015-04-16	—	—
北京视记云科技创业投资有限公司	2015-04-14	—	—
北京水平投资管理有限公司	2014-12-10	—	—
北京天翼汇融投资管理有限公司	2009-11-09	www.the-capital.com.cn	010-85872472
北京同创金鼎投资管理有限公司	2013-08-09	www.jindingcapital.com.cn	—
北京同创九鼎投资管理股份有限公司	2013-12-12	—	010-63221188
北京万禾创新投资管理有限公司	2014-09-11	—	—
北京沃康资本管理有限公司	2013-05-16	www.beyondfund.com	010-82483542
北京五岳世纪投资有限公司	2012-11-19	www.n5capital.com	—
北京信中利投资股份有限公司	1999-05-17	www.chinaequity.net	010-85550509
北京亦庄普丰国际创业投资管理有限公司	2009-08-17	—	010-67875167
北京用友幸福投资管理有限公司	2010-05-12	www.ufcap.com	—
北京智银投资管理有限公司	2010-12-14	www.wiste.cn	—
北京中投建华投资管理有限公司	2011-09-22	—	010-64685181
北京中兴华建投资管理有限公司	2015-08-12	—	010-64685181
毕节市科技创业投资有限公司	2014-12-29	—	—
滨州北海创业投资有限公司	2011-12-26	—	0543-2258709
滨州高新技术创业投资有限公司	2010-05-07	—	0543-8191177
滨州市慧立创业投资有限公司	2011-06-20	—	—
博辰创业投资管理（苏州）有限公司	2007-11-26	—	0512-66969661
博汇源创业投资有限合伙企业	2009-05-26	—	—

公司名称	成立时间	网址	电话
常创（常州）创业投资合伙企业（有限合伙）	2013-09-03	—	0519-85228057
常创天使（常州）创业投资中心（有限合伙）	2014-03-04	—	0519-85228057
常德合金生物科技投资中心（有限合伙）	2015-12-31	—	021-66316757
常德沅澧产业投资控股有限公司	2014-01-22	—	0736-7133995
常熟博瀚创业投资有限公司	2009-11-23	—	0512-52351556
常熟博融创业投资有限公司	2016-08-12	—	0512-52351556
常熟金茂创业投资管理有限公司	2010-11	www.jolmo.com	025-84730375
常熟经济开发区高新技术创业投资有限公司	2009-06	—	0512-52292926
常熟市国发创业投资有限公司	2010-11-25	—	0512-52876487
常州常金创业投资有限公司	2014-12-12	—	—
常州常荣创业投资有限公司	2009-09-08	www.ndinvest.cn	0519-89816672
常州常以创业投资管理有限公司	2009-12-31	—	0519-89629972
常州常以创业投资中心（有限合伙）	2010-01-12	—	0519-89629972
常州创业投资集团有限公司	2013-12-27	www.eccjt.com	0519-86680622
常州德丰杰清洁技术创业投资中心（有限合伙）	2009-12	www.dfjcompass.com	0519-89182227
常州德丰杰投资管理有限公司	2009-12	www.dfjcompass.com	0519-89182227
常州德丰杰正道创业投资中心（有限合伙）	2012-03	www.dfjcompass.com	0519-89182227
常州德丰杰正道投资管理有限公司	2012-02-20	www.dfjcompass.com	0519-89182227
常州东方产业引导创业投资有限责任公司	2016-04-01	—	—
常州沣时扬创业投资中心（有限合伙）	2017-11-07	www.xcap.com.cn	—
常州蜂鸟创业投资合伙企业（有限合伙）	2012-06-21	—	0519-81231818
常州高睿创业投资管理有限公司	2007-09-24	—	0519-85150557
常州高投创业投资有限公司	2008-07-22	—	0519-85150557
常州高新创业投资有限公司	2012-01-18	—	0519-81235008
常州高新技术风险投资有限公司	2000-12-22	www.cz—vc.com	0519-85150557
常州高新区印刷电子产业基金创业投资有限公司	2013-09-05	—	0519-88850176
常州高新投创业投资有限公司	2012-08-13	—	0519-81235008
常州和泰股权投资有限公司	2001-10-29	—	0519-85176186
常州和裕创业投资有限公司	2011-04	—	0519-85176186
常州红土人才投资合伙企业（有限合伙）	2017-11-27	www.szvc.com.cn	0519-86318682
常州华软投资管理有限公司	2010-07-07	—	010-65505560
常州嘉和达创业投资中心（有限合伙）	2016-12-12	—	—
常州金陵华软创业投资合伙企业（有限合伙）	2010-08-05	—	010-65535560

公司名称	成立时间	网址	电话
常州金码创业投资管理合伙企业（有限合伙）	2011-11-30	www.jolmo.net	025-84730211
常州金茂经信创业投资管理企业（有限合伙）	2013-12-31	www.jolmo.net	025-84730211
常州金茂新兴产业创业投资合伙企业（有限合伙）	2011-09	www.jolmo.net	025-84730375
常州力合创业投资有限公司	2008-10-10	www.leaguercapital.com	0519-86220138
常州力合投资管理有限公司	2008-08	www.leaguercapital.com	0519-86220138
常州领创创业投资有限公司	2016-05-11	—	—
常州牡丹江南创业投资有限责任公司	2010-03-15	—	0519-68866908
常州青枫云港投资中心（有限合伙）	2017-05-26	—	—
常州青年创业投资中心（有限合伙）	2012-12-20	—	0519-85228057
常州青企联合创业投资合伙企业（有限合伙）	2013-01-05	—	0519-85228057
常州瑞烁创业投资合伙企业（有限合伙）	2017-06-15	—	—
常州睿泰创业投资管理有限公司	2012-01-06	—	0519-81081861
常州睿泰创业投资中心（有限合伙）	2012-01-09	—	—
常州睿泰贰号创业投资中心（有限合伙）	2017-07-20	—	0519-81081861
常州睿泰叁号创业投资中心（有限合伙）	2017-10-18	—	0519-81081861
常州赛富高新创业投资管理有限公司	2009-10-28	www.sbaif.com	0519-89606122
常州赛富高新创业投资中心（有限合伙）	2009-12	www.sbaif.com	0519-89606122
常州市久益股权投资中心（有限合伙）	2010-07-30	www.nd-invest.cn	0519-89816672
常州天创股权投资中心（有限合伙）	2016-12-15	—	—
常州天融股权投资中心（有限合伙）	2016-06-30	—	—
常州武进红土创业投资有限公司	2008-08-19	www.szvc.com.cn	0519-86318682
常州武岳峰创业投资管理有限公司	2011-03-03	www.summitviewcapital.com	0519-86620218
常州武岳峰创业投资合伙企业（有限合伙）	2011-03-23	www.summitviewcapital.com	0519-86220218
常州鑫未来创业投资有限公司	2017-11-07	—	—
常州信辉创业投资有限公司	2007-05-11	—	0519-88137096
常州悦石科泰思投资合伙企业（有限合伙）	2017-09-28	—	010-62188360
常州智造新兴产业创业投资中心（有限合伙）	2016-10-31	—	0519-81235008
常州钟楼红土创业投资有限公司	2013-08-23	www.szvc.com.cn	0519-86318682
宸科创业投资（深圳）有限公司	2017-06-14	—	—
成都创新风险投资有限公司	2001-06-08	www.cd-vc.com.cn	028-85337115
成都德同银科创业投资合伙企业（有限合伙）	2010-03-03	www.dtcap.com	028-85231897
成都电科鹰熊创业投资中心（有限合伙）	2015-11-26	—	028-68902966
成都高投创业投资有限公司	2004-05-17	www.cdhtivc.com	028-85335111
成都硅谷天堂通威银科创业投资有限公司	2010-12-22	—	028-83202890

公司名称	成立时间	网址	电话
成都合力蓉信股权投资基金管理有限公司	2015-12-16	—	—
成都阶梯创业投资合伙企业（有限合伙）	2016-03-09	—	028-65471211
成都阶梯创业投资有限公司	2015-04-15	—	028-65471211
成都凯晟投资管理中心（有限合伙）	2010-11-19	—	—
成都老鹰易真创业投资有限公司	2015-06-05	—	—
成都晟唐银科创业投资企业（有限合伙）	2011-01-30	—	028-85987150
成都银科创业投资有限公司	2009-03-18	www.ykvc.cn	028-85336380
成都盈创德弘创业投资合伙企业（有限合伙）	2015-09-23	—	028-85335111
成都盈创德弘股权投资基金管理有限公司	2015-09-08	—	—
成都盈创兴科创业投资合伙企业（有限合伙）	2014-09-26	—	028-85988444
成都盈创兴科股权投资基金管理有限公司	2014-09-23	—	028-85988444
成都招商局银科创业投资有限公司	2010-12-31	—	—
成都真然股权投资基金管理有限公司	2015-01-30	www.zhenranziben.com	—
诚承投资控股有限公司	2013-10	—	—
池州中安创业投资基金合伙企业（有限合伙）	2016-06-01	—	—
崇德弘信（北京）投资管理有限公司	2012-12	—	—
滁州浚源创业投资中心（有限合伙）	2011-06	www.jycapital.cn	010-82661938
楚商领先（武汉）创业投资基金管理有限公司	2013-06-25	www.chushang-invest.cc	027-87750827
创业时代创业投资（深圳）有限公司	2017-07-14	www.chhuangyesd.com	—
大连北方科技企业孵化基地	2003-06-12	www.bffhjd.cn	0411-87505839
大连创业工坊科技服务有限公司	2002-08-07	www.chuangyegongfang.com	—
大连海融高新创业投资管理有限公司	2008-02-18	—	—
大连海融高新创业投资基金有限公司	2007-12-29	—	—
大连嘉创投资集团有限公司	2003-09-24	—	0411-88120533
大连精石文化产业投资有限公司	2014-04-28	—	0411-83792186
大连科技风险投资基金有限公司	2000-02	www.dstvc.com.cn	0411-82781352-11
大连赛伯乐创业投资中心（有限合伙）	2013-09-13	—	400-6761188-1037
大连天使创业投资有限公司	2006-04-14	—	0411-84753186
大连万融天使投资有限公司	2010-11-30	—	—
大连网信创业投资管理有限公司	1999-06-28	—	0411-82859969
大连银信创业投资有限公司	2006-09-13	—	0411-84802259-8001
大连知你小巢科技服务有限公司	2016-04-18	—	—
大连中以英飞投资管理有限公司	2014-03-04	www.zhongyifund.com	0411-39576019
大连众创空间企业管理有限公司	2015-07-10	—	—

公司名称	成立时间	网址	电话
大庆市高新技术产业投资企业（有限合伙）	2016-07-22	—	0451-51920801
丹阳市高新技术创业投资有限公司	2010-12-31	—	0511-86922610
德晟创业投资有限公司	2011-03-09	—	0411-82779477
德阳盈创阳光天使创业投资管理有限公司	2015-09-14	—	0838-6939393
鼎信博成创业投资有限公司	2010-08-26	—	0851-85806514
东方汇富创业投资管理有限公司	2017-09-01	www.orica.com.cn	0755-83515166
东莞红土创业投资有限公司	2013-03-15	www.szvc.com.cn	0769-26622138
东营经济开发区斯博特创业投资有限公司	2012-06-04	—	0546-8300909
丰厚资本	2012-11-26	www.fhcapital.com	010-89508968
佛山创业投资有限公司	2009-05-13	—	0757-22216839
佛山市博古科技投资有限公司	2009-09-14	—	0757-87380711
佛山市科海创业投资有限公司	2002-05-15	—	0757-86683130
佛山市三水高新创业中心有限公司	2004-09-29	www.fscyzx.comcn	0757-87380711
佛山市优势集成创业投资合伙企业（有限合伙）	2010-06-08	—	0757-86290169
佛山拓展创业投资有限公司	2010-12-10	—	0757-22216839
福建北辰星投资管理有限公司	2014-12-12	www.poritarcap.com	—
福建华兴创业投资有限公司	2000-12-26	www.fjhxvc.com	0591-87858275
富海永成基金	2014-09-22	www.ofcapital.com	021-50581867
甘肃低碳产业科技发展投资基金（有限合伙）	2017-09-05	—	0931-8735351
甘肃锋创创新创业产业投资基金（有限合伙）	2016-12-15	—	—
甘肃兰白试验区张江创新创业投资基金合伙企业（有限合伙）	2017-01-10	—	—
甘肃普高创业投资基金（有限合伙）	2016-09-14	www.gspgct.com	—
甘肃省科技风险投资有限公司	2001-08	—	0931-8537887
甘肃中睿泰德新兴农业投资基金（有限合伙）	2016-07-11	—	—
高能天汇创业投资有限公司	2007-01-29	www.powercapital.cn	—
高榕资本（深圳）投资中心（有限合伙）	2014-05-14	www.banyanvc.com	010-84442279
高投名力成长创业投资有限公司	2007-04-29	www.mcgf.com.cn	021-62889166
高瞻（无锡）创业投资有限公司	2011-04	www.tallwoodvc.com	0510-85228386
高瞻（无锡）企业管理有限公司	2011-05	www.tallwoodvc.com	0510-81814997
冠誉创业投资管理（深圳）有限公司	2004-03-28	www.itechvc.com	0755-83733664
广东创华投资有限公司	2010-12-22	—	—
广东德运创业投资有限公司	2013-05-03	www.dmkjy.com	0757-22908821
广东国科创业投资有限公司	2010-10-28	—	—

公司名称	成立时间	网址	电话
广东国科蓝海创业投资企业（有限合伙）	2015-06-17	—	—
广东恒健创业投资有限公司	—	—	—
广东弘德恒顺新材料创业投资合伙企业（有限合伙）	2017-06-19	—	—
广东红土创业投资有限公司	2012-03-27	—	—
广东猎投创业投资基金合伙企业（有限合伙）	2014-10-28	—	0757-86680996
广东南方星辰创业投资有限公司	2009-05-26	—	020-87329436
广东三泽投资管理有限公司	2015-11-23	—	0731-82768320
广东省科技创业投资有限公司	1992-11-05	www.gvcgc.com	—
广东省科技风险投资有限公司	1998-01-08	www.gvcgc.com	020-87684955
广东省粤科金融集团有限公司	2000-09-21	www.gvcgc.com	020-87682766
广东粤科惠华电子信息产业创业投资有限公司	2013-12-20	—	020-87683211
广西海东科技创业投资有限公司	2010-04-14	—	0772-3867268
广西中小企业创业投资有限公司	2009-08-12	www.gxfi.net	0771-5586630
广州元禾原点投资管理有限公司	2015-09-21	—	0512-66969533
广州长策投资管理有限公司	2015-05-29	www.ccinv.cn	020-85235200
贵阳博实火炬新兴产业创业投资企业（有限合伙）	2013-07-30	—	—
贵阳成创合力创业投资管理企业（有限合伙）	2011-03-25	—	0851-84757198
贵阳创新天使投资基金有限公司	2014-03-01	—	0851-85806514
贵阳高科创业投资有限责任公司	2009-09-03	www.guiyanggk.com	0851-84391972
贵阳高新创业投资有限公司	2011-04-27	—	0851-82203995
贵阳工投生物医药产业创业投资有限公司	2013-02-19	—	0851-84757198
贵阳花溪科技创业投资有限公司	2011-07-19	—	0851-83863159
贵阳甲秀创业投资中心（有限合伙）	2011-04-08	—	0851-84757198
贵阳市创业投资有限公司	2010-12-28	www.gyvc.cn	0851-84757198
贵阳市大数据安全产业创业投资基金有限公司	2017-10-19	—	0851-84757198
贵阳市服务外包及呼叫产业创业投资基金有限公司	2016-02-19	—	0851-84757198
贵阳市工业和信息化产业发展引导基金有限公司	2016-12-26	—	0851-84757198
贵阳市星火现代服务业创业投资有限公司	2014-05-13	—	—
贵阳市引凤高技术产业创业投资基金有限公司	2014-05-13	—	0851-84757198
贵州得天汇信创业股权投资中心（有限合伙）	2013-09-23	—	—
贵州德欣禾悦创业投资管理有限公司	2014-04-08	—	—
贵州鼎信博成投资管理有限公司	2009-09-16	www.gztvc.net	0852-85806514
贵州鼎信卓越创业投资有限公司	2013-12-6	—	—
贵州贵孵一起创天使基金投资中心（有限合伙）	2015-09-25	—	—

公司名称	成立时间	网址	电话
贵州国喜投资有限公司	2011–09–06	—	0851–82264888
贵州红土创业投资有限公司	2014–08–22	—	—
贵州金通达投资有限公司	2012–10–22	www.jtd.cc	0592–5140333
贵州经开创业投资管理有限公司	2012–06–01	www.gzjkct.com	0851–3890646–804
贵州经开创业投资有限公司	2012–08–21	—	0851–3890646–804
贵州省科技风险投资有限公司	1998–12	www.gzstvc.net	0851–85806514
贵州中鼎投资管理有限公司	2004–09–04	www.gzzd.cn	0851–86824648
贵州中水建设管理股份有限公司	2004–02–17	www.gsgcgw.com	0851–85610887
贵州筑银资本管理有限公司	2012–03–02	—	0851–84757198
国本创业投资江苏有限公司	2012–11–09	—	0516–8268995
国科嘉和（北京）投资管理有限公司	2011–08–24	www.cashcapital.cn	010–57636599
国科瑞祺物联网创业投资有限公司	2010–07–22	www.casim.cn	010–82607629–802
国润创业投资（苏州）管理有限公司	2008–05	www.guorun.com	0512–62998663
哈尔滨阿里汇富创业投资管理有限公司	2014–08–15	—	—
哈尔滨爱立方投资管理有限公司	2016–03–31	—	—
哈尔滨创新投资有限公司	2002–06–28	—	0451–84686552
哈尔滨创业投资集团有限公司	2009–02–26	www.hrbvc.com.cn	0451–84858002
哈尔滨大正鼎新投资管理有限公司	2012–08–21	—	—
哈尔滨东方汇富创业投资管理有限公司	2015–07–10	—	—
哈尔滨东方汇富创业投资企业	2015–11–26	—	—
哈尔滨富德恒创业投资企业	2014–01–24	—	—
哈尔滨富德恒利创业投资管理有限公司	2014–01–02	—	—
哈尔滨华滨创业投资管理有限公司	2014–12–02	—	—
哈尔滨华滨光辉创业投资企业（有限合伙）	2014–12–29	—	—
哈尔滨嘉玺创业投资管理有限公司	2012–12–27	—	0451–51854933
哈尔滨经济技术开发区新兴产业股权投资企业（有限合伙）	2016–06–24	—	0451–51920808
哈尔滨君丰创业投资企业	2015–01–29	—	—
哈尔滨君瑞投资管理有限公司	2014–11–18	—	—
哈尔滨凯致辰风投资管理有限公司	2015–08–19	—	0451–51920707
哈尔滨科力创业投资管理有限公司	2016–05–19	—	0451–51920801
哈尔滨朗江创新股权投资企业	2015–04–01	—	0451–84865258
哈尔滨朗江创新股权投资企业（有限合伙）	2015–04–01	—	0451–84865258
哈尔滨朗江创业投资管理有限公司	2015–03–26	—	0451–84865258
哈尔滨联创创业投资企业（有限合伙）	2015–12–03	—	010–65288289

公司名称	成立时间	网址	电话
哈尔滨市阿里聚旺创业投资企业（有限合伙）	2015-11-30	—	—
哈尔滨市科技风险投资中心	1998-05	—	0451-84686552
哈尔滨市天琪创业投资企业	2014-07-30	—	0451-82287805
哈尔滨市天琪创业投资企业（有限合伙）	2014-07-30	—	0451-82287805
哈尔滨市天琪股权投资基金管理企业（有限合伙）	2014-07-25	www.tqtz.com.cn	0451-82287805
哈尔滨越榕先锋创业投资有限责任公司	2014-12-15	—	—
哈尔滨越榕阳光创业投资企业（有限合伙）	2014-12-25	—	—
哈尔滨云谷创业投资企业	2013-07-10	—	—
海安达志创业投资有限公司	2016-09-18	www.dzct.cn	0513-88856600
海安得一创业投资有限公司	2015-12-14	—	021-64178726
海安东阳创业投资有限公司	2015-03-31	—	0513-88776222
海安丰睿创业投资有限公司	2015-08-20	—	—
海安峰融创业投资有限公司	2014-12-18	—	—
海安峰融投资管理有限公司	2014-10-15	—	—
海安富阳创业投资有限公司	—	—	0513-88826567
海安海高创业投资有限公司	2016-03-28	—	—
海安海开创业投资有限公司	2016-03-28	—	—
海安晗泰创业投资有限公司	2016-06-29	—	0513-88651598
海安和灵创业投资有限公司	2016-08-24	—	0513-88869883
海安恒益创业投资有限公司	2016-06-23	—	0513-88600692
海安金鑫创业投资有限公司	2016-10	—	—
海安开泰创业投资有限公司	2016-03-28	—	—
海安蓝天创业投资有限公司	2016-11-15	—	0513-88869873
海安青蓝创业投资有限公司	2015-03-26	—	—
海安申海创业投资有限公司	2016-11-03	—	—
海安泰港创业投资有限公司	2015-06-24	—	—
海安信拓创业投资有限公司	2016-06-30	—	0513-88833885
海安中海创业投资有限公司	2017-12-15	—	—
海硅（上海）创业投资合伙企业（有限合伙）	2011-08-05	—	021-65650817
海门国仟天使投资基金合伙企业（有限合伙）	2017-08-11	—	—
海门时代伯乐创富股权投资合伙企业（有限合伙）	2017-08-29	—	—
海门时代伯乐股权投资合伙企业（有限合伙）	2014-09-26	—	0513-82197321
海门天外望创业投资基金合伙企业（有限合伙）	2017-10-09	—	—
海南青创投资管理有限公司	2014-03-17	www.joyoty.com	0898-65319797

公司名称	成立时间	网址	电话
海南师范大学科技园管理有限公司	2014-07-01	www.hkdsp.com	—
海南雨点小额贷款有限公司	2016-04-06	—	—
海宁工程大科技园有限公司	2014-05-05	www.jb98.cnkj	0573-89263785
海宁力合天使创业投资合伙企业（有限合伙）	2014-09-30	—	—
海宁三仁腾兴股权投资合伙企业（有限合伙）	2015-06-02	—	—
海宁三仁望岳股权投资合伙企业（有限合伙）	2015-06-02	—	—
杭州安丰宸元创业投资合伙企业（有限合伙）	2016-01-21	—	0571-87633580
杭州安丰杭盈创业投资合伙企业（有限合伙）	2017-04-20	—	0571-87633580
杭州安丰慧元创业投资合伙企业（有限合伙）	2016-03-15	—	0571-87633580
杭州安丰玖号创业投资合伙企业（有限合伙）	2015-09-28	—	0571-87633580
杭州安丰上盈创业投资合伙企业（有限合伙）	2015-01-09	—	0571-87633580
杭州安丰盛科创业投资合伙企业（有限合伙）	2017-06-15	—	—
杭州安丰新千投创业投资合伙企业（有限合伙）	2017-01-09	—	0571-87633580
杭州安丰鑫元创业投资合伙企业（有限合伙）	2017-01-10	—	—
杭州拔萃投资管理有限公司	2017-12-20	—	—
杭州帮创投资合伙企业（有限合伙）	2016- 01-29	—	—
杭州帮实投资管理有限公司	2014-04-03	www.vcchina.com	—
杭州葆光投资管理有限公司	2012-10-18	—	0571-85455412
杭州滨江众创投资合伙企业（有限合伙）	2015-04-24	—	—
杭州博谊投资合伙企业（有限合伙）	2017	—	—
杭州辰弘投资合伙企业（有限合伙）	2016-06-14	—	0571-88771697
杭州诚和创业投资有限公司	2006-06-01	—	0571-88219849
杭州崇石投资合伙企业（有限合伙）	—	—	—
杭州德同创业投资合伙企业（有限合伙）	2010-07-08	—	0571-86690981
杭州德同投资管理有限公司	2010-04-21	—	0571-86690981
杭州鼎聚芥园创业投资合伙企业（有限合伙）	2011-05-28	—	—
杭州鼎聚景远创业投资合伙企业（有限合伙）	2016-05-23	—	—
杭州鼎聚坤华创业投资合伙企业（有限合伙）	2011-12-21	—	—
杭州鼎聚茂华创业投资合伙企业（有限合伙）	2013-01-07	—	—
杭州鼎聚投资管理有限公司	2011-04-06	—	—
杭州独角兽投资管理有限公司	2015-03-25	—	—
杭州敦和创业投资有限公司	2011-04-11	www.dunhevc.com	0571-87789050
杭州飞来投资管理有限公司	2007-06-28	www.flyvc.com	0571-88868827
杭州福生创业投资管理有限公司	2016-04-27	—	0571-86166991

公司名称	成立时间	网址	电话
杭州复朴共进投资合伙企业（有限合伙）	2015-03-31	—	0571-86690981
杭州复朴投资管理有限公司	2014-09-17	—	0571-86690981
杭州富海银涛投资管理合伙企业（有限合伙）	2011-07-27	—	0755-82588181
杭州广润创业投资有限公司	2007-11-28	—	0571-86951902
杭州贵巨创业投资合伙企业（有限合伙）	2015-09-23	—	0571-86951902
杭州海邦沣华投资管理有限公司	2017-10-15	—	—
杭州海邦巨擎创业投资合伙企业（有限合伙）	2016-03-14	—	—
杭州海邦新湖人才创业投资合伙企业（有限合伙）	2013-08-02	www.hbvc.com.cn	0571-81022997
杭州海邦药谷从正创业投资合伙企业（有限合伙）	2015-06-05	—	0571-81022997
杭州海邦羿谷创业投资合伙企业（有限合伙）	2017-12-28	—	—
杭州汉洋友创投资合伙企业（有限合伙）	2015-01-29	—	0571-87397929
杭州杭商宝石创业投资合伙企业（有限合伙）	2011-02-21	—	0571-86586927
杭州好望角车航投资合伙企业（有限合伙）	2016-06-30	—	0571-28178269
杭州好望角启航投资合伙企业（有限合伙）	2011-07-28	www.gsxt.zjaic.gov.cn	0571-28239066
杭州好望角投资管理有限公司	2007-08-22	www.gsxt.zjaic.gov.cn	0571-88236955
杭州好望角苇航投资合伙企业（有限合伙）	2015-11-23	—	0571-28239066
杭州好望角引航投资合伙企业（有限合伙）	2014-05-05	—	0571-28239066
杭州好望角禹航投资合伙企业（有限合伙）	2015-04-09	—	0571-28239066
杭州好望角越航投资合伙企业（有限合伙）	2014-12-25	—	0571-28239066
杭州浩宣投资合伙企业（有限合伙）	2017-03-09	—	—
杭州厚初创业投资合伙企业（有限合伙）	2014-05-22	—	0571-87988858
杭州金投智远创业投资合伙企业（有限合伙）	2017-07-21	—	—
杭州金永信创业投资合伙企业（有限合伙）	2009-12-21	—	0571-85279925
杭州金永信润禾创业投资合伙企业（有限合伙）	2010-05-04	—	0571-85279925
杭州金永信天时创业投资合伙企业	2010-04-07	—	0571-85279925
杭州锦聚投资管理有限公司	2014-07-21	www.jinju-capital.com	0571-28205211-8004
杭州锦聚新能源壹号投资合伙企业（有限合伙）	2017-12-12	—	0571-28205211-8004
杭州锦杏谷创业投资合伙企业（有限合伙）	2015-02-13	—	0571-28205211-8004
杭州经济技术开发区创业投资有限公司	2008-10-09	www.hedaventures.com	0571-88062089
杭州君知投资合伙企业（有限合伙）	2017-02-01	—	—
杭州君志投资合伙企业（有限合伙）	2017-02-10	—	—
杭州科发创业投资合伙企业（有限合伙）	2013-01-09	www.zdkfcapital.com	0571-88250427
杭州科发金鼎创业投资合伙企业（有限合伙）	2017-10-11	www.zjkfcapital.com	0571-88250328
杭州科发天使投资合伙企业（有限合伙）	2015-02-12	www.zdkfcapital.com	0571-88250427

公司名称	成立时间	网址	电话
杭州兰德润广投资管理有限公司	2010-12-20	—	0571-86963977
杭州兰德优势创业投资合伙企业（有限合伙）	2011-07-07	—	—
杭州蓝贝壳帮实创业投资合伙企业（有限合伙）	2015-11-26	—	—
杭州浪淘沙势弘投资合伙企业（有限合伙）	2016-06-14	—	0571-88771697
杭州浪淘沙投资管理有限公司	2014-09-19	www.ltsvc.com	0571-88771697
杭州浪淘沙智选创业投资合伙企业（有限合伙）	2014-11-06	—	0571-88771697
杭州立晟佳悦创业投资合伙企业（有限合伙）	2016-05-11	www.ls-vc.com	—
杭州立元创业投资股份有限公司	2006-12-08	www.cnlyjt.com	0571-87769018
杭州联创投资管理有限公司	2008-10-07	www.newmargin.com	0571-28130555
杭州联创永津创业投资合伙企业（有限合伙）	2009-09-01	—	—
杭州联创永润投资合伙企业（有限合伙）	2012-03-14	—	—
杭州联创永溢创业投资合伙企业（有限合伙）	2010-10-08	—	—
杭州灵琰投资合伙企业（有限合伙）	2013-06-03	—	0571-85455412
杭州纳泽投资合伙企业（有限合伙）	2017-03-15	—	0571-88122783
杭州普华博帆投资合伙企业（有限合伙）	2016-01-21	—	—
杭州普华帆顺投资合伙企业（有限合伙）	2016-10-26	—	—
杭州普华锐昆创业投资合伙企业（有限合伙）	2017-10-26	—	—
杭州普华顺程投资合伙企业（有限合伙）	2016-10-26	—	—
杭州普华智顺股权投资合伙企业（有限合伙）	2016-10-25	—	—
杭州钱江浙商创业投资合伙企业（有限合伙）	2009-06-03	—	0571-89922221
杭州庆诚投资合伙企业（有限合伙）	2015-08-20	—	—
杭州容胜投资合伙企业（有限合伙）	2015-12-01	—	—
杭州如山创业投资有限公司	2007-08	www.crestvalue.com	0571-87896213
杭州润琰投资合伙企业（有限合伙）	2013-04-08	—	0571-85455412
杭州赛伯乐瓦特投资合伙企业（有限合伙）	2016-08-23	—	—
杭州赛宸吉盛投资合伙企业（有限合伙）	2015-01-26	—	—
杭州赛硅银投资合伙企业（有限合伙）	2014-04-11	www.cybernaut.com.cn	0571-89939834
杭州赛久投资合伙企业（有限合伙）	2016-02-04	—	—
杭州赛麓股权投资合伙企业（有限合伙）	2016-06-27	—	—
杭州赛智君锐投资合伙企业（有限合伙）	2017-05-19	—	—
杭州十维创业投资合伙企业（有限合伙）	2015-06-01	—	—
杭州市高科技投资有限公司	2000-08	—	0571-86699729
杭州数创创业投资合伙企业（有限合伙）	2013-11-13	—	0571-97960022
杭州硕石投资合伙企业（有限合伙）	2015-11-17	—	—

公司名称	成立时间	网址	电话
杭州松观投资管理有限公司	2017-09-22	—	—
杭州天帮投资合伙企业（有限合伙）	2014-06-26	—	—
杭州天赋投资管理合伙企业（有限合伙）	2016-04-29	—	—
杭州天联投资管理合伙企业（有限合伙）	2014-03-14	—	—
杭州天璞创业投资合伙企业（有限合伙）	2013-07-05	—	—
杭州天跃投资管理合伙企业（有限合伙）	2016-01-25	—	—
杭州万豪投资管理有限公司	2006-01-09	—	0571-88129640
杭州维思投资合伙企业（有限合伙）	2012-07-17	—	—
杭州文诚创业投资有限公司	2012-07-09	—	—
杭州文广创业投资有限公司	2010-12-29	—	0571-89870615
杭州文广股权投资管理有限公司	2010-11-10	—	0571-89870615
杭州西创股权投资合伙企业（有限合伙）	2015-12-30	—	0571-87174979
杭州信倍股权投资合伙企业（有限合伙）	2016-05-31	—	—
杭州宣弘投资合伙企业（有限合伙）	2016-06-14	—	0571-88771697
杭州言和投资管理合伙企业（有限合伙）	2015-07-22	—	—
杭州以弘投资合伙企业（有限合伙）	2017-01-18	—	0571-88122783
杭州银杏海股权投资合伙企业（有限合伙）	2016-08-01	—	—
杭州银杏数股权投资合伙企业（有限合伙）	2015-03-13	—	0571-87174979
杭州英选投资合伙企业（有限合伙）	2016-06-14	—	0571-88771697
杭州盈动悦创创业投资合伙企业（有限合伙）	2015-09-10	—	0571-87960022
杭州友创天辰投资合伙企业（有限合伙）	2017-07-06	—	0571-87952529
杭州友创天使投资合伙企业（有限合伙）	2016-07-20	—	0571-87397929
杭州原质连客创业投资合伙企业（有限合伙）	2015-04-21	www.yuanzhivc.com	0571-88579775
杭州云创创业投资合伙企业（有限合伙）	2014-10-24	—	0571-87960022
杭州云栖创投股权投资合伙企业（有限合伙）	2017-11-20	—	0571-87174979
杭州云卓投资合伙企业（有限合伙）	2016-04-22	—	0571-87960022
杭州长江创业投资有限公司	1996-01-06	—	0571-86624323
杭州哲创投资合伙企业（有限合伙）	2016-12-04	—	—
杭州浙科汇福创业投资合伙企业（有限合伙）	2016-10-12	—	0571-88869550
杭州浙科汇经创业投资合伙企业（有限合伙）	2017-06-30	—	0571-88869550
杭州浙科汇庆创业投资合伙企业（有限合伙）	2013-04-10	—	—
杭州浙科盛元创业投资合伙企业（有限合伙）	2017	—	0571-88869550
杭州浙欣投资合伙企业（有限合伙）	2014-10-24	—	—
杭州中来锦聚新能源合伙企业（有限合伙）	2015-04-20	—	0571-20285211-8004

公司名称	成立时间	网址	电话
航天科工高新投资管理（北京）有限公司	2012-09-11	www.casicfund.com	—
航众控股集团有限公司	2012-05	www.hangzhong.com.cn	010-66167600
合肥高特佳创业投资有限责任公司	2010-04-19	www.szgig.com	0551-65310817
合肥高新产业投资有限公司	2016-07-12	—	0551-65326509
合肥高新创业投资管理合伙企业（有限合伙）	2015-08-21	www.hfgxt.com.cn	0551-65326509
合肥高新科技创业投资有限公司	2012-10-19	www.gxkt.hfgxjt.com	0551-65326509
合肥广电投资有限责任公司	2003-08-06	www.hfbtv.com	0551-63509205
合肥赛富合元创业投资中心（有限合伙）	2011-01-13	—	—
合肥世纪创新投资有限公司	2002-09-11	—	0551-66195765
合肥市创新科技风险投资有限公司	2000-08-28	www.hfgk.com	0551-62675471
合肥市高科技风险投资有限公司	2000-04-18	—	—
合肥同安创业投资基金行	2010-09-06	—	0551-63677135
合肥兴泰资本管理有限公司	1997-06-02	www.xtkg.com	0551-63758980
合和达投资管理有限公司	2011-11-04	—	—
合之力蓉盛成都创业投资中心（有限合伙）	2015-12-31	—	—
河北国创创业投资有限公司	2012-06	www.guochuangchuangtou.com	0311-67663758
河北慧谷投资有限公司	2012-09	—	0311-85969599
河北金冀达创业投资有限公司	2009-08-31	—	0311-85961613
河北科技投资集团有限公司	2001-02-15	www.hebvc.com	0311-85961613
河北科润杰创业投资有限公司	2013-07-25	—	0311-69053128
河北领创嘉盛创业投资有限公司	2015-10-19	—	0311-67667379
河北玛雅股权投资基金管理有限公司	2012-05-30	www.mayape.com	0311-67267294
河北天鑫创业投资有限公司	2011-07-04	—	—
河北天煜投资有限公司	2015-07-24	—	0311-89928602
河北为润股权投资基金管理有限公司	2015-05-12	—	0311-68037206
河北兴石创业投资有限公司	2009-12-21	—	—
河北燕郊燕胜创业投资有限公司	2011-05-27	—	0316-3357676
河南宝祥民营科技创业投资有限公司	2012-12-05	—	0371-55011760
河南创业投资股份有限公司	2002-08	www.hnvc.cn	0371-67897012
河南德瑞恒通高端装备创业投资基金有限公司	2013-05-15	—	0371-55698755
河南高科技创业投资股份有限公司	2001-04-29	www.hnvc.com.cn	0371-67895090
河南华祺节能环保创业投资有限公司	2013-06-20	www.haiyuqi.com	0371-86684801
河南华夏海纳创业投资集团有限公司	2009-06-18	www.huaxiahn.com	86-0371-86068198
河南赛淇高技术服务创业投资基金（有限合伙）	2017-11-25	—	0371-68599029

公司名称	成立时间	网址	电话
河南省国控基金管理有限公司	2012-10-31	—	0371-86556706
河南省留学创业投资有限公司	2006-08-10	www.hnchuangtou.com	—
河南信科股权投资基金管理有限公司	2016-03-28	—	—
河南兴豫生物医药创业投资基金（有限合伙）	2014-05-26	—	0371-86661004
河南隐阳汇金股权投资中心（有限合伙）	2017-04-28	—	—
河南中创信环保产业创业投资基金（有限合伙）	2016-10-21	—	0371-53369659
河南中证开元创业投资基金（有限合伙）	2013-09-17	—	0371-86545368
鹤壁发展投资基金管理有限公司	2015-10-22	—	—
鹤壁市海创产业转型发展投资基金（有限合伙）	2017-06-13	—	—
黑龙江红土科力创业投资有限公司	2011-07-11	—	0451-55553193
黑龙江凯致天使创业投资企业（有限合伙）	2015-11-04	—	—
黑龙江科力天使创业投资有限公司	2014-07-11	—	—
黑龙江省大正泽霖投资企业（有限合伙）	2017-11-24	—	—
黑龙江省工研院创业投资管理有限公司	2017-08-04	—	—
黑龙江省工研院创业投资企业（有限合伙）	2017-11-15	—	0451-87171034
黑龙江省科力高科技产业投资有限公司	2003-06-25	www.hljkl.com	—
黑龙江信泰投资有限公司	2014-09-03	—	0451-82336222
衡阳高新南粤基金管理有限公司	2016-12-26	—	0734-8168559
衡阳岳涵新材料投资有限公司	2016-04-21	—	—
弘森（天津）资产管理有限公司	2015-04-16	www.tjhsamc.cn	022-89357730
弘信创业工场投资集团股份有限公司	1996-10-30	—	0592-5627310
红榕创业投资股份有限公司	2010-07-16	—	—
红塔创新投资股份有限公司	2000-06-15	—	010-58555666
洪泰天创投成都创业投资中心（有限合伙）	2015-12-31	www.angelplus-cd.com	—
洪泰天使（成都）股权投资基金管理有限公司	2015-09-06	www.angelplus-cd.com	—
湖北当代高投创业投资基金合伙企业（有限合伙）	2015-09-07	—	027-65026436
湖北九派创业投资有限公司	2010-09-09	www.jiupaivc.com	027-59339178
湖北军融高技术服务创业投资基金中心（有限合伙）	2015-06-24	—	—
湖北科创天使投资有限公司	2014-07-11	—	027-87440849
湖北省齐信达投资管理有限公司	2014-05-05	—	027-87571051
湖北盛世高金创业投资有限公司	2011-03-24	—	027-87440849
湖北新能源投资管理有限公司	2010-08-18	—	027-65796340
湖北中元九派产业投资基金合伙企业（有限合伙）	2016-11-23	—	027-59339177
湖南财富同超创业投资管理股份有限公司	2010-07-19	—	0731-82567348

公司名称	成立时间	网址	电话
湖南财富同超创业投资有限公司	2010-10-10	—	0731-82567348
湖南达晨财鑫创业投资有限公司	2011-03-28	—	0736-7133995
湖南迪策创业投资有限公司	2002-12-05	—	0731-89952741
湖南鼎信泰和股权投资管理有限公司	2012-06-07	—	0731-85123296
湖南高科发创智能制造装备创业投资有限公司	2013-02-05	—	0731-28861596
湖南高新创业投资管理有限公司	2011-03-10	www.hhtvc.com	0731-85165395
湖南高新创业投资集团有限公司	2007-06-28	www.hhtvc.com	0731-85165400
湖南国微集成电路创业投资基金合伙企业（有限合伙）	2015-12-24	—	0731-89952611
湖南海捷投资有限公司	2010-04-09	www.hiyield.cn	0731-88780198
湖南海捷先进装备创业投资有限公司	2013-05-08	www.hiyield.cn	0731-88780198
湖南汉坤股权投资管理有限公司	2012-02-17	—	0731-89917899
湖南弘高高技术服务创业投资有限公司	2015-07-07	—	0731-62190624
湖南湖大海捷津杉创业投资有限公司	2011-04-29	www.hiyield.cn	0731-88780100
湖南华鸿景开投资管理有限公司	2010-06-08	—	0731-88186795
湖南华菱津杉投资管理有限公司	2010-03-25	—	—
湖南华曦资产管理有限公司	2015-02-12	www.huaxizichan.com	0731-85580510
湖南汇垠天星股权投资私募基金管理有限公司	2014-11-26	—	0731-82290362
湖南金科投资担保有限公司	2003-11-27	—	0731-85810466
湖南浚源鼎立创业投资管理有限公司	2015-06-25	—	—
湖南力合创业投资有限公司	2016-07-21	—	0731-55515503
湖南力合天使私募股权基金管理有限公司	2016-10-17	—	0731-55515503
湖南美雅资本管理有限公司	2008-08-21	—	0731-82226297
湖南摩根信通投资有限公司	2014-09-25	www.mgxtinvest.com	0731-84166383
湖南蒲公英私募股权基金管理有限公司	2017-07-25	—	—
湖南省广信创业投资基金有限公司	2012-06-05	—	—
湖南省中小微企业产业投资基金管理有限公司	2014-08-11	—	—
湖南天巽投资管理有限公司	2015-08-31	—	0731-84110275
湖南同超投资股份有限公司	2008-01-23	www.hntctz.com	0731-82567348
湖南湘投高科技创业投资有限公司	2000-02-23	www.hnhvc.com	0731-85188649
湖南新能源创业投资基金企业（有限合伙）	2010-05-14	—	0731-82768320
湖南兴湘投资有限公司	2008-12-18	www.hnxxtz.com	0731-84815981
湖南永创伟业创业投资企业（有限合伙）	2015-10-28	—	—
湖南兆富投资控股（集团）有限公司	2009-08-24	www.zaffer.cn	0731-88737722
湖南浙商嘉立创业投资有限公司	2010-08-06	—	0731-85696977

公司名称	成立时间	网址	电话
湖南正银投资管理有限公司	2011-07-07	www.zytzjj.com	—
湖南中大联合创业咨询有限公司	2013-08-09	www.zdlhcy.com	—
湖南中大融港投资管理有限公司	2015-12-28	—	—
湖南中科高科动力产业创业投资基金企业（有限合伙）	2017-11-30	—	0731-28861596
华控（天津）投资管理有限公司	2016-07-19	www.techtransfer-vc.com	010-82150099
华菱津杉（湖南）创业投资有限公司	—	—	—
华软创业投资无锡合伙企业（有限合伙）	2009-08	www.csinvestmentgroup.com	010-82525169
华软创业投资宜兴合伙企业（有限合伙）	2010-08-28	www.csinvestmentgroup.com	010-82825169
华晟投资管理有限责任公司	2012-05-14	—	0551-63533681
华穗食品创业投资企业	2009-04-13	—	021-62898817
华芯（上海）创业投资管理有限公司	2011-03-17	—	021-31352499
华章天地传媒投资控股集团有限公司	2013-04-28	—	0791-86895379
淮南市创业风险投资有限公司	2011-11-26	—	0554-6679199
淮南市天使投资基金（有限合伙）	2016-07-26	—	—
洹水资产管理（上海）有限公司	2014-01-29	www.huanshuicapital.com	—
黄河三角洲投资管理有限公司	2009-04-03	—	0546-7768881
黄蓝创业投资有限公司	2012-08-06	—	0543-5164888
黄山市天使投资基金	2016-07-25	—	0559-2528715
汇智创业投资有限公司	2009-04-29	—	0551-65321476
惠州红土创业投资有限公司	2016-03-03	www.szvc.com.cn	0752-7191886
霍尔果斯嘉泽创业投资有限公司	2012-11-28	—	—
霍尔果斯凯风进取创业投资有限公司	2014-08-05	www.cowinvc.com	—
济南财金立达股权投资管理有限公司	2017-04-05	www.sdcjld.com	0531-88822186
济南华科创业投资合伙企业（有限合伙）	2013-11-12	—	0531-88887576
济南科技风险投资有限公司	2001-04	www.jnvc.com.cn	0531-88879277
济南科信创业投资有限公司	2011-10	—	0531-88879277
济南云海创业投资有限公司	2013-05-24	—	0531-85106246
济宁共创投资有限公司	2013-09-29	—	—
济宁市惠达财丰创业投资有限公司	2014-03-11	www.huidatouzi.com	—
济宁市圈带新兴产业发展基金管理有限公司	2017-10-31	—	—
济宁市圈带新兴产业发展基金合伙企业（有限合伙）	2017-12-29	—	—
济宁英飞尼迪创业投资管理有限公司	2010-12-22	www.infinity-equity.com	0537-3281510
济宁英飞尼迪创业投资中心（有限合伙）	2011-04-21	www.infinity-equity.com	0537-3281505
嘉兴豪真投资合伙企业（有限合伙）	2015-08-20	—	—

公司名称	成立时间	网址	电话
嘉兴华聚投资管理有限公司	2016-06-30	www.huajuvc.com	0296-8255421
嘉兴华睿布谷鸟创业投资合伙企业（有限合伙）	2014-08-14	—	—
嘉兴联创汉德投资合伙企业（有限合伙）	2015-06-02	—	—
嘉兴市领汇创业投资管理有限公司	2010-12-21	—	0575-87153786
嘉兴天禀投资合伙企业（有限合伙）	2014-05-16	—	—
嘉兴天浩投资管理有限公司	2014-12-10	—	—
嘉兴天澜投资合伙企业（有限合伙）	2014-11-17	—	—
嘉兴天禄投资合伙企业（有限合伙）	2014-12-22	—	—
嘉兴天叶投资合伙企业（有限合伙）	2016-06-24	—	—
建湖县建科创业投资有限公司	2010-12	www.4408499.czvv.com	0515-86233503
江东控股集团有限责任公司	1999-03-15	www.jdkgjt.com.cn	—
江山市恒创投资合伙企业（有限合伙）	2016-01-19	—	—
江苏艾利克斯投资有限公司	2006-01-19	—	0511-86900801
江苏鼎信咨询有限公司	1998-04-27	www.do-think.com	025-86586898
江苏鼎信资本管理有限公司	2009-06-25	—	025-86586898
江苏东恒环境控股有限公司	2011-08-26	www.eeholdings.cn	0511-87560393
江苏风行天下创业投资有限公司	2017-08-08	—	—
江苏高鼎科技创业投资有限公司	2007-08-31	www.js-vc.com	025-85529900
江苏高弘投资管理有限公司	2006-09	—	025-52313062
江苏高晋创业投资有限公司	2008-06-12	—	0519-85150557
江苏高科技投资集团有限公司	1992-07- 30	www.js-vc.com	025-85529999
江苏高投成长创业投资有限公司	2008-01	—	025-85529900
江苏高投成长价值股权投资合伙企业（有限合伙）	2011-05	—	025-85529999
江苏高投创新价值创业投资合伙企业（有限合伙）	2011-05-19	—	025-85529900
江苏高投创新科技创业投资合伙企业（有限合伙）	2011-04	—	025-85529900
江苏高投创新天使创业投资合伙企业（有限合伙）	2013-11-01	—	025-85529900
江苏高投创新中小发展创业投资合伙企业（有限合伙）	2012-12-25	—	025-85529900
江苏高投创业投资管理有限公司	1999-01-29	—	025-85529999
江苏高投发展创业投资有限公司	2010-07-16	—	025-85529999
江苏高投科贷创业投资合伙企业（有限合伙）	2013-12-31	—	025-85529900
江苏高投宁泰创业投资合伙企业（有限合伙）	2012-01-30	—	025-85529900
江苏高投中小企业创业投资有限公司	2009-05	—	025-85529900
江苏高新创业投资管理有限公司	2005-01-14	www.js-vc.com	025-85529900
江苏高新创业投资有限公司	2005-08-15	www.js-vc.com	—

公司名称	成立时间	网址	电话
江苏弘瑞科技创业投资有限公司	2002-09	—	025-52313062
江苏红黄蓝创业投资有限公司	2014-02-19	—	025-88869883
江苏华控创业投资有限公司	2008-07-10	www.huakongpe.com	025-87716620-801
江苏华控投资管理有限公司	2008-01-15	—	025-87716220-801
江苏华全创业投资有限公司	2013-01-05	—	0523-80959672
江苏华睿投资管理有限公司	2010-06-12	—	—
江苏汇鸿创业投资有限公司	2004-07-06	—	025-86770714
江苏嘉睿创业投资有限公司	2008-03-28	—	025-88160137
江苏金茂低碳产业创业投资有限公司	2010-11-19	www.jolmo.net	025-84730375
江苏金茂环保产业创业投资有限公司	2010-12-17	www.jolmo.net	025-84730375
江苏津通创业投资有限公司	2007-06-25	www.jinton.com	0519-86226016
江苏九洲投资集团创业投资有限公司	2007-09-19	www.jiuzhouinvest.com	0519-85228057
江苏聚融创业投资有限公司	2011-11-16	—	0511-87899196
江苏科泉高新创业投资有限公司	2012-10-31	www.kequanvc.com	025-85589174
江苏联发创业投资有限公司	2011-12-13	—	0513-88869069
江苏隆鑫创业投资有限公司	2006-05	—	025-84401201
江苏人才创新创业投资二期基金（有限合伙）	2015-05-19	—	025-85529900
江苏人才创新创业投资合伙企业（有限合伙）	2014-03-25	—	025-85529900
江苏如东高新创业投资有限公司	2014-05-05	—	0513-88158132
江苏瑞明创业投资管理有限公司	2009-12-30	www.jsrm2009@yeah.net	025-83172132
江苏桑夏投资有限公司	2010-04-28	—	—
江苏省无锡江大大学科技园有限公司	2001-12-30	www.j-park.jiangnan.edu.cn	0510-85189107
江苏省现代服务业发展创业投资基金（有限合伙）	2015-05-29	—	025-85529900
江苏盛泉创业投资有限公司	2007-06	www.vc-century.com	025-58071508
江苏盛宇丹昇创业投资有限公司	2008-10-28	—	0511-86929333
江苏苏大天宫创业投资管理有限公司	2010-10-08	www.sdkjy.suda.edu.cn	0512-62925790
江苏苏大投资有限公司	2001-02	—	0512-67504016
江苏苏豪投资集团有限公司	1999-05-06	—	—
江苏天氏创业投资有限公司	2005	—	025-87752270
江苏新材料产业创业投资企业（有限合伙）	2013-11-13	www.jolomo.net	025-84730375
江苏新创投资有限公司	2007-10-17	—	0523-84623002
江苏新顶旭科技创业投资有限公司	2010-04-27	—	—
江苏信泉创业投资管理有限公司	2006-12-30	—	025-58071508
江苏兴科创业投资有限公司	2007-08-20	www.jsxkct.com	0519-86302628

公司名称	成立时间	网址	电话
江苏盐城龙湖文化产业发展有限公司	2013-05-28	—	0515-88459606
江苏毅达成果创新创业投资基金（有限合伙）	2015-05-19	—	—
江苏毅达股权投资基金管理有限公司	2014-02-18	—	025-85529900
江苏鹰能创业投资有限公司	2007-08-28	—	025-85529900
江苏智光创业投资有限公司	2015-04-22	—	—
江苏中关村科技产业园创业投资有限公司	2016-04-26	—	—
江苏中科物联网科技创业投资有限公司	2010-07-14	www.casiot.com	0510-85380859
江苏紫金文化产业二期投资基金（有限合伙）	—	—	—
江苏紫金文化产业发展基金（有限合伙）	2010-03-15	—	025-85529900
江苏紫金文化创业投资合伙企业（有限合伙）	2011-08-04	—	025-85529900
江西高技术产业投资股份有限公司	2002-03	www.jxvc.com.cn	0791-88110252
江西立达新材料产业创业投资中心（有限合伙）	2011-08-03	www.reitercapital.com	0791-83851565
江西省创东方科技创业投资中心（有限合伙）	2014-09-24	—	—
江阴市高新技术创业投资有限公司	2007-02-06	—	0510-81602090
姜堰市高新实业投资有限公司	2010-12-23	—	0523-88117969
金华市博观科华股权投资合伙企业（有限合伙）	2015-06-04	—	—
金华市普华海纳股权投资合伙企业（有限合伙）	2015-07-28	—	—
金华市普华济帆股权投资合伙企业（有限合伙）	2016-02-17	—	—
金华市普华济兴股权投资合伙企业（有限合伙）	2016-02-03	—	—
金华市天勤科华股权投资合伙企业（有限合伙）	2015-06-03	—	—
金库（杭州）创业投资管理有限公司	2011-08-23	www.kymcocapital.com	0571-86693015
晋商世纪山西股权投资管理有限公司	2013-08-07	www.jssjjt.com	—
京科新材智投资管理（北京）有限公司	2015-08-26	—	010-88029660-8008
菁英汇投资管理（天津）有限责任公司	2015-12-15	www.jingyinghuitj.com	022-28389033
靖江市高新技术创业投资有限公司	2010-03	—	0523-89181480
句容市高新创业投资有限公司	2014-10-10	—	0511-87272670
凯撒世嘉股权投资管理股份有限公司	—	—	—
科华（宜都）科技创业投资基金（有限合伙）	2015-12-02	—	—
科华银赛创业投资有限公司	2009-07-30	www.khysct.com	027-59817377
克雷（深圳）资本管理有限公司	2015-06-11	—	—
昆山银桥投资中心（有限合伙）	2016-11-24	—	—
莱芜科融投资管理合伙企业（有限合伙）	2013-08-16	—	0531-67803781
兰溪普华聚力股权投资合伙企业（有限合伙）	2015-12-01	—	—
兰州高科创业投资担保有限公司	2003	—	0931-8711879

公司名称	成立时间	网址	电话
兰州科技产业发展投资基金	2016-07-28	www.hljczb.com	0931-8784061
兰州科技创新创业风险投资基金（有限合伙）	2016-07-28	—	—
廊坊市高科创新创业投资有限公司	2006-10-19	—	0316-2235190
力合科创集团有限公司	1999-08-31	www.leaguer.com.cn	0755-26550303
连云港金海创业投资有限公司	2006-07-19	www.lygjhvc.com	0518-85523512
连云港市润财创业投资发展有限公司	2010-10-22	—	0518-85520303
联创策源投资咨询（北京）有限公司	2005-06-14	www.ceyuan.com	010-84020999
联合创业集团有限公司	2005-07-07	—	0411-88009300
联想创投	2016-03-18	www.capital.lenovo.com	010-5886-3933
辽宁诚泰投资有限公司	2012-10-31	—	—
辽宁科技创业投资有限责任公司	2000-02-28	www.lnvc.com.cn	024-23244922
辽宁联盟中资创业投资企业（有限合伙）	2012-09-03	www.c-vc.com.cn	024-83769078
辽宁青创空间企业管理咨询有限公司	2017-06-30	www.qcspace.com	—
辽宁星云朵朵投资管理有限公司	2014-12-01	—	—
柳州开元创业投资有限公司	2011-12-30	—	0771-5715238
六安高科创业投资有限公司	2011-10-20	—	0564-3323933
六安中安天使基金合伙企业（有限合伙）	2016-06-21	—	0551-63677211
六盘水市科技创业投资有限公司	2011-04-14	—	—
罗普特（厦门）投资管理有限公司	2013-05-30	—	0592-3662225
洛阳创业投资有限公司	2011-10-28	—	—
洛阳宏科创新创业投资有限公司	2014-12-19	www.lyguohongtouzi.com	—
洛阳盈科智能装备投资管理有限公司	2017-03-20	—	—
马鞍山市创业天使投资引导基金	2015-12-31	—	0555-8323429
麦克逊创业投资海安有限公司	2016-09-28	—	0513-88856583
绵阳金慧通股权投资基金管理有限公司	2014-12-02	—	—
绵阳久盛科技创业投资有限公司	2004-03-05	—	0816-2316521
绵阳市金慧丰股权投资基金管理中心（有限合伙）	2014-03-26	—	—
明石创业投资江苏有限公司	2015-01-13	—	—
牡丹江水平科技投资基金（有限合伙）	2016-12-27	—	—
南安市红桥创业投资有限公司	2010-08-13	www.hqcapital.com.cn	0595-86392990
南昌创业投资有限公司	2005-12	www.ncct.com.cn	0791-82286261
南京高达资本管理有限公司	2011-09-22	www.goodvc.cn	025-83153546
南京高新创业投资有限公司	2012-06-01	—	025-58696594
南京红土创业投资有限公司	2010-05-31	www.szvc.com.cn	025-58867560

公司名称	成立时间	网址	电话
南京科源投资管理有限公司	2012-08-22	—	025-85589174
南京市高新技术风险投资股份有限公司	2001-02-24	www.nj-vc.com	025-86579660
南京市栖霞区科技创业投资有限公司	2009-07-31	—	025-85329822
南京外滩明珠创业投资有限公司	2011-03-17	—	025-89669155
南京文化创业投资有限公司	2011-02-24	—	025-86579660
南京协立创业投资有限公司	2009-05-11	—	025-86816826
南京毅达股权投资管理企业（有限合伙）	—	—	—
南京中成创业投资有限公司	2009-08-28	—	025-86579660
南京中原创业投资有限公司	2010-12-17	—	025-86579660
南通爱福七龙投资中心（有限合伙）	2014-12-17	—	0513-81288095
南通邦融二期股权投资基金中心（有限合伙）	—	—	—
南通高特佳汇金投资合伙企业（有限合伙）	2013-05-24	—	0513-81288026
南通国泰创业投资有限公司	2006-10-20	www.ntgtvc.com	0513-85288204
南通恒富创业投资合伙企业（有限合伙）	2013-12-16	—	0513-86126133
南通红土伟达创业投资管理有限公司	2014-04-21	www.szvc.com.cn	0513-83562508
南通红土伟达创业投资有限公司	2014-04-21	www.szvc.com.cn	0513-83562508
南通金德投资有限公司	2016-06-30	—	0513-88857333
南通金源汇富投资合伙企业（有限合伙）	2015-04-07	—	025-86816826
南通康融创业投资有限公司	2016-04-08	—	0513-88355999
南通科创创业投资管理有限公司	2013-04-23	—	0513-85728713
南通科技创业投资有限公司	2011-04-22	—	—
南通蓝海投资有限公司	2010-11-11	—	0513-86639999
南通蓝湾壹号创业投资合伙企业（有限合伙）	2017-10-25	—	—
南通鲤鱼高新技术创业服务有限公司	2014-12-25	www.innovationpark.cn	—
南通玲珑湾天使投资基金合伙企业（有限合伙）	2017-01-16	—	—
南通七龙景华投资中心	2015-07-07	—	—
南通启华生物医疗产业基金合伙企业（有限合伙）	2017-02-23	—	—
南通时代伯乐创业投资合伙企业（有限合伙）	2016-09-12	—	—
南通时代伯乐汇邦股权投资合伙企业（有限合伙）	2017-08-17	—	—
南通时代伯乐众邦股权投资合伙企业（有限合伙）	2017-08-17	—	—
南通松禾创业投资合伙企业（有限合伙）	2009-01	—	0513-85507237
南通松禾资本管理有限公司	2009-01-05	—	0513-85507237
南通天外望天玑投资基金合伙企业（有限合伙）	2017-04-01	—	—
南通天外望天狼投资基金合伙企业（有限合伙）	2017-04-01	—	—

公司名称	成立时间	网址	电话
南通五水投资发展有限公司	2013-06-17	—	0513-85609598
内蒙古生产力促进中心有限公司	2004-12-08	—	0471-6280864
宁波安丰和众创业投资合伙企业（有限合伙）	2011-03-10	—	0571-87633580
宁波安丰汇群创业投资合伙企业（有限合伙）	2011-08-12	—	0571-87633580
宁波安丰汇盈创业投资合伙企业（有限合伙）	2011-08-12	—	0571-87633580
宁波安丰领先创业投资合伙企业（有限合伙）	2011-04-26	—	0571-87633580
宁波安丰添富创业投资合伙企业（有限合伙）	2012-07-13	—	0571-87633580
宁波安丰众盈创业投资合伙企业（有限合伙）	2010-04-27	—	0571-87633580
宁波北岸智谷海邦创业投资合伙企业（有限合伙）	2016-07-07	—	0574-83088686
宁波北远创业投资中心（有限合伙）	2010-08-27	—	0574-27706565
宁波创业风险投资有限公司	1999-05-06	—	0574-86881546
宁波东元创业投资有限公司	2005-05-16	www.nbvc.com.cn	0574-87294001
宁波高新区华桐恒德创业投资合伙企业（有限合伙）	2016-06-29	—	0574-87294001
宁波海邦人才创业投资合伙企业（有限合伙）	2011-09-29	—	0574-83088686
宁波海达鼎兴投资管理有限公司	2011-11-11	—	0574-89019226
宁波海达睿盈股权投资管理有限公司	2017-01-08	—	022-59852168
宁波华慈蓝海创业投资有限公司	2011-03-15	—	0574-63903036
宁波华建风险投资有限公司	2010-07-12	—	—
宁波华建汇富创业投资有限公司	2011-07-08	—	—
宁波华建投资管理有限公司	2010-06-21	—	—
宁波华桐创业投资管理有限公司	2016-02-24	—	0574-87294001
宁波华桐恒泰创业投资合伙企业（有限合伙）	2017-05-15	—	0574-87294001
宁波开云融汇创业投资合伙企业（有限合伙）	2015-05-18	—	0574-88182007
宁波科发宝鼎创业投资合伙企业（有限合伙）	2016-11-16	www.zjkfcapital.com	0571-88250328
宁波科发海鼎创业投资合伙企业（有限合伙）	2014-05-30	www.zdkfcapital.com	0571-88250427
宁波梅花天使投资管理有限公司	2014-04-28	www.plumventures.cn	—
宁波梅山保税港区顺赢股权投资合伙企业（有限合伙）	2017-08-10	—	—
宁波民和风险投资有限公司	2010-06-03	—	—
宁波明光投资控股集团有限公司	2017-05-22	—	—
宁波普华友实股权投资合伙企业（有限合伙）	2016-07-22	—	—
宁波普华元顺股权投资合伙企业（有限合伙）	2016-07-22	—	—
宁波杉杉望新科技创业投资有限公司	2009-12-14	—	0574-56801577
宁波市伯乐开图创业投资合伙企业（有限合伙）	2013-06-19	—	0574-88182007
宁波市科发二号股权投资基金合伙企业（有限合伙）	2012-09-18	www.zdkfcapital.com	0571-88250427

公司名称	成立时间	网址	电话
宁波市科发股权投资基金合伙企业（有限合伙）	2012-03-01	www.zdkfcapital.com	0571-88250427
宁波市蓝洋成长投资合伙企业（有限合伙）	2010-12-03	—	—
宁波市蓝洋投资管理合伙企业（有限合伙）	2010-12-03	—	—
宁波首创成长股权投资合伙企业（有限合伙）	2010-11-18	—	—
宁波天骥赢和股权投资管理有限公司	2016-04-18	—	0574-87359666
宁波天堂硅谷合众股权投资合伙企业（有限合伙）	2012-02-16	—	0571-86483535
宁波天堂硅谷融创股权投资合伙企业（有限合伙）	2014-01	—	—
宁波天堂硅谷融正股权投资合伙企业（有限合伙）	2014-01-08	—	0571-87089718
宁波天堂硅谷新风股权投资合伙企业（有限合伙）	2015-12-17	—	—
宁波天堂硅谷新健股权投资合伙企业（有限合伙）	2015-12-23	—	—
宁波天堂硅谷新象股权投资合伙企业（有限合伙）	2015	—	—
宁波万豪铭山投资合伙企业（有限合伙）	2016-10-26	—	—
宁波新以创业投资管理有限公司	2010-01-13	www.infinty-equity.com	0574-87993884
宁波新以创业投资合伙企业（有限合伙）	2010-01-29	www.infinity-equity.com	0574-87993884
宁波英飞伯乐创业投资管理有限公司	2015-06-25	www.infinity-equity.com	0574-8799384
宁波英飞伯乐创业投资合伙企业（有限合伙）	2015-09-10	—	0574-87993884
宁波浙科汇聚创业投资合伙企业（有限合伙）	2014-07-16	—	—
宁波浙科永强创业投资合伙企业（有限合伙）	2015-12-09	—	0571-88869350
宁夏国投基金管理有限公司	2002-08-26	—	0951-3026390
宁夏穆坤投资基金管理有限公司	2014-03-19	www.mukunpe.com	—
宁夏宁东科技创业投资有限公司	2016-06-07	—	—
宁夏中财高新投资管理有限公司	2013-04-17	www.nxzcgx.com	0951-8507997
盘锦建银股权投资基金管理有限公司	2016-06-30	—	0427-2680603
盘锦中以英飞投资管理有限公司	2016-06-29	—	0427-2680603
齐齐哈尔市科技成果转化创业投资合伙企业（有限合伙）	2017-09-20	—	0451-51920801
黔西南州创业投资基金有限公司	2015-07-31	—	—
秦皇岛市科技投资公司	2000-02-18	www.qhdktgs.com	0335-3639739
秦皇岛燕大产业集团有限公司	1996-12-23	www.ysusp.com.cn	0335-8500962
青岛迪凯投资管理有限公司	2014-11-27	—	—
青岛高创澳海股权投资管理有限公司	2016-07-21	—	—
青岛高创投资管理有限公司	2009-12-25	—	—
青岛高新联合投资管理有限公司	2012-12-10	www.gaoxinlianhe.com.cn	0532-55678337
青岛里程碑创业投资管理有限公司	2011-05-20	www.ms-vc.com	0532-80931757
青岛市科技风险投资有限公司	2000-08-17	www.huatongvc.com	0532-85063780

公司名称	成立时间	网址	电话
青海国科创业投资基金（有限合伙）	2013-10-23	—	0971-5115081
青海汇富科技成果转化投资基金（有限合伙）	2015-12-21	—	0971-5115081
青海科技创新投资基金（有限合伙）	2013-12-25	—	010-88555416
衢州隆启润泽股权投资合伙企业（有限合伙）	2017-05-17	—	—
泉州市红桥创业投资有限公司	2010-02-22	www.hqcapital.com.cn	0595-28292990
泉州市红桥民间资本管理股份有限公司	2008-10-29	www.hqcapital.com.cn	0595-82032092
人保（苏州）科技保险创业投资企业（有限合伙）	2016-10-09	—	—
日亚（天津）创业投资管理有限公司	2011-06-13	www.jaic-vc.co.jp	—
日亚创业投资企业	2009-01-06	—	021-61976299
日照华和科技创业投资有限责任公司	2010-05-28	—	0633-8339288
荣盛创业投资有限公司	2007-09-08	—	010-59232688-804
融鑫谷（北京）投资基金管理有限公司	2015-04	—	010-59773804
软库博辰创业投资企业	2008-03-03	—	0512-66969661
三泽创业投资管理有限公司	2008-02-28	www.sunzfund.com	0731-82768320
厦门保金股权投资基金管理有限公司	2012-12-24	—	0592-2239515
厦门博芮投资股份有限公司	2012-05-29	www.xmbory.com	0592-5021184
厦门创翼创业投资有限公司	2008-06-20	—	0592-2360798
厦门创翼德晖股权投资合伙企业（有限合伙）	2011-02-11	www.divinecapital.com.cn	0592-2915616
厦门创兆地产投资管理有限公司	2012-03-26	—	—
厦门高新技术创业中心有限公司	1996-12-18	www.xmibi.com	0592-3923999
厦门高新技术风险投资有限公司	1998-12-09	—	—
厦门高新科创天使创业投资有限公司	2013-03-11	www.xmibi.com	0592-3923999
厦门国海坚果投资管理有限公司	2013-03-28	www.capitalnuts.com	0592-2577216
厦门海西创业投资有限公司	2015-06-09	www.hxvc.cn	0592-3929888
厦门海峡科技创新股权投资基金管理有限公司	2015-08-11	—	0592-6275076
厦门红土创业投资有限公司	2010-06-08	—	0592-5778290
厦门红土投资管理有限公司	2010-06-12	—	0592-5770650
厦门华登创业投资有限公司	2008-08-13	www.xmerqing.com	0592-2219232
厦门火炬集团创业投资有限公司	2004-04-05	www.xmhjtz.com	0592-5711818
厦门嘉壹创业投资有限公司	2014-09-12	—	0592-5134308
厦门坚果投资管理有限公司	2012-08-07	www.capitalnuts.com	0592-2577216
厦门金拾股权投资基金管理有限公司	2015-06-05	—	0592-5311500
厦门科技创业投资有限公司	2011-04-06	—	0592-5711818
厦门隆领投资合伙企业（有限合伙）	2011-03-29	www.lognling.com	—

公司名称	成立时间	网址	电话
厦门铭源红桥投资管理有限公司	2011-08-31	—	0592-2278628
厦门七匹狼创业投资有限公司	2009-07-03	www.sw-gh.com	0592-5377752
厦门七匹狼节能环保产业创业投资管理有限公司	2012-12-28	—	0592-5377752
厦门青瓦投资管理有限公司	2014-05-05	www.greytile.cn	0592-2387226
厦门软件产业投资发展有限公司	1998-12-02	www.xsoft.com.cn	0592-2519997
厦门市弘磐投资管理有限公司	2016-06-27	—	—
厦门天鉕基业股权投资合伙企业（有限合伙）	2011-06-17	—	—
厦门伟泰晟弘股权投资合伙企业（有限合伙）	2017-03-02	—	0592-5655853
厦门携合创业投资合伙企业（有限合伙）	2013-08-01	—	0592-2278628
厦门信诚通创业投资有限公司	2015-03-27	—	0592-5952900
厦门英诺嘉业股权投资基金合伙企业（有限合伙）	2016-08-12	—	—
厦门永红创业投资有限公司	2006-12-19	—	0592-5058092
山东德泰创业投资有限公司	2010-03-29	www.sddetai.cn	0535-3942685
山东多盈节能环保产业创业投资有限公司	2014-01-07	—	—
山东府新创业投资有限公司	2012-10-23	—	0543-3199899
山东恒发创业投资有限公司	2012-02-28	—	0543-5077698
山东弘利创业投资有限公司	2009-12-31	—	0539-8385619
山东红桥创业投资有限公司	2011-12-22	—	0531-67803781
山东红桥股权投资管理有限公司	2011-11-30	—	0531-67803781
山东红土创业投资有限公司	2012-01-19	—	—
山东华峰创业投资有限公司	2012-07-23	—	—
山东黄河三角洲创业发展集团有限公司	2010-03-30	www.sdhsjcy.com	0543-3199899
山东黄金创业投资有限公司	2015-08-20	—	0531-67711071
山东汇益创业投资有限公司	2014-01-13	—	0531-82912988
山东嘉华盛裕创业投资股份有限公司	2009-08-27	www.jhsytz.com	0535-6869999
山东嘉瑞创业投资集团有限公司	2012-08-06	—	0539-6012023
山东江诣创业投资有限公司	2010-08-12	—	0535-6719638
山东科创投资有限公司	2010-10-22	—	0537-3292806
山东科融天使创业投资合伙企业（有限合伙）	2015-02-06	—	0531-67803781
山东利泰投资有限公司	2009-03-24	—	—
山东宁信投资管理有限公司	2014-12-04	—	0537-2269315
山东旗城科技创业投资股份有限公司	2009-08-19	—	0536-2139207
山东麒津创业投资管理有限公司	2015-12-17	—	—
山东融裕金谷创业投资有限公司	2014-08-22	www.sdryjg.com	0531-88821351

公司名称	成立时间	网址	电话
山东省方正创业投资有限责任公司	2010-10-29	—	0543-6782271
山东省科技创业投资有限公司	2009-07-27	—	0531-86569598
山东天地共富创业投资基金合伙企业（有限合伙）	2016-08-10	—	—
山东天齐创业投资有限公司	2010-03-24	—	0533-3598500
山东中泰天使创业投资基金企业（有限合伙）	2015-12-17	—	—
山西 TCL 汇融创业投资有限公司	2010-09-26	—	—
山西佰世投资管理有限公司	2010-07-05	—	—
山西大正元投资咨询有限公司	2007-06-12	www.tdrcap.com	—
山西典石股权投资管理有限公司	2011-11-28	—	0351-7672281
山西丰创投资管理有限公司	2016-02-02	—	—
山西高新产业投资基金管理有限公司	2017-07-05	—	—
山西国电创业投资有限公司	2011-04-14	www.tzgs.sxgjdl.com	—
山西国金股权投资管理有限公司	2015-01-29	—	0351-5628152
山西弘道投资管理有限公司	2016-02-02	—	—
山西黄河股权投资管理有限公司	2017-10-11	—	—
山西金丰承树投资管理有限公司	2010-08-03	—	—
山西金丰汇智创业投资有限公司	2009-04-10	www.jfhjzvc.com	0351-3343158
山西晋财惠晋资本管理有限公司	2017-01-05	—	—
山西晋尚博银股权投资管理有限公司	2013-03-13	—	—
山西龙城燕园创业投资管理有限公司	2012-02-15	—	—
山西龙翔基金管理有限公司	2017-03-24	—	—
山西省创业风险投资引导基金有限责任公司	2008-08-06	—	0351-8330500
山西省创业投资基金管理集团有限公司	2012-11-01	www.sxcxt.com.cn	0351-5628151
山西省创业投资基金管理有限公司	2012-11-01	www.sxcxt.com.cn	0351-5628151
山西省高新技术创业中心	1992-07	www.sxbi.org	0351-7039502
山西省科技基金发展有限公司	1993-06	www.sxstf.com	0351-2026370
山西省山投新能源产业集团有限公司	2007-09-20	www.stny.com.cn	0351-7775218
山西省文化产业股权投资管理有限公司	2015-10-21	—	0351-7190803
山西兴创达股权投资管理有限公司	2015-01-29	—	—
山西中盈洛克利创业投资有限公司	2011-03-14	—	0351-8225532
山证基金管理有限公司	2013-06-05	—	0351-7028554
陕西大同创业投资有限公司	2016-03-14	www.oneworldcapital.net	029-81100979
陕西敦敏投资合伙企业（有限合伙）	2017-02-14	—	029-86262570-820
陕西高端装备高技术创业投资基金（有限合伙）	2013-06-28	—	0917-3322919

公司名称	成立时间	网址	电话
陕西供销知守基金管理有限公司	2015-11-16	—	—
陕西和灵投资管理有限公司	2012-06-12	—	029-68295950
陕西鸿创投资管理有限公司	2014-03-04	—	029-68200936
陕西金控知守基金管理有限公司	2017-03-10	—	—
陕西金资基金管理有限公司	2016-12-12	—	—
陕西科技创业投资管理有限公司	2012-09-18	www.cycn.net	029-88446713
陕西科控启元创业投资管理合伙企业（有限合伙）	2017-01-19	—	—
陕西科控投资管理有限责任公司	2016-02-04	—	—
陕西科迈投资管理合伙企业（有限合伙）	2015-08-31	—	029-81107657
陕西秦商投资管理有限公司	2011-03-09	—	—
陕西荣厚源创业投资有限公司	2012-07-12	—	—
陕西省西咸新区信息产业园投资发展有限公司	2012-05-30	—	029-38020608
陕西省现代能源创业投资基金有限公司	2012-12-20	—	029-68295800
陕西省新材料高技术创业投资基金（有限合伙）	2014-03-21	—	—
陕西文化产业投资基金（有限合伙）	2014-06-25	www.scgpimc.com	—
上创普盛（天津）创业投资管理有限公司	2015-12-29	—	022-58951595
上海邦明投资管理股份有限公司	2010-05-14	www.bmc-sh.com	021-65105827
上海漕河泾创业投资有限公司	2002-05-22	—	021-64951721
上海常石投资管理有限公司	2014-10	www.longcapital.cn	—
上海达晨恒胜创业投资中心（有限合伙）	2012-04-06	—	021-68886698
上海德丰杰龙升创业投资合伙企业（有限合伙）	2012-11-01	www.dfjdragon.com	021-62800585
上海鼎嘉创业投资管理有限公司	2003-10-30	www.dj-vc.com	021-50801918
上海复旦创业投资有限公司	2000-11-09	—	021-65642533
上海复旦医疗产业创业投资有限公司	2003-01-24	www.fudanmed.com	021-64738465
上海亘元创业投资有限公司	2009-03-02	—	021-67103305
上海国盛古贤创业投资管理有限公司	2012-12-12	www.gsgx-capital.com	021-58303168
上海国盛古贤创业投资合伙企业（有限合伙）	2013-04	www.gsgx-capital.com	021-58303168
上海海脉德衍禧创业投资合伙企业（有限合伙）	2015-11-12	—	—
上海洪峰创业投资合伙企业（有限合伙）	2015-01-14	www.crestvc.com	—
上海惠畅投资管理合伙企业（有限合伙）	2015-01-27	—	021-68453169
上海绩亮创业投资有限公司	2016-04-05	—	—
上海晋燃惠赋投资管理有限公司	2016-04-14	—	—
上海晋燃能源投资有限公司	2015-01-30	www.shjrtz.com	—
上海科技创业投资股份有限公司	1993-06-30	www.sstic.com.cn	021-64330776

公司名称	成立时间	网址	电话
上海力合清源创业投资管理合伙企业（有限合伙）	2012-08-22	www.leaguercapital.com	021-62370021
上海力合清源创业投资合伙企业（有限合伙）	2012-08-22	www.leaguercapital.com	021-62370021
上海联创永钦创业投资企业（有限合伙）	2011-08-31	www.newmargin.com	021-62123900
上海联升创业投资有限公司	2010-04-09	www.atlas-venture.com	021-64718011
上海林涌投资咨询有限公司	2011-12-14	www.linyonginvestment.com	021-61069081
上海麦腾永联创业投资合伙企业（有限合伙）	2014-08-15	www.mytechchina.com	021-66057991-26
上海南翔创业投资有限公司	2013-03-07	—	021-33510022
上海欧奈而创业投资有限公司	2010-03-17	—	021-50801918
上海欧奈尔创业投资中心（有限合伙）	2011-06-28	—	021-50801918
上海磐石商联创业投资管理有限公司	2012-08-17	—	021-60758996
上海浦东科技投资有限公司	1999-06	www.pdsti.com	021-50276385
上海汽车创业投资有限公司	2001-06-19	—	021-22011669
上海千骥创业投资管理有限公司	2010-01-07	www.cenova.com	021-64375623
上海千骥创业投资中心（有限合伙）	2012-07-12	www.cenova.com	—
上海千骥诺格医药创业投资管理有限公司	2012-05-30	www.cenova.com	—
上海千骥生物医药创业投资有限公司	2010-04-29	www.cenova.com	—
上海千骥星鹤创业投资管理有限公司	2015-02-11	www.cenova.com	—
上海千骥星鹤创业投资中心（有限合伙）	2015-06-26	www.cenova.com	—
上海荣顾创业投资有限公司	2015-12-17	—	021-61273919
上海瑞经达创业投资有限公司	2010-02-10	—	025-83172132
上海上创新微投资管理有限公司	2011-01-20	www.shcapital.com.cn	021-60932618
上海上创信德创业投资有限公司	2008-03-05	www.shcapital.com.cn	021-60932618
上海上创信德投资管理有限公司	2007-11-23	—	021-60932618
上海时空五星创业投资管理有限公司	2009-11-18	—	021-61218707
上海时空五星创业投资合伙企业（有限合伙）	2009-12-31	—	021-61218709
上海市北科技创业投资有限公司	2011-11-23	—	021-62505267
上海思佰益仪电股权投资管理有限公司	2012-11-14	—	021-68776823
上海沃燕创业投资合伙企业（有限合伙）	2015-10-13	—	021-87758066
上海无穹创业投资中心（有限合伙）	2015-01-28	—	—
上海物联网创业投资基金合伙企业（有限合伙）	2010-11-22	—	021-60932618
上海星杉创业投资有限公司	2007-07-18	www.starryfir.com	021-63352666
上海星湾创业投资合伙企业（有限合伙）	2015-04-03	—	—
上海寅福创业投资有限公司	2010-05-06	—	021-65650817
上海寅嘉创业投资管理有限公司	2010-06-22	www.incufortune.com	021-65650817

公司名称	成立时间	网址	电话
上海闸北创业投资有限公司	2011-11-09	—	021-62505267
上海张江创业投资有限公司	2000-07-12	www.zj-vc.com	021-50801918
上海张科领弋升帆创业投资中心（有限合伙）	2015-11-17	—	021-50777596
上海正海聚弘创业投资中心（有限合伙）	2014-08-21	—	021-50937905
上海正海资产管理有限公司	2008-01-31	www.royalsea-capital.com	021-50937905
上海正赛联创业投资管理有限公司	2011-01-31	www.cacfund.com	021-64275106
上海正赛联创业投资有限公司	2010-10-22	www.cacfund.com	021-64275106
上海中嘉兴华创业投资管理有限公司	2012-10-17	www.c-vc.com.cn	—
上海中嘉兴华创业投资合伙企业（有限合伙）	2012-12-31	www.c-vc.com.cn	—
邵阳市思考投资有限公司	2014-09-16	—	0739-5026767
绍兴海邦人才创业投资合伙企业（有限合伙）	2017-07-07	www.hbvc.com.cn	—
绍兴柯桥锦聚创业投资合伙企业（有限合伙）	2016-02-24	—	0739-28205211-8004
绍兴市上虞区安丰盈元创业投资合伙企业（有限合伙）	2017-07-03	—	—
绍兴天堂硅谷恒煜股权投资合伙企业	2016-09-27	—	—
深圳德威精选股权投资有限公司	2013-11-25	—	0755-83861078
深圳鼎正股权投资基金企业（有限合伙）	2013-08-26	—	0755-26551906
深圳国成世纪创业投资有限公司	2003-04-16	www.ciamvc.com	0755-82967097
深圳国金纵横投资管理有限公司	2013-12-06	www.guojin.com	—
深圳力合清源创业投资管理有限公司	2010-04-28	www.leaguercapital.com	0755-86363823
深圳诺辉岭南投资管理有限公司	2015-03-05	—	—
深圳鹏德创业投资有限公司	2010-07	—	0755-26525681
深圳前海同威资本有限公司	2013-04-10	—	—
深圳清源投资管理股份有限公司	2011-11-25	www.leaguercapital.com	0755-86363823
深圳市帮而为实天使投资企业（有限合伙）	2015-06-10	—	—
深圳市保腾创业投资有限公司	2007-12-03	www.platinumvc.cn	—
深圳市保中太创业投资有限公司	2007-04-06	—	0755-83264501
深圳市贝石创业投资有限公司	2008-03-05	—	0755-82876373
深圳市博爱生投资管理有限公司	2003-06-30	—	—
深圳市创东方投资有限公司	2007-08-21	www.cdfcn.com	0755-88316757
深圳市达晨财智创业投资管理有限公司	2008-12-15	—	0755-83515115
深圳市达晨创业投资有限公司	2000-04	www.fortunevc.com	0755-83515115
深圳市达实股权投资发展有限公司	2014-09-01	—	0755-26588332
深圳市鼎正投资咨询有限公司	2003-04-23	—	0755-26551907
深圳市东方现代产业投资管理有限公司	2005-04-22	www.orica.com.cn	0755-82789371

公司名称	成立时间	网址	电话
深圳市分享创业投资管理有限公司	2009-04-28	www.sharecapital.cn	0755-86331909
深圳市分享投资合伙企业（有限合伙）	2007-08-27	www.sharecapital.cn	0755-86331909
深圳市孚威创业投资有限公司	2007-10-15	www.szfuweivc.com	0755-25771505
深圳市富坤创业投资集团有限公司	2008-04-11	www.rlequities.com	0755-88311638-8019
深圳市高特佳投资集团有限责任公司	2001-03-02	www.szgig.com	0755-86332710
深圳市高新投创业投资有限公司	1994-12-29	www.szhti.com.cn	0755-82852555
深圳市国成科技投资有限公司	1997-09-08	www.szgcvc.com	0755-83516944
深圳市和康投资管理有限公司	2010-09-17	—	0755-26776191
深圳市红岭创投股权投资基金管理有限公司	2012-03-22	—	0755-82038849
深圳市红土创客创业投资管理有限公司	2016-01-25	—	0755-82912880
深圳市红土孔雀创业投资有限公司	2015-07-15	—	0755-82912880
深圳市红土星河创业投资管理有限公司	2016-03-16	—	—
深圳市华信创业投资有限公司	2011-05-19	—	0755-86410783
深圳市吉财投资咨询有限公司	2010-11-09	—	—
深圳市佳利泰创业投资有限公司	2009-07-20	www.jialitai.com	0755-25312056
深圳市金域九鼎股权投资中心（有限合伙）	2012-05-23	—	0755-26551907
深圳市君丰创业投资基金管理有限公司	2009-09-30	www.jfamc.com	0755-82823635
深圳市南桥资本投资管理合伙企业（有限合伙）	2012-05-08	—	—
深圳市年利达创业投资有限公司	2007-09-20	—	0755-23993622
深圳市朋年投资有限公司	2007-03-17	www.pn1970.com	—
深圳市坪山新区红土创新发展创业投资有限公司	2015-12-24	—	0755-82912880
深圳市前海独角兽资本管理企业（有限合伙）	2015-11-22	—	—
深圳市前海乐途资本管理有限公司	2015-06-20	—	—
深圳市前海鹏德移动互联网创业投资基金（有限合伙）	2014-09	—	0755-26525681
深圳市融创创业投资有限公司	2008-01-23	www.szrci.com	—
深圳市时代伯乐创业投资管理有限公司	2011-04-25	—	—
深圳市天图创业投资有限公司	2002-04-11	www.tiantu.com.cn	0755-36909834
深圳市天图投资管理股份有限公司	2010-01-11	www.tiantu.com.cn	0755-36909834
深圳市同创伟业创业投资有限公司	2000-06-26	www.cowincapital.com.cn	0755-82879025
深圳市鑫海泰投资咨询有限公司	2008-06-23	—	—
深圳市阳和生物医药产业投资有限公司	2013-01-25	—	—
深圳市倚锋创业投资有限公司	2007-08-22	www.efung.cc	0755-88308601
深圳市优元东欧投资有限公司	2015-02-126	—	0755-25102707
深圳市悦享资本管理有限公司	2010-08-06	www.szyxzbgl.com	0755-23819923

公司名称	成立时间	网址	电话
深圳市招商局银科投资管理有限公司	2011-01-26	www.cmykcapital.com	0755-26677220
深圳市中和春生壹号股权投资基金合伙企业（有限合伙）	2010-11-18	—	0755-26776191
深圳市中金富创业投资管理有限公司	2009-07-30	—	0755-29089397
深圳市中兴创业投资基金管理有限公司	2010-10-18	—	0755-26776191
深圳市纵之横创业投资管理有限公司	2007	—	0755-86219383
深圳优元投资有限公司	2002-10-16	—	—
深圳中新创业投资管理有限公司	2001-12-19	www.szvc.com.cn; www.uobgroup.com	0755-82904093
沈阳德鸿创展股权投资有限公司	2017-02-22	—	024-83780528
沈阳高新创业投资有限公司	2004-11-08	—	024-66608365
沈阳禾诚科技项目投资合伙企业（有限合伙）	2016-04-01	—	—
沈阳恒信安泰股权投资基金管理有限公司	2012-11-23	www.hxatvc.com	024-83839929
沈阳浑南科技城发展有限公司	2011-05-06	www.sycx360.com	024-83766158
沈阳科技风险投资有限公司	1998-11-04	—	024-22790061
沈阳起点创业投资有限公司	2013-06-19	—	024-25822668
沈阳青果投资管理有限公司	2011-01-28	—	—
沈阳日亚创业投资管理有限公司	2011-11-16	www.jaic-vc.co.jp	024-83773215
沈阳赛伯乐绿科股权投资管理有限公司	2015-07-13	—	—
沈阳梧桐谷创业投资管理有限公司	2014-04-08	—	024-89577776
沈阳星科汇创业投资有限公司	2017-09-14	—	024-83766158
沈阳兴途股权投资基金管理有限公司	2016-10-13	—	024-82514862
圣康世纪投资控股（北京）有限公司	2013-11-05	www.skgf.com.cn	010-83020098
石家庄高新区科发投资有限公司	2010-03-23	—	0311-66699013
石家庄科创投资有限公司	2002-09-19	—	0311-66685160
石家庄科技创业投资有限公司	2002-09-19	—	0311-66685160
石家庄石以创业投资管理有限公司	2009-11-30	—	0311-66699011
石家庄鑫汇金投资有限公司	2003-04-23	—	—
首科开阳（北京）科技服务有限公司	2016-11-23	—	—
四川雅惠新材料创业投资基金有限公司	2015-09-22	—	0831-2400925
四川中物创业投资有限公司	2007-02-08	www.caep-vc.com	028-85311576
苏州创东方富诚投资企业（有限合伙）	2010-09-20	—	0512-68322281
苏州创元高投创业投资管理有限公司	2010-08-27	—	0512-68322738
苏州创元高新创业投资有限公司	2010-11-15	—	0512-68322738
苏州达泰创业投资管理有限公司	2010-05	www.delta-capital.cn	0512-66969930
苏州达泰创业投资中心（有限合伙）	2010-08	www.delta-capital.cn	0512-66969930

公司名称	成立时间	网址	电话
苏州荻溪文化创意产业投资中心（有限合伙）	2012-04-28	—	0512-65808803
苏州东方汇富创业投资企业（有限合伙）	2012-12-6	—	0512-65126380
苏州敦行价值投资合伙企业（有限合伙）	2017-06-23	—	0512-68158093
苏州敦行投资管理有限公司	2017-03-22	—	0512-68158093
苏州方广创业投资管理合伙企业（有限合伙）	2012-05-28	www.fgventure.com	021-54245723
苏州方广创业投资合伙企业（有限合伙）	2012-09-25	www.fgventure.com	021-54245723
苏州斐然向风创业投资中心（有限合伙）	2011	—	—
苏州富丽东方能源股权投资企业（有限合伙）	2011-07-28	—	0512-68322281
苏州富丽高新投资企业（有限合伙）	2010-11-10	—	0512-68322281
苏州富丽明康投资企业（有限合伙）	2011-07-26	—	0512-68322281
苏州富丽启康投资企业（有限合伙）	2011-07-25	—	0512-68322281
苏州富丽泰泓投资企业（有限合伙）	2010-12-24	—	0512-68322281
苏州富丽投资有限公司	2010-07-29	www.fuli-capital.com	0512-68322281
苏州高创天使电子商务产业投资合伙企业（有限合伙）	2016-10-24	—	—
苏州高创天使二号投资合伙企业（有限合伙）	2016-10-21	—	—
苏州高新创业投资集团融联管理有限公司	2012-02-08	—	0512-68081156
苏州高新创业投资集团新麟管理有限公司	2008-12-04	—	0512-68762955
苏州高新国发创业投资有限公司	2009-05-22	—	0512-65126380
苏州工业园区禾源北极光创业投资合伙企业（有限合伙）	2011	—	010-59696185
苏州工业园区华穗创业投资管理有限公司	2008-07-18	—	021-62898817
苏州工业园区康力机器人产业投资有限公司	2016-03-08	www.kl-invest.com	0512-63290000
苏州工业园区太浩成长二期创业投资合伙企业（有限合伙）	2016-01-22	—	—
苏州工业园区元禾原点创业投资管理有限公司	2013-09-24	—	—
苏州工业园区原点正则壹号创业投资企业（有限合伙）	2013-11-19	—	0512-66969533
苏州工业园区原点种子创业投资企业（有限合伙）	2017-12-07	—	0512-66969533
苏州国发创富创业投资企业（有限合伙）	2010-07-14	—	0512-65126380
苏州国发东方创业投资管理有限公司	2008-11-14	—	0512-65126380
苏州国发服务业创业投资企业（有限合伙）	2012-04-23	—	0512-65126380
苏州国发高铁文化创业投资管理有限公司	2013-08-19	—	—
苏州国发高铁文化创业投资中心（有限合伙）	2013-09-29	—	—
苏州国发高新创业投资管理有限公司	2008-12-17	—	0512-65126380
苏州国发股权投资基金管理有限公司	2012-11-21	—	0512-65126380
苏州国发宏富创业投资企业（有限合伙）	2011-04	—	0512-65126380
苏州国发建富创业投资企业（有限合伙）	2010-06-30	—	0512-65126380

公司名称	成立时间	网址	电话
苏州国发聚富创业投资有限公司	2010-03-25	—	0512-65126380
苏州国发黎曼创业投资有限公司	2010-05-19	—	0512-65126380
苏州国发融富创业投资管理企业（有限合伙）	2009-12-28	—	0512-65126380
苏州国发融富创业投资企业（有限合伙）	2010-01-20	—	0512-65126380
苏州国发天使创业投资企业（有限合伙）	2011-06	—	0512-65126380
苏州国发添富创业投资企业（有限合伙）	2012-05-09	—	0512-65126380
苏州国发文化产业创业投资企业（有限合伙）	2012-12-17	—	—
苏州国发涌富创业投资企业（有限合伙）	2011-06	—	0512-65126380
苏州国发源富创业投资企业（有限合伙）	2011-01	—	0512-65126380
苏州国发智富创业投资企业（有限合伙）	2010-03	—	0512-65126380
苏州国润创业投资发展有限公司	2008-07	www.guorunpe.com	0512-62998661
苏州国润瑞祺创业投资企业（有限合伙）	2011-07	www.guorunpe.com	0512-62998663
苏州华创赢达创业投资基金企业（有限合伙）	2012	—	0512-63936955
苏州华沛投资合伙企业（有限合伙）	2017-11-15	—	—
苏州金茂创业投资管理企业（有限合伙）	2011-05	www.jolmo.net	025-84730375
苏州金茂投资管理有限公司	2007-12-27	www.jolmo.net	025-84730211
苏州金茂新兴产业创业投资企业（有限合伙）	2011-06	www.jolmo.net	025-84730375
苏州聚展创业投资企业（有限合伙）	2016-06-30	—	—
苏州君实协立创业投资有限公司	2014-01-06	—	025-86816823
苏州君玄创业投资中心（有限合伙）	2011	—	025-86816826
苏州凯风万盛创业投资合伙企业（有限合伙）	2011	www.cowinvc.com	0512-66969533
苏州科技创业投资公司	1993-07	—	0512-69330076
苏州龙瑞创业投资管理有限公司	2009-12	—	0512-66969306
苏州龙跃投资中心（有限合伙）	2010-01	—	0512-66969306
苏州清研汽车产业创业投资企业（有限合伙）	2014-10-18	—	0512-63936955
苏州清研资本管理企业（有限合伙）	2014-03-07	—	0512-63936955
苏州融联创业投资企业（有限合伙）	2012-03-15	www.sndvc.com	0512-68081156
苏州瑞华投资合伙企业（有限合伙）	2015-07-06	—	025-83172132
苏州瑞璟创业投资企业（有限合伙）	2010-11-17	—	0512-68326637
苏州瑞曼投资管理有限公司	2010-03-17	—	0512-68326637
苏州盛泉百涛创业投资管理有限公司	2010-12-15	—	025-58071508
苏州盛泉海成创业投资合伙企业（有限合伙）	2014-10-23	—	025-58071508
苏州盛泉万泽创业投资合伙企业（有限合伙）	2011-03-03	—	025-58071508
苏州市吴江创迅创业投资有限公司	2014-12-04	—	0512-63493186

公司名称	成立时间	网址	电话
苏州市吴江创业投资有限公司	2008-09-16	—	0512-63493186
苏州市相城创新产业创业投资中心（有限合伙）	2017-11-13	—	0512-65808803
苏州市相城创业投资有限责任公司	2008	—	0512-65808803
苏州市相城埭溪创业投资有限责任公司	2016-06-17	—	0512-65808803
苏州市相城高新创业投资有限责任公司	2009-03-12	—	0512-65808803
苏州市相城基金管理有限公司	2009-01-16	—	0512-65808803
苏州顺融创业投资管理合伙企业（有限合伙）	2014-09-10	www.shunrongvc.com	—
苏州顺融进取创业投资合伙企业（有限合伙）	2016-11-12	www.shun rong venture capital	—
苏州顺融瑞腾创业投资合伙企业（有限合伙）	2015-06-10	www.shunrongvc.com	—
苏州顺融天使二期创业投资合伙企业（有限合伙）	2014-11-19	www.shunrongvc.com	0512-67902058
苏州顺融天使三期创业投资合伙企业（有限合伙）	2015-10-16	www.shunrongvc.com	0512-67902058
苏州苏科创投资管理有限公司	2016-05-04	—	—
苏州太浩成长创业投资合伙企业（有限合伙）	2014-11-05	—	—
苏州天宫号投资管理有限公司	2016-07-21	www.sudatiangong.com	0512-62925790
苏州天宫一号投资中心（有限合伙）	2016-01-14	www.sudatiangong.com	0512-62925790
苏州吴中国发创业投资管理有限公司	2008-08-28	—	0512-65126380
苏州吴中国发创业投资有限公司	2008-08-28	—	0512-65126380
苏州相渭汽车产业投资中心（有限合伙）	2015-12-08	—	0512-65808803
苏州协立创业投资有限公司	2013-04-28	—	025-86816826
苏州协立宽禁带创业投资中心（有限合伙）	2017-09-17	—	025-86816826
苏州协立投资管理有限公司	2011-03	—	025-86816826
苏州协睿创业投资管理有限公司	2011-08-15	—	025-86816826
苏州新麟创业投资有限公司	2009-01-22	—	0512-68762955
苏州新麟二期创业投资企业（有限合伙）	2011-11	—	0512-68762955
苏州新麟三期创业投资企业（有限合伙）	2017-03-08	—	0512-68762955
苏州新晟信息产业投资企业（有限合伙）	2017-12-15	—	—
苏州新协创业投资有限公司	2006-05-16	—	0512-62620019
苏州信慧成创业投资管理有限公司	2014-07-28	—	025-58071508
苏州亿和创业投资有限公司	2009-12-29	—	0512-65214770
苏州亿文创新资本管理有限公司	2007-12-03	—	0512-65214770
苏州亿文投资有限公司	2007-12-17	—	0512-65214770
苏州银基美林创业投资管理有限公司	2012-09-03	—	0512-36830119
苏州兆戎空天创业投资合伙企业（有限合伙）	2015-02-26	—	025-58071508
苏州紫荆华创创业投资合伙企业（有限合伙）	2017-08-09	—	0512-67509067

公司名称	成立时间	网址	电话
睢宁县天使创业投资有限责任公司	2013-03-06	—	0516-88037115
台州科金创业投资合伙企业（有限合伙）	2014-11-12	—	0571-89939766
太仓生物医药创业投资有限公司	2012-09-20	www.bip.taicang.gov.cn	0512-33019923
太湖县企业公有资产经营管理有限公司	2005-12-01	www.thzcgs5506@sina.com	0556-4162643
太原高新区股权投资有限公司	2014-01-02	—	0351-2799797
太原市海信小微企业创业基金管理有限公司	2016-09-14	—	—
泰州华诚高新技术投资发展有限公司	2005	www.tzibi.com	0523-86196007
泰州华健创业投资有限公司	2007-06-08	—	—
泰州健鑫创业投资有限公司	2012-12-14	—	0523-82216000
泰州市创业风险投资有限公司	2001-08	—	0523-86196199
泰州市高港高新区开发投资有限责任公司	2010-08	—	0523-86118800
泰州中国医药城融健达创业投资有限公司	2013-03-19	—	0523-82216000
唐山高新创业投资有限公司	2007-07-02	—	0315-3858385
唐山科技创业投资管理有限责任公司	2009-04-22	—	—
特地世界（大连）科技股份有限公司	2015-03-17	www.tediword.com	0411-82740076
天创博盛（天津）股权投资基金合伙企业（有限合伙）	2011-10-18	—	022-86259326
天津滨海财富股权投资基金有限公司	2007-08-21	www.behycapital.com	022-23374077
天津滨海创业投资管理有限公司	2007-09-18	www.binhaicapital.com	022-58909361
天津滨海天创众鑫股权投资基金有限公司	2010-02-04	—	022-86259326
天津滨海天使创业投资有限公司	2006-09-11	—	022-58909386
天津滨海新区创业风险投资引导基金有限公司	2008-02-04	www.bhsf.com.cn	022-65831777
天津财富嘉绩投资合伙企业（有限合伙）	2014-10-22	—	022-23374077
天津琛琰投资有限公司	2010-12-20	—	022-23374055
天津陈塘海天创业投资合伙企业（有限合伙）	2017-01-25	—	022-58909361
天津创业投资管理有限公司	2003-03-28	www.tjvcm.com	022-86259326
天津创业投资有限公司	2001-03-30	www.tjvc.com.cn	022-58785806
天津迪恩投资管理有限公司	2012-06-13	—	022-59385952
天津东虹科技创业投资发展有限公司	2011-04-28	—	022-58785820
天津蜂巢投资管理合伙企业（有限合伙）	2011-09-15	—	—
天津阜通乾元股权投资基金管理有限公司	2015-09-09	—	022-87455108
天津海量重度大数据企业孵化器有限公司	2016-05-06	—	—
天津海泰滨海创业投资有限公司	2008-04-16	—	—
天津海泰戈壁创业投资管理有限公司	2008-02-21	www.htgvc.com	—
天津海泰红上创新投资有限公司	2008-05-28	—	022-59902569-8009

公司名称	成立时间	网址	电话
天津海泰科技投资管理有限公司	1997-05-08	www.hitech-investment.com	022-83715773
天津虹桥天使投资有限公司	2017-08-24	—	022-23374077
天津火石信息服务业创业投资合伙企业（有限合伙）	2013-02-06	—	022-59385952
天津科创天使投资有限公司	2006-06-19	www.tjacco.com	022-87893289
天津科技融资控股集团有限公司	2010-11-24	www.tjstgroup.com	022-58785820
天津科技投资集团有限公司	1997-12	www.stic.com.cn	022-28355110
天津科源创业投资管理有限公司	2010-09-13	—	022-88259117
天津锟桥创业投资有限公司	2003-08-07	www.kqvc.com	022-87893441
天津联想之星创业投资有限公司	2012-01-09	—	022-82982400
天津南开区苑鑫创业投资有限公司	2012-10-12	—	022-58785820
天津普银天使创业投资有限公司	2017-06-20	—	022-58951595
天津清启陆石股权投资中心（有限合伙）	2016-05-04	—	022-84395995
天津清研陆石投资管理有限公司	2016-05-03	—	022-84395995
天津市武清区信邦科技创业投资发展有限公司	2011-05-23	—	022-58785820
天津水星创业投资有限责任公司	2010-05-10	—	022-59852168
天津泰达科技投资股份有限公司	2000-10-13	www.tedavc.com.cn	022-66297288
天津天保成长资产管理有限公司	2007-03-06	—	022-86259326
天津天创华鑫现代服务产业创业投资合伙企业（有限合伙）	2012-12-04	—	022-86259326
天津天创盈讯创业投资合伙企业（有限合伙）	2011-09-26	—	022-86259326
天津天地酬勤创业投资合伙企业（有限合伙）	2016-05-19	—	022-23708158
天津天地酬勤股权投资管理有限公司	2015-11-16	www.tianjinvc.net	022-23708158
天津天地酬勤天使创业投资有限公司	2016-05-24	—	022-23708158
天津天富创业投资有限公司	2007-12-04	—	022-86259326
天津天以生物医药股权投资基金有限公司	2010-11-25	—	022-86259326
天津天英创业投资管理有限公司	2010-06-22	—	022-86259326
天津蜗牛天使创业投资有限公司	2016-08-08	—	—
天津浔渡创业投资合伙企业（有限合伙）	2011-04-08	—	0510-80708899
天津燕山航空创业投资有限公司	2013-03-28	—	022-58087222
天津友和投资管理有限公司	2015-09-25	www.uohope.com	—
天津沅渡创业投资合伙企业（有限合伙）	2010-08-11	—	0510-80708899
天津中科达创业投资管理有限公司	2015-10-28	www.zkdcap.com	—
天津中汽瑷睿创业投资有限公司	2017-06-01	—	—
天翼科技创业投资有限公司	2012-07-23	www.189chuangyi.com	021-20989590
桐乡桐创投资管理有限公司	2015-06-01	www.19220232.pe168.com	0573-88100999

公司名称	成立时间	网址	电话
铜陵市中融大有天源创业投资有限合伙企业（有限合伙）	2016-08-23	—	010-50860999
铜陵天源股权投资集团有限公司	2007-02-01	—	0562-2885077
铜仁梵净山科技创业投资有限公司	2013-04-09	—	—
皖江产业转移投资基金（安徽）管理有限公司	2009-01-15	—	—
万联道一（天津）创业投资合伙企业（有限合伙）	2017-07-13	—	—
万向创业投资股份有限公司	2000-12	—	0571-87153792
威海北创投资管理有限公司	2015-09-11	—	—
威海创新投资有限公司	2003-07-16	—	0631-5231709
潍坊创业投资有限公司	2001	—	0536-8865276
潍坊鲁信厚源创业投资中心（有限合伙）	2014-06-13	—	—
潍坊市国维创业投资有限公司	2014-11-13	—	—
潍坊市国信创业投资有限公司	2012-07-17	—	0536-5166710
潍坊万通创业投资有限公司	2009-09-28	—	—
乌鲁木齐高新技术融资担保有限公司	2007-05-09	www.uhdz.gov.cn	0991-3834189
乌鲁木齐市科技投资经营中心	2001-07-25	—	0991-4538283
无锡 TCL 爱思开半导体产业投资基金合伙企业（有限合伙）	2015-09-01	—	0510-82800509
无锡 TCL 创业投资合伙企业（有限合伙）	2010-07	—	—
无锡滨湖科技创业投资有限责任公司	2006-07-18	—	0510-85898528
无锡创业投资集团有限公司	2000-10-26	www.wxvcg.com	0510-82700936
无锡高新技术风险投资股份有限公司	2000-08	www.wxvc.com.cn	0510-85226431
无锡国弘尚理投资管理有限公司	2010-03-19	—	0510-85213378
无锡国联厚泽创业投资企业（有限合伙）	2011-10-28	—	021-61631098
无锡国联浚源创业投资中心（有限合伙）	2010-04-16	www.jycapital.cn	0510-82700340
无锡航天国华物联网投资企业（有限合伙）	2012-06-11	—	0510-85386420
无锡红土创业投资有限有限公司	2009-04-29	—	0510-82800637
无锡厚泽成长创业投资企业（有限合伙）	2011-07-05	—	021-61631098
无锡厚泽创新创业投资企业（有限合伙）	2011-06-27	—	021-61631098
无锡华软投资管理有限公司	2009-06	www.csinvestmentgroup.com	010-82525169
无锡江南大学国家大学科技园有限公司	2009-04-03	www.j-park.jiangnan.edu.cn	0510-85189107
无锡金茂二号新兴产业创业投资企业（有限合伙）	2011-12-21	www.jolmo.net	025-84730211
无锡均衡创业投资有限公司	2007-11-14	—	0510-86216651
无锡浚源资本管理中心（有限合伙）	2010-04-16	www.jycapital.cn	0510-82700340
无锡力合创业投资有限公司	2008-11	www.leaguercapital.com	0510-83590286
无锡力合清源创业投资合伙企业（有限合伙）	2011-09-09	www.leaguercapital.com	0510-83590296

公司名称	成立时间	网址	电话
无锡力合投资管理咨询有限公司	2009-04-17	www.leaguercapital.com	0510-83590296
无锡领峰创业投资有限公司	2009-12-11	—	0510-85213378
无锡清研投资有限公司	2009-08-14	—	0510-83591879
无锡瑞明博创业投资有限公司	2010-12-15	—	025-83172132
无锡世铭国联创业投资企业	2010-05-13	—	021-53752208
无锡市金惠创业投资有限责任公司	2006-11	—	0510-83590163
无锡市锡山创业投资有限公司	2007-08	—	0510-88705868
无锡市新区科技金融创业投资集团有限公司	2008-01-31	www.wxvc.com.cn	0510-85226431
无锡新区领航创业投资有限公司	2009-08-03	www.wxvc.com.cn	0510-85226431
无锡源清创业投资有限公司	2012-06-28	—	0510-81801998
无锡源清盛华创业投资有限公司	2013-04-28	—	0510-81801998
无锡耘杉创业投资中心（有限合伙）	2013-07-12	—	—
无锡正海联云投资企业（有限合伙）	2012-12-04	—	—
无锡中科汇盈创业投资有限责任公司	2008-03-07	—	0510-85383122
无锡中科汇盈二期创业投资有限责任公司	2010-04-07	—	0510-85383122
无锡众合投资发展有限公司	2006-12	—	0510-85386981
芜湖达成创业投资中心（有限合伙）	2010-04-28	—	—
芜湖富海浩研创业投资基金（有限合伙）	2012-12-27	—	0553-3850713
芜湖奇瑞科技有限公司	2001-11-21	www.mychery.com	0553-5922267
芜湖瑞建汽车产业创业投资有限公司	2010-07-01	—	0553-3812768
芜湖瑞业股权投资基金（有限合伙）	2009-12-21	—	021-64151936
芜湖市科创融资担保有限公司	2004-05-28	—	0553-5965868
芜湖市世纪江东创业投资中心（有限合伙）	2009-08-18	www.jd-capital.cn	0553-5772022
芜湖远大创业投资有限公司	2009-04-23	—	0553-5992194
吴江东方创富创业投资企业（有限合伙）	2012-10-29	—	—
吴江东方国发创业投资有限公司	2008-11-11	—	0512-65126380
吴江东方融富创业投资管理企业（有限合伙）	2012-10-12	—	—
吴江海博科技创业投资有限公司	2010-08-20	www.haiboinvestment.net	0512-63010566
吴江华业创业投资管理中心（有限合伙）	2011-12-21	—	0512-63936955
武汉创星汇天使投资基金合伙企业（有限合伙）	2017-08-18	—	—
武汉点亮创业投资基金合伙企业（有限合伙）	2017-01-09	—	027-81658878
武汉东湖高新硅谷天堂股权投资合伙企业（有限合伙）	2017-03-03	www.ggttvc.com	027-84842228
武汉东湖华科投资中心（有限合伙）	2014-12-22	—	027-87180181
武汉斐然源通中以科技股权投资基金合伙企业（有限合伙）	2013-09-24	—	—

公司名称	成立时间	网址	电话
武汉公牛创业投资有限公司	2011-11-12	—	—
武汉固德银赛创业投资管理有限公司	2009-04-21	www.gdysct.com	027-59817377
武汉光电工研育成创业投资基金合伙企业（有限合伙）	2015-06-17	—	027-87936898
武汉光谷博润二期生物医药投资中心（有限合伙）	2017-01-06	—	027-68419102
武汉光谷创投基金管理有限公司	2008-05-09	www.chinaovvc.com	027-87618808
武汉光谷高新成长创业投资合伙企业（有限合伙）	2013-12-31	—	—
武汉光谷新三板股权投资基金合伙企业（有限合伙）	2013-01-25	—	027-87440849
武汉硅谷天堂晨曦股权投资基金合伙企业（有限合伙）	2012-09-07	www.ggttvc.com	027-84842228
武汉硅谷天堂恒誉创业投资基金合伙企业（有限合伙）	2012-09-07	www.ggttvc.com	—
武汉红土创新创业投资有限公司	2012-03-20	—	027-87339809
武汉华工创业投资有限责任公司	2000-09-11	www.hustvc.com.cn	027-81338733
武汉金科互联产业投资基金合伙企业	2016-02-04	—	—
武汉科创青桐创业投资有限公司	2015-10-30	—	—
武汉科技创业天使投资基金合伙企业（有限合伙）	2014-01-10	—	—
武汉普华真新股权投资合伙企业（有限合伙）	2017-01-06	—	—
武汉赛伯乐妇女创新创业股权投资基金合伙企业（有限合伙）	2014-04-15	—	—
武汉同鑫力诚创业投资中心（有限合伙）	2017-07-11	—	—
武汉同鑫力诚投资管理有限公司	2017-07-11	—	—
武汉誉达通创业投资基金合伙企业（有限合伙）	2016-08-22	—	—
武汉中科建联产业投资基金合伙企业（有限合伙）	2017-08-03	—	—
武汉中元九派产业投资管理有限公司	2016-07-25	www.vchubei.com	027-59339177
西安创业园投资管理有限公司	2003-07-04	—	029-81113511
西安德蒙投资有限公司	2017-09-22	—	—
西安德同迪亚士投资管理有限公司	2011-09-28	—	029-88894881
西安敦成投资管理有限公司	2017-01-12	—	—
西安高新盈峰创业投资管理有限公司	2016-11-23	—	—
西安海通安元投资管理有限公司	2015-06-01	—	029-61812210
西安航天基地创新投资有限公司	2009-07-08	www.xaibfs.com	—
西安军融电子卫星基金投资有限公司	2016-05-13	—	—
西安科耐特投资管理有限公司	2014-07-08	—	—
西安迈朴投资发展有限公司	2002-01-08	—	029-81113288
西安迈朴资本管理有限公司	2012-11-29	www.mapsxa.com	029-81113288
西安青实资本管理有限公司	2017-10-26	www.xaeeq.com	—
西安曲江文化产业风险投资有限公司	2009-12-01	www.xaqjvc.com	029-85427802

公司名称	成立时间	网址	电话
西安同创博润创业投资管理中心（有限合伙企业）	2011-11-16	www.xatcbr.com	029-86486599
西安同泽投资有限公司	1995-05-05	—	029-88312715
西安西交一八九六资本管理有限公司	2017-06-12	—	—
西安西旅创新投资管理有限公司	2008-06-24	—	029-8919563
西安熙信科创资本管理合伙企业（有限合伙）	2016-04-25	—	—
西安知守创业投资管理有限公司	2017-03-24	—	—
西证重庆股权投资基金管理有限公司	2013-07-18	www.swsc.com.cn	023-63786322
湘潭智造谷产业投资管理有限责任公司	2016-03-15	—	—
新疆创投资本管理有限责任公司	2010-07-15	www.xjvc.net	0991-3682873
新疆大藏资产管理股份有限公司	2015-04-17	—	0991-3821497
新疆合赢成长股权投资有限合伙企业	2011-05-23	—	020-87553579
新疆红山基金管理股份有限公司	2015-07-16	www.hongshanfund.com	—
新疆火炬创业投资有限公司	2012-08-09	www.tvcxj.com	0991-3678085
新疆融汇鑫创业投资管理有限公司	2011-11-30	—	0991-6990026
新疆赛科森投资咨询有限责任公司	2002-04	—	6611966
新疆天裕华盛股权投资管理有限公司	2011-10-27	—	0991-2612357
新疆维吾尔自治区国有资产投资经营有限责任公司	1998-04-23	—	0991-2810861
新疆浙新股权投资有限合伙企业	2011-11-02	—	—
新疆中科援疆创新创业私募基金管理有限公司	2015-10-09	—	0991-3820157
新疆中小企业创业投资股份有限公司	2010-01-26	www.xjvc.cn	0991-4583310
信阳汇盈创业孵化有限公司	2016-03-03	www.xyhycyfh.com	—
兴化市高新投资有限公司	2010-07-16	—	0523-83242633
宿迁国发创业投资企业（有限合伙）	2011-07-22	—	0527-87031252
宿迁科技创业投资有限公司	2012-03-23	—	0527-87031252
宿迁市开创创业投资有限公司	2010-09-07	—	0527-88859628
宿州天使投资合伙企业（有限合伙）	2016-03-20	—	—
徐州博灏创业投资管理有限公司	2014-01-06	www.bohoasset.com	—
徐州风彩创业投资有限公司	2016-12-26	—	—
徐州高新创业投资有限公司	2010-02-24	—	0516-85906737
徐州国盛鸿运创业投资有限公司	2014-01-21	—	—
徐州淮海红土创业投资有限公司	2014-01-14	www.szvc.com.cn	—
徐州环晟创业投资有限公司	2016-02-17	—	—
徐州汇尔康创业投资有限公司	2016-12-26	www.xzhek.com	0516-85777288
徐州嘉禾农业投资基金（有限合伙）	2016-01-12	—	—

公司名称	成立时间	网址	电话
徐州中金创业投资有限公司	2016-09-29	—	0516-89656788
许昌市发展创业投资有限公司	2006-06-20	—	—
许昌市开源股权投资基金管理有限公司	2016-09-06	—	—
宣城火花科技创业投资有限公司	2017-06-15	—	—
亚杰天使投资管理（北京）有限公司	2012-04-11	www.aama-fund.com	010-62680817
烟台安芙兰创业投资中心（有限合伙）	2015-12-11	—	—
烟台创新创业投资有限公司	2014-05-08	—	—
烟台富春九鼎创业投资中心（有限合伙）	2011-12-13	—	—
烟台鲁创恒富创业投资中心（有限合伙）	2012-06-06	—	0531-86969598
烟台泰达创业投资管理有限公司	2014-01-23	—	022-66297288
烟台泰达生物及新医药产业创业投资中心（有限合伙）	2015-01-22	—	022-66297288
烟台文化发展创业投资基金有限公司	2014-05-27	—	0531-86155699
烟台源创科技投资中心（有限合伙）	2014-07-17	—	010-58143806
烟台源创现代服务业创业投资合伙企业（有限合伙）	2017-01-04	—	—
盐城高新区投资集团有限公司	2009-09-23	—	0515-88638063
盐城盐龙创业投资有限公司	2011-01-14	—	0515-88457508
扬中市创新投资有限公司	2015-10-09	—	—
扬州富海国龙影视投资中心（有限合伙）	2014-04-21	www.ofcapital.com	021-50581867
扬州富海扬帆互联网文化投资中心（有限合伙）	2015-08-14	www.ofcapital.com	021-50581867
扬州广陵区科技镇长团创业投资基金合伙企业（有限合伙）	2016-06-03	—	0514-82073568
扬州海圣创业投资中心	2012-07-09	—	0514-87991537
扬州邗江高新创业投资有限公司	2011-08-05	—	0514-87770259
扬州经信新兴产业创业投资基金	2013-01-08	—	025-84730375
扬州巨谷创投财富管理有限公司	2017-04-14	—	—
扬州平衡宜创创业投资基金中心（有限合伙）	2014-12-22	—	025-51889757
扬州平衡资本管理中心（有限合伙）	2014-11-25	—	025-51889757
扬州市创业投资有限公司	2007-05-21	www.jrjt.yangzhou.gov.cn	—
扬州英飞玛雅创业投资中心（有限合伙）	2013-12-25	—	0514-87785521
扬州英飞尼迪创业投资管理有限公司	2010-11-08	—	0514-87785512
扬州长晟安众创业投资基金合伙企业	2017-03-06	—	—
扬州长晟创业投资有限公司	2014-11-25	—	0514-82058968
杨凌东方富海现代农业生物产业股权投资企业（有限合伙）	2011-06-17	—	—
仪征高新技术产业投资发展有限公司	2005	—	0514-80852107
义乌科发创业投资合伙企业（有限合伙）	2016-01-21	www.zjkfcapital.com	0571-88250328

公司名称	成立时间	网址	电话
义乌浙科汇富创业投资合伙企业（有限合伙）	2016-01-25	—	0571-88869550
英诺天使基金	2013-04-01	www.innoangel.com	—
鹰潭联浙商投创业投资合伙企业（有限合伙）	2016-01-14	—	0701-88771697
盈富泰克创业投资有限公司	2000-04-20	www.infovc.com	0755-82966479
盈富泰克国家新兴产业创业投资引导基金（有限合伙）	2016-09	—	0755-23884280
榆林能源产业基金管理有限公司	2016-11-21	www.ylnyfund.com	—
原子（上海）投资股份有限公司	2012-04-01	www.atomvc.com	021-65055235
圆基（重庆）股权投资基金管理有限公司	2010-02-05	—	023-63329022
云南宁祥股权投资基金管理有限公司	2012-10-19	—	—
云南省现代农林投资有限公司	2009-05-27	www.cnynai.com	0871-68338757
云南信产智华股权投资基金管理有限公司	2015-12-23	—	—
云南银河之星金融服务有限公司	2014-10-22	—	0871-67419042
云南云投股权投资基金管理有限公司	2013-05-09	www.yigfund.com	—
泽星投资管理（大连）有限公司	2015-11-09	—	0411-88079959
张家口宣科双创天使创业投资基金有限公司	2017-11-01	—	—
长春科技大市场创业投资有限公司	2017-02-23	—	—
长春市科技发展中心	1997-06-06	www.ccfengxian.com	0431-88578575
长汉共同合作基金	2007-09-18	—	025-85529900
长沙高新技术创业投资管理有限公司	2000-09-09	www.cshvc.com	0731-88286898
长沙麓谷高新移动互联网创业投资有限公司	2014-03-25	—	—
长沙启泰创业投资管理有限公司	2017-05-25	—	—
长沙市科技风险投资管理有限公司	2000-05-18	www.csvcc.cn	0731-88286892
长沙天巽投资合伙企业（有限合伙）	2017-05-24	—	0731-84110275
长沙通程投资管理有限公司	2014-07-14	www.d-fin.cominvest	0731-84140499
长沙先导产业投资有限公司	2009-05-15	www.cpih.cn	0731-88768823
长沙兴创投资管理合伙企业（有限合伙）	2007-11-13	—	0731-82953007
长兴科创投资管理合伙企业（有限合伙）	2015-10-19	—	0571-89939766
长兴科商创业投资合伙企业（有限合伙）	2015-06-15	—	0571-88869317
长兴科威创业投资合伙企业（有限合伙）	2014-12-30	—	—
长兴启航投资管理合伙企业（有限合伙）	2015-10-09	—	0571-89939765
长兴天使投资管理合伙企业（有限合伙）	2015-10-22	—	0571-89939766
招商局科技集团有限公司	1995-12-20	www.cmtech.net	0755-26888628
肇庆市粤科金瑞投资管理有限公司	2010-08-19	—	0758-2321528
肇庆市粤科金叶创业投资有限公司	2010-10-18	—	0758-2260355

公司名称	成立时间	网址	电话
浙江安丰进取创业投资有限公司	2009-03-25	—	0571-87633580
浙江春晖创业投资有限公司	2007-10-17	—	0575-82150888
浙江大学创新技术研究院有限公司	2012-09-29	www.zjuiti.com	0571-58122629
浙江大学科技创业投资有限公司	2008-10-29	—	0571-87397929
浙江东翰高投长三角投资合伙企业（有限合伙）	2010-09-20	—	025-85529900
浙江菲达股权投资基金合伙企业（有限合伙）	2016-03-14	—	0575-87776660
浙江海邦创智投资管理有限公司	2017-09-01	www.hbvc.com.cn	0571-26237933
浙江海邦人才创业投资合伙企业（有限合伙）	2011-12	www.hbvc.com.cn	0571-81022997
浙江海宁天玑创业投资管理合伙企业（有限合伙）	2015-06-19	—	—
浙江海宁天擎创业投资管理合伙企业（有限合伙）	2015-07-06	—	—
浙江海洋经济创业投资有限公司	2010-01-19	—	0580-2036865
浙江浩誉创业投资有限公司	2011-01-14	—	0571-85814767
浙江合力创业投资有限公司	2011-03-09	—	0571-87988858
浙江红石创业投资有限公司	2007-11-27	—	—
浙江红土创业投资有限公司	2010-04-21	—	0573-83710180
浙江华瓯创业投资有限公司	2007-11-16	www.hovc.cn	0571-87988858
浙江华瓯股权投资管理有限公司	2011-05-17	—	0571-87988858
浙江华睿北信源数据信息产业投资合伙企业（有限合伙）	2015-08-19	—	—
浙江华睿布谷鸟创业投资合伙企业（有限合伙）	2015-06-03	—	—
浙江华睿产业互联网股权投资合伙企业（有限合伙）	2015-04-13	—	—
浙江华睿德银创业投资有限公司	2010-05-04	—	0571-88163180
浙江华睿点金创业投资有限公司	2009-08-10	—	—
浙江华睿点石投资管理有限公司	2007-11-14	—	0571-88163180
浙江华睿富华创业投资合伙企业（有限合伙）	2012-07-03	—	—
浙江华睿海越光电产业创业投资有限公司	2009-12-23	—	—
浙江华睿海越现代服务业创业投资有限公司	2010-01-28	—	0571-88163180
浙江华睿弘源智能产业创业投资有限公司	2010-03-22	—	0571-88163180
浙江华睿胡庆余堂健康产业投资基金合伙企业（有限合伙）	2015-11-27	—	—
浙江华睿互联投资有限公司	2010-10-20	—	0571-88163180
浙江华睿火炬创业投资合伙企业（有限合伙）	—	—	—
浙江华睿金石投资合伙企业（有限合伙）	—	—	—
浙江华睿控股有限公司	2002-08	www.sinowisdom.cn	0571-88163180
浙江华睿蓝石创业投资有限公司	2014-09-02	—	—
浙江华睿庆余创业投资有限公司	2013-12-30	—	—

公司名称	成立时间	网址	电话
浙江华睿如山创业投资有限公司	2010-12-07	—	0571-88163180
浙江华睿如山装备投资有限公司	2009-10-13	—	—
浙江华睿睿银创业投资有限公司	2007-03-28	—	—
浙江华睿盛银创业投资有限公司	2009-08-11	—	—
浙江华睿泰信创业投资有限公司	2008-07-21	—	—
浙江华睿泰银投资有限公司	2009-07-20	—	—
浙江华睿祥生环境产业创业投资有限公司	2010-11-15	—	0571-88163180
浙江华睿兴华股权投资合伙企业（有限合伙）	2012-12-24	—	—
浙江华睿医疗创业投资有限公司	2011-01-24	—	0571-88163180
浙江华睿中科创业投资有限公司	2010-07-05	—	0571-88163180
浙江嘉海创业投资有限公司	2010-01-13	—	0571-89922221
浙江嘉庆投资有限公司	2010-06-29	—	0571-86821212
浙江嘉银投资有限公司	2006-05-24	—	0571-88163180
浙江金永信投资管理有限公司	2005-03-24	—	0571-85279925
浙江科金天使启航股权投资合伙企业（有限合伙）	2011-11-14	—	0571-89939766
浙江蓝石创业投资有限公司	2008-05-15	—	—
浙江蓝源投资管理有限公司	2011-10-21	www.bluesource.hk	0574-89019226
浙江美林创业投资有限公司	2008-07-11	www.merrillcapital.cn	0571-85455412
浙江瓯联创业投资有限公司	2009-05-12	—	0571-87988858
浙江瓯盛创业投资有限公司	2008-06-03	—	0571-87988858
浙江瓯信创业投资有限公司	2009-04-02	—	0571-87988858
浙江品利股权投资基金管理有限公司	2013-09-25	—	—
浙江普发科技开发中心	1991-08-12	—	0571-88911708
浙江普华天勤股权投资管理有限公司	2011-06-20	www.puhuacapital.com	0571-87755559
浙江如山成长创业投资有限公司	2008-08-18	www.crestvalue.com	0571-87896213
浙江如山高新创业投资有限公司	2010-11-10	www.crestvalue.com	0571-87896213
浙江如山汇金资本管理有限公司	2010-09-26	www.crestvalue.com	0571-87896213
浙江如山汇鑫创业投资合伙企业（有限合伙）	2015-11-05	www.crestvalue.com	0571-87896213
浙江如山新兴创业投资有限公司	2012-09-11	www.crestvalue.com	0571-87896213
浙江若溪投资合伙企业（有限合伙）	2014-08-14	—	—
浙江赛伯乐科创股权投资管理有限公司	2011-08-09	www.cybernautvc.com	0571-88085123
浙江绍兴普华兰桥文化投资合伙企业（有限合伙）	2015-11-10	—	—
浙江绍兴普华兰亭文化投资合伙企业（有限合伙）	2015-12-07	—	—
浙江省创业投资集团有限公司	2000-09-30	www.zjvc.cn	0571-88259222

公司名称	成立时间	网址	电话
浙江省科技风险投资有限公司	1993-06	www.zvc-zj.com	0571-88869550
浙江省天堂硅谷创业创新投资服务中心有限公司	2008-05	www.vcpes.com	0571-86483535
浙江泰银创业投资有限公司	2007-10-26	—	—
浙江天使湾创业投资有限公司	2010-09-29	www.tisiwi.com	0571-89715708
浙江天堂硅谷朝阳创业投资有限公司	2007-04-16	—	0571-86483535
浙江天堂硅谷晨曦创业投资有限公司	2007-10-16	—	0571-86483535
浙江天堂硅谷海天汇缘创业投资合伙企业（有限合伙）	2013-03-04	—	0571-86483535
浙江天堂硅谷合丰创业投资有限公司	2009-10-13	—	0571-86483535
浙江天堂硅谷合胜创业投资有限公司	2009-10-20	—	0571-87089718
浙江天堂硅谷合众创业投资有限公司	2007-10-24	—	0571-86483523
浙江天堂硅谷恒通创业投资有限公司	2008-05-26	—	0571-86483535
浙江天堂硅谷久和股权投资合伙企业（有限合伙）	2012-03-01	—	0571-86483535
浙江天堂硅谷久融股权投资合伙企业（有限合伙）	2011	—	0571-86483535
浙江天堂硅谷久晟股权投资合伙企业（有限合伙）	2011	—	0571-87089718
浙江天堂硅谷久盈至臻股权投资合伙企业（有限合伙）	2012-02-13	—	—
浙江天堂硅谷开创产业投资管理合伙企业（有限合伙）	2014-09	—	—
浙江天堂硅谷鲲诚创业投资有限公司	2006-12-01	—	0571-86483535
浙江天堂硅谷鲲鹏创业投资有限公司	2009-06-26	—	0571-86483535
浙江天堂硅谷七弦股权投资合伙企业（有限合伙）	2011	—	0571-86483535
浙江天堂硅谷时顺股权投资合伙企业（有限合伙）	—	—	—
浙江天堂硅谷台州合盈股权投资有限公司	2011	—	0571-86483535
浙江天堂硅谷阳光创业投资有限公司	2006-06-20	—	0571-86483535
浙江天堂硅谷银嘉股权投资合伙企业（有限合伙）	2010-11-16	—	0571-86483523
浙江天堂硅谷银泽股权投资合伙企业（有限合伙）	2010-10-19	—	0571-86483523
浙江天堂硅谷盈丰股权投资合伙企业（有限合伙）	2010-07-30	—	0571-87089718
浙江天堂硅谷盈通创业投资有限公司	2010-06-01	—	0571-86483535
浙江天堂硅谷长泰股权投资合伙企业（有限合伙）	2011-07-15	—	0571-86483535
浙江维科创业投资有限公司	2008-02-28	—	0571-87207613
浙江新安创业投资有限公司	2011	—	0571-88050547
浙江信德丰创业投资有限公司	2010-05-27	—	0571-87225400
浙江以琳创业投资有限公司	2014-08-08	—	—
浙江亿都创业投资有限公司	2007-11	—	0571-85310058
浙江银泰睿祺创业投资有限公司	2009-11-09	—	0574-87093878
浙江盈瓯创业投资有限公司	2010-11-05	—	0571-87988858

公司名称	成立时间	网址	电话
浙江长兴科金投资管理有限公司	2015-10-09	—	0571-89939766
浙江浙大大晶创业投资有限公司	2001-01-03	—	0571-87382889
浙江浙大友创投资管理有限公司	2001-01-21	—	0571-87397929
浙江浙科汇丰创业投资有限公司	2010-09	—	—
浙江浙科汇利创业投资有限公司	2010-05	—	—
浙江浙科汇涛创业投资合伙企业（有限合伙）	2011-05-09	—	—
浙江浙科汇盈创业投资有限公司	2009-08	—	—
浙江浙科美林创业投资有限公司	2011-04	—	—
浙江浙科升华创业投资有限公司	2010-10	—	—
浙江浙科银江创业投资有限公司	2010-10-14	—	—
浙江浙能创业投资有限公司	2003-03-11	—	—
浙江浙商创业投资股份有限公司	2007-11	www.zsvc.com.cn	0571-89922221
浙江浙商海鹏创业投资合伙企业（有限合伙）	2008-06-03	—	0571-89922221
浙江浙商诺海创业投资合伙企业（有限合伙）	2010-04-14	—	0571-89922221
浙江浙商长海创业投资合伙企业（有限合伙）	2010-12-14	—	0571-89922221
浙江中宇科技风险投资有限公司	2003-10-10	—	0571-88217703
浙江众盛创银投资有限公司	2016-06-23	—	0571-87282592
浙江舟山如山汇盈创业投资合伙企业（合伙企业）	2016-04-28	www.crestvalue.com	0571-87896213
浙江诸暨惠风创业投资有限公司	2008-08-06	—	0575-87026018
浙商创投（沈阳）有限公司	2013-08-21	www.zsvc.com.cn	024-31857212
浙商万嘉（北京）创业投资管理有限公司	2010-12-22	www.entworks.com.cn	—
浙银富海（深圳）资本管理有限公司	2016-01-15	—	—
镇江创业园有限公司	2015-10-15	—	—
镇江高科创业投资有限公司	2012-03-16	—	0511-87056055
镇江高投创业投资有限公司	2008-08	—	025-85529900
镇江高新创业投资有限公司	2010-06-11	—	0511-83179317
镇江国投创业投资有限公司	2011-10-19	—	0511-85606910
镇江红土创业投资有限公司	2011-04-22	www.szvc.com.cn	0511-85988773
镇江君鼎协立创业投资有限公司	2013-02-04	—	025-86816826
镇江君舜协立创业投资中心（有限合伙）	2016-09-08	—	025-86816826
镇江凯普斯创业投资中心（有限合伙）	2015-06-03	—	—
镇江康成亨创业投资管理有限公司	2013-07-23	—	—
镇江康成亨创业投资合伙企业（有限合伙）	2013-08-12	—	—
镇江力合天使创业投资企业（有限合伙）	2012-12-13	—	0511-88884035

公司名称	成立时间	网址	电话
镇江领军人才创新创业股权投资有限公司	2016-10-20	—	—
镇江乾鹏创业投资基金企业（有限合伙）	2012-11-20	—	0511-80896166
镇江亿致能源科技孵化器有限公司	2010-10-18	—	0511-85630166
镇江银河创业投资有限公司	2012-06-11	—	010-66568253
镇江中科金山创业投资企业（有限合伙）	2011-08-24	www.csm-inv.com	0510-85383122
郑州海归孵化器管理中心（有限合伙）	2014-12-22	—	—
郑州市产业发展引导基金有限公司	2015-01-07	—	0371-67186167
郑州优埃富欧投资管理有限公司	2015-10-29	www.ufovc.com.cn	—
郑州中惠融金创业投资管理中心（有限合伙）	2017-11-22	—	—
中鼎开源创业投资管理有限公司	2012-02-08	—	—
中广核银创一期股权投资有限公司	2011-12-07	—	—
中合盛资本管理有限公司	2014-12-04	—	—
中节能南通合同环境管理投资基金中心（有限合伙）	2013-04-03	—	0513-81288030
中科图灵洛阳投资管理中心（有限合伙）	2017-11-10	—	0379-69697796
中企汇安资产管理有限公司	2014-03-26	—	—
中天辽创投资管理有限公司	2016-08-11	—	024-23213206
中兴众创空间（西安）投资管理有限公司	2017-09-15	—	—
重庆贝信投资有限公司	2014-02-21	—	023-86713575
重庆渤溢股权投资基金管理有限公司	2014-09-30	—	023-67468572
重庆辰龙股权投资基金管理有限公司	2012-03-05	—	023-63218290
重庆宸西股权投资基金管理有限公司	2014-05-19	—	023-63080193
重庆大乘股权投资基金管理有限公司	2014-05-23	—	023-63507862
重庆大石投资管理有限公司	2013-09-17	www.upcubator.com	—
重庆道微投资管理有限公司	2013-11-11	—	—
重庆德同创业投资中心（有限合伙）	2010-04-01	—	023-67889905
重庆德同领航创业投资中心（有限合伙）	2014-04-30	—	023-67889905
重庆德同投资管理有限公司	2009-12-29	—	023-67889905
重庆德众合元股权投资基金管理有限公司	—	www.dezhongfund.com	023-63056452
重庆峰瑞卓越一期股权投资基金合伙企业（有限合伙）	2016-04-19	—	023-65308717
重庆富坤创业投资中心（有限合伙）	2009-09-22	www.rlequities.com	023-67030600
重庆富坤新智能交通投资合伙企业（有限合伙）	2014-04-08	www.rlequities.com	023-67030700
重庆高新创投红马资本管理有限公司	2014-04-14	www.cqrhcapital.com	023-67990972
重庆高新创业投资有限公司	2007-08-03	—	023-67570797
重庆和亚化医投资管理有限公司	2014-03-10	—	023-63428005

公司名称	成立时间	网址	电话
重庆恒锐源股权投资基金管理有限公司	2009-12-23	www.chinahry.com	023-86798500
重庆鸿曜股权投资基金管理有限公司	2014-12-29	—	—
重庆华犇创业投资管理有限公司	2010-04-16	www.chinarunvc.com	023-63318955
重庆华犇电子信息创业投资中心（有限合伙）	2010-11-16	www.chinarunvc.com	023-63318955
重庆环保产业股权投资基金管理有限公司	2015-10-12	www.cqeppe.com.com	—
重庆洹杉股权投资基金管理有限公司	2015-01-15	—	—
重庆皇极股权投资基金管理有限公司	2014-08-05	www.ff2020.com	023-60369188
重庆汇涌金股权投资基金管理有限公司	2014-04-04	www.cqhyj.cn	—
重庆开创高新技术创业投资有限公司	2005-03-25	—	023-68601100
重庆科技风险投资有限公司	1993-01-16	www.cqskjvc.com	023-67516883
重庆科兴股权投资管理有限公司	2011-10-28	—	023-67516883
重庆科兴乾健创业投资有限公司	2011-12-01	—	—
重庆两江新区创新创业投资发展有限公司	2011-09-26	www.chinaljcapital.com	023-61757903
重庆临云股权投资基金管理有限公司	2014-08-22	www.linyunziben.com	023-88796706
重庆诺鼎资产管理有限公司	2015-01-13	—	023-62388929
重庆清研股权投资基金管理中心（有限合伙）	2016-03-15	—	—
重庆三屋领秀创业投资有限公司	2012-11-22	—	023-62611660
重庆三屋投资有限公司	2009-12-02	www.cqswtz.com	023-62611660
重庆深渝创新投资管理有限公司	2007-06-26	—	023-88609961
重庆市大渡口区科技产业创业投资有限公司	2013-01-21	—	023-67516108
重庆泰豪渝晟股权投资基金中心（有限合伙）	2011-08-05	—	023-63022990
重庆天使科技创业投资有限公司	2010-01-25	—	023-67516883
重庆天使投资引导基金有限公司	2009-07-17	www.cqvcgf.com	023-67516108
重庆同弘股权投资基金管理有限公司	2014-08-26	www.tonghongpe.com	023-63669961
重庆拓景股权投资基金管理有限公司	2014-12-01	—	—
重庆万业美科股权投资基金管理有限公司	2011-01-30	www.wanyec.com	023-67741365
重庆文化股权投资基金管理有限责任公司	2012-10-22	—	—
重庆西证渝富股权投资基金管理有限公司	2012-05-10	www.cqxzyf.com	023-67760963
重庆星耀辉腾股权投资基金管理有限公司	2016-02-01	—	023-88658889
重庆业如红土股权投资基金管理有限公司	2017-02-13	—	—
重庆逸百年股权投资基金管理有限公司	2015-09-21	—	—
重庆英飞尼迪创业投资中心（有限合伙）	2011-08-16	www.infinity-equity.com	023-63051585
重庆圆基新能源创业投资基金合伙企业（有限合伙）	2011-01-27	—	023-63329022
重庆兆信股权投资基金管理有限公司	2014-12-17	—	—

公司名称	成立时间	网址	电话
重庆致业源科技有限公司	2017-06-20	—	023-63055586
重庆众利商贸流通产业股权投资基金管理有限公司	2014-12-17	—	023-63656929
珠海高科创业投资管理有限公司	2017-09-28	—	—
珠海高新创业投资有限公司	2015-09-29	—	—
珠海高新技术创业投资管理有限公司	2017-08-25	—	—
珠海高新天使创业投资有限公司	2017-01-25	—	—
珠海红杉资本股权投资中心（有限合伙）	2010-03-26	—	010-84475669
珠海虹峰创业投资有限公司	2016-02-26	—	010-56767880
珠海金控高新产业投资中心（有限合伙）	2014-04-23	—	—
珠海九控投资有限公司	2015-04-16	—	—
珠海领先互联高新技术产业投资中心（有限合伙）	2014-09-03	—	0756-3333838
珠海清华科技园创业投资有限公司	2001-07	www.tspz.com	0756-3612000
珠海市锐盛创业投资企业（有限合伙）	2015-12-17	—	—
珠海招商银科股权投资中心（有限合伙）	2012-01-21	—	0755-26677220
株洲高新动力产业投资发展有限公司	2016-11-12	—	—
株洲高新天诚先进装备制造创业投资合伙企业（有限合伙）	2016-08-24	—	—
株洲广信兆富投资管理有限公司	2012-02-28	—	0731-88737722
株洲科创创业投资管理有限公司	2015-04-26	—	—
株洲科聚创业投资企业（有限合伙）	2016-11-21	—	—
株洲时代创新投资企业（有限合伙）	2016-10-19	www.timesinvest.cn	0731-22877368
株洲市国投创新创业投资有限公司	2015-11-27	www.zzgtct.com	0731-28688892
株洲市青年创业引导投资合伙企业（有限合伙）	2016-12-06	—	—
株洲市世富投资管理有限公司	2009-12-14	www.zzsafer.com	0731-22727013
株洲新动力众创天使投资企业	2017-01-23	—	—
株洲云创投资管理有限公司	2017-09-26	—	—
株洲兆富成长企业创业投资有限公司	2010-10-13	—	0731-88737722
株洲兆富投资咨询有限公司	2009-08-24	www.zaffer.cn	0731-22857751-8008
株洲中车时代高新投资有限公司	2003-05-12	www.timesinvest.cn	0731-22877368
诸暨鼎信创业投资有限公司	2008-07-29	—	0571-87896213
诸暨富华中云投资合伙企业（有限合伙）	2017-11-17	—	—
诸暨贵银创业投资有限公司	2014-05-14	—	—
诸暨华睿嘉银创业投资合伙企业（有限合伙）	2014-11-21	—	—
诸暨华睿庆丰创业投资合伙企业（有限合伙）	—	—	—
诸暨华睿文华股权投资合伙企业（有限合伙）	2015-06-10	—	—

公司名称	成立时间	网址	电话
诸暨华睿新锐投资合伙企业（有限合伙）	2015-06-01	—	—
诸暨华睿钻石投资合伙企业（有限合伙）	2017-10-17	—	—
诸暨嘉维创业投资合伙企业（有限合伙）	2016-04-18	—	—
诸暨如山汇安创业投资合伙企业（有限合伙）	2017-05-02	www.crestvalue.com	0571-87896213
淄博创新资本创业投资有限公司	2007-05	—	—
淄博高新技术风险投资股份有限公司	2003-07- 10	www.zbvc.net	0533-3586969
淄博齐鲁创业投资有限责任公司	2002-12-06	www.zbqlct.com	0533-6206621
淄博市高新技术创业投资有限公司	2007-07-25	—	0533-6206621
紫腾投资有限公司	2010-07-20	—	0991-4528202
自贡创新基金管理有限公司	2017-03-24	—	—
遵义科技创业投资有限公司	2010-11-05	—	0851-28922337